The Federal Contract

The Federal Contract

A Constitutional Theory of Federalism

STEPHEN TIERNEY

OXFORD
UNIVERSITY PRESS

OXFORD
UNIVERSITY PRESS

Great Clarendon Street, Oxford, OX2 6DP,
United Kingdom

Oxford University Press is a department of the University of Oxford.
It furthers the University's objective of excellence in research, scholarship,
and education by publishing worldwide. Oxford is a registered trade mark of
Oxford University Press in the UK and in certain other countries

First Edition published in 2022

Impression: 1

Published in the United States of America by Oxford University Press
198 Madison Avenue, New York, NY 10016, United States of America

British Library Cataloguing in Publication Data

Data available

Library of Congress Control Number: 2021950735

ISBN 978–0–19–880674–5

DOI: 10.1093/oso/9780198806745.001.0001

Printed and bound in the UK by
Clays Ltd, Elcograf S.p.A.

To Liam, Daniel, and James

Preface

Federalism is a very familiar form of government. It characterises the first modern constitution—that of the United States—and has been deployed by constitution-makers to manage large and internally diverse polities at various key stages in the history of the modern state: nineteenth- and twentieth-centuries nation-building and decolonisation; post-war reconstruction; post-1989 constitutional realignment; and, most recently, an ongoing period of fluid and troubling conflicts grounded in the politics of identity. Despite its pervasiveness in practice, this book argues that federalism has been strangely neglected by constitutional theory. It has tended either to be subsumed within one default account of modern constitutionalism, or it has been treated as an exotic outlier—a *sui generis* model *of the state* rather than a form of constitutionalism *for the state*. This neglect is both unsatisfactory in conceptual terms and problematic for constitutional practitioners, obscuring as it does the core meaning, purpose, and applicability of federalism as a discrete model of constitutionalism with which to manage complex states.

The federal turn in modern constitutional theory—what I call the federal contract—represents nothing less than an alternative form of social contract: a distinct register of constitutional government, adapting public law to the management of territorial pluralism. Territorial pluralism has always been, and continues to be, a challenging but unavoidable backdrop to the design of many polities, and yet its political significance has largely been ignored in pursuit of a uniform approach to state-making and constitution-building. Federalism offers a radical alternative to unitary constitutionalism; but so unsettling are its potential implications for the monistic elision of people, state, and constitution (a relationship that has characterised modern constitutionalism), that its true meaning as a categorically distinct type of democratic government has been blurred.

The federal contract offers an alternative account of many of the most fundamental concepts with which constitutionalists and political actors have traditionally operated: constituent power, the nature of sovereignty, subjecthood and citizenship, the relationship between institutions and constitutional authority, and ultimately the legitimacy link between constitutionalism and democracy. This book contends that each of these categories requires to be recalibrated through the calculus of federal constitutionalism in order to draw out its distinctive meaning and mode of application specific to a federal constitutional setting.

This is a matter of practical as well as conceptual importance. Constitution-makers in some of the most unsettled regions of the world turn to federalism today as a possible solution to the territorial difficulties with which they are confronted.

In doing so they find an idea of government that has been constricted by institutional assumptions stemming from eighteenth- and nineteenth-centuries constitutional practice, when what they need is a pliable and practical schema for government that can be tailored to their own circumstances. Only through a fundamental reassessment of the core constitutional purpose of federalism can its capaciousness and flexibility as a consistent and rational genus of authority be fully appreciated.

In rethinking the idea and practice of federalism, this book adopts a root and branch reappraisal of the federal contract. It does so by analysing federalism through the conceptual categories which characterise the nature of modern constitutionalism: Foundations, Authority, Subjecthood, Purpose, Design, and Dynamics. This approach seeks to explain and in so doing revitalise federalism as a commodious and adaptable concept of rule that can be deployed imaginatively to facilitate the deep territorial variety and complexity of the contemporary state in the twenty-first century.

Acknowledgements

This book is the culmination of reflections over a number of years on the relationship between territory and authority. I have developed these ideas through many academic papers and am very grateful for the helpful comments of attendees at events in Oxford, the London School of Economics, University College London, the European University Institute, the University of Quebec at Montreal, Leuven, Ghent, Ottawa, Texas, Oslo, Seoul National University, Toronto, the University of Montreal, Notre Dame, and Yale. I have also benefited from events organised by the Edinburgh Centre of Constitutional Law, including the annual symposium we run with International IDEA on constitution-building in situations of territorial complexity.

I am indebted to Pau Bossacoma Busquets, Gary Jacobsohn, Geneviève Nootens, and James Tully for insightful comments on the manuscript. At Oxford University Press I would like to thank Jamie Berezin and Alex Flach who each showed strong support for the project, anonymous reviewers for their encouragement, and the production team led by Iona Jacob for their professionalism. The research assistance I received from Noah Brown at Notre Dame and Peter Reid at Edinburgh was also invaluable. Much of the book was written during the trying circumstances of pandemic lockdown and I am deeply grateful for the support and forbearance of my wife Ailsa and my children to whom the book is dedicated.

Over many years I have benefited greatly from reading the work of and discussing ideas with so many colleagues that I cannot possibly name them all, but I wish to note the particular influence of Martin Loughlin, Peter Oliver, James Tully, Neil Walker, Michael Keating, Erin Delaney, Jeff King, Mark Elliott, Adam Tomkins, Alison Young, Robert Schütze, David Armitage, Nicholas Aroney, Margaret Moore, Richard Simeon, Richard Albert, and Asanga Welikala. At the start of my academic career I was encouraged to study federalism by Alain Gagnon. I owe Alain a great debt for the kindness and collegiality he showed to a young scholar from another country and another discipline. Alain worked closely with Michael Burgess—a wonderful man whose humanity and generosity are very much missed—and the diverse networks which they have both established over the years are emblematic of the federal spirit at its best.

I am also appreciative of the students I have taught and from whom I have learned. I introduced a new course on comparative federalism at Notre Dame in 2020 which was a very valuable testing ground for my ideas. Over the years my students at Edinburgh have also offered challenging and exciting insights on federalism and constitutionalism, constantly reminding me with their passion and enthusiasm of the importance of bringing to constitutional rule theoretical analysis grounded in the hinterland of precise empirical detail.

My work for the House of Lords Select Committee on the Constitution over the past seven years has been both fascinating and immensely rewarding in demonstrating how constitutionalism encapsulates, and cannot be meaningfully understood in the absence of, the most intimate interaction between theory and practice; how each informs and shapes the other; and how the territorial nature of any constitution is in large part a thing unto itself, only comprehensible through the very specific and nuanced interaction of the history, received wisdom, institutional design, and popular sentiment that characterises each polity.

In writing this book I seek neither to praise nor to bury federalism but rather to explain it through the prism of constitutional theory. The journey to its completion has taken me in many different directions, through a series of intellectual adventures and across a range of disciplines and traditions. I have been guided by maps made by others, but in the end I have arrived at a different destination from most. The reader will decide whether the journey and its conclusion were well-directed, or misconceived; and for this assessment, while appreciative of those who have led the way, I accept full responsibility.

Contents

1
The Federal Contract

I. Introduction

It is customary to begin any book on federalism by observing its ongoing significance and recent proliferation as a form of government.[1] But more notable than the resilience, growth, and adaptability of federalism over time is the very creation and constitutional entrenchment of multiple systems of government within one polity in an era of otherwise centralised and demotically homogenising nation-states. Since the eighteenth century the state has been the dominant site of lawful authority over territory; in essence, the exclusive locus for the ordering of political power across large polities and their empires. A key feature of the process of state-building has been the unification of disparate territories within a singular constitutional system and the husbanding of all political power under the authority of one, all-encompassing, sovereign order of rule. Accordingly, modern constitutionalism has come to be conceived as a single, universalisable model of democratic government, premised upon a monistic construction of both the people and the constitution as a unified legal-normative project.

In this context, federalism appears to irritate against, if not directly contradict, the core integrationist purpose of the modern constitution. Federalism is a categorically different model of rule from unitary constitutionalism. It is based upon collective, territorially located sites of constitutional personhood, manifest in a plurality of governments embedded within the constitution of the state, rather than upon a uniform and unitary conception of the demos encapsulated in one governmental form. Federalism as an idea is therefore deeply troubling to a simple and seemingly comprehensive account of modern public law that strives to reduce the legal-normative conception of modern politics to one state, one constitution, one people.

Although federalism is a remarkable innovation in an era of constitutional monism, the radical dissonance which it strikes within the otherwise harmonious symphony of modern government has largely gone unconsidered by constitutional theory. This book aims to correct this omission, examining federalism as a discrete

[1] W. Riker, *Federalism: Origin, Operation, Significance* (Boston: Little, Brown and Company, 1964), 1; R.L. Watts, 'The Federal Idea and its Contemporary Relevance', in T.L. Courchene et al., *The Federal Idea: Essays in Honour of Ronald L. Watts* (Kingston-Montreal: McGill-Queen's, 2011), 13–27, 14; M. Feeley and E. Rubin, *Federalism: Political Identity and Tragic Compromise* (Ann Arbor: University of Michigan Press, 2008), 1.

The Federal Contract. Stephen Tierney, Oxford University Press. © Stephen Tierney 2022.
DOI: 10.1093/oso/9780198806745.003.0001

idea of rule for the modern state and one which fundamentally unsettles the notion that the conceptual and institutional tools developed to facilitate state- and nation-building can be understood as a singular and exclusive narration of, and *modus operandi* for, modern constitutionalism. The neglect of federalism within constitutional theory has resulted in a failure to elicit its conceptual essence as a specific genus of government. The consequence has been the marrying of conceptual misconstruction with political inhibition. Federalism is so conceptually vexing that modern constitutional theory, in its purported universalism and in pursuit of an inherently narrow and standardising mind-set, has tended to downplay both its theoretical implications and its institutional potential. In this way federalism has suffered from intellectual stultification as a constitutional idea and political enfeeblement as an order of rule when it should in fact be deployed imaginatively to facilitate the deep complexity of contemporary societies in the twenty-first century.

In this book I seek to retrieve the anatomy of federalism as an alternative and comprehensive theoretical and practical constitutional project, arguing that the 'federal contract' should be conceived as a distinct, viable, and indeed vital alternative to the standard conception of the social contract that so dominates the contemporary nexus between constitution and state.[2] This is an essential task at a time when the state remains the primary site of legitimate public law but one which in many places struggles to adapt to demotic pluralism, institutional transformation, and shifting patterns of normative authority within and beyond its boundaries. Federalism has the potential to facilitate such adaptation, but in order for this to be fulfilled the federal contract must be recovered and rearticulated as a discrete, generic, conceptually coherent, and institutionally capacious order of constitutional rule for the contemporary state.

II. Federalism: an idea of government

Although its endurance may be less remarkable than its very emergence, federalism has proven to be highly durable: indeed, its persistence and dissemination around the world constitutes one of the most dramatic transformations in government of

[2] D. Hume, 'Of the Original Contract', in *Essays: Moral, Political, and Literary* (Oxford: Oxford University Press, 1963), 457; S. Holmes, 'Precommitment and the Paradox of Democracy', in J. Elster and R. Slagstad (eds), *Constitutionalism and Democracy* (Cambridge: Cambridge University Press, 1988), 195–240; J.E. Lane, *Constitutions and Political Theory* (Manchester: Manchester University Press, 1996),; T. Ginsburg, 'Constitutions as Contract, Constitutions as Charter', in D. Galligan and M. Versteeg (eds), *Social and Political Foundations of Constitutions* (Cambridge: Cambridge University Press, 2013), 182–204; D.S. Grewal and J. Purdy, 'The Original Theory of Constitutionalism' (2018) 127 *Yale Law Journal* 665–705.

the past seventy-five years.[3] And yet this development and, in particular, recent attempts to adapt federalism to some of the most fraught territorial problems of our time highlight the conceptual and definitional imprecision which has beset the study of the federal constitution for more than two centuries. Scholars have tended to study federalism as a form of governmental, political, and social practice, without according sufficient significance to the fact that it is fundamentally a form of constitutionalism, and without a thorough exposition of its essence as an idea of constitutional rule. The key aim of this book is to strip back federalism to its ideational core as a particular legal-normative project that occupies its own discrete space upon the register of constitutionalism; an essential task if the conceptual confusion and subsequent institutional constriction that attend the subject are to be overcome.

Since the second half of the twentieth century commentators have disagreed radically even on the question of how many constitutions are federal or federalising. The late Michael Burgess, a passionate advocate of federalism, argued in 2012 that since 1945 approximately one-third of states had adopted or were moving towards a federal constitutional system.[4] Daniel Elazar, an earlier pioneer in the revival of federal studies in the latter part of the twentieth century—and in many ways Burgess' intellectual inspiration—went further, asserting in the mid-1990s that over half of the world's 180 states, with approximately 80 per cent of the global population, were federal or had some kind of federal arrangement.[5] But these claims seem to be confronted by radical disagreement. Another giant of federal scholarship, Ronald Watts, declaimed in the same period that there were merely twenty-four 'federations' in the world.[6] It is extraordinary that leading scholars working in any field should arrive at such conspicuous divergence on the very scope of their discipline. However, on closer inspection, it transpires that very different meanings were being accorded by these scholars to the respective terms 'federal', 'federalism', and 'federation'; the last representing, for Watts, a subset of yet another category, 'federal political systems'.[7] In fact, commentators were oscillating between, on the one hand,

[3] R.L. Watts, *Comparing Federal Systems*, 3rd edn (Montreal, QC, Canada: McGill-Queen's University Press, 2008), Preface and 7; L. Hooghe and G. Marks, 'Types of Multi-level Governance', in L. Hooghe and G. Marks (eds), *Multi-level Governance and European Integration* (London: Rowman and Littlefield, 2001), 17–31, 17.

[4] He called this the 'federal tendency'. M. Burgess, *In Search of the Federal Spirit: New Theoretical and Empirical Perspectives in Comparative Federalism* (Oxford: Oxford University Press, 2012), 2.

[5] D. Elazar, *Federal Systems of the World: A Handbook of Federal, Confederal and Autonomy Arrangements*, 2nd edn (Harlow: Longman, 1994), xv, xvi–xvii.

[6] R.L. Watts, *Comparing Federal Systems*, 2nd edn (Montreal, QC, Canada: McGill-Queen's University Press, 1999), 4. In 2008 he adjusted this to twenty-five countries 'each exhibiting the fundamental characteristics of a functioning federation'. Watts, *Comparing Federal Systems*, 3rd edn, 1. See also T.O. Hueglin and A. Fenna, *Comparative Federalism: A Systematic Inquiry*, 2nd edn (Toronto: University of Toronto Press, 2015), 47–48.

[7] R.L. Watts, 'Federalism, Federal Political Systems, and Federations' (1998) *Annual Review of Political Science* 117–137. Watts' broader notion of 'federal political systems' allowed him to conclude that a much greater number of countries merited this constitutional description, bringing him closer to

an open-ended elision of federalism as an idea with 'multi-level' government[8] and, on the other, a tight, institutionally focused definition of 'federal government'. By the turn of the millennium the consequence of this empirical bipolarity was an increasingly inward-looking terminological debate around the very meaning of these terms, rather than a deep (and at that time vitally necessary) engagement with the fundamental constitutional idea they together bore.

This vignette, and the degree of fundamental classificatory dispute that it betokens, exemplifies the broader conceptual imprecision that has beleaguered the study of federalism within both political studies and doctrinal constitutional law. A byzantine lexicon came to supplant the real issue that confronted scholars in an age when the need for a proper understanding of the meaning and potential of federalism was greater than ever: the constitutional purpose of federalism as a discrete order of rule for, and tool with which to manage the territorial complexity of, the modern state.

Although taxonomy has largely displaced ontology, it is clear nonetheless that the federal turn, and the application of the term 'federal' to describe territorial government, is an increasingly prominent constitutional feature of contemporary statehood.[9] Many of the most vivid moves towards federal government have occurred very recently, with federalism being adapted to accommodate complex territorial pluralism in many of the world's most troubled regions, from south eastern Europe to the Middle East.[10] The diversity, and indeed the individual distinctiveness, of each of the governmental arrangements that have emerged during this period of constitution-making in divided societies[11] together posit a fresh conceptual challenge to the subject. The established options for institutional design derived from the classical cases—the United States of America, Switzerland, Canada, Australia, and Germany—were adapted with very mixed success to

the numbers advanced by Elazar and Burgess. These and other definitional approaches to federalism are discussed further in Chapter 2.

[8] A particularly vague and confusing term, much in vogue over the past two decades. I. Bache and M. Flinders, *Multi-level Governance* (Oxford: Oxford University Press, 2004).

[9] Reflected in an upsurge in scholarship addressing its different sites of application: R. Saxena (ed.), *Varieties of Federal Governance: Major Contemporary Models* (New Delhi, India: Foundation Books, 2012); M. Seymour and A.G. Gagnon, *Multinational Federalism: Problems and Prospects* (United Kingdom: Palgrave MacMillan, 2012); A. Benz and J. Broschek, *Federal Dynamics: Continuity, Change, and the Varieties of Federalism* (Oxford: Oxford University Press, 2013); J. Kincaid (ed.), *A Research Agenda for Federalism Studies* (Cheltenham: Edward Elgar, 2019); A. Lev (ed.), *The Federal Idea: Public Law between Governance and Political Life* (Oxford: Hart Publishing, 2019); A.-G. Gagnon and A. Tremblay (eds), *Federalism and National Diversity in the 21st Century* (United Kingdom: Palgrave MacMillan, 2020).

[10] S. Keil, *Multinational Federalism in Bosnia and Herzegovina* (Farnham and Burlington: Ashgate, 2013); D. Stjepanovic, *Multiethnic Regionalisms in Southeastern Europe: Statehood Alternatives* (United Kingdom: Palgrave, 2017); L.M. Anderson, 'Theorizing Federalism in Iraq' (2007) 17 *Regional and Federal Studies* 159–171.

[11] S. Choudhry (ed.), *Constitutional Design for Divided Societies: Integration or Accommodation* (Oxford: Oxford University Press, 2008); R. Dixon, R. Levy, and M. Tushnet, 'Theories and Practices of Federalism in Deeply Divided Societies' (2019) *Federal Law Review* 481–490.

accommodate the emergence of new states and new constitutions in the post-war period of Western decolonisation.[12] The inadequacy of this approach in the 1950s and 1960s,[13] and its evident failure by the 1970s,[14] made clear that in the post-1989 era of deepening and intensifying territorial heterogeneity, complacent assumptions about the transferability of orthodox federal models would no longer serve.[15] Early federal polities, with the partial exceptions of Switzerland and Canada, were largely homogeneous, and their success was indeed widely attributed to societal uniformity.[16] With the collapse of authoritarian rule in deeply pluralised states, original thinking was needed as radically new forms of territorial democracy bearing the adjective 'federal' were adapted to manage the complex cultural diversity and attendant tensions in South Africa, Ethiopia, Bosnia-Herzegovina, and Iraq;[17] while centripetal tendencies continued to affect some of the world's largest states, such as India, Nigeria, and Russia, which were themselves already sites of plural government.

Despite the need for a root and branch rethinking of federalism as a constitutional idea, disagreements stemming from a strict terminological empiricism continue to trouble the use of the term 'federal'. We see this in relation to radical transformations in the territorial government of older states such as the United Kingdom, Belgium, and Spain. Much of the work in politics and constitutional law has sought to reduce the distinction between 'devolution' and 'federalism' to a dogmatic, and at times casuistic, formalism, despite the existential uncertainty upon which the very term federalism rests.[18] The result is an approach to federal

[12] T.M. Franck,(ed.), *Why Federations Fail: An Inquiry into the Requisites for Successful Federalism* (New York: New York University Press, 1968); D.J. Elazar, *Exploring Federalism* (Tuscaloosa: University of Alabama, 1987), 240–244; B. O'Leary, 'An Iron Law of Nationalism and Federation? A (NeoDiceyian) Theory of the Necessity of a Federal Staatsvolk and of Consociational Rescue' (2001) 7 *Nations and Nationalism* 273–296, 283–284.

[13] Watts, 'The Federal Idea and its Contemporary Relevance', 20.

[14] Resulting in a new focus upon the 'pathology' of federal systems: Franck, *Why Federations Fail* and U.K. Hicks, *Federalism, Failure and Success: A Comparative Study* (London: Macmillan, 1978).

[15] As Burgess comments: 'The post-Cold War world has changed to such an extent that we find most of the classic theories of federal state formation and their subsequent maintenance simply redundant.' M. Burgess, 'Opening Pandora's Box: Process and Paradox of the Federalism of Political Identity', in A. López-Basaguren and L.E.S. Epifanio (eds) *The Ways of Federalism in Western Countries and the Horizons of Territorial Autonomy in Spain* (Berlin: Springer, 2013), vol. 1, 3–14, 11.

[16] J.S. Mill, *Considerations on Representative Government* (London: Parker, Son and Bourn, 1861), 289; J. Bryce, *The American Commonwealth, 2 vols* (London: Macmillan and Co. Ltd, 1919), vol. I, 357, ascribing American federal success to a 'community in blood, in language, in habits and ideas, a common pride in the national history and the national flag'.

[17] So-called 'post-conflict federalism': S. Choudhry and N. Hume, 'Federalism, Devolution and Secession: From Classical to Post-conflict Federalism', in T. Ginsburg and R. Dixon (eds), *Comparative Constitutional Law* (Cheltenham: Edward Elgar, 2011), 356–386, 363.

[18] Scholars adopting an institutionalist approach to federalism have found it difficult to classify complex constitutional solutions that have emerged to manage territorial diversity. In relation to both the United Kingdom and Spain, the nebulous term 'quasi-federalism' has been applied: V. Bogdanor, *Devolution in the UK* (Oxford: Oxford University Press, 2001); M. Flinders, 'Constitutional Anomie' (2010) 44 *Government and Opposition* 383–409 and L. Moreno, *The Federalization of Spain* (London, Portland: Frank Cass, 2001). For discussion see Stephen Tierney, 'Federalism in a Unitary State: A Paradox too Far? (2009) 19 *Regional and Federal Studies* 237–254.

thinking that is didactic and yet hazy. While territorial government within states continues to expand and diversify, this process is accompanied by entrenched and ongoing contestation surrounding when and how a particular division of territorial authority can legitimately be described as 'federal'.[19] As we will explore later in the book, the search for definitions in much of the literature tends to be circular in orientation, with conceptual definition founded implicitly or explicitly upon a pre-conceived notion of institutional form.

The doctrinal positivism that has inhibited explication of the constitutional essence of federalism is inherently unsatisfactory as a matter of legal science; more significantly, it is also damaging to the pursuit of practical constitution-making. In fact, federalism, as a particular form of modern constitutional government, can only be defined and explained by constitutional theory. Constitutional theory is the study of the specific task performed by constitutions: the transformation of political power into normative authority. The modern state has been built upon such a process, allowing control over territory to acquire the legitimacy of lawful rule. Since the essential contention of this book is that federalism is a distinct order of rule for the modern state, it follows that it must be understood as transforming political power into legal authority *for a particular purpose*. Federalism gives foundational recognition and accommodation to the state's constituent territorial pluralism. The purpose of the federal constitution is both to foster this foundational pluralism and to maintain the constitutional relationship between pluralism and union in the creation and reconciliation of different orders of government. It is the centrality of territorial pluralism to the federal idea that makes it a discrete genus of rule within the constitutional species. Consequently, it is necessary to take full account of the foundationally fundamental step that is made in the process of constitutionalisation: the creation of a new order of legal rule founded upon the territorial multiplicity of the polity.

The neglect of federalism by constitutional theory and the fundamental failure to articulate and explain its constitutional essence has left the federal idea obscured and its nature open to categorical disagreement. Before explaining how, in this book, I will seek to retrieve and articulate the anatomy of the federal idea,

Spain has meanwhile been described as 'a unitary state engaged in devolutionary federalization'. Watts, *Comparing Federal Systems*, 3rd edn, 42. Another frequently used formulation is that 'Spain is a federation in all but name'. Watts, *Comparing Federal Systems*, 3rd edn, 42. Moreno and Colino use the same expression: L. Moreno and C. Colino, 'Kingdom of Spain', in L. Moreno and C. Colino (eds), *Diversity and Unity in Federal Countries* (Montreal/Kingston: McGill-Queen's University Press, 2010), 289–319, 302; while other approaches replace the word 'federal' with 'regional state' or 'compound state': E. Aja, *Estado autonómico y reforma federal* (Madrid: Alianza, 2014). Moreno has even called Spain a 'federation in disguise', L. Moreno, 'Federalization in Multinational Spain', in M. Burgess and J. Pinder (eds), *Multinational Federations* (London: Routledge, 2007), 86–107.

[19] S. Tierney, 'The Territorial Constitution and the Brexit Process' (2019) 72 *Current Legal Problems* 59–83, 66–67.

it is necessary first to explore how the concept of federalism has proven to be so challenging to constitutional theory and the ways in which, consequently, its distinctive essence has come to be obscured.

III. A journey without a map: the federal idea and the road from Philadelphia

The principal reason for the conceptual confusion that distorts the study of federalism is that it has been described, explained, justified (or refuted), and ultimately defined exclusively by reference to practice; in particular, to the practice of American constitutionalism which is seen as the progenitor of, and consequently the institutional benchmark for, federalism in the modern state. This is problematic not only because a description of the practice of federalism (in particular, one instance of its practice) is no substitute for a broader inter-temporal theoretical study of the constitutional purpose federal government as a genus of rule is designed to serve, but also because the American experience is an unhelpful, indeed distorting, yardstick. The nascent United States created a constitutional system to fit its particular societal conditions. More than this, the drafting of the constitution was so contested that its text left unclear and ultimately inchoate how public authority was intended to be divided or shared between the states and the federal government.[20]

The elemental disputes that characterised the Philadelphia process remained unresolved in the early nineteenth century, fuelling the conditions for civil war in the 1860s.[21] This in turn led ultimately to a deep transformation (and defederalisation)

[20] We will explore the detail of the US constitution's federal provisions in later chapters but for now it is noteworthy that it was born from deep disagreement and resulted in uneasy compromise, often hidden in obscure textual provisions. For example, one proposition ('the Virginia Plan'), led by James Madison, argued for a strong central government, while another, 'the New Jersey Plan', presented by the 'anti-federalists', sought greater authority for the states within the constitution. T. Anderson, *Creating the Constitution: The Convention of 1787 and the First Congress* (Pennsylvania: Penn. State Press, 1993), 50–59. See also B. Ackerman, *We the People II: Transformations* (Cambridge MA: The Belknap Press of Harvard University Press, 1998), 49–51. This resulted in 'the Connecticut Compromise', which shaped bicameralism and the allocation of powers in a way that, by seeking to meet both demands, left the balance of power between states and federal government ultimately under-determined: A.L. LaCroix, *The Ideological Origins of American Federalism* (Cambridge MA: Harvard University Press, 2011), 155–156. For an account of the fierce critique presented by 'anti-federalists' of the centralising trajectory which they anticipated the draft constitution would take, see C. Kenyon, *Men of Little Faith* (Amherst: University of Massachusetts Press, 2003).

[21] In many ways textual obfuscation was a deliberate strategy, to paper over irresoluble differences in intention among the founders as to the future direction of the Union; to seek 'compromise via silence and ambiguity'. R. Smith, *Civic Ideals: Conflicting Visions of Citizenship in U. S. History* (New Haven: Yale University Press, 1997), 133. This is not surprising per se. Jacobsohn and Roznai observe that in many constitutions born amidst deep disagreement, 'radical change is deferred to a distant time': G. Jacobsohn and Y. Roznai, *Constitutional Revolution* (New Haven: Yale University Press, 2020), 57. Carl Schmitt makes a similar point in relation to 'dilatory formal compromise' (*dilatorische Formelkompromiß*) in relation to the Weimar constitution of 1919. See D. Kelly, 'Introduction: Carl Schmitt's Critique of Friedrich Meinecke' (2017) 17 *Max Weber Studies* 48–53, 53.

of the polity during and after Reconstruction.[22] Further radical reconceptions of the Constitution's core purpose occurred during the New Deal and Civil Rights periods,[23] whereby a unification and nationalisation of the American demos was accompanied by, and in turn further encouraged through, the institutional centralisation of the national polity.[24] The point was thereby reached where the very characterisation of the United States as a federal polity has for decades been called into question.[25]

This is not in any way to criticise the trajectory of American constitutional history. The constitutional practice of the United States adapted itself, as any should, to the societal realities of the polity. The point is that a highly complex and very particular constitutional experience should not lightly be viewed as a prototype for a genus of constitutionalism and certainly not as a procrustean *coda* with which to understand, far less shape, the constitutions of other societies, even if these constitutions bear a superficial similitude through the shared constitutional label: 'federalism'.[26]

[22] R. Bensel, *Yankee Leviathan: The Origins of Central State Authority in America 1859–1877* (Cambridge: Cambridge University Press, 1990); Kimberley S. Johnson, *Governing the American State: Congress and the New Federalism, 1877–1929* (Princeton: Princeton University Press, 2007). See also Ackerman, *We the People II: Transformations*, 198–200 and 204–205, where Ackerman argues that during Reconstruction the USA went through a 're-founding' that shifted American constitutional identity from federalism to a demotically monist form of nationalism.

[23] S. Beer, 'The Modernization of American Federalism' (1973) 3 *Publius* 49–95.

[24] J. Sexton, *A Nation Forged by Crisis: A New American History* (New York: Basic, 2018).

[25] Harold Laski asserted, after seven years of the New Deal, that 'the epoch of federalism is over'. H.J. Laski, 'The Obsolescence of Federalism' (1939) 98 *New Republic* 367. That the F.D. Roosevelt presidency was key to this conclusion is evident when we note Laski's earlier and much more positive endorsement of plural forms of government in 'The Pluralistic State' (1919) 28 *Philosophical Review* 562–575. The New Deal period is indeed widely seen as the catalyst for the centralisation of American politics: Samuel H. Beer, 'The Modernization of American Federalism'; J.J. Wallis and W.E. Oates, 'The Impact of the New Deal on American Federalism', in M.D. Bordo, C. Goldin, and E.N. White (eds), *The Defining Moment: The Great Depression and the American Economy in the Twentieth Century* (Chicago: University of Chicago Press, 1998), 155–180. Others argue that 'cooperative federalism', which is characterised by a blurring of the borders of federal/state governmental competences, dates back to the post-Civil War period: Kimberley S. Johnson, *Governing the American State: Congress and the New Federalism*, 1877–1929. In a recent study, this long period of centralisation led Feeley and Rubin to conclude that 'federalism is no longer an operative principle in the United States'. Rather, 'what now passes for federalism in the United States is actually managerial decentralization'. Feeley and Rubin, *On Federalism: Federalism as Tragic Choice*, Preface ix and 152. Others have taken a similar view: K.E. Whittington, 'Dismantling the Modern State? The Changing Structural Foundations of Federalism' (1998) 25 *Hastings Constitutional Law Quarterly* 483–528, 483; D.J. Hopkins, *The Increasingly United States: How and Why American Political Behavior Nationalized* (Chicago: University of Chicago Press, 2018); H. Gerken, 'Federalism as the New Nationalism: An Overview' (2014) 123 *Yale Law Journal* 1626–2133; J. Kincaid, 'Dynamic De/Centralization in the United States, 1790–2010' (2019) 49 *Publius: The Journal of Federalism* 166–193; N. Jacobs, 'An Experimental Test of How Americans Think about Federalism' (2017) 47 *Publius: The Journal of Federalism* 572–598; E. Zackin, 'What's Happened to American Federalism?' (2011) 43 *Polity* 388–403. As Zackin puts it (at 392), in discussing Feeley and Rubin's book: 'The American state now operates as a single polity. It may be a decentralized republic, but it is not a federalized system.'

[26] It is also notable that the drafting of the American constitution itself was not an exercise in ideal 'federalisation' (were such an ideal to exist). Rather it was influenced by an eclectic range of comparative sources, both ideational and institutional—LaCroix, *The Ideological Origins of American Federalism*, 6–9, 34. This 'bricolage', or grabbing of what came to hand (M. Tushnet, 'The Possibilities of Comparative

It is also the case that the origins of the Constitution of the United States are viewed today as 'federal' only through a retrospective prism. The words 'federal' and 'federalism' do not appear in the title or text of the American constitution as promulgated,[27] and indeed these very terms were interpreted by the founders of that constitution in ways very different from those in which they are used today.[28] Ironically, federalism came in the late nineteenth and twentieth centuries to be conceptualised intellectually, not by reference to what the American constitution was intended to be, but by what it became.[29] This in itself is unsurprising. It is important that historical constitutional analysis is not driven by terminology. Forms of government which come over time to be classified as constitutional *genera* can emerge at first opaquely and developmentally in any state, only later to be definable as archetypes in the wider context of subsequent international institutional extrapolations which draw upon, and through practice re-mould, the conceptual edifice of this precedent: neologisms of usage if not of taxonomy. As Tocqueville observed, a new type of government did emerge at Philadelphia, even if its essence was not at that time fully unveiled: 'Human understanding more easily invents new things than new words … a form of government has been found which is neither exactly national nor federal; but no further progress has been made, and the new word which will one day designate this novel invention does not yet exist.'[30] The Philadelphia process was truly developmental. LaCroix notes: 'a set of ideas about government that was later called "federalism" began to coalesce at the convention.'[31]

Constitutional Law' (1999) 108 *Yale Law Journal* 1225–1309, 1229), also made the American constitutional founding very much the product of its time. 'To appreciate the significance and novelty of American federalism, we must connect it to larger eighteenth century debates about the nature, location and ultimate hierarchy of political and legal authorities.' LaCroix, 221.

[27] The word 'federal' did not enter the Constitution until the ratification in January 1964 of the 24th amendment prohibiting poll taxes. This makes reference to 'Federal Elections'.

[28] It has been observed that the authors of *The Federalist* papers 'were not even clear about the distinctiveness of the institutions they were fashioning'. P. King, *Federalism and Federations* (London: Croom Helm, 1982), 22. LaCroix discusses how American federalism emerged in initially shapeless form around the core idea of 'divided governmental authority' and that the framers 'drew from several strands of political, legal, and constitutional thought, some of which originated in the late sixteenth and early seventeenth centuries' (LaCroix, 11). In tracing a range of influences: Anglo-American constitutional debates, European continental ideas around sovereignty and unions, early experiments of union among the American states themselves, and Great Britain's formation through English union with Scotland and Ireland, LaCroix notes how the very idea of divided authority posed deep conceptual problems for those attempting to articulate the nature of the nascent constitution: LaCroix, 18.

[29] For the sense in which Wheare saw federalism as a nation-building project through the retrospective lens of constitutional and social development, first in the United States, and then extrapolated through the later constitutions of Canada, Australia, and Switzerland, see K.C. Wheare, 'Federalism and the Making of Nations' in A.W. Macmahon (ed.), *Federalism: Mature and Emergent* (New York: Columbia University Press, 1955), 28–43. See also K.C. Wheare, *Federal Government* (Oxford: Oxford University Press, 1946) (4th edn, 1963).

[30] A. de Tocqueville, *Democracy in America* (New York: Vintage, 1990), 158–159. See also D. Karmis, 'Fédéralisme et relations intercommunautaires chez Tocqueville: entre prudence et négation des possibles' (1998) 17 *Politique et Sociétés* 59–91, 67–72.

[31] LaCroix, *The Ideological Origins of American Federalism*, 2. She also observes that: 'A new conception of layered governmental authority had been invented during the colonists' struggles with

Instrumental in all of this was a series of newspaper articles published by Alexander Hamilton, John Jay, and James Madison, who together adopted the collective pen name Publius. These polemics, brought together as *The Federalist* papers, intervened in the constitutional debate following the Philadelphia Constitutional Convention of 1787, promoting the ratification of the draft constitutional text which it had produced. In doing so, and displaying, archetypically, the iterative interplay between constitutional practice and theory, the authors fashioned a new intellectual framework for the emerging idea of federal government as a distinct category of constitutional rule. As Rossiter puts it: '*The Federalist* converted federalism from an expedient into an article of faith, from an occasional accident of history into an enduring expression of the principles of constitutionalism.'[32]

What emerged at Philadelphia was a constitutional model that was in effect a hybrid (for James Madison, a 'compound'[33]) between two very different visions, one unitary and centralising, the other pluralist and diversifying.[34] The American foundation was a huge step forward for federal constitutionalism, conceiving as it did of the very possibility of multiple governments co-existing and co-operating within the modern state, despite the inherently unifying and centralising impetus with which the nation-state was otherwise emerging and consolidating in this period.[35] In doing so, it located federalism firmly as a constitutional form for the modern state and not, as it had hitherto been understood, as a loose governing arrangement for a composite of independent states.[36]

The birth of the US constitution was indeed a landmark in the emergence of federal constitutionalism. But the fact remains that no individual constitution, designed to meet the very specific needs of a particular polity, should be treated as itself definitive of a broader family of constitutional rule, without skewing the essence of that generic idea within wider constitutional theory. Contemporary understandings of the American system as a blueprint for federalism are largely

metropolitan powers and refined during the early republicans' debates over the institutional mechanisms by which that authority would operate. That conception ended up bearing the name 'federalism', a theoretically and historically significant label that immediately began to accumulate new meanings and new significances as it rolled onward in time.' LaCroix, 220

32 C. Rossiter (ed.), *The Federalist Papers* (New York: The New American Library, 1961), Preface xii.

33 James Madison, Federalist No. 51, Rossiter (ed.), *The Federalist Papers*, 320–325.

34 Madison called these, respectively, 'national' and 'federal' visions of the Constitution, reflecting a broader conceptual tension that manifested itself in the institutional battle between the Virginia and New Jersey plans. James Madison, Federalist No. 39, Rossiter (ed.), *The Federalist Papers*, 240–246.

35 A.D. Smith, *Nationalism and Modernism* (London: Routledge, 1998).

36 In this regard, the move away from the existing constitutional model was conceptually radical. The union encapsulated in the Articles of Confederation from 1781 to 1787 was, like the Confederations in Germany, the Netherlands, and Switzerland of the sixteenth and seventeenth centuries, essentially a league of independent states: D.S. Lutz, 'The Articles of Confederation as the Background to the Federal Republic' (1990) 20 *Publius: The Journal of Federalism* 55–70. It is therefore no exaggeration to argue that: 'The history of modern federal government … begins with the adoption of the US Constitution in 1789 and the break with the historical practice of confederalism.' Hueglin and Fenna, *Comparative Federalism*, 2nd edn., 73.

due to the later adoption of territorial systems of rule which used it as a principal referent. In the nineteenth century, and despite the ways in which its own constitutional self-understanding had so radically changed in the intervening decades, the deeply unsettled American model was a major influence—'the decisive model'[37]—upon processes of constitution-building in the British Dominions. We see this in the birth of the modern Canadian constitution in 1867,[38] where the American experience served as a very powerful backdrop to the foundational debates,[39] even if the recently concluded internal conflict tended to accentuate the vices rather than the virtues of the Philadelphia precedent.[40] But what the Canadian process also served to demonstrate was the lack of any conceptual agreement about the idea of federalism or even of the use of the word 'federal'. Unlike the Constitution of the United States, the British North America (BNA) Act did make one reference to its federal nature, in the first clause of the preamble: 'Whereas the Provinces of Canada, Nova Scotia, and New Brunswick have expressed their Desire to be federally united into One Dominion . . .'.[41] But no other use of the word occurs in the Act. Indeed, the 'idiosyncratic'[42] adoption of the term 'confederation' in relation to the BNA Act to describe what is today considered to be a quintessentially *federal* system, denotes the ongoing conceptual and lexical fluidity of the federal idea— 'a polyhedron'[43]—by the mid-nineteenth century.[44]

Earlier, the Swiss had adopted the term 'Federal Constitution' for their new system of government in 1848 which bound the twenty-two cantons more closely together. However, again we find an internationally settled nomenclature to be

[37] H. Sidgwick, *The Development of European Polity*, 2nd edn (London: Macmillan and Co., Ltd, 1903), 430.

[38] British North America Act (BNA), 1867, 30–31 Vict., c. 3 (UK); renamed the Constitution Act, 1867 by the Canada Act, 1982, c. 11 (UK).

[39] R. Chagnon, 'The Fathers of Confederation and the BNA Act: Constitutional Visions and Models', in E. Brouillet, A.-G. Gagnon, and G. Laforest (eds), *The Quebec Conference of 1864: Understanding the Emergence of the Canadian Federation* (Kingston/Montreal: McGill-Queen's University Press, 2018), 29–48, 40–43.

[40] E. Brouillet, A.-G. Gagnon, and G. Laforest, '1864, a Pivotal Year in the Advent of the Canadian Confederation', in E. Brouillet, A.-G. Gagnon, and G. Laforest (eds), *The Quebec Conference of 1864: Understanding the Emergence of the Canadian Federation* (Kingston/Montreal: McGill-Queen's University Press, 2018), 3–25, 11–12. See also S. Tierney, 'Misconceiving Federalism: Canada and the Constitutional Idea', in R. Albert (ed.), *Canada in the World* (Cambridge: Cambridge University Press, 2017), 34–58.

[41] Preamble, British North America (BNA) Act, 1867, 30–31 Vict., c. 3 (UK).

[42] Hueglin and Fenna, *Comparative Federalism* 2nd edn, 109.

[43] M. Chevrier, 'The Idea of Federalism among the Founding Fathers of the United States and Canada', in A.-G. Gagnon (ed.), *Contemporary Canadian Federalism: Foundations, Traditions, Institutions* (Toronto: University of Toronto Press, 2007), 11–52, 41.

[44] Rachel Chagnon, discussing the process leading to the BNA Act 1867, observes, 'a clear definition of federalism proved impossible to formulate during the debates even when the definitive version of the project was drawn up in London. The terms federation, confederation, or federal union, apparently squaring the circle, were used indiscriminately.' Rachel Chagnon, 'The Fathers of Confederation and the BNA Act: Constitutional Visions and Morals', 36. This echoes the American process. LaCroix also notes the 'slipperiness' of terms such as federal and confederal 'used by commentators in the founding and ratification periods, and the rapidity with which meanings could change'. LaCroix, *The Ideological Origins of American Federalism*, 217.

elusive. According to Nicolas Schmitt, this process transformed 'a centuries' old confederation into a federal state',[45] but the constitutional design of this model was in many ways more decentralised than Canadian *confederation*, and the term confederation was, and continues to be, used in the Swiss constitution as a form of self-description.[46] One point ishowever clear. Despite its own long (and at times quixotically) vernacular history of territorial union, the Swiss constitution of 1848 was clearly influenced by the architectural innovations of Philadelphia, for example in the adoption of a bicameral legislature.[47] So too were the legal orders of various Latin American countries in the nineteenth century—Venezuela (1811), Mexico (1824), Argentina (1853), and Brazil (1891) —each of which adopted presidential-congressional forms of government[48] and more broadly 'adopted federal structures in imitation of the U.S. federation'.[49]

Half a century after the Swiss constitutional reorganisation, another British Dominion, Australia, explicitly adopted the term 'federal' to describe the nature of the new constitution and the institutions it created.[50] However, the term 'Commonwealth' (Article 1 of the 1900 Act) was a more prominent descriptor. Despite its confusingly mixed terminology, the Commonwealth of Australia Constitution Act 1900 followed the American federal model more faithfully—or 'slavishly'[51]—than did the Canadian founders in 1867.[52] Both the Canadian and

45 N. Schmitt, 'Swiss Confederation', in J. Kincaid and G. Alan Tarr (eds), *Constitutional Origins, Structure, and Change in Federal Countries*, (Montreal/Kingston: McGill-Queen's University Press, 2005) *vol. 1*, 347–381, 376. And see J. Wayne Baker, 'The Covenantal Basis for the Development of Swiss Political Federalism: 1291–1848' (1993) 23 *Publius* 19–41.

46 'The People and the Cantons ... form the Swiss Confederation', Constitution of Switzerland, (1999), art. 1.

47 Hueglin and Fenna note that, despite Switzerland's longevity as a polity and pre-modern confederal character, 'modernizing elites essentially adopted the American model of second-chamber representation when Switzerland changed from confederal to federal governance in the nineteenth century'. Hueglin and Fenna, *Comparative Federalism* 2nd edn, 67. Watts also observes that the legislative division of powers and a popularly elected second chamber with equal cantonal representation also echo the American constitution. See Watts, *Comparing Federal Systems*, 3rd edn, 69.

48 Jose A. Cheibub et al., 'Latin American Presidentialism in Comparative and Historical Perspective' (2011) 89 *Texas Law Review* 1707–1731, 1710, 1712, n. 42.

49 Watts, *Comparing Federal Systems*, 3rd edn, 3. See also K.S. Rosenn, 'Federalism in the Americas in Comparative Perspective' (1994) 26 *The University of Miami Inter-American Law Review* 1–50. Colombia also experimented with federalism in the nineteenth century, becoming the United States of Colombia in 1863.

50 The preamble to the Commonwealth of Australia Constitution Act 1900 commences: 'WHEREAS the people of New South Wales, Victoria, South Australia, Queensland, and Tasmania, humbly relying on the blessing of Almighty God, have agreed to unite in one indissoluble Federal Commonwealth under the Crown of the United Kingdom of Great Britain and Ireland, and under the Constitution hereby established: ... '. Its institutions are also described in federal terms. The legislative power is vested in 'a Federal Parliament'. Constitution of Australia (1901), chap. 1, pt 1. This contrasts with the national legislature of Canada which is simply called 'the Parliament of Canada', British North America Act (BNA), 1867, 30–31 Vict., c. 3 (UK), art. IV., s. 17.

51 Hueglin and Fenna, *Comparative Federalism: A Systematic Inquiry*, 2nd edn, 161.

52 The Australian federal system was nevertheless the product of a very wide range of intellectual influences: N. Aroney '"A Commonwealth of Commonwealths": Late Nineteenth-Century Conceptions of Federalism and Their Impact on Australian Federation, 1890–1901' (2002) 23 *The Journal of Legal History* 253–290. See also C. Saunders, 'Commonwealth of Australia', in J. Kincaid and G. Alan Tarr (eds), *Constitutional Origins, Structure, and Change in Federal Countries, vol. 1*, 12–47. American

Australian systems are of course distinguishable from the American constitution on one fundamental register, adopting as they did British-style parliamentary, rather than presidential, systems of government. So too did India in 1950. Indian constitution-makers were primarily influenced by the structure of government bequeathed by the UK Parliament through the Government of India Act 1935, which was itself modelled on the BNA Act 1867.[53] The Indian constitution in fact avoided the term 'federal', using 'union' instead.[54]

The American precedent was throughout this period hugely influential in conceptual as much as institutional ways, helping to shape the mindset of later constitution-makers.[55] Indeed, given that it was set to travel across the globe to

constitutionalism was influential in some ways directly, and in others indirectly, through the work of James Bryce, A.V. Dicey, Edward Freeman, and others. Peter Oliver observes: 'Bryce had a particularly strong influence in Australia, where his *The American Commonwealth* (London, Macmillan, 1888) had been required reading for participants in the Conventions of the 1890s which drafted the Australian Constitution.' P. Oliver, 'Parliamentary Sovereignty, Federalism and the Commonwealth', in R. Schutze and S. Tierney (eds), *The United Kingdom and the Federal Idea* (Oxford: Hart, 2018), 49–72, 58. Aroney agrees, describing Bryce's work as: 'the most profound of the influences on the Australian framers'. Aroney, '"A Commonwealth of Commonwealths": Late Nineteenth-Century Conceptions of Federalism and Their Impact on Australian Federation, 1890–1901', 263.

Modern systems also influenced each other in diverse and often *ad hoc* ways. The historic attachment to direct democracy within Swiss constitutionalism was attractive to Australian constitution-makers who adopted the use of double majority referendums for constitutional amendment in the 1901 Act.

Alone among modern federal systems, the origins of German federalism were largely indigenous and hence relatively unaffected by the American exemplar. In 1871, the North German Federation of 1867 was expanded to include south German states, building the modern German state. This was based upon the discrete historical unions of the German lands and in time the constitution would establish the very distinctive model of German 'administrative federalism' which we explore in later chapters. However, we will also discuss how the more modern manifestation of German federalism, in 1949, was in part shaped by American practice.

[53] Watts, *Comparing Federal Systems*, 3rd edn, 36; A. Majeed, 'Republic of India', in J. Kincaid and G. Alan Tarr (eds), *Constitutional Origins, Structure, and Change in Federal Countries, vol. 1*, 180–207. Canada in its turn influenced constitution-making in a number of other former colonies including Malaysia as they moved to independence within the British Dominions. Watts, *Comparing Federal Systems*, 3rd edn, 69.

[54] Article 1 declares India to be a 'union of states'. The only context in which 'federal' is used is in relation to the 'Federal Court' (*inter alia*, art. 366(11)), an institution which predated the constitution, being originally constituted under the Government of India Act, 1935.

[55] It is important to recall that for Americans themselves, the adoption of a federal system was first of all a dramatic step-change in mentality rather than merely a new institutional structure for government. LaCroix talks of 'an American ideology of federalism'. For her: 'This ideology was larger and more profound than a constitutional doctrine or a structural principle of government. Rather, it was the frame through which Americans came to view their political and legal world, as well as the foundation of the nation itself.' LaCroix, *The Ideological Origins of American Federalism*, 221. Its role as a prototype was aided by important early commentaries upon the federal form of government that drew upon the American system as a model. A very influential early work was James Bryce's three-volume study. This was primarily concerned with America but also drew comparisons with Canada in its final sections: J. Bryce, *The American Commonwealth, 3 vols* (London: MacMillan and Company, 1888). We have noted his influence on Australian federalism. Henry Sidgwick was a nineteenth-century scholar who cast his net more widely, studying the Germanic and Swiss traditions of plural government. H. Sidgwick, *The Elements of Politics* (London: Macmillan, 1891); *The Development of European Polity* (London: Macmillan, 1903). In these nineteenth-century studies, and others by Dicey, Mill, and others, a blending of theory and practice came, by the turn of the twentieth century, to form a sharper idea of federalism from its early, and still embryonic institutional manifestations.

a range of very different societies with contrasting political histories and traditions and embed itself through very different constitutional models, the American model could only do so as a constitutional idea, not as an institutional standard. Its key role therefore was to create the very possibility that territorial pluralism could be accommodated constitutionally within a nation-state. In this way, the American system, despite its incipient and unresolved foundational disagreements, its pathological failings by the mid-nineteenth century, and its subsequent transformation in a centralising way, became effectively synonymous with the very term 'federalism' and the totem of a universalisable constitutional idea of federal government.

In the twentieth century this term 'federal government' was most famously deployed by Kenneth Wheare. The evangelical influence of Wheare, an Australian constitutionalist working in Oxford, should not be underestimated for the way in which he, by mid-century (and on the eve of Western decolonisation through which federalism was set to enjoy a new lease of life), helped consolidate an institutionalist approach to federalism, in a way analogous to Dicey's influence upon British and Commonwealth constitutionalism, while at the same time eliding the idea underpinning federal practice with the American constitution: for Wheare, the prototype of an empirical federal species. His *magnum opus* of 1946 treated American constitutionalism and 'federal government' as, in effect, synonyms.[56] Watts, another adherent of federal institutionalism and both a student and a (not uncritical) follower of Wheare, was moved to observe some sixty years later that this intellectual tendency to see the US constitution as the institutional pole star for federal theory was mirrored in practice: 'Virtually all subsequently attempted federations have taken some account of the constitutional design and operation of the United States in developing their own federal structures.'[57]

As a consequence, in the twentieth century, federal systems were also constructed adopting or at least adapting this original constitutional precedent. States emerging from colonial rule including not only India (1950) but also Malaya (1948), Pakistan (1956), Malaysia (1963), Nigeria (1954), Rhodesia and Nyasaland (1953), the West Indies (1958), Indochina (1945–47), the Mali Federation (1959), and Indonesia (1945–49) all experimented with federalism[58] and were influenced both by the constitutions of existing federal Dominions and, either directly or through these British imperial precedents, by the American template.

[56] The innovation that resulted from Philadelphia 'justifies us in describing the new principle, which distinguishes the US constitution so markedly and so significantly, as the "federal" principle'. K.C. Wheare, *Federal Government* (New York: Oxford University Press, 1946), 11.

[57] Watts, *Comparing Federal Systems*, 3rd edn, 30. Working at the same time as Wheare, H.R.G. Greaves also argued that the USA was 'the outstanding example of a federal union'. H.R.G. Greaves, *Federal Union in Practice* (London: George Allen & Unwin, 1940), 16.

[58] Watts' was a pioneer of the study of those countries, particularly of the British Commonwealth, that adopted federalism in the process of decolonisation. R.L. Watts, *New Federations: Experiments in the Commonwealth* (Oxford: Oxford University Press, 1966). See also R.L. Watts, 'The Federal Idea and its Contemporary Relevance', in T.L. Courchene et al., *The Federal Idea: Essays in Honour of Ronald L. Watts* (Kingston-Montreal: McGill-Queen's, 2011), 13–27, 19–20.

This influence was also felt in a second wave of Latin American federalism. South American states (Brazil (1946), Venezuela (1947), and Argentina (1949)) 'where the federal structure of the United States had often been imitated',[59] resorted again to federalism in the course of a new post-war turn in constitution-making, and once again the shadow of Philadelphia was felt.[60]

This was a propitious time for federalism which was enjoying 'a popularity such as it had never known before',[61] as Western empires collapsed and new states looked with some admiration to the success of existing federal systems in North America and Australia. A further reason was the search for constitutional solutions to the political pathologies of 1930s Europe. After the Second World War, Germany (1949) and Austria (1945) adopted models of federalism that did to some extent recall early-modern experiences of shared territorial rule in the German lands.[62] But in the post-war world, victor's constitutionalism also played its part as the political power of *Pax Americana* helped shape state reconstruction in the territories of the Holy Roman Empire. Although the German lands had been characterised by a particular tradition of segmented, and largely unstructured, territorial rule for centuries up to the mid-nineteenth century, the post-war models took on the trappings of embedded constitutionalism and juridification under the influence of American constitutional architects.[63] This influence also extended to breaking up historic territories within Germany, in particular Prussia, to create new federal *Länder*, thereby helping to ensure German federalism did not consolidate strong

[59] Watts, 'The Federal Idea and its Contemporary Relevance', 20. Another example is the federal constitution for Mexico, promulgated in 1824; its federal status was restated in the constitution of 1917.

[60] 'In terms of institutional set-up, the federal systems of Mexico, Venezuela, Brazil and Argentina are strongly American in character.' Hueglin and Fenna, *Comparative Federalism* 2nd edn, 67. It is however also important to observe that the constitutions adopted in these Latin American countries tended, as they always had, to be federal more in form than reality; the central branch of government rarely relinquishing any real powers to the territories. E.L. Gibson (ed.), *Federalism and Democracy in Latin America* (Baltimore: John Hopkins University Press, 2004).

[61] M. Beloff, 'The "Federal Solution" in the Application to Europe, Asia and Africa' (1953) 1 *Political Studies* 114–131, 114.

[62] Hueglin and Fenna, *Comparative Federalism*, 2nd edn, 196; H.W. Koch, *A Constitutional History of Germany in the Nineteenth and Twentieth Centuries* (London: Longman, 1984). The German constitution of 1949 also built upon both the federal model Germany had adopted in 1871 and the re-worked version contained in the Weimar constitution in 1919. Constitution of the German Empire (1919), *inter alia* arts 12–19 and 60–67. The post-war constitution of Austria reinstated the federal model that characterised the Austrian constitution of 1920. Constitution of Austria (1920), chs 2–4. M. Stelzer, *The Constitution of the Republic of Austria: A Contextual Analysis* (Oxford: Hart Publishing, 2011). Even Communist systems adopted at least the form of federalism if not the reality of meaningful territorial pluralism. This was a feature of the USSR from 1918, Soviet Russia Constitution (1918), and was adopted by the Socialist Federal Republic of Yugoslavia in 1946 and the Constitution of Czechoslovakia in 1960.

[63] Despite the discrete tradition of earlier German federalism it is also the case that American constitutionalism influenced the constitutional development of German territories in the nineteenth century: H. Steinberger, 'Historic Influences of American Constitutionalism upon German Constitutional Development: Federalism and Judicial Review' (1998) 36 *Columbia Journal of Transnational Law* 189–208, 196.

regional identities.[64] This approach tended to turn the federal idea on its head—aiming to eradicate rather than accommodate territorial diversity. But the lack of deep territorial attachments had always been a social reality of American federalism and, to those helping to constitute a new Germany, the securing of liberal rights and the distribution of sites of government as a way of containing the power of the centre were prioritised over, and indeed seen as preferable to, the nurturing of territorial identities.

The German experience highlights an inherent problem with the pervasive influence of American federalism (perceived of course as a strength by J S Mill, Bryce, and others as I will discuss in later chapters): its design to serve—and to foster—a very homogeneous population would limit its utility as a model for the more demotically diverse states that would later turn to federalism as a way to accommodate difference.[65] Indeed the US model was already of limited precedential value in the nineteenth century where federalism in both Switzerland and Canada evolved to manage deep, territorially located, cultural diversity. We see the fundamental shortcomings of its value as a prototype more starkly when we turn to the failures of federalism as the initial bubble of post-colonial optimism began to deflate during the second half of the twentieth century. From the late 1960s through to the 1980s it became apparent that a number of post-war federations were degenerating, and indeed a number, such as the West Indies, Pakistan/Bangladesh, and Malaya, either collapsed into separate states or adopted a unitary constitutional form in the face of separatist pressures.[66]

Since 1989 we have seen many attempts to adapt federal rule to societal situations of deep complexity, from the former Yugoslavia to Iraq and Sri Lanka.[67] The Belgian constitution changed in 1993 to declare the state federal,[68] South Africa experimented with federalism in its interim constitution in 1994 and in the final,

[64] C. Clark, *Iron Kingdom: The Rise and Downfall of Prussia, 1600-1947* (Cambridge MA: Harvard University Press, 2006), 687.

[65] Although Madison extolled federalism as a good system of government for a large and diverse population (*The Federalist*, 10), the founding of the Constitution took place at a time in which the revolutionary war had helped forge a strong sense of an American national self. J.M. Murrin, 'A Roof without Walls: The Dilemma of American National Identity', in R. Beeman, S. Botein, and E.C. Carter II (eds), *Beyond Confederation: Origins of the Constitution and American National Identity* (Chapel Hill: University of North Carolina Press, 1987), 333–348. See also Chief Justice Chase: 'The Union of the States never was a purely artificial and arbitrary relation. It began among the Colonies, and grew out of common origin, mutual sympathies, kindred principles, similar interests, and geographical relations.' *Texas v White* 74 U.S. (7 Wall.) 700 (1869), 724.

[66] Watts, having catalogued post-colonial dabbling with federalism, comments: 'Most of the post-war federal experiments experienced difficulties and a number of these were abandoned or temporarily suspended.' Watts, 'The Federal Idea and its Contemporary Relevance', 20.

[67] D. Stjepanović, 'Multiethnic Regionalisms in Southeastern Europe: Statehood Alternatives' (London: Palgrave MacMillan, 2018); L.M. Anderson, 'Theorizing Federalism in Iraq' (2007) *Regional and Federal Studies* 159–171; R. Edrisinha and A. Welikala (eds), *Essays on Federalism in Sri Lanka* (Colombo: Centre for Policy Alternatives, 2008).

[68] Constitution of Belgium (1831), tit. 1, art. 1.

promulgated version in 1996 it established a complex system that both established territorial levels of government and integrated these closely with the centre.[69] In 1978 Spain adopted a constitution which expressly provided for plural governments,[70] while South America witnessed yet another series of federal constitution-making initiatives in Brazil (1988), Argentina (1994), and Venezuela (1999).[71] Mexico reformed its already federal constitutional system in 2000, while Russia promulgated a new federal legal order in 1993, as did Nigeria in 1999. Federalism has also been deployed in innovative ways to try to resolve serious conflicts, for example in Bosnia and Herzegovina,[72] Iraq,[73] and Nepal,[74] with decentralised government also now a feature of the Democratic Republic of Congo.[75] Other countries such as Myanmar and the Philippines have long debated federal constitutional reform.[76]

Many of these countries have turned to federalism in response to the often intense political problems that stem from deep territorial pluralism within their borders: 'as a way of ending acute civil ethno-cultural conflict and of avoiding utter political collapse'.[77] A recurrent problem however is that, despite the precedential weight it bears, the American system and the value-based superstructure that has been built upon it do not always travel well, largely because what should be a capacious constitutional idea has been delimited by an ideological disposition towards strong cultural unity, a normative elision with liberalism,[78] particularly a narrowly individualist account of liberalism,[79] and an empirical packaging by way of a highly particular institutional blueprint. It is no surprise that this 'template', adopted for the culturally, nationally, and ideologically harmonious United States, and adapted to a similarly congenial demotic environment in Australia (and the institutional endeavour to engineer such an environment in Germany) simply could

[69] Constitution of the Republic of South Africa (1996), ch. 6.

[70] The Spanish Constitution (1978), pt VIII.

[71] Edward Gibson, *Federalism and Democracy in Latin America*.

[72] Constitution of Bosnia and Herzegovina, (1995), art. III. Bosnia-Herzegovina contains within it the Federation of Bosnia and Herzegovina as one of two entities, all within a wider federal structure. S. Keil, *Multinational Federalism in Bosnia and Herzegovina* (Farnham and Burlington: Ashgate, 2013).

[73] Constitution of Iraq (2005), art. 1, 109–125.

[74] Constitution of Nepal (2015), pt 13–20. H. Bhattacharyya, *Federalism in Asia: India, Pakistan, Malaysia, Nepal and Myanmar*, 2nd edn (London: Routledge, 2021).

[75] The Constitution of the Democratic Republic of Congo (2005). This creates 'decentralized territorial entities', art. 3 and see arts 203–206.

[76] M.G. Breen, *The Road to Federalism in Nepal, Myanmar and Sri Lanka: Finding the Middle Ground* (Abingdon: Routledge, 2018); E. Araral (Jr), P.D. Hutchcroft, G.M. Llanto, J.E. Malaya, R.U. Mendoza, and J.C. Teehankee, *Debate on Federal Philippines: A Citizen's Handbook* (Manila: Ateneo de Manila University Press, 2017).

[77] Watts, 'The Federal Idea and its Contemporary Relevance', 23.

[78] Hueglin and Fenna argue that within American federalism, a 'strong ideological commitment to individual liberalism generally overrides concerns of regional or state authority'. Hueglin and Fenna, *Comparative Federalism*, 2nd edn, 56. We return to the ideological underpinnings of American federalism in Chapters 2 and 7.

[79] C. Taylor, 'The Politics of Recognition', in A. Gutman (ed), *Multiculturalism: Examining the Politics of Recognition* (Princeton: Princeton University Press, 1994), 25–73.

not operate as a roadmap for the constitutional management of highly complicated and often deeply fraught situations of cultural and national pluralism.[80]

When constitution-makers in more recent times have tried to adapt federal solutions to their own situations they find, instead of the commodious array of institutional tools which they need, rather an idea overlain by a thick epistemic empiricism that sets out, as definitive of the federal concept, an institutional apotheosis which was itself designed by, and then refined for, an entirely more straightforward popular environment in states which shared a very specific socio-political heritage: the liberal west, and in particular the Anglo-American world as it passed through decolonisation. This reality was already apparent in the nineteenth century as a very different institutional model took root in Canada, producing a constitutional system that has played out in a very different, less homogenising and less centralising way, than American or Australian federalism.

The combination of heavy empiricism and ideational presupposition means that systems which diverge from the institutional and ideological *idée fixe* which federal scholarship has assimilated over 200 years are often described as not federal, or at best partly federal.[81] But such an orientation in fact both distorts and constrains the federal idea through inappropriate registers. Political and moral instrumentalism latch onto, and in doing so misdirect, what is in reality a *constitutional* idea. This is a category error. *Contra* these approaches, the core constitutional purpose of federalism requires to be distilled in a conceptual way. Federalism is designed to manage political power for a highly specific, but inherent, purpose: the construction of a constitutional union founded upon the foundational significance of territorial pluralism. Accordingly, federalism as a system of rule must be sufficiently flexible to adapt to such pluralism from polity to polity in accordance with the specific territorial conditions of the state in question. There is no reason why federalism should not be a broad conceptual resource with which to manage the political conditions of complex societies today. However, in its attempt to box societal specificities into a fixed institutional and ideological schema, modern federal

[80] In 1999 Stepan noted that 'American-style federalism embodies some values that would be very inappropriate for many democratizing countries, especially multinational polities'. Alfred Stepan, 'Federalism and Democracy: Beyond the U.S. Model' (1999) 10 *Journal of Democracy* 19–34. One of these values is an insistence upon a symmetrical distribution of institutional roles and competences. Maja Sahadžić focuses upon the increasingly anachronistic blind-spot within federal theory that glosses over recent asymmetrical approaches to federal institution-building: 'traditional federal scholarship appears to have not kept up with the dynamics of the internal structure of states by assuming that the federal state is made up of equal constituent units. Not only does traditional federal scholarship limit the potential of dynamic federalism, it also hinders opportunities to confront challenges that are linked to changes in the understanding of autonomy claims.' M. Sahadžić, *Asymmetry, Multinationalism and Constitutional Law: Managing Legitimacy and Stability in Federalist States* (London: Routledge, 2021). See also F. Requejo, *Multinational Federalism and Value Pluralism* (London: Routledge, 2005).

[81] The term 'quasi-federal' has been discussed at n 18 above. It is no surprise that Watts uses this opaque description in labelling systems that do not possess all of the institutional essentials he considers necessary to be a federation: Watts, 'The Federal Idea and its Contemporary Relevance', 16. The inflexibility of federal theory is further explored in Chapter 2.

theory has tended to turn this core purpose on its head: federalism as a model of government should not adapt beyond fixed institutional limits to fit the needs of the societies which turn to it; rather these societies should constrain and package their constitutional and institutional imaginations if they wish to buy a constitutional franchise from the federal brand.[82]

What we are left with from the evolution of the federal idea since Philadelphia is both description, and indeed prescription, masquerading as definition or, more problematically, as ontology; and one highly stylistic instance of government posited as a universalisable model. Valuable though institutional analysis of federalism is, on its own—and when so heavily reliant upon one dominant and distorting example—it does not and cannot take us to the essence of the federal idea as a particular and generalisable order of rule for the modern state in all its territorial variation and complexity.

IV. The federal contract as a constitutional idea: towards a conceptual framework

My core methodological claim therefore is that, since federalism is a subset of the specific area of social activity we call constitutionalism, the federal idea needs to be reconceived through constitutional theory in order to unearth its core purpose in managing political power within a multi-territorial state. Constitutional theory has developed exponentially as a discipline in recent decades,[83] and yet we find that

[82] Ronald Watts in one of his later papers, in which he engaged with 'multinational federations', noted a paradox within traditional theory encapsulated in the work of Daniel Elazar. Elazar he observed 'often maintained that in a world marked by fragmentation, ethnic conflict and heightened nationalism, various forms of federal political arrangements combining self-rule and shared rule might provide a key to peace. At the same time, however, he saw ethnic nationalism as one of the strongest forces arrayed against federalism.' Ronald Watts, in J. Pinder and M. Burgess (eds), *Multinational Federations* (Oxford: Routledge, 2007), 225–247, 228 citing D.J. Elazar, *Federalism and the Way to Peace* (Kingston: Queen's University Press, 1994), 167–168. This is in fact not a paradox. Federalism, to be of value for modern pluralistic states, must be able to engage with and overcome revanchist nationalism through the accommodation of difference. Stepan alights upon how the 'classical model' approach has constrained imaginative institutional design within the federal idea: 'some of the most influential works in political science today offer incomplete or insufficiently broad definitions of federalism and thereby suggest that the range of choices facing newly democratising states is narrower than it actually is'. Stepan, 'Federalism and Democracy: Beyond the U.S. Model', 21. Talking of some of the challenging arenas in which federalism has been attempted, such as Iraq, Watts also says: 'the problem in these cases has been a lack of what previous experience has suggested are prerequisites for an effective federal system: respect for constitutionalism, and a prevailing spirit of tolerance and compromise. Until these necessary underlying conditions are created, efforts to create sustainable federal systems are likely to prove simply futile.' Watts, 'The Federal Idea and its Contemporary Relevance', 23. The category error here is the sense that social conditions should adapt to the federal form, rather than the need for the federal form to be sufficiently imaginative that *it* can adapt to facilitate challenging social conditions. As Aroney puts it 'federal bargains are a function of the unique conditions of each country'. N. Aroney, 'Constituent Power and the Constituent States: Towards a Theory of the Amendment of Federal Constitutions' (2017) 17 *Jus Politicum: Revue De Droit Politique* 5–31, 5.

[83] M. Loughlin, 'Constitutional Theory: A 25th Anniversary Essay' (2005) 25 *Oxford Journal of Law and Society* 183–202; D.J. Galligan, 'Constitutional Paradox or the Potential of Constitutional

federalism remains under-studied as a category of constitutionalism. As Amnon Lev points out: 'The surge of interest in the foundations of public law has yet to extend to federalism . . . As a result, we know very little about the intellectual foundations of the federation; what the values and ideas are that underpin this type of polity, inform its government and shape the normative expectations of the governed.'[84] Of course, the institutional manifestations of federalism have been widely studied, but this work tends either to be subsumed within the standard account of default unitary constitutionalism,[85] or to be seen as an outlier that does not fit within 'state constitutionalism'.[86]

My task is to move away from formulations of the federal idea that superimpose upon it a thick ideological or empirical conditioning and/or which see it merely as an institutional variant within one model of constitutionalism. I also seek to retrieve its essence as a *constitutional* idea rather than merely the constitutional manifestation of a *political* idea. Throughout the book I seek to do this through the conceptual categories—or discrete organs—which together constitute what I take to be the essential anatomy of constitutionalism: Foundations, Authority, Subjecthood, Purpose, Design, and Dynamics.

Chapter 2 takes forward the argument that federalism is a distinctive constitutional category that can only be explained through constitutional theory. In a review of the literature on federalism that brings out various strands of empirical analysis, I argue that each of these has failed to alight upon the constitutional essence of the federal idea. This chapter then addresses those theories of federalism that do exist, contending that these have been overlain by a moral normativism that tends to view federalism instrumentally as the conveyor of, or threat to, broader value systems. Against these approaches, the chapter posits an alternative constitutionalist methodology which begins by noting the essential function of a constitution: to transform political power into lawful authority. The essential task for the constitutional theorist of federalism is to explore what is done in the creation of a federal constitution that transforms political power into lawful authority *in a federal way*.

This leads in Chapter 3 to consideration of the foundations of federal constitutionalism. In this chapter I adopt a different approach from that which has tended to be taken in political or historical studies of federalism. Rather than considering

Theory' (2008) 28 *Oxford Journal of Legal Studies* 343–367; N.W. Barber, *The Constitutional State* (Oxford: Oxford University Press, 2010); D. Grimm, *Constitutionalism: Past, Present and Future* (Oxford: Oxford University Press, 2019).

[84] A. Lev, 'Introduction: Federalism and Public Law Theory', in A. Lev (ed.), *The Federal Idea: Public Law between Governance and Political Life* (Oxford: Hart Publishing, 2019), 1–26, 1.

[85] Carl Friedrich, like many other commentators, treated federalism as merely 'a subdivision of the general kind of process involved in modern constitutionalism'. C.J. Friedrich, 'Federal Constitutional Theory and Emergent Proposals', in A.W. Macmahon (ed.), *Federalism: Mature and Emergent* (New York: Russell & Russell, 1962), 510–533, 528–529.

[86] O. Beaud, *Théorie de la Fédération* (Paris: PUF, 2007).

the political motives or social forces active in the decision to federalise, the constitutional theorist is more concerned with what, in legal normative terms, is done in that moment of constitutional creation: the 'what' of constitution-making rather than the 'why' of constitution-making. An act of constitution-making is of great significance, it is a pact or a contract in which the parties to it are bound by their foundational legal commitment. There may be different reasons why each polity emerges as a federal constitution. What is significant for the constitutional theorist is the consequence of this in legal terms. Here I explore how the act of federal founding is fundamentally different from the birth of a unitary constitution. Collective territorial subjects come together to seal the federal contract; it is they, rather than merely the individualised populace, who provide a federal constitution with the underpinning legitimacy upon which its authority is based. Given the centrality of constituent territories to the formation of the federal constitutional contract, the relationship between constituent power and constitutional form which has been a primary focus of the constitutional theory of foundations needs to be fundamentally reworked in the context of a federal constitutional contract. The foundational constituent power of a federal constitution must be characterised in an entirely different way from foundational constituent power in a unitary constitution. This, as I explore in later chapters, has profound implications for how we must conceive of 'constitutional constituent authority' in the federal constitution going forward.

The very specific normative framework through which a federal constitution is founded leads me in Chapters 4 and 5 to consider the implications of the federal constitutional moment for the nature of authority within the federal contract. In Chapter 4 I trace the emergence of the concept of sovereignty in the context of the modern state, demonstrating how sovereignty has served instrumentally to provide a legal bulwark supporting the construction of the state, and offering a strong, coherent, and unified conception of ultimate rule in both its external, international dimension, and its inward-facing, constitutional aspect. This conception of sovereignty is however founded upon an essentially monist demotic base; a unifying nexus of one individualised people forming the constitutional nation. In Chapter 5 I discuss how federalism does not fit comfortably within default monist constitutionalism and in fact represents a potentially radical alternative to it. Having argued in Chapter 3 that the foundation of a federal constitution is based upon territorially situated demotic pluralism rather than demotic homogeneity, what flows from this is a radically different way of conceiving the nature of authority and the relations of authority within the constitution. In this chapter I therefore confront the ill-fitting relationship between federalism and sovereignty. Some have argued that sovereignty in federal context is 'divisible', while others have sought to reconceive relations of authority within a federal constitution without reliance upon sovereignty theory at all. I reject both approaches. Sovereignty is as meaningful a concept for the federal constitution as for any other, and as the category of ultimate constitutional rule it cannot be divided. However, just as the moment of federal constitutional origins is fundamentally distinguishable from the unitary constitutional moment, so too must sovereign authority within a federal constitutional order be conceived in very different ways from that within a unitary constitution. I return to the distinction introduced in Chapter 3 between 'foundational constituent power' and 'constitutional constituent authority', exploring how the latter plays out very differently in the context of federalism from the way it manifests itself in a unitary constitution, resting as it does upon pluralised territorial sources of constitutional constituent power. The chapter notes the potential implications of this for the very essence of federal constitutionalism.

If the legitimation of political rule is the underlying purpose of contemporary constitutionalism, the key source of legitimacy for any polity is its subjects. In Chapter 6 I discuss how it is in framing the relevant subjects of federal democracy within the federal idea that perhaps the most stark contrast arises between federal constitutional theory and that of default monist constitutionalism. In this chapter I advance the claim that, in constitutional terms, the primary subjects of the federal constitution are its constituent territories. The legal-normative implication of this reality, which marks a category distinction with unitary constitutionalism and the exclusive subjecthood it attributes to individuals, is a fundamental challenge to established constitutional theory. It is remarkable that constitutional theory has in general failed to address the implications of the collective territorial constitutional subject for standard constitutional concepts such as constituent power, sovereignty, and citizenship. In this chapter I begin this task.

In Chapter 7 I build upon these accounts of foundations, authority, and subjecthood to elicit the purpose of federalism. I distinguish the idea of constitutional purpose from that of political purpose, the former asserting the creation of legally conditioned path dependencies as of greater legal-normative significance than the political motivations involved in doing so. Strategic political aims are of course a relevant and important consideration in the framing of any constitution, but constitutionalism is by its nature about the *regulation* of political power more than the impulses behind its exercise. On this basis I ask why it is that political power is husbanded by certain constitutions in a federal way. An attempt is made in the chapter to define the meta-purpose of federalism as the foundational recognition and accommodation of a constitution's constituent territorial pluralism through a union relationship that both creates and reconciles different orders of government. I discuss how this fundamental constitutional purpose of federalism contains within it a tension between two different dynamics: pluralism and union. Rather than being a pathology of federalism, leading to its inevitable demise, I argue that this iterative relationship provides the dynamic resource through which a healthy federal constitutional system forges its own path. It is also the case that the fundamental purpose of federalism leads to principles, by which is meant the logical implication or chain of reasoning that flows from the foundational character of federalism as a particular form of constitutional rule. It is argued that there are four principles of federal constitutionalism: recognition, autonomous government, associational government, and reciprocity, the last of these manifesting itself in both vertical and horizontal dimensions.

In Chapters 8 and 9 I turn to design. The foundations, purpose, and principles of federalism bear implications for how the institutional structure of the constitution should be fashioned. But in abjuring heavily empirical approaches to federalism, I contend that it is not possible to lay out an institutional template as the definitive representation of federal design. Much of the focus of political studies and constitutional law scholarship on federalism centres upon institutional form. A dominant strain has involved an attempt to arrive at the essential institutional framework that makes a polity either federal or non-federal. The consequence is that the nature of federalism is distorted by an approach that is institutionally led rather than focused upon the idea of federalism that derives from its immanent constitutional purpose. In lived constitutional experience, the institutionalisation of federalism manifests itself very differently from one constitution to another. And it is perfectly appropriate that it should do so, given that the primary purpose of federalism is to accommodate territorial pluralism as it manifests itself from polity to polity: just as the nature of demotic pluralism differs from state to state, so too will the institutional design of the constitution.

In these two chapters I build upon my account of principles in Chapter 7 to show how these can be given effect in a very broad range of ways from one federal constitution to another. I also consider how the various principles of federalism manifest themselves in very different ways from one federal constitution to another. In chapter 8 I address the principles of recognition and autonomous government; in Chapter 9 I turn to associational government and both vertical and horizontal reciprocity. The purpose of these chapters is to explore how the federal contract can come to be constituted in a range of different ways; these chapters do not purport to be a comprehensive exercise in empirical comparative politics or constitutional law nor an account of the institutional design of every federal system.[87]

A final issue is the dynamics of the federal polity and, in particular, how constitutional change is effected. This is addressed in Chapter 10. Constitutional theory is increasingly concerned with the issue of constitutional amendment in a world of ever more elaborate and more deeply entrenched constitutions. A key question in contemporary debates is how best to reach an appropriate balance between open democratic decision-making on the one hand and constitutional entrenchment on

[87] For such accounts see Watts, *Comparing Federal Systems*; Hueglin and Fenna, *Comparative Federalism*; F. Palermo and K. Kössler, *Comparative Federalism: Constitutional Arrangements and Case Law* (Oxford: Hart Publishing, 2017), a recent and particularly comprehensive account.

the other. The federal model complicates this debate, which again of course has hitherto largely adopted the unitary, or at least the monist, constitution as its default case study.

An important question that arises is whether within the federal idea a different relationship exists or should exist between constitutional rigidity and open democracy than prevails within liberal-unitary constitutionalism. On the one hand, to what extent do constituent territories rely upon entrenchment to protect their original contract? On the other, does the tension between pluralism and union that characterises the federal contract require a more open field of political deliberation and decision-making in order to manage this tension and avoid constitutional gridlock and political atrophy? Constitutional change is also examined in broad relief, addressing the vital role judicial interpretation has played in shaping federal constitutions and how, at a deeper level, changes in constitutional culture can change and even fundamentally transform federal polities.

V. Conclusions

Federalism has both proliferated and diversified greatly in recent decades, and at the same time it has been the subject of renewed interest by scholars seeking to understand both its essence and its adaptability to new situations. One recurring difficulty is that early analysis, which has remained deeply influential, was built upon previous practice, in particular that of the American constitution which turned out to be an ill-fitting template for a potentially broad constitutional category. Another drawback is that those looking for the federal idea have tended to do so in the wrong places—by way of institutional or behavioural analysis on the one hand or normative political theory on the other, neither of which brings us to the conceptual essence of the federal idea. In this book I argue that only constitutional theory can uncover the fundamental nature of federalism as a specific genus of constitutional rule. Applying constitutional theory we will find that the federal idea marks a radical fork in the road in the development of the modern state: the federal constitutional contract contrasting sharply with the demotically monist mentality and institutional instantiation that characterises the unitary constitution. That said, the monist mindset has come to permeate understandings of federal constitutionalism to the point of assimilation within it. The methodology of constitutional theory therefore allows us to reset the distinctiveness of federal constitutionalism, drawing out the conceptual and functional components immanent within, and specific to, the federal idea. Constitutional theory also offers the tools with which to overcome the conceptual, classificatory, and terminological essentialism that has gripped much of the political studies and constitutional law scholarship in this area. It is surprising that the elements that comprise the anatomy of constitutionalism—foundations, authority, subjecthood, purpose, design, and dynamics—have not hitherto been subjected to a detailed conceptual study of the constitutional essence of federalism. The price has been ideational confusion and the empirical and practical constriction of federalism as a constitutional and political resource. The exposition of the federal idea by constitutional theory is a vital task and it is the aim of this book to take it forward.

2
Reconceiving Federalism

I. Introduction

In this chapter I address the definitional disagreement that has proven so debilitating to federal scholarship and so inhibiting to government practitioners who seek to adapt federalism to their own societal requirements. A principal cause of terminological discord has been a tendency to address federalism in a narrow empirical way, describing its political, social, and economic practice and effects rather than analysing its constitutional purpose and functions. I begin the chapter by addressing three main trends in federal scholarship which have done so much to explain the political practice of federalism but which have at the same time served to obscure the constitutional essence of the federal idea itself: definitionalism, institutionalism, and behaviouralism.

Since federal scholarship is largely observational in nature, it largely eschews theoretical enquiry into the conceptual underpinnings of the federal idea. However, when turning later in the chapter to the theoretical accounts of federalism that do exist, we still do not arrive firmly at the constitutional idea that encapsulates federalism. Attempts to explain the federal idea have been influenced by an implicit or explicit moral normativism that tends to view federalism either in expansive terms as a facilitator (or indeed personification) of the good life, or in an enervating way as a mere instrument whose value (and hence purpose) derives from its utility in furthering externally derived moral norms, in particular those of liberalism. In fact, empirical and theoretical accounts of federalism share an instrumentalist disposition that leaves both of these approaches incapable of arriving at the discrete conceptual essence of federalism as a constitutional form.

In the final section of the chapter I argue that it is necessary to move beyond empirical and moral-normative approaches in order to address federalism as a genus of government through the specific discipline of constitutional theory. Only in this way can we begin to piece together the anatomy of federal constitutional law and alight upon its inherent purpose as a species of modern constitutionalism.

The Federal Contract. Stephen Tierney, Oxford University Press. © Stephen Tierney 2022.
DOI: 10.1093/oso/9780198806745.003.0002

II. Empirical instrumentalism: definitionalism, institutionalism, and behaviouralism in the study of federalism

Within the scholarly traditions of political studies and constitutional law, a vast literature on federalism has scrutinised the political and constitutional structures of particular states;[1] addressed the comparative dimension of federalism;[2] analysed its institutional design;[3] offered assessments of the behavioural underpinnings of federal systems;[4] considered the implications of federalism for the functioning of political systems and state economies;[5] and addressed how federal

[1] For example, I. Morgan and P. Davies (eds), *The Federal Nation: Perspectives on American Federalism* (USA: Palgrave MacMillan, 2008); N. Aroney, *The Constitution of a Federal Commonwealth: The Making and Meaning of the Australian Constitution* (Cambridge: Cambridge University Press, 2007); A.-G. Gagnon (ed.), *Contemporary Canadian Federalism* (Toronto: University of Toronto Press, 2009); M. Umbach (ed.), *German Federalism: Past, Present and Future* (London: Palgrave MacMillan, 2002); L. Tillin, *Indian Federalism* (Oxford: Oxford University Press, 2019); H. Bhattacharyya, *Federalism in Asia: India, Pakistan, Malaysia, Nepal and Myanmar*, 2nd edn (London: Routledge, 2021).

[2] Comparative work on federalism by English-speaking scholars first emerged in the nineteenth century. Notable publications include Edward Augustus Freeman, *History of Federal Government: From the Foundation of the Achaian League to the Disruption of the United States* (London: MacMillan, 1863)—(Freeman originally intended to author four volumes, but he only completed one); J. Bryce, *The American Commonwealth, 3 vols* (London: MacMillan and Company, 1888); A.V. Dicey, *Introduction to the Study of the Law of the Constitution*, 8th edn (London: Macmillan and Co., 1915 [1st edn, 1885]). The first detailed twentieth-century study was undertaken by Kenneth Wheare: K.C. Wheare, *Federal Government* (Oxford: Oxford University Press, 1946). In recent decades comparative study has dominated the literature: R. Watts, *Comparing Federal Systems*, 3rd edn (Montreal/Kingston: McGill-Queens University Press, 2008); M. Burgess and A.-G. Gagnon (eds), *Comparative Federalism and Federation: Competing Traditions and Future Directions* (Hemel Hempstead, UK: Harvester Wheatsheaf, 1993); M. Burgess, *Comparative Federalism: Theory and Practice* (London: Routledge, 2006); T.O. Hueglin and A. Fenna, *Comparative Federalism: A Systematic Enquiry*, 2nd edn (Broadview Press: Peterborough, Ont., 2006); J. Erk, *Explaining Federalism: State, Society and Congruence in Austria, Belgium, Canada, Germany and Switzerland* (London: Routledge, 2007); M. Burgess, *In Search of the Federal Spirit: New Theoretical and Empirical Perspectives in Comparative Federalism* (Oxford: Oxford University Press, 2012); R. Saxena, *Varieties of Federal Governance: Major Contemporary Models* (Cambridge: Cambridge University Press, 2012). Most of these accounts are by scholars in political studies. A recent detailed study in comparative constitutional law is offered by F. Palermo and K. Kössler, *Comparative Federalism: Constitutional Arrangements and Case Law* (Oxford: Hart Publishing, 2017). This latter work is particularly rich in offering historical and contemporary approaches to federalism in both the Anglo-American and German traditions; on the latter see also Umbach, *German Federalism* and W. Swenden, *Federalism and Regionalism in Western Europe: A Comparative and Thematic Analysis* (United Kingdom: Palgrave, 2006); I. Härtel, *Handbuch des Föderalismus. Föderalismus als demokratische Rechtsordnung und Rechtskultur in Deutschland, Europa und der Welt* (Berlin: Springer, 2012).

[3] As we will discuss later in the chapter, institutionalism represents a strong tradition within federal scholarship. For a recent focus upon the relationship between institutional design and the sustainability of federal systems, see M. Filippov, P.C. Ordeshook, and O. Shvetsova, *Designing Federalism: A Theory of Self-Sustainable Federal Institutions* (Cambridge: Cambridge University Press, 2004). See also J. Bednar, *The Robust Federation: Principles of Design* (Cambridge: Cambridge University Press, 2009); A. Benz and J. Broschek, *Federal Dynamics Continuity, Change, and the Varieties of Federalism* (Oxford: Oxford University Press, 2013).

[4] Bryce was an early exponent of this tradition (*The American Commonwealth*). See also W.S. Livingston, *Federalism and Constitutional Change* (Oxford: Clarendon Press, 1956); Erk, *Explaining Federalism*.

[5] W. Riker, *Federalism: Origin, Operation, Significance* (Boston: Little, Brown, 1964); R.P. Inman and D.L. Rubinfield, 'Economics of Federalism', in F. Parisi (ed.), *The Oxford Handbook of Law and Economics: Volume 3: Public Law and Legal Institutions* (Oxford: Oxford University Press, 2017), 84–105.

relations play out in practice through party politics,[6] political culture,[7] and political attitudes and identities.[8] Much of this work has served greatly to illuminate the practice of federalism and, in particular, the tensions and strains which attend it. But as we review and map the main strands of this scholarship we find that it has not in the end produced a clear conceptualisation of federalism's legal-normative purpose.

There are three main approaches taken by scholars within this literature: definitionalism, institutionalism, and behaviouralism. The first involves institutionally focused attempts (largely of a lexical nature) to arrive at a definition of the word federal, and of related terms: federalism, federal political system, federation, and federal state. Indeed federal scholarship, perhaps more than any other constitutional category, has been troubled by deeply contested, often confused and latterly 'tired'[9] or 'sterile'[10] efforts to define the nature of the subject. One consequence of this is that—as discussed in Chapter 1—commentators disagree even about the number of 'federal states' that exist.[11] In essence, the definitional approach has been one of distinction-drawing.

One significant division upon which commentators have concentrated is that between a 'federal' and a 'confederal' system of government. This distinction demonstrates how definitional approaches to explaining federalism are ultimately subjective and circular. That the emerging American constitutional system was neither a unitary constitution nor a league or alliance of effectively sovereign and independent states was clear to the authors of the Federalist papers.[12] What has been less clear over time is exactly how to conceive of the American system as a *via media* between these two poles. And from this vague starting point, confusion has grown. Attempts to find a universal or universalisable account of the terms 'federal' or 'federation' is inevitably distorted by the notion of institutional practice from

[6] K. Detterbeck, *Multi-Level Party Politics in Western Europe* (Switzerland: Springer, 2012); A. Albala and J.M. Reniu (eds), *Coalition Politics and Federalism* (Switzerland: Springer, 2018).

[7] P. Fafard, F. Rocher, and C. Cote, 'The Presence (or Lack Thereof) of A Federal Culture in Canada: The Views of Canadians' (2010) 20 *Regional and Federal Studies* 19–43; M. Burgess, *In Search of the Federal Spirit: New Theoretical and Empirical Perspectives in Comparative Federalism* (Oxford: Oxford University Press, 2012), 252–279.

[8] J. Kincaid and R.L. Cole, 'Citizen Attitudes Toward Issues of Federalism in Canada, Mexico, and the United States' (2011) 41 *Publius* 53–75.

[9] Burgess, *Comparative Federalism*, 9.

[10] Palermo and Kössler, *Comparative Federalism*, 6.

[11] For a discussion of ongoing classificatory confusion in the contemporary federalism literature see B.A. Radin, 'Varieties of Federal Governance: Major Contemporary Models' (2012) 42 *Publius* 493–538. Palermo and Kössler conclude: 'the debate on classification of federal countries remains partisan and cannot lead to shared conclusions'. Palermo and Kössler, *Comparative Federalism*, 4.

[12] Madison made this point at the Constitutional Convention: M. Farrand, *Records of the Federal Convention of 1787, 4 vols* (New Haven: Yale University Press, 1911–37), I, 37. See also James Madison, Federalist No. 39 in C. Rossiter (ed.), *The Federalist Papers* (New York: The New American Library, 1961), 240–246; and for discussion, I. Hampsher-Monk, 'Democracy and Federation in the Federalist Papers', in A.-G. Gagnon and M. Burgess (eds), *Federal Democracies* (London: Taylor and Francis, 2010), 29–45.

which one starts;[13] and where the underpinning rationale of that exemplar is itself inchoate and contested, we are led down a definitional rabbit hole that is inevitably subjective, case-study led, and ultimately self-fulfilling.

One feature of the contrast between federalism and confederalism has been an attempt to define federalism by what it is not. For Thomas Franck it was 'a tendency that is neither unitary nor separatist'.[14] A concomitant problem with the federalism/confederalism binary has been a failure to distinguish constitutional law from statehood. Positing American federalism as a middle path between a league of states and a unitary state is fundamentally misconceived because it brings into play two different registers of normative authority simultaneously. The term 'unitary *state*' is in fact a misnomer, subsuming within it the actual vector of relevance: 'unitary *constitution*'. A state is an entirely different animal from a league of states, regardless of the type of constitution through which its government is organised. We therefore need to distinguish two fundamental steps taken by the Philadelphia process. The first was to constitute the United States, unequivocally, as one *state* within a nascent international community of states. The second distinct move was a constitutional one, establishing *internally* a federal system of government as the constitutional characterisation of the polity of that state. In practice the two certainly overlapped in time, but at a conceptual level this distinction is of the first importance. Federal theory has suffered from a tendency to elide these distinct concepts of state and constitution. We see the confusion more clearly in the continental tradition where the distinction between *bundesstaat*, as a form of 'federal state' which assumed also the title 'federation', and *staatenbund* (and more recently, *staatenverbund*), as league or confederacy of independent states, has left the concept of federalism, as a form of constitutional design for a modern, sovereign state, blurred.[15]

The confusion of state and constitution in a federal context was a feature of the literature from the late nineteenth into the twentieth century. Edward Augustus Freeman published the first volume of his *History of Federal Government* in 1863.[16] He viewed federalism in instrumental terms as an aid to building nation-states across territories sharing one nascent nationality, such as Italy and Germany: for him, federalism was a device with which to construct states for unified peoples rather than a form of constitutional law serving demotic pluralism.[17] Henry Sidgwick

[13] As Birch observes, federalism is 'defined by the student in a manner which is determined by the approach which he wishes to make to his material'. A.H. Birch, 'Approaches to the Study of Federalism', (1966) 14 *Political Studies* 15–33, 15.

[14] T.M. Franck (ed.), *Why Federations Fail: An Inquiry into the Requisites for Successful Federalism* (New York: New York University Press, 1968), Preface, x.

[15] The implications of this elision for further confusion over the nature of authority within federal constitutions is explored in Chapter 5.

[16] Freeman, *History of Federal Government*.

[17] As Lang puts it: 'Freeman was preoccupied with nation-building, with organizing Europe into large states that would bring peace and stability to the continent while extending its frontiers.' T. Lang, 'The Limits of Victorian Federalism: E.A. Freeman's History of Federal Government' (2018) History Open Access Publications <https://scholarworks.umass.edu/history_oapubs/3>, 1–18, 18.

took a similar approach to Freeman. In his notion of 'federality'—an umbrella category encompassing many different forms of rule involving multiple territories—he largely dismissed any clear distinction between *bundesstaat* and *staatenbund*. In this work the 'federal state' emerges as a category *sui generis*, distinct from both unitary states on the one hand and leagues or confederations on the other. Sidgwick, as did others in the nineteenth century, also viewed 'federal states' in a highly contingent way, as a transitional arrangement on the road to strong, unitary statehood.[18] He too concluded, somewhat unhelpfully, that no clear lines could necessarily be drawn in attempting to distinguish among *bundesstaat*, *staatenbund*, and federal state,[19] a conclusion that detracts from the very essence of definitionalism. And so from this nineteenth-century work, largely focused upon early German federal models, we see a tradition emerge that treats federalism as a distinct category of state and in doing so presents it as an outlier in relation to the burgeoning modern discourse on constitutional law.[20]

Using the American federal system as a template has led inevitably to definitionalism being superseded by institutionalism. In Chapter 1 we traced how, in the nineteenth and twentieth centuries, both federal constitution-making and federal scholarship were shaped by an assumption that the American constitutional model of 1787 represents the default prototype of federalism.

It is no surprise that nineteenth-century accounts of federalism were heavily influenced by the American experience.[21] But it is a curiosity that for much of the twentieth century, in particular during the revival in federal scholarship from the late 1940s, this remained the case.

Although interest in federalism had largely faded within Anglo-American constitutional studies in the first half of the last century, this changed with the end of the Second World War when Germany and Austria were reconstituted in a federal way, while federalism also gained traction in Africa, Asia, and the West Indies—decolonisation producing new states characterised by complex territorial pluralism: an era of 'federalism-as-panacea'.[22] At this time the publication of Kenneth Wheare's

[18] H. Sidgwick, *The Development of European Polity* (London: Macmillan, 1903), 433

[19] Henry Sidgwick, *The Development of European Polity*, 507.

[20] A tradition we continue to see today: O. Beaud, *Théorie de la Fédération* (Paris:, PUF, 2007); S. Rehling Larsen, *The Constitutional Theory of the Federation and the European Union* (Oxford: Oxford University Press, 2021).

[21] Bryce, *The American Commonwealth*. J.S. Mill's account of federalism was also largely framed by his account of American government: J.S. Mill, *Considerations on Representative Government* (Cambridge: Cambridge University Press, 1958), 305–319. In referring to adapting the general principles of representative government to a federal system, Mill took the view that 'the provision of the American Constitution seems exceedingly judicious'. Mill, 314. See also R.B. Porter, 'John Stuart Mill and Federalism' (1977) 7 *Publius* 101–124. Dicey too set out to compare sovereignty 'as it exists in England' with federalism as it existed in several parts of the world 'and especially in the United States of America'. A.V. Dicey, *Introduction to the Study of the Law of the Constitution*, 8th edn (London: Macmillan and Co., 1915), 138.

[22] 'a remedy for a great variety of political, economic, social, cultural, and other ailments and at all levels of organization'. Thomas M. Franck, *Why Federations Fail*, ix.

influential book, *Federal Government*,[23] was especially timely. Wheare, Gladstone Professor of Government and Public Administration at Oxford University, offered a positivist analysis of federalism which was, in Michael Burgess's estimation, narrowly 'legalistic'.[24] Wheare's approach was to define largely by description. He addressed federalism squarely through the register of institutional design, producing a comparative analysis of four federal systems (the USA, Canada, Australia, and Switzerland), the only states he considered properly federal.[25] Although this work was avowedly comparative, wide-ranging, and detailed in its analysis, the spectre of Philadelphia looms particularly large in Wheare's overall conception of the federal idea. Building upon the work of Bryce and Dicey, Wheare argued that: 'The modern idea of what federal government is has been determined by the United States of America.'[26] Therefore, it was appropriate '... in seeking a legitimate and convenient definition of federal government, to begin by examining the Constitution of the United States'.[27] But rather than simply beginning from such an investigation, Wheare relied upon the American system as a template, which he called the 'classical' form of federalism.[28]

Wheare's approach therefore was to search for the generic idea of federalism through empirical observation. The 'federal principle' was 'the method of dividing powers so that the general and regional governments are each, within a sphere, coordinate and independent'.[29] This approach, which sought to derive definition from practice, became a fixed characteristic of later work.[30] The problem with this approach is not only that it substitutes institutional design for conceptual clarity, but that the 'classical' governmental model from which it begins is wide and inexact. We see this in the defining properties of federalism which Rufus Davis derives from Wheare's definition: 'co-equal jural status; self-sufficient governmental machinery; fiscal autonomy, and some viable balance in the distribution

[23] K.C. Wheare, *Federal Government* (New York: Oxford University Press, 1946).

[24] Burgess, *In Search of the Federal Spirit*, 1. For Burgess, Wheare's account, dwelling 'largely in the language of constitutional law', missed the wider political implications of federalism. Livingston similarly charged Wheare with 'legal formalism'. W.S. Livingston, *Federalism and Constitutional Change* (Oxford: Oxford University Press, 1956), 1. Riker was characteristically more brusque, branding Wheare's approach 'extreme legalism'. W. Riker, 'Federalism', in F.I. Greenstein and N. Polsby (eds), *Handbook of Political Science. Volume V: Government Institutions and Process* (Reading MA: Addison-Wesley, 1975), 103.

[25] Wheare, *Federal Government*, 16.

[26] Wheare, *Federal Government*, 1.

[27] Wheare, *Federal Government*, 1.

[28] A focus which Burgess considers 'excessive'. Burgess, *In Search of the Federal Spirit*, 556.

[29] Wheare, *Federal Government*, 11. Wheare's definition in fact echoed that of the US Supreme Court's own post-Civil War account of the American constitutional settlement: 'The government of the United States and the government of a state are distinct and independent of each other within their respective spheres of action, although existing and exercising their powers within the same territorial limits. Neither government can intrude within the jurisdiction, or authorize any interference therein by its judicial officers with the action of the other.' *Tarble's Case*, 80 U.S. (13 Wall.) 397, 407 (1871).

[30] Half a century later Rufus Davis was still adopting a very similar approach. S. Rufus Davis, *Theory and Reality: Federal Ideas in Australia, England and Europe* (Queensland: University of Queensland Press, 1995), 46.

of functions'.[31] These efforts to generalise from this starting point could only end in failure: the American federal system which was framed so laconically by its own constitution, and which left open to political development how the system would operate in practice, could never perform such an ambitious role.[32] The problem however was, in methodological terms, more fundamental than merely tying the definition of federalism to one example. As federalism proliferated in diverse ways, such attempts to define a generic constitutional idea through description of practice fell hostage to changes in practice across the world. For example, early definitions of federalism based upon 'watertight'[33] divisions of rule between central and territorial governments became redundant, with the development of more and more shared competences as the size of the modern state (at all levels) continued to grow. New accounts of federalism therefore had to take account of increasingly shared and overlapping federalism, the so-called 'marble cake' nature of public law in a modern federal system.[34] Any definition by description was now buffeted by transformational developments in the contemporary polity, barely envisaged in 1787.[35] As Burgess put it, with the emergence of new federal forms in the era of post-war decolonisation, 'practice had outstripped theory'.[36]

After Wheare, institutionalist approaches to federalism lost credibility.[37] Indeed, in the post-war era, where federalism was deployed to manage the territorial pluralism of numerous and diverse emerging states, the focus of research moved from institutional design to the political, economic, and social roles federalism performed. This occurred at a time when behaviouralism was supplanting institutionalism within social studies and a new 'realism' became fashionable.[38] This wave of scholarship, beginning in the late 1950s, argued that what really mattered was not institutional form but the underpinning forces of power within constitutional systems.

31 Rufus Davis, *Theory and Reality: Federal Ideas in Australia, England and Europe*, 72. His work is discussed further in Chapter 7.

32 As Hueglin and Fenna argue: 'While American federalism remains the classical model, it ever more appears to us as a case of exceptionalism, posing limits to the extent that other federations might imitate or learn from it.' Hueglin and Fenna, *Comparative Federalism*, Preface, xiii.

33 *A.G. Canada v. A.G. Ontario* [1937] AC 326, 354.

34 M. Grodzins, *The American System* (D.J. Elazar ed.) (Chicago: Rand McNally & Company, 1966).

35 For example, in the new era of 'cooperative federalism', writers such as Maurice Vile in 1961 suggested that Wheare's notion of independence be replaced by 'interdependence'. M.J.C. Vile, *The Structure of American Federalism* (Oxford: Oxford University Press, 1961).

36 Burgess, *Comparative Federalism*, 36.

37 In a 1977 essay Maurice Vile was particularly scathing. For him a theory of federalism by this point 'hardly exist[ed]' because 'much of the theoretical effort of the last thirty years has been devoted to the discussion of the definition of federalism in such a way as to leave little or no basis upon which to build any sustained theoretical structure'. M.J.C. Vile, 'Federal Theory and the "New Federalism"' in D. Jaensch (ed.), *The Politics of New Federalism* (Adelaide: Australian Political Studies Association, 1977), 1.

38 H. Eulau, *The Behavioral Persuasion in Politics* (New York: Random House, 1963).

Particularly in the American federalism literature this type of behaviouralism came to dominate, with William Livingston leading this shift in approach.[39] Livingston was concerned not with the constitutional nature of federalism but rather with the social purposes federalism serves and the outcomes it produces: 'The essential nature of federalism is to be sought for not in the shading of legal and constitutional terminology but in forces economic, social, political and cultural that makes the outward forms of federalism necessary. The essence of federalism lies not in the constitutional or institutional structure but in the society itself.'[40] The institutional structure of federalism was viewed entirely instrumentally, as 'a device by which the federal qualities of a society are articulated and protected'.[41] In this way, Livingston sought to move federal scholarship entirely away from legal theory; constitutional concepts and even structures were of little concern, the real action was now located in social behaviour.

In 1964 William Riker published a study in which he applied rational choice theory in constructing a dense experimental and observational account of federalism.[42] Riker's approach, like Livingston's, was behaviouralist in disposition, but his work focused more upon patterns of political power than broader social forces. Turning his attention to the operation of federal systems, Riker like Livingston eschewed the institutionalist legalism of Wheare, which for him neglected or at least underplayed the significance of political realities.[43] But *contra* Livingston, he believed that the role of political actors trumped ideology or economic and social forces as the real determinants of political behaviour in federal systems. As Burgess puts it, Riker 'swung the pendulum of interpretation back from constitutional law, sociology and contemporary systems theory to political studies—or to "the political" ... with a focus that was avowedly "non-normative empirical analysis"'.[44] Riker's core concern was the motivation of political actors in creating a federal system, assessing from a 'rationalist' perspective the calculations that informed this decision.

[39] W.S. Livingston, *Federalism and Constitutional Change* (Oxford: Clarendon Press, 1956). It is possible to find strains of behaviouralism in earlier work, such as that of Bryce. In *American Commonwealth* he adopted a political-sociological approach in assessing the different centrifugal and centripetal pressures that play upon federal systems. J. Bryce, *Studies in History and Jurisprudence*, 2 vols (Oxford: Clarendon Press, 1901), discussed by Burgess, *Comparative Federalism* 18–19.

[40] W.S. Livingston, *Federalism and Constitutional Change*, 1–2. S. Rufus Davis was similarly dismissive of Wheare's institutionalism, taking more interest in the underpinning structure of society. S. Rufus Davis, 'The "Federal Principle" Reconsidered', Part II (1956) 1 *Australian Journal of Politics and History* 223–244, 243.

[41] W.S. Livingston, *Federalism and Constitutional Change*, 1–2.

[42] Riker, *Federalism: Origin, Operation, Significance*.

[43] An earlier account anticipated both Livingston and Riker. H.R.G. Greaves published a comparative account of federalism in *Federal Union in Practice* (London: George Allen & Unwin, 1940). His focus however was not primarily upon institutions but rather the causes and conditions of federal union. This book was largely neglected in a literature increasingly dominated by the American academy.

[44] Burgess, *Comparative Federalism*, 37.

There is considerable value in analysing political and other social forces within federal constitutions. But behavioural study brings us no closer to the essence of federalism as a constitutional idea. As a later significant player in federal studies, Preston King, pointed out: 'Attempts to measure the behaviour of federations ... must inevitably involve some tacit or explicit conventions or agreements about what a federation actually is.'[45] For King, '[d]escription always implies analysis.'[46] But this tended to be overlooked in the 1950s and '60s. The analysis that interested behaviouralists was largely an assessment of the political and social manifestations of the federal idea rather than the essence of the idea itself.

In the end this fundamental question could not be avoided. Riker's approach, although impatient with the very notion of seeking a constitutional definition of federalism, relied implicitly upon a particular conception of what a 'federal' system was. And, ironically, despite his contempt for Wheare's institutionalist approach, he fell back upon the American model as a synonym for federalism.[47] This highlights another general weakness with many behaviouralist accounts in the post-war tradition. Not only do they fail to take us further in the quest for a generic idea of federalism but, emanating as most did within American scholarship, the default institutional backdrop against which they worked served subliminally to reinforce the idea that American federalism is the paradigm masterplan for federal government in general.

The upshot of these behaviouralist accounts, which built upon, while trying to distance themselves from, the institutionalism of Wheare, is an understanding of federalism as an idea that is in fact formulated not from first principles but from first practice. The search for the federal idea therefore stalled, either distracted by institutional essentialism or relegated by behaviouralism as an issue of no consequence. Nearly two centuries after the Philadelphia convention, Ivo Duchacek in 1970 offered a damning assessment of progress to date in arriving at a definition of federalism: 'There is no accepted theory of federalism. Nor is there an agreement as to what federalism is exactly.'[48] It is also the case that, after the wave of

[45] P. King, *Federalism and Federation* (London: Croom Helm, 1982), 11.

[46] King, *Federalism and Federation*, 11.

[47] Riker 'deemed the derivation of modern federalism to be singularly located in the United States', Burgess, *In Search of the Federal Spirit*, 92.

[48] I.D. Duchacek, *Comparative Federalism: The Territorial Dimension of Politics* (New York: Holt, Rinehart and Winston, 1970), 191. He continued: 'We see the term applied to almost any successful combination of unity with diversity, to almost any form of pluralism and cooperation within and among nations.' (Duchacek, 191). A similar suggestion that federal studies had hit an existential crisis was expressed by Maurice Vile in 1973: 'The particular game is played out ... The time has now come to reassess federal systems in terms of a definition which actually does help us distinguish between differing kinds of political system.' M.J.C. Vile, *Federalism in the United States, Canada and Australia* (London: H.M. Stationery Office, 1973), 35. In fact, Vile identified definitionalism itself as an impediment to finding the essence of federalism. A theory of federalism 'hardly exists today, largely it is suggested, because much of the theoretical effort of the last thirty years has been devoted to the discussion of the definition of federalism in such a way as to leave little or no basis upon which to build any sustained theoretical structure'. M.J.C. Vile, 'Federal Theory and the "New Federalism"' in D. Jaensch (ed.), *The Politics of New Federalism* (Adelaide: Australian Political Studies Association, 1977), 1.

behaviouralism that had characterised scholarship in the 1950s and '60s started to 'peter out',[49] federalist study itself went into abeyance. As Michael Stein generously puts it: 'After this rather fertile period in the theoretical evolution of federalism from the late 1940s to the 1970s, there was a dearth of innovative and influential Anglo-American contributions to federal theory.'[50] Michael Burgess' assessment was more blunt but surely more accurate: by the end of the 1960s, the literature had 'stagnated'.[51]

Following a scholarly hiatus in the 1970s, a fresh wave of study turned once more to federal institutions as the key to extracting the federal idea. This 'new institutionalist' move in federal scholarship introduced the distinction between 'federalism' as an idea and 'federation' as its institutional manifestation; the former normative, the latter descriptive. This move, begun by Preston King in 1982, was certainly a step forward.[52] We see this approach developed most clearly in the work of Ronald Watts.[53] Watts was a Canadian politics scholar who had been a student and protégé of Wheare at Oxford. This influence showed as he set out to challenge behaviouralism within federal scholarship for the radical break it had made with earlier institutional analysis. Watts argued that institutions matter not least for the role they play in shaping behaviour, identities, attitudes, etc.;[54] an example of the irresoluble chicken and egg debate between institutionalists and behaviouralists within social studies. It was he who, building upon Preston King's analysis, introduced a distinction between 'federal political systems', as a wide category of multi-level government, and 'federations' which, for Watts, fitted a particular institutional design and were, accordingly, far fewer in number. Watts' approach was not only institutionalist but comparative. He began by trawling widely among the large number of 'multi-level' systems around the world, creating an expansive schema of 'federal political systems'. For Watts, a 'federal political system' is:

> a broad category of political systems in which, by contrast to the single central source of authority in unitary systems, there are two (or more) levels of government thus combining elements of *shared-rule* (collaborative partnership) through common institutions and *regional self-rule* (constituent unit autonomy) for the governments of constituent units.[55]

[49] Burgess, *Comparative Federalism*, 48.

[50] M. Stein, 'Federalism', in B. Badie, D. Berg-Schlosser, and L. Morlino (eds), *International Encyclopaedia of Political Science* (New York: Sage Publications, 2016), vol. 1, 897.

[51] Burgess, *Comparative Federalism*, 48.

[52] King, *Federalism and Federation*. Preston King abjured behaviouralist accounts that focused upon the degree of centralization or decentralization within a federal system, arguing that the main issue in seeking to define federalism is the 'representation of regional units in the national legislature'. King, *Federalism and Federation*, 19.

[53] R.L. Watts, *Comparing Federal Systems*, 3rd edn (Kingston/Montreal: McGill-Queens University Press, 2008), 20–21.

[54] Watts, *Comparing Federal Systems*, 3rd edn, 20–21.

[55] Watts, *Comparing Federal Systems*, 3rd edn, 8.

By this he meant the very wide genus of political organisation which Elazar had adopted in his work on federalism beginning in the 1960s,[56] embracing, as Watts put it, 'unions, constitutionally decentralized unions, federations, confederations, federacies, associated states, condominiums, leagues, and joint functional authorities' and 'hybrids'.[57] Watts then whittled this list down to a much narrower category of 'federations', concluding that, among federal political systems, there were only twenty-five federations in the world. The term 'federation' he reserved for a specific category within the genus of federal political systems:

> 'federations' represent a particular species in which neither the federal nor the constituent units of government are constitutionally subordinate to the other, i.e. each has sovereign powers derived from the constitution rather than another level of government, each is empowered to deal directly with its citizens in the exercise of its legislative, executive and taxing powers and each is directly elected by its citizens.[58]

As did Wheare, Watts alighted upon a crucial feature of a fully federal system—the way in which territorial pluralism is recognised *constitutionally* as a vital dimension of the constitution's authority and source of constitutional identity. But he does not go on to explain what this means for the constitutionality of the federal polity or for constitutionalism more broadly. Instead, like earlier institutionalists, he turns to institutional observation, arriving at several institutional features which taken together constitute the nature of a 'federation', as opposed to the wider and looser category of 'federal political system'.[59] We must recall that Watts turned to institutionalism due to the failure of behaviouralism to arrive at a definition of federalism. But his research is in itself a form of behaviouralism—what we might call 'institutional behaviouralism'—which attempts to derive definition by observing the political dynamics that built federal institutions.[60] From this

[56] Elazar, *Exploring Federalism*.

[57] R.L. Watts, 'Federalism, Federal Political Systems, and Federations' (1998) 1 *Annual Review of Political Science* 117–137, 120.

[58] Watts, *Comparing Federal Systems*, 3rd edn, 9.

[59] Watts sets out six essential features of a federation: 'at least two orders of government ... each acting directly on its citizens'; 'a supreme written constitution not unilaterally amendable'; 'representation of distinct regional views within the federal policy-making institutions, usually provided by the particular form of the federal second chamber'; an umpire to resolve disputes, and 'processes and institutions to facilitate inter-governmental collaboration' in areas where powers overlap. Watts, *Comparing Federal Systems*, 3rd edn, 9. For a discussion of Watts' schema see also M. Burgess, 'Federalism and Federation', in M. Burgess and A.-G. Gagnon (eds), *Comparative Federalism and Federation: Competing Traditions and Future Directions* (Hemel Hempstead, UK: Harvester Wheatsheaf, 1993), 3–14.

[60] It would be a mistake therefore to locate Watts' work as a Manichean counterpoint to behaviouralism. In fact, he saw the relationship between institutions and political behaviour as symbiotic, the two interacting and each in doing so shaping the development of the other: Watts, *Comparing Federal Systems*, 3rd edn, 21.

he sought to derive a generalizable idea of federalism as a form of constitutional government.[61]

In the end however, Watts offers us simply another detailed institutional template which had 'the effect of subordinating federation to a mere species of a genus [federal political systems] that itself remains somewhat ambiguous'.[62] Watts was correct that within behaviouralist scholarship the search for federalism had collapsed into a vague or amorphous decentralisation. But ultimately his work does not fully explain the relationship between federal constitutional practice, which Watts observes lucidly, and the constitutional idea of federalism, which he did not really pursue.[63]

The approach taken by Watts, and before him Preston King, has been very influential to the present day, where even very recent accounts tend to eschew definition in preference for description[64] or pragmatism ('I know it when I see it'[65]). Watts has also been influential in taking the institutional turn in a comparative direction: if we are to define the subject by looking at its practice, then it makes sense to cast the observational net as widely as possible.

Comparative study has indeed proliferated since the 1990s.[66] This work has been encouraged by global political changes: the collapse of the USSR and the SFRY spawned new constitutions founded upon territorial pluralism; further troubled states such as Iraq have turned, often despairingly, to federal solutions; while the intensification of sub-state cultural identities within otherwise settled states such as Belgium, Canada, Spain, and the United Kingdom has led to a decades-long period of constitutional upheaval. Recent and insightful comparative work has been conducted by Michael Burgess, Alain Gagnon, Thomas Hueglin, and Michael

[61] An example of this self-referential circularity comes with Watts' account of the United Kingdom: '[In] the United Kingdom, devolutionary processes have incorporated some federal features, although by no means all the features of a full-fledged federation.' R.L. Watts, 'The Federal Idea and its Contemporary Relevance', in T.L. Courchene et al., *The Federal Idea: Essays in Honour of Ronald L. Watts* (Kingston-Montreal: McGill-Queen's, 2011), 15The UK is not federal because its institutional composition does not match those polities which Watts asserts to be federal. That this conclusion has become a trope highlights just how pervasive the new institutional approach has been in proffering a narrow, institutional template as a proxy for federalism as an idea: S. Tierney, 'Federalism in a Unitary State: A Paradox too Far?' (2009) *Regional and Federal Studies* 237–254; 'The Territorial Constitution and the Brexit Process' (2019) 72 *Current Legal Problems* 59–83.

[62] Burgess, *Comparative Federalism: Theory and Practice*, 48.

[63] As Hueglin and Fenna put it when reflecting upon federal scholarship in general: 'What is particularly confusing is that there is only one term, federalism, comprising both a commitment to federal principles ... and the existence of complex federal arrangements in practice ... Collapsing these two meanings into one discourages a critical examination of how well federal practices live up to their principles.' Hueglin and Fenna, *Comparative Federalism: A Systematic Inquiry*, 2nd edn, 23.

[64] J. Kincaid, 'Introduction', in John Kincaid (ed.), *A Research Agenda for Federalism Studies* (Cheltenham: Edward Elgar, 2019), 1–14, 2.

[65] F. Palermo and K. Kössler, *Comparative Federalism: Constitutional Arrangements and Case Law* (Oxford: Hart Publishing, 2017), 3—drawing an analogy with obscenity, per J. Stewart in *Jacobellis v. Ohio* 378 US 184 (1964).

[66] See n 2 above.

Keating among others.[67] In many ways this work is part of a 'post-ontological' turn. With a rise of dedicated federal research centres, often situated within the energetic International Association of Centres for the Study of Federalism (IACFS), it is clear that politics and constitutional law scholars are increasingly content to park theoretical questions about the essence of federalism and turn instead to a combined institutionalist/behaviouralist approach to how systems, which are taken to be federal, play out in practice, and how political behaviour interacts with their institutional design in more or less effective ways.[68] This approach focuses upon the utility of federalism as a framework for a territorially diversifying world. It combines behaviouralism and institutionalism, sharing the former's impatience with the quest to define federalism.[69] Accordingly, attention has turned to broader and more amorphous categories of 'territorial polities'[70] or 'multi-level governance'.[71] It is common now to encounter a brushing over of, or indeed irritation with, the definitional question. As Hueglin puts it, 'For most people, federalism simply is a form of divided government.'[72] Or, in Dardanelli's curt assessment, '[i]n essence, federalism is a constitutional device to divide powers between at least two levels of government.'[73]

Overall, despite all of the work in definitionalism, institutionalism, and behaviouralism, from the eighteenth century to the present day, the concept of federalism remains obscured and under-theorised within political studies and constitutional law. Burgess's conclusion was that, by the early twenty-first century, we were left

[67] Burgess, *Comparative Federalism*; Burgess and Gagnon, (eds), *Comparative Federalism and Federation*; Gagnon (ed.), *Contemporary Canadian Federalism*,; Hueglin and Fenna, *Comparative Federalism*; and M. Keating, *Plurinational Democracy: Stateless Nations in a Post-Sovereignty Era* (Oxford: Oxford University Press, 2001).

[68] This new pragmatic turn with its focus upon efficacy is exemplified by U.M. Amoretti and N. Bormeo (eds), *Federalism and Territorial Cleavages* (Baltimore: Johns Hopkins University Press, 2004), the aim of which is 'to assess why some territorial cleavages are more easily accommodated than others' and examine 'whether this goal is facilitated by federal state structures', Amoretti, 'Introduction: Federalism and Territorial Cleavages', 2.

[69] Burgess himself finally described the search for such a definition as 'futile'. *Comparative Federalism*, 2.

[70] J. Broschek, B. Petersohn, and S. Toubeau, 'Territorial Politics and Institutional Change: A Comparative-Historical Analysis' (2018) 48 *Publius* 1–25.

[71] The blurring of the idea of federalism with the nebulous idea of 'multi-level governance' is partly a response to 'globalisation' and the engagement of states within international structures that assert growing levels of governmental authority. It is a model of analysis frequently seen within European scholarship: L. Hooghe and G. Marks, *Multi-level Governance and European Integration* (London: Rowman and Littlefield, 2001). This term has however served merely to obscure further the essence of federalism as a specific idea of constitutional rule for states, with the notion being applied indiscriminately 'to any complex and multifaceted political process'. I. Bache, *The Politics of European Union Regional Policy: Multi-Level Governance or Flexible Gatekeeping?* (Sheffield: Sheffield University Press, 1998), 153–154.

[72] T.O. Hueglin, 'Federalism and Political Theory: A Case of Mutual Neglect?' in John Kincaid (ed.), *A Research Agenda for Federalism Studies* (Cheltenham: Edward Elgar, 2019), 15–26, 15.

[73] P. Dardanelli, 'De/centralization', in J. Kincaid (ed.), *A Research Agenda for Federalism Studies* (Cheltenham: Edward Elgar, 2019), 106–116, 106. Dardanelli places federalism on a scale of relative centralization/decentralization, recalling earlier accounts such as Franck's, n 14 above and indeed the nineteenth-century approaches of Bryce and Freeman.

with 'conceptual ambiguity' and 'the absence of impermeable watertight compartments between the standard conceptual categories'.[74] This is something of an understatement. What is in fact still lacking is any meaningful account of the essence of federalism as a discrete and generic order of constitutional rule for the modern state.

III. Theorising federalism

It would be unfair to lay blame for the dearth of theory at the door of political studies. The principal concern of political scientists is always the practice of public power. The failure fully to analyse the proliferation of federalism as a form of government in both the post-war and post-1989 periods is a more notable lacuna within political theory, which has tended not to identify in federalism a subject of distinctive theoretical interest.

It is of course important not to over-state this point. Politics scholars working in the area have brought important theoretical insights to the study of federalism, for example addressing its relationship to democracy[75] and to the recent turn in "plurinational' theory,[76] and the interface between federalism and multiculturalism.[77] Others have taken strides in re-exploring the historical origins and traditions of federalism,[78] while further interventions attempt to take stock of the proliferation of federalism in a time of globalisation.[79] But it is frequently noted nonetheless that more comprehensive theoretical interventions are missing. Burgess, for example, argued in 2006 that as yet there was 'no fully fledged theory of federalism',[80] an observation also made by

[74] Burgess, *Comparative Federalism*, 24.

[75] A. Stepan, 'Federalism and Democracy: Beyond the U.S. Model' (1999) 10 *Journal of Democracy* 18–33; M. Burgess and A-G. Gagnon (eds), *Federal Democracies* (London: Routledge, 2010); M. Forsyth, *Union of States: The Theory and Practice of Confederations* (New York: Leicester University Press, 1981).

[76] A.-G. Gagnon and J. Tully (eds), *Multinational Democracies* (Cambridge: Cambridge University Press, 2001); A. Midwinter and M. Keating, *Nations Against the State: The New Politics of Nationalism in Quebec, Catalonia and Scotland* (London: Palgrave MacMillan, 2001); W. Norman, *Negotiating Nationalism: Nation-Building, Federalism, and Secession in the Multinational State* (Oxford: Oxford University Press, 2006); A.-G. Gagnon and M. Seymour, *Multinational Federalism: Problems and Prospects* (United Kingdom: Palgrave MacMillan, 2012).

[77] J. Tully, *Strange Multiplicity: Constitutionalism in an Age of Diversity* (Cambridge: Cambridge University Press, 1995).

[78] T.O. Hueglin, *Early Modern Concepts for a Late Modern World: Althusius on Community and Federalism* (Waterloo: Wilfrid Laurier University Press, 1999); Hueglin and Fenna, *Comparative Federalism*.

[79] A. Gamper, 'A "Global Theory of Federalism": The Nature and Challenges of a Federal State' (2005) 6(10) *German Law Journal* 1297–1318.

[80] Burgess, *Comparative Federalism*, 1. He continued: 'At best there is partial theory based upon rigorous conceptional analysis and the pursuit of terminological precision. At worst there is crass empiricism rooted in the failure to develop concepts and define the key terms.' Ibid.

others,[81] some of whom contrast this gap with the plethora of theory on other systems of government.[82]

As we address the theoretical approaches to federalism which do exist, it is evident furthermore that political and moral theory has supplanted constitutional theory in the analysis and assessment of federalism. Turning to the canon of political theory, federalism has tended not to feature in theories of democracy,[83] and this omission has not been corrected in the past few decades, despite federalism becoming such a significant feature of constitutional practice. For example, federalism is rarely if ever discussed in the work of contemporary political philosophers as a factor which might impact upon their notions of justice; the subject remaining 'understudied and poorly understood'.[84] This is so even for scholars such as John Rawls[85] or Jürgen Habermas[86] who came from, and spent their academic lives working within, federal states. In discussing Rawls, Margaret Moore notes that his work tends to ignore the territorial dimension of government altogether: 'In *A Theory of Justice* Rawls begins with the convenient simplifying assumption that the just society is closed: that it is a "self-sufficient association of persons", thereby abstracting from the issue of the territory to which "the just society" is entitled and the relationship of that territory to other territories.'[87] She observes further that: 'little attention was drawn to the fact that Rawls also assumed that justice operated within a *territorially* delimited political community (a state) and the territorial dimension of the state was not addressed in anything like adequate terms'.[88]

[81] In 2011 Scott argued: 'there is no theory of federalism'. Kyle Scott, *Federalism: A Normative Theory and its Practical Relevance* (New York: Continuum, 2011), 1. Hueglin and Fenna agree: 'a general theory of federal state formation does not exist'. Hueglin and Fenna, *Comparative Federalism: A Systematic Inquiry*, 2nd edn, 98.

[82] Wayne Norman observes: 'the role of the federal ideal in the standard histories of political thought has been *unjustifiably* neglected in our intellectual tradition'. Norman, *Negotiating Nationalism*, 82. Feeley and Rubin share this view: 'In light of its prominence as a governing arrangement and of the many and varied benefits advocates claim for it, one might expect there to be a vast and robust literature on federalism. Yet there is not. There is certainly no shortage of literature on federalism—in fact, there has been a deluge of it in recent decades—but virtually none of it presents a theory of the subject.' M. Feeley and E. Rubin, *Federalism: Political Identity and Tragic Compromise* (University of Michigan Press, 2008), 1–2; and see M. Feeley, 'The Political Theory of Federalism' (2012) 28 *Flinders Journal of History and Politics* 1–15, 2.

[83] D. Weinstock, 'Towards a Normative Theory of Federalism' (2001) 53 *International Social Science Journal* 75–83, 77, 79.

[84] J.T. Levy, 'Federalism, Liberalism, and the Separation of Loyalties' (2007) 101 *American Political Science Review* 459–477, 459; T.O. Hueglin, 'Federalism and Democracy: A Critical Reassessment', in G. Skogstad et al. (eds), *The Global Promise of Federalism* (Toronto: University of Toronto Press 2013), 25.

[85] J. Rawls, *A Theory of Justice* (Oxford: Oxford University Press, 1972), 102 and 357; and *The Law of Peoples* (Cambridge MA: Cambridge University Press, 1999).

[86] J. Habermas, *Between Facts and Norms: Contributions to a Discourse Theory of Law and Democracy* (Cambridge: Polity Press, 1996).

[87] M. Moore, *A Political Theory of Territory* (Oxford: Oxford University Press, 2015), 4.

[88] M. Moore, *A Political Theory of Territory*, 4. See also F. Requejo, *Multinational Federalism and Value Pluralism* (Oxford: Routledge, 2004); S. Tierney, *Constitutional Law and National Pluralism* (Oxford: Oxford University Press, 2004); M. Canovan, 'Sleeping Dogs, Prowling Cats and Soaring Doves: Three Paradoxes in the Political Theory of Nationhood' (2001) 49 *Political Studies* 203–215, 205–206. Norman, *Negotiating Nationalism*, 80 discusses a similar lacuna in Habermas' work. Ironically, Habermas has recently addressed the subject of federalism not in relation to his native German federal

In a related way, Wayne Norman observes that he and other political philosophers turning to address federal theory in the 1990s 'knew that our "mentors"—philosophers like Rawls, Nozick, and Dworkin—were silent on the mysteries of federalism. So too were almost all of their communitarian, feminist, and socialist critics during the 1970s and 1980s ... Standard texts in democratic theory generally avoided the topic, as did our field's principal journals, *Ethics* and *Philosophy and Public Affairs*.'[89] A helpful collation of those accounts of federalism which do appear within political theory is offered by Norman in a collection edited with Dimitri Karmis.[90] However, the paucity of 'greats' in this collected volume bears out Norman's observation.

IV. Normative instrumentalism: two types of moral theorising about federalism

Where political theory does address federalism it tends to bring a normative and hence a prescriptive approach to the federal idea. This disposition towards normative evaluation manifests itself in two ways. One approach does not allude so much to the inherent normative merits of federalism, but focuses instead upon its instrumental utility as a constitutional tool with which to achieve wider political goals: a 'defence of federalism to mask the advocacy of particular substantive goals that in themselves do not flow from federalism at all'.[91] A second approach finds intrinsic rather than instrumental value in federalism, viewing it as a model of government well suited to the nature of the human condition, in particular to the range of social interconnections that reflect the needs of people for community and society. I will address each in turn, arguing that neither is a substitute for a constitutional theory of federalism.

(i) Federalism and externally derived values

Federalism is often presented as an instrumentally useful way of achieving broader moral goods. This approach is analogous to the behavioural turn in political studies

republic but more tangentially in discussing the multi-state European Union: J. Habermas, 'Democracy in Europe: Why the Development of the EU into a Transnational Democracy Is Necessary and How It Is Possible' (2015) 21 *European Law Journal* 546–557; 'Citizen and State Equality in a Supranational Political Community: Degressive Proportionality and the Pouvoir Constituant Mixte' (2017) 55 *Journal of Common Market Studies* 193–202.

[89] Norman, *Negotiating Nationalism*, 80.

[90] D. Karmis and W. Norman (eds), *Theories of Federalism: A Reader* (New York: Palgrave-Macmillan Publishing, 2005). See also S. Mogi, *The Problem of Federalism; A Study in the History of Political Theory* (New York: The Macmillan Company, 1931).

[91] Feeley and Rubin, *Federalism: Political Identity and Tragic Compromise*, 2.

since it tends to focus upon the political, economic, and social effects of federalism, rather than upon its conceptual essence as a genus of government. But unlike behaviouralism, which seeks to describe and explain the social and political impact of federalism from an avowedly empirical perspective, instrumental normative theory assesses federalism for the moral consequences of its effects. In doing so it adopts a number of benchmarks for evaluating the moral efficacy of federalism. We will return to this issue in more detail in Chapter 7 but for now let us take two examples of these evaluative tools: one concerned with strong democracy, another with strong statehood. In terms of democracy, virtue is often found in federalism for its usefulness in diffusing the power of government and thereby serving as an institutional check, moderating the risk of over-large and potentially tyrannical government.[92] It is also argued that by creating an additional layer of government, and indeed the competition among governments within the system, federalism can foster competition, help expand citizen opportunities to exercise choice, and in a related way enhance the economic performance of the polity. A variation on this latter dimension of the argument is that federalism allows for policy experimentation in one or more regions, facilitating innovations to be tested and then rolled out if successful: federalism as laboratory.[93] In relation to effective statehood, evaluations focus upon whether a federal system is better or worse at helping to foster a strong and secure state, particularly in the context of its international relations: for some, federalism is considered advantageous in allowing a group of territories to unite, thereby establishing a larger and more strategically powerful entity; for others, a federal system is perceived to produce weak central government which poses problems of efficiency and may even represent a threat to the very stability of the state.[94]

Arguments that use democracy and/or strong statehood as their referents tend to merge with a broader ideological orientation which asks, in essence, whether federalism is a boon or a hindrance to the pursuit of liberal goals, in particular individual freedom *from* government, and freedom *to* pursue individual ends, each to be nurtured within a viable and properly functioning state. The premise behind these approaches is that individual freedom is best advanced by way of limited government. Federalism, which divides and/or shares governmental authority, and in

[92] This is an argument that has come to characterise the constitutional historiography of the emergent United States, e.g. A. Hamilton, Federalist No. 28, C. Rossiter (ed.), *The Federalist Papers* (New York: The New American Library, 1961), 178–182.

[93] James Madison, Federalist No. 56, C. Rossiter (ed.), *The Federalist Papers* (New York: The New American Library, 1961), 346–350; *New State Ice Co. v. Liebmann* 285 U.S. 262, 311 (1932) (Brandeis, J. dissenting). For an account that both reviews the historical sources of these instrumentalist arguments and which is itself an engaging modern take on this approach see Levy, 'Federalism, Liberalism, and the Separation of Loyalties'.

[94] Again these arguments are as old as federalism itself, being a core concern of the Federalists. Federalist, Nos 15–28, C. Rossiter (ed.), *The Federalist Papers* (New York: The New American Library, 1961).

so doing constrains its exercise, is therefore a useful option from a liberal perspective, particularly for large polities.

It is my broader contention in this book that moral normativism cannot take us to the essence of federalism as a constitutional idea. But even by its own lights an instrumental normative approach suffers from a number of drawbacks. One is over-inclusiveness. The moral standards by which federalism is assessed are not specific to federalism and could in general be applied to any constitutional form of governmental decentralisation. In the American tradition, the opinion of Justice O'Connor in *Gregory v. Ashcroft* is often considered to be a classic statement of the value of federalism. Focusing upon the American system, she states: 'This federalist structure . . assures a decentralized government that will be more sensitive to the diverse needs of a heterogeneous society; it increases opportunity for citizen involvement in democratic processes; it allows for more innovation and experimentation in government; and it makes government more responsive by putting the States in competition for a mobile citizenry.'[95] Feeley and Rubin observe: 'All these advantages, however, flow from decentralization, and none have much to do with the federalist principle that geographically defined governmental subunits must be granted partial autonomy in particular areas of governance.'[96] In short, the value of federalism for individual freedom can collapse into a broader argument for subsidiarity, local or multi-level government. This approach says nothing about the foundational territorial personhood that characterises federal constitutionalism.

A second weakness of normative instrumentalism is that the value ascribed to federalism as an idea is susceptible to the vagaries of practice. For example, if one or more of the constituent territorial governments in a particular polity is considered by liberals to offer a weaker context for individual freedom than the central government, then it may be concluded that there is in fact no value in having a federal system at all, or that any value it has is outweighed by its political outcomes or side-effects. This can render federalism's value vulnerable to short-term concerns: for example, the emergence for a brief time of an illiberal government in one or more sub-state territory. It is a short journey from here to the conclusion that a unitary system would be preferable.[97] No one put this more bluntly than Riker in the 1960s: 'if in the United States one approves of Southern white racists, one should approve of American federalism [... If] one disapproves of racism, one should disapprove of federalism.'[98] In such an account, federalism is not ascribed any inherent and discrete constitutional purpose; the assessment of its value is driven by either extraneous ideology or its apparent effects at a particular time in

[95] *Gregory v. Ashcroft* 501 U.S. 452, 458 (1991), per Justice O'Connor.

[96] Feeley and Rubin, *Federalism: Political Identity and Tragic Compromise*, 22.

[97] It has been argued that ideological disaffection with the outcomes of federalism in the USA helps explain the disdain for the subject within American political theory. Levy, 'Federalism, Liberalism, and the Separation of Loyalties', 468.

[98] Riker, *Federalism: Origin, Operation, Significance*, 155.

a particular place rather than a consideration of its inherent character as a generic order of constitutional rule.

A further issue arising from normative instrumentalism is that liberal arguments can sit in considerable tension with one another. A federal system may be considered to be very useful in fulfilling the function of facilitating rational choice and enhancing economic opportunities for individuals, but it may also be seen as a danger to other rights, particularly those of minorities within certain sub-state territories.[99] Or again, it may be considered useful in limiting and diffusing governmental power but precisely for that reason the state's power as an international actor may be diminished because the central government's international relations are hamstrung by dissent among territorial governments. These contradictions serve to confuse the search for the meaning of federalism, dependent as they are upon such fluctuating contingencies.[100] Seeking to elicit what federalism might (or might not) *be useful for* in political, social, or economic terms takes us no closer to knowing what federalism *is*.

(ii) Federalism and inherent moral value

A second normative tradition posits the inherent moral worth of federalism as an ideal system of government. This is a perspective that transcends ideological and empirically situated political theory, turning instead to the evaluative register of moral political philosophy. This approach does not suffer from the shortcomings of instrumental normativism since it is not subject to the same caprices of outcome that flow from ideological assessments founded in political culture, the particularities of institutional design, or the policy outcomes that stem from these. As such, intrinsic normativism is a more self-contained and hence coherent approach with which to try to uncover the nature of the federal idea. However, despite the insights it delivers, it also ultimately fails to take us to the heart of federalism as a *constitutional* rather than a moral idea.

In essence, the intrinsic normative theory of federalism contends that federalism is a model of government well suited to the nature of the human condition, in particular to the range of social interconnections that characterise the communal and social dimensions of human nature. The philosophical provenance of this idea can be traced back to Johannes Althusius.[101] Among contemporary federal theorists,

99 W. Kymlicka, 'Federalism, Nationalism and Multiculturalism', in Karmis and Norman (eds), *Theories of Federalism: A Reader*, 269–292.

100 A trap which Levy himself falls into: 'I want to suggest that there is nothing intrinsically illiberal about federalism at all. Federalism as a limit on the power of the central state is a case of illiberal means in the service of liberal ends only if liberalism is identified from the outset with a strict formal universalism, rationalism, and egalitarianism.' Levy, 'Federalism, Liberalism, and the Separation of Loyalties', 474.

101 J. Althusius, *Politica Methodice Digesta, Atque Exemplis Sacris et Profanis Illustrata*, [1603], F.S. Carney (ed. and trans.) (Indianapolis: Liberty Fund, 1995).

Thomas Hueglin has done more than anyone to resuscitate Althusius, that curious character of early modernity who lived in Emden between 1557 and 1638. In his highly engaging work, which seeks to draw themes from Althusius' obscure and often self-contradictory pronouncements, and locate them in the context of post-modernity,[102] Hueglin makes much of Althusius' main claim, namely that: 'Politics is the art of consociating men for the purpose of establishing, cultivating, and conserving social life among them.'[103] For Hueglin and Fenna, Althusius offers valuable insights into both the human condition and the forms of government best suited to it. Federalism is articulated as an inter-temporal and potentially universalisable model of government, appropriate to manage the complex pluralism of human attachments in any social setting. It follows that federalism is, in itself, an essentially 'normative proposition with its own intellectual history'.[104]

Nicholas Aroney, in work that marries the study of federalism with natural law, tends to agree with Hueglin that Althusius' work reflects a penetrating insight into human nature; an understanding of people as social beings who form their associations from, as it were, the ground up: initially in the realm of intimate private life, rather than through the exclusively 'public' context of the state.[105] Both Hueglin and Aroney are attracted by Althusius' premise that the strongest bonds people form are with the family and through the family in tight local communities; it is from these that more attenuated public attachments flow. As Aroney explains, it is in Althusius that we find the origin of the idea that 'all federative systems presuppose a set of political and constitutional values that build from the local outwards because they treat the local as in some sense historically, logically *and* normatively prior'.[106] From close personal relationships other attachments develop organically in a range of both private associations and, consequently, public relationships

[102] Hueglin, *Early Modern Concepts for a Late Modern World: Althusius on Community and Federalism*.

[103] Hueglin and Fenna, *Comparative Federalism*, 91.

[104] Hueglin and Fenna, *Comparative Federalism*, 73. Hueglin and Fenna's work on comparative federalism is heavily influenced by Althusius. Unsurprisingly therefore, their notion of the federal idea is explicitly normative. Federalism 'is not only a description of the way in which power and governance are sometimes organized; it is also a set of values and prescriptions about how communities should be structured'. Hueglin and Fenna, *Comparative Federalism*, 73.

[105] For Aroney, Althusius offers an understanding of the human condition 'in which expressions of human sociality and political ordering work their way outwards, from the local to the universal, in a nested association of communities within communities'. N. Aroney, 'The Federal Condition: Towards a Normative Theory' (2016) 61 *The American Journal of Jurisprudence* 13–31, 14. For the deeper roots of Aroney's conception of the federal idea in the natural law tradition see also N. Aroney, 'Before Federalism? Thomas Aquinas, Jean Quidort and Nicola Casanus', in A. Ward and L. Ward (eds), *The Ashgate Research Companion to Federalism* (Farnham: Ashgate, 2009), 31–48. Michael Burgess was also attracted by the notion that federalism is a model of government apposite for the human condition. He too viewed Althusius as the key intellectual progenitor of the 'federal tendency'. Burgess, *Comparative Federalism*, 1–2 and 172–175; *In Search of the Federal Spirit: New Theoretical and Empirical Perspectives in Comparative Federalism* (Oxford: Oxford University Press, 2012), 159–164.

[106] N. Aroney, 'The Federal Condition', in Amnon Lev (ed.), The *Federal Idea: Public Law between Governance and Political Life* (Oxford: Hart Publishing, 2019), 29–51, 50.

encapsulated in specific and often pluralised forms of government.[107] It is this account of the spontaneous interweaving of human nature, communal attachments, and government growth that leads federal normativists to the essence of the 'federal condition', encapsulating the human instinct to socialise, in which 'expressions of human sociality and political ordering work their way outwards, from the local to the universal, in a nested association of communities within communities'.[108]

Another claim that flows from the approaches taken by Hueglin and Aroney is that the significance of both the wide range and fluidity of human associations was largely side-lined, or indeed traduced, by the homogenising impetus that characterises the nation-building project of modernity. Aroney is attracted by the potential of Althusian thought to enlighten us to the path not taken, a journey that should have elevated the federal idea as one better suited to the social complexity of modernity than the unitary constitution with its instrumental focus upon centralisation and demotic singularity.[109]

In this approach, which links the philosophy of Althusius to an account of the best form of government for the socially situated individual, federalism is in effect co-opted in service of a deeper moral project. 'From a more "normative" perspective ... federalism is a means by which our legitimate orientations to *both* locality and universality—each of them characteristics of the human condition generally—can best be accommodated.'[110] This modern Althusianism—tying federalism to a communal and relationally pluralised image of human identity—is of critical significance for moral political philosophy; in particular, for the methodological individualism that is an often subliminal preconception of its very ontology.[111] It calls into question the default account of modern government which, as we have seen in the implicit or explicit elision of liberalism with so much federal theory, presupposes the atomised individual as the exclusive bearer of *a priori* normative value.

[107] As Aroney explains, Althusius offers a vision of a political society that 'rests on a covenant between its constitutive members. These members are not simply individuals, but include towns, cities and provinces.' Aroney, 'The Federal Condition', in Lev, *The Federal Idea*, 33–34.

[108] Aroney, 'The Federal Condition, in Lev, 38–45.

[109] As Aroney explains: 'For Althusius, the priority of families, cities and realms was not only historical. It was also normative. He understood each such association to be formed by an explicit agreement among its constituent members, which agreement constituted a kind of fundamental law which defined and limited the responsibilities, powers and jurisdiction of the association.' Aroney, 'The Federal Condition: Towards a Normative Theory', 24. As Aroney also puts it, our attachments to family and locality matter hugely: 'although contemporary political theory has tended to overlook this due to its focus on the nation-state as the locus of political authority, there is a real sense in which cooperation and coordination existing at a neighborly and local scale provide the foundations for its existence on a wider scale'. Aroney, 'The Federal Condition: Towards a Normative Theory', 20.

[110] Aroney, 'The Federal Condition: Towards a Normative Theory', 31.

[111] 'Federalism as a broad social philosophy' assumes 'that forming relationships in a variety of communities is part of human nature. Belonging to one or several communities is regarded as part of individual liberty and identity. In other words, the most general principle of federalism holds that human beings possess by nature individual as well as group identities.' Hueglin and Fenna, *Comparative Federalism*, 25. See also C. Taylor, *Sources of the Self: The Making of the Modem Identity* (Cambridge, MA: Harvard University Press, 1989).

This turn in federal theory opens up an important avenue through which federal thought can penetrate and challenge many of the monistic and indeed universalist assumptions that underpin so much contemporary political philosophy. A plurality of modern normative theorists 'implicitly assume that, once one has determined what justice requires, there can be no interesting argument for allowing it to vary from place to place'.[112] The stress placed by modern Althusianism upon the social, territorially situated, layered, and nuanced nature of human attachments, as these vary from one locus to another, poses nothing less than an existential challenge to the homogenising epistemology of contemporary liberalism.

The origins of modern Althusianism, which links federalism to the human condition, are traceable back to Daniel Elazar, whose advocacy of federalism's intrinsic worth was encapsulated in his account of a metaphysical human inclination towards covenant and, through covenant, to federal forms of government.[113] In Elazar, we are reminded of another key move in this normative tradition: locating the federal idea inter-temporally, ascribing to it a common thread of meaning running back from modernity not only to the early modern period in which Althusius worked but even to the ancient world. Elazar, as we have seen, tracks the federal idea back to the tribes of Israel.[114] Watts agrees[115] and casts his net even more widely,[116] while Aroney identifies sources of federal thinking in the work of Augustine[117] and Aquinas.[118] Hueglin goes further than anyone in imagining the inter-temporality of the federal idea, linking Althusias' Reformationist political philosophy to a post-modern conception of federalism, and positing it as a still salient template with

[112] Levy, 'Federalism, Liberalism, and the Separation of Loyalties', 463.

[113] Elazar traces the idea of covenant, and hence his idea of federalism, to a divine plan for humanity. D.J. Elazar, 'Covenant and Polity in Biblical Israel', in *The Covenant Tradition in Politics* (New Brunswick: Transaction Publishers, 1995), 1. See also I.L. Horowitz, 'Daniel J. Elazar and the Covenant Tradition in Politics' (2001) 31 Publius 1–7; Burgess, *In Search of the Federal Spirit: New Theoretical and Empirical Perspectives in Comparative Federalism*, 183. As a concept, the idea of covenant influenced the early history of the Swiss union which dates to the Middle Ages. J.W. Baker, 'The Covenantal Basis for the Development of Swiss Political Federalism: 1291–1848' (1993) 23 *Publius* 19–41.

[114] Elazar, 'Covenant and Polity in Biblical Israel' and D.J. Elazar, *Federalism: An Overview* (Pretoria: HSRC Publishers, 1995), 19.

[115] Watts, *Comparing Federal Systems*. See also Palermo and Kössler, *Comparative Federalism*, 67–68.

[116] Watts also sees 'federal' ideas in the political organisation of the Hellenic city states, the Roman republic, the Bedouin and the Native confederacies of North America: Watts, *Comparing Federal Systems*, 2–3. He then turns to early modern examples of what he takes to be a conceptually interconnected federal impetus in Switzerland and the United Provinces of the Netherlands, the Holy Roman Empire, and the British settlements of New England: Watts, *Comparing Federal Systems*, 3. See also H. Beck and P. Funk (eds), *Federalism in Greek Antiquity*, (Cambridge: Cambridge University Press, 2015). References to a line from modern federalism back to Native American associations are indeed common. See, e.g., D.S. Lutz. 'The Iroquois Confederation Constitution: An Analysis' (1998) 28 *Publius* 99–127, a phenomenon also discussed by Freeman, *History of Federal Government V1*.

[117] N. Aroney, 'Christianity, Sovereignty, and Global Law', in R. Domingo and J. Witte, Jr (eds), *Christianity and Global Law* (Abingdon: Routledge, 2020), 267–286, 281.

[118] N. Aroney, 'The Federal Condition: Towards a Normative Theory' (2016) 61 *The American Journal of Jurisprudence* 13–31, 23.

which to engage the territorial complexity of modern government, particularly in Europe.[119]

One major advance made by the normative turn in federal studies is that it has helped to broaden the horizon of the subject after a period in which empirical work had reduced scholarship either to definitionalism at the micro-level of institutional design or to institutionally decontextualised behavioural observation. The work of Elazar, Burgess, Aroney, and Hueglin has come to characterise a new tradition of modern Althusianism which sees in federalism the embodiment of Aristotelean virtue-ethics adapted to the deep territorially located pluralism that characterises many contemporary polities. This approach to federalism focuses attention on the need to resuscitate federalism as a discrete idea of constitutional rule, one that should be actively engaged within broader theoretical debates about the nature of government and the constitutional purposes for which it is instituted.

Despite the fresh and insightful interventions made by these 'intrinsic normativists', one negative consequence of this turn has been a tendency to veer too far from the path of explanation and evaluation to that of advocacy.[120] This is not a new phenomenon. Alvin Jackson observes that nineteenth and early twentieth-century commentators on federalism 'were more concerned with earnest evangelism than with rigorous theology'.[121] A more recent example is Ronald Watts, whose very definition of federalism is overtly normative. In distinguishing federalism from 'federal political systems' and 'federations', he argues: 'In this distinction, "federalism" is used basically not as a descriptive but a normative term and refers to the advocacy of multi-tiered government combining elements of shared-rule and regional self-rule.'[122] A problem which attends such an approach is that those who have proven to be federalism's most earnest promoters (or detractors) have often failed fully to explain precisely what it is that they endorse or refute.

In essence therefore, while both instrumental normative and intrinsic normative approaches are insightful in explaining why federalism has proven so

[119] T.O. Hueglin, 'Federalism: An Alternative Category in Political Thought?', in R. Saxena (ed.), *Varieties of Federal Governance: Major Contemporary Models* (Cambridge: Cambridge University Press, 2012), 3–17. Although, notably, he thinks the idea began with Althusius and cannot be traced back to Greece or Rome: 'I would in fact want to advance that it [Althusius' theory] was the first significant and systematic theory of federalism altogether.' Hueglin, *Early Modern Concepts for a Late Modern World: Althusius on Community and Federalism*, 133.

[120] It is important to emphasise however that Hueglin and Aroney themselves can scarcely be accused of such a lapse. For each of these writers the normative essence of federalism is accompanied by exhaustive empirical study of the subject.

[121] A. Jackson, 'The Failure of British and Irish Federalism, Circa 1800–1950', in R Schütze and S Tierney (eds), *The United Kingdom and the Federal Idea* (Oxford: Hart, 2018), 29–47, 30. As an example, we might note that Freeman introduced his sweeping late nineteenth-century book with a reference to federalism as a teleological ideal: 'That ideal, in its highest and most elaborate development, is the most finished and the most artificial production of political ingenuity.' E.A. Freeman, *History of Federal Government in Greece and Italy*, 2nd edn (London: MacMillan, 1893), 1. Feeley and Rubin also note, and indeed warn against, the distorting effects of prescriptive accounts: Feeley and Rubin, *Federalism: Political Identity and Tragic Compromise*, 5–6.

[122] Watts, *Comparing Federal Systems*, 3rd edn, 8.

attractive to human societies or political actors, they do not of themselves tell us *what federalism is* as a form of government for the modern state. Instead, we find that across the field of federal scholarship, institutional analysis elides with normative theorising in a way that leaves the essence of the federal concept obscured.[123] Michael Burgess noted that a pathological failing of federal scholarship was its tendency to deal 'simultaneously with fundamental moral questions as well as with amoral matter-of-fact issues'.[124] He also identified correctly that the respective approaches brought to the study of federalism by political theorists and politics scholars are in fact incommensurable:

> The moral basis to federalism derives from certain inherent virtues, such as respect, tolerance, dignity and mutual recognition, which lead to a particular form of human association, namely, the federal state or federation. The amoral foundation suggests that no such qualities inhere in federalism at all and that it is nothing more than a particular constitutional and/or political technique for achieving certain overarching goals such as territorial expansion or economic benefits and security.[125]

While these instrumentalist approaches, whether institutionalist/behaviouralist or normative, can be rich and insightful in describing how federalism works or in highlighting its potential benefits, they do not go to the essence of federalism as a constitutional idea. Of these accounts, the intrinsic moral assessment offers the clearest and most specific explanation of the value of federalism by focusing upon its inherent essence and the societal pluralism upon which it is built. But its intertemporal approach, ranging from the ancient to the pre-modern to the modern (and for Hueglin, the post-modern), and the failure to locate federalism's essential purpose firmly within constitutional law, leaves a gap in our search for the federal contract as an essentially modern constitutional project. I now take up the argument that only constitutional theory can fill this explanatory gap, locating the idea of federalism firmly within the story of the modern state and the constitutional forms that have been fashioned to its service.

V. Federal theory as constitutional theory

Constitutional theory is categorically distinguishable from political studies for its specifically constitutional focus. It is concerned with analysing and evaluating a

[123] As Feeley and Rubin put it: 'Despite the alleged tough-mindedness of political scientists... and legal scholars, their treatment of the subject remains mired in sentimental attachment to the idea of federalism.' Feeley and Rubin, *Federalism: Political Identity and Tragic Compromise*, 2.

[124] Burgess, *Comparative Federalism*, 1.

[125] Burgess, *Comparative Federalism*, 1.

particular area of social activity: the framing, founding, practice, and changing of constitutions, operational through internationally comparable institutions and rules. Unlike political studies, constitutional theory is not simply the study of political forces, actors, attitudes, or behaviours. Rather, it is a self-contained, indeed immanent, study of the constitutional transformation of the political into constitutional authority and of the resulting legal-normative regime through which it is husbanded and managed by law.

Constitutional theory can also be contrasted with political philosophy. As we have seen, the latter locates the purpose of political rule in externally generated ideological values. Constitutional theory certainly has an evaluative dimension, but unlike political philosophy constitutional theory is not an exercise in ideal theorising from first, abstract principles, and unlike more instrumental applications of political theory nor does it accept that constitutional practice is simply a vehicle for ideologically generated political and economic goals. Constitutionalism understands the inherent purposes of any constitutional system to be those that are generated by the constitution itself; concomitantly, the inherent purpose of any genus of constitutionalism stems from the nature of that genus. Constitutionalism explains the alchemy by which political legitimacy is converted into lawful authority, whereupon legitimacy and authority operate symbiotically in a mutually supportive relationship within any constitutional system. Constitutional theory therefore unlocks the essence of the federal idea by identifying what federalism is, and then how and why it is deployed to manage political power in a particular way and for a particular purpose, as well as the particular way in which the legitimacy-authority relationship manifests itself in federal context.

Evaluation is an essential feature of this exercise. Constitutional theory is an endeavour both to understand constitutional law as the legal-normative conditioning of political practice, and a benchmark with which to measure how such a legal order works against its own internal logic.[126] Constitutional theory is concerned with synthesising the practice and theory of constitutional law. It is the integral relationship between these two dimensions that opens the door to evaluation: how well does the practice of constitutional law meet its theoretical aims? This approach differs however from normative political philosophy in that this evaluative dimension is internally generated from the purposes of the constitution in question. A constitutional theorist asks what the purpose of a particular constitution is and how this purpose is reflected in the constitution's institutional formation and practice. A 'good' constitution is one that represents faithfully the purpose or purposes for which it was created. In this way constitutional practice, both in terms of how the constitution is initially framed and how its legal-normative authority plays out, is central to the normative evaluation that constitutional theory brings to bear. This

[126] S. Tierney, 'Federalism and Constitutional Theory', in G. Jacobsohn and M. Schor (eds), *Comparative Constitutional Theory* (Cheltenham: Edward Elgar, 2018), 45–65.

evaluative dimension is essentially about function. What is the function that the constitution is intended to serve? Kelsen wrote: 'The validity of a legal order cannot be questioned on the ground that its contents are incompatible with some moral or political value.'[127] This is only partially true. The continuing validity of a constitution depends upon its *constitutional value*, namely ongoing fidelity to the function or purpose for which the constitution was promulgated.[128] Through the methodology of 'functional normativity' a constitutional theorist's key enquiry is how well a particular constitution does in fact meet that function or purpose.

I have previously applied the methodology of constitutional theory to the study of the constitutional accommodation of national pluralism[129] and in turn to constitutional referendums,[130] and as a method of analysis it is also ideally placed to help unpack the federal idea. A search for the essence of federalism is complex because, unlike other political ideas such as 'democracy' or 'liberalism' which remain comparatively abstract and open to a vast array of widely different conceptual and institutional forms, the federal idea informs, and is in turn further shaped by the practice of, a specific form of government. Federalism is not just a political idea or ideological proposition, it is a particular category of constitutional practice. As a result, federalism must be located within the theory-practice nexus that characterises constitutional law itself. The symbiosis of its inherent bi-dimensional nature—a constitutional concept encapsulating a specific genus of constitutional practice—must be understood if it is to be meaningfully analysed.[131]

The notion of normative functionalism can, for example, help us surmount the ultimately irresoluble debate as to whether federalism is at root an empirical or normative category by explaining the connection between the two in the very conceptualisation of modern constitutionalism. The key reason why federalism has never been adequately defined is due to a rigid binary in the approaches taken within political theory and political studies which has engendered a bi-polar zigzagging between, on the one hand, externally generated normative assessments

[127] H. Kelsen, *General Theory of Law and State* (New Brunswick: Transaction, 2006), 113.

[128] And this can of course be informed by morality. As the Supreme Court of Canada has stated: 'Our law's claim to legitimacy . . . rests on an appeal to moral values, many of which are imbedded in our constitutional structure.' *Reference re Secession of Quebec* [1998] 2 SCR 217, para. 67

[129] S. Tierney, *Constitutional Law and National Pluralism* (Oxford: Oxford University Press, 2004), 12–17.

[130] S. Tierney, *Constitutional Referendums: The Theory and Practice of Republican Deliberation* (Oxford: Oxford University Press, 2012), 2–4.

[131] LaCroix captures neatly the essentially iterative engagement between theory and practice that shaped the emergence of the United States' federal constitution. 'The federal idea has origins because it was created; it is an intellectual artefact, not a transcendent or timeless idea that has always hovered around waiting to be applied to a particular project.' A.L. LaCroix, *The Ideological Origins of American Federalism* (Cambridge, MA: Harvard University Press, 2011), 220. In broader relief, this process reflects Hermann Heller's idea of the constitution as a dialectical construction and as an unending interaction of legal form and political action. See discussion of Heller's work in M. Loughlin, 'The Concept of Constituent Power' (2013) 13 *European Journal of Political Theory* 218–237, 230–231. See also H. Heller, *Sovereignty: A Contribution to the Theory of Public and International Law*, D. Dyzenhaus (ed.) (Oxford: Oxford University Press, 2019).

and, on the other, deductive reasoning founded upon narrow and often partial empirical observations derived from either definitionalism, institutionalism, or behaviouralism. This Manichean polarisation, identified by Burgess,[132] stems from a failure to understand federalism in its relationship between theory and practice as a *constitutional* idea. It is only through articulation of this idea that we can both arrive at federalism's inherent purpose in the management of political power, and thereupon evaluate particular constitutional systems in light of this.

There have been attempts by politics scholars to arrive at a synthesis of the idea of federalism and its institutionalisation. Burgess was one commentator who struggled with the federal idea, trying to marry it in a coherent way to federation as the encapsulation of federal practice. Where Burgess's account differs from an approach founded in constitutional theory, as indeed do those of so many politics scholars looking at federalism, is that he does not identify the specific discipline of constitutional theory as a way through the dichotomy between normative theory and empirical practice. In the end Burgess falls back upon the binary he seeks to avoid, reaching for political theory as the only way to encapsulate the normative dimension of federalism: 'the federal principle is an organising principle and its fundamental purpose is essentially moral. Its *raison d'être* is to furnish the basis for order and stability but in a framework that formally acknowledges, protects and promotes human dignity, difference and diversity. This is its moral content and purpose.'[133]

This approach is at once both over-inclusive and insufficiently precise. In offering up values that are as open-ended as 'human dignity, difference and diversity', Burgess, like Justice O'Connor in *Gregory v. Ashcroft*, could be describing any modern democratic form of government: one struggles to imagine a democratic system that would not claim to protect and promote these values. The key question remains. What is it about the federal idea that distinguishes federalism from other modern democratic forms of government? In the end, the failure to answer this question lies not in Burgess's analysis; political theory simply cannot fill this gap. The search for the normative dimension of federalism cannot be an exercise in abstract political reasoning or a draw-down from a master list of generalisable political values. Rather it must be a functionalist approach that locates the inherent normative dimension of federalism in the constitutional functions it performs.

What then is the inherent purpose of federal constitutionalism? In this book I argue that it is to establish a constitutional union that gives foundational recognition and accommodation of the state's constituent territorial pluralism. A federal constitution serves both to foster this foundational pluralism and to maintain the constitutional relationship between pluralism and union in the creation and reconciliation of different orders of government. This purpose and the related principles

132 See above n 124.
133 Burgess, *Comparative Federalism*, 3.

which together characterise the normative functionalism of the federal idea will be unpacked in Chapter 7 and thereafter deployed in analysis of the institutionalisation of the federal idea. The key point at this stage of the book is to reiterate that this purpose and the principles that flow from it are immanent to the technique of federal government and are not ordained by ideologically driven normative values.

VI. Concluding remarks

The anatomy of the constitutional idea of federalism lies veiled within a literature that is characterised by two approaches to the subject which are seemingly rivals but which are, in a shared instrumentalist focus, in fact often fused. Each of these approaches has, in its own way, served to distort the essence of the federal idea. One is a strict empiricism, describing federalism's particular institutional manifestation from place to place, or observing its behavioural effects and from there deducing its nature by way of comparative analysis; the other is moral normativism, assessing federalism for its instrumental efficacy in promoting particular political, social, or economic values or goals. Neither approach takes us to the essence of federal constitutionalism. *Contra* institutionalism and behaviouralism, federalism must be addressed as a particular order of rule rather than simply an observable product of lived political life; and *contra* moral normativism, this genus must be recognised as an ontological rather than a moral template for government: a discrete model of constitutional rule, the value of which must be assessed immanently for its constitutional praxis rather than abstractly as a useful conduit for ideologically derived political ideals. Federalism may of course also be viewed by many to be a politically ideal form of rule; that is a matter of taste. But to elide description and prescription is to run together the constitutional essence of federalism with the merits of such an order of rule and, in the end, to confuse the nature of the subject.

It is the aim of this book to draw out the functionalism of federalism as an instance of normatively informed constitutional practice. This approach is more modest than an exercise in ideal political morality, but it is nonetheless capable of critique. The methodology of constitutional theory—the functional normativity that drives it—compels us also to address the 'conditions of possibility'[134] embedded within the federal idea. In other words, assessing federalism as a normatively informed sub-set of constitutional practice can lead to an evaluative turn that explores how the idea might be better institutionalised in practice from place to place, depending upon the foundational and ongoing terms of any federal contract. Freeing the federal idea from narrow institutionalism certainly opens up institutional possibilities. But the constitutional idea of federalism facilitates critique and

[134] J. Tully, *Public Philosophy in a New Key: Volume I: Democracy and Civic Freedom* (Cambridge: Cambridge University Press, 2008), 16.

prescription with a crucial caveat. The essence of federalism cannot be detached from moral value, nor from political or social behaviour, and certainly not from institutional design. But each of these is ultimately ancillary to the core function of federalism as a discrete form of constitutional rule; as a legal technique for management of territorial pluralism within the modern state.

3
The Foundations of Federalism

I. Introduction

Constitutional foundations are the logical starting point in our attempt to uncover the essence of federalism through the register of constitutional theory. The other building blocks which form our conceptual understanding of federal constitutionalism are layered explicitly or implicitly upon the constitution's foundational act, wherein the identity and purpose of the constitution emerge and the contours of its normative authority are shaped. In this chapter I argue that the federal foundational act is a specific category of constitutional beginning, and that understanding the nature of this 'federal moment', and its path-defining potential, is central to a broader appreciation of the discrete nature of federal constitutionalism. I also contend however that the specificity of the federal moment has largely been subsumed within one universalising theoretical account of constitutional foundations ('monist constitutionalism') and therefore that the particular implications of the federal constitutional moment for the identity, purpose, and normative authority of the federal constitution remain either underdeveloped or misunderstood.

In light of their normative significance, constitutions also take on a symbolic role that extends beyond their practical legal effect. As the source of authority for the public life of the polity, the constitution can become the focal point for a new civic identity, assuming a 'demos'-defining or 'nation'-defining character: the constitution does not merely establish institutions of government, it also transforms its creators into subjects, establishing their foundational civic status and the public space within which a collective constitutional identity forms and develops. Therefore, in the foundation of a constitution we see a complex interaction between the agency of the contingent, pre-constitutional people, and the new, and ongoing, agency of the constitutional people who in later relief give a more complete meaning to the founding act.

Constitutional theory approaches constitutional foundations in a very different way from other disciplines. Historians or politics scholars tend to focus upon the specific political and societal circumstances that shape the emergence of each constitutional system at a particular time in a territory's history: in temporal terms their attention centres therefore upon the pre-constitutional period. Constitutionalists on the other hand address constitutional history in conceptual terms, focusing not so much upon the background environment from which the constitution emerges but more upon its legal-normative consequences: upon constitution-making as an

The Federal Contract. Stephen Tierney, Oxford University Press. © Stephen Tierney 2022.
DOI: 10.1093/oso/9780198806745.003.0003

authority-generating act that functions as the legitimate source for a new, self-circumscribed legal order.[1] Our principal focus is therefore later in time, addressing the constitutional moment itself—the big bang—rather than the pre-constitutional environment from which it comes. In this way constitutionalists search less for the background circumstances that inform a *particular* constitution's foundations and more for a generic explanation of the legal-normative commonality that links *all constitutions* as authority-bearers. This difference in emphasis can be explained by distinguishing the term 'constitutional foundations' from 'constitutional origins'. History and political studies are more concerned with the latter: from where does the impetus for this particular constitution at this particular time stem, and what are the political conditions or motivations behind its original creation? The constitutionalist is interested less in *why* a particular constitution originates at a particular time, and more in *what* is done—and *by whom*—in the constitutional moment of normative re-ordering that founds a new legal system. And it is this latter approach—the establishment of constitutional authority at the moment of constitutional naissance—that is the concern of this chapter.

From a constitutionalist perspective, there are two key issues that flow from this emphasis upon normative re-ordering: one is of course the normative authority that the emerging constitution acquires, but a second and equally important concern is the *a priori* issue of the political legitimacy that attends that moment. As was argued in the last chapter, the latter is the alchemy that transforms foundational power into post-foundational authority: the sanction required to give the modern polity its validation, turning might into right; a feature that ties the moment of creation to the key subject-forming role which a modern constitutional founding plays. In other words, the constitutionalist in fact does, like the historian or political scientist, take an interest in the pre-constitutional period, but that interest is more narrowly focused: concentrated upon the conceptual register of normative authority in the passage from the pre-constitutional regime to the new constitutional order and its interplay with foundational legitimacy.

In this chapter I address how the initial and enduring importance of the foundational act of a modern constitution involves a deep interconnection between legitimacy of the constitutional moment and the normative authority it produces. I argue that the idea of constituent power offers a bridge between the two that remains a vital resource for the life of any legitimate constitution. In doing so however, I will also explore how constituent power specifically, and constitutional foundations more broadly, have been conceptualised against one default model, the monist account of constitutions. My task therefore is to retrieve from this

[1] Dicey drew a distinction between the historian's method of 'ascertaining the steps by which a constitution has grown to be what it is' and the lawyer's aim to discern 'the law as it now stands'; that is, between 'political understandings' and 'rules of law'. A.V. Dicey, *Lectures Introductory to the Study of the Law of the Constitution* (London: Macmillan 1885). See also J.W.F. Allison (ed.), *The Oxford Edition of Dicey* (Oxford: Oxford University Press, 2013), vol. 1, 15–16, 20.

account the specific tradition of federal foundations, and in doing so to draw out a discrete and significant conception of federal constituent power.

In the next section of the chapter I begin by exploring the issue of legitimacy in constitutional foundations—*by whom* or *in whose name* is a constitution founded? In Section III I turn to the normative authority of constitutional foundations—*what* is done at that moment and what is its normative significance? Each section begins by addressing the monist default within modern constitutionalism and attempts to explain how this story has been built implicitly—and often unselfconsciously—upon a particular conception of the demos. In each section I then seek to elicit the particular account of federal constitutional foundations in relation to legitimacy and normativity respectively, exploring how federalism poses a radical challenge not only to the standard account of constitutional foundations, but also to the very notion that there is one universalisable model of modern constitutionalism.

II. The legitimacy of constitutional foundations

(i) Agency, foundational act, and validation

The subject of foundations has been a fraught one for constitutional theorists because it calls into question the very coherence of constitutional authority. This is an existential challenge to constitutional theory as an explanatory discipline since constitutional theory is premised upon the notion that constitutional authority is a meaningful idea, distinguishable from, and transformative of, political power. This challenge therefore concerns the legitimacy claims of constitution-makers: who possesses the authority to found a constitution and from where does this authority to authorise and endow a binding normative regime derive?[2] In the era of the modern state the legitimacy question is tied inextricably to the idea of the demos, bringing to the table a conceptualisation of 'the people' as authors (at least symbolically) of the constitution, and as bestowers of the constitution's political authenticity, and hence of its lawful validity.[3] This connection between foundation and

[2] This is a perennial problem for constitutionalists attempting to conceptualise the people as both founder and subject. Arato identifies this paradox in Kelsen's work: 'To derive ... validity from the order itself, as its transcendental condition of possibility, in Kelsen's famous Grundnorm, for example, is deeply question begging, or circular. Such attempted derivation only poses the question of legitimacy, without at all solving it.' A. Arato, *The Adventures of the Constituent Power: Beyond Revolutions?* (Cambridge: Cambridge University Press, 2017), 12.

[3] For a number of contemporary scholars, constituent power is an inherently democratic concept: 'Constituent power ... has an important connection with the democratic ideal. In its modern and contemporary foundations, constituent power is attributed to the nation, the people or the community; in short, to all those who will become subject to the future constitutional regime. Constituent power points toward a democratic constitution-making power, and its popular and collective character makes it incompatible with given or imposed constitutions.' J.I. Colón Ríos, *Weak Constitutionalism: Democratic Legitimacy and the Question of Constituent Power* (Oxford: Routledge, 2012), 102. See also G. Jeffrey Jacobsohn and Yaniv Roznai, *Constitutional Revolution* (New Haven: Yale University Press, 2020), 14.

demos has, I would submit, three intertwined dimensions: agency, the nature of the foundational act, and validation. I explore each in turn.

Agency at the moment of constitutional foundation is often articulated in modern constitutional theory through the language of constituent power: the idea that constitutional authority stems from, and remains vested in, the people.[4] Recalling how constitutional theory differs from empirical historicism, such an articulation of popular agency may be, in any particular constitutional experience, a historical fiction.[5] Few instances of constitutional formation are traceable back to a nationwide deliberative conversation and genuine mobilisation of national self-consciousness. In many cases, the historical reality is constitution-drafting by a selective elite. Furthermore, the people may also be engaged only notionally in a constitution's ratification.[6] At a deeper conceptual level, it is also arguably impossible to make sense of the very idea of 'the people' until the constitution itself moulds this collective political personality from the clay of the pre-constitutional multitude.[7] Hans Lindahl discusses how the constitutional moment is one of 'rupture' that 'does not—and cannot—reveal a people immediately present to itself as a collective subject'.[8] The nature of the people is only disclosed—or is itself only fully cast—within, and by, the constitution itself. But whether the political mobilisation of a self-conscious people was a real pre-constitutional phenomenon or merely a myth designed to cement constitutional self-justification *ex post facto*, constituent power is still highly significant for the role it plays in legitimising the process.[9] It

[4] A.E. Sieyès, 'What Is the Third Estate? (1789)', in O.W. Lembcke and F. Weber (eds), *Emmanuel Joseph Sieyès: The Essential Political Writings* (Leiden: Brill, 2014); L. Rubinelli, *Constituent Power: A History* (Cambridge: Cambridge University Press, 2020), 33–74.

[5] In the American context, see E. Morgan, *Inventing the People: The Rise of Popular Sovereignty in England and America* (New York: Norton, 1988). See also R. Hirschl, *Comparative Matters: The Renaissance of Comparative Constitutional Law* (Oxford: Oxford University Press, 2014), 174. And in fact the very idea of constituent power can be used instrumentally to foster oppression rather than democratic agency: H. López Bofill, *Law, Violence and Constituent Power: The Law, Politics And History of Constitution Making* (Abingdon: Routledge, 2021).

[6] Or not at all. The Japanese constitution uses the language of popular sovereignty even though it was in effect imposed by a victorious USA. C. Hahm and S.H. Kim, 'To Make "We the People": Constitutional Founding in Postwar Japan and South Korea' (2010) 8 *International Journal of Constitutional Law* 800–848. On the general problem of concretising the people, Morgan writes: 'A king, however dubious his divinity might seem, did not have to be imagined. He was a visible presence, wearing his Crown and carrying his sceptre. The people, on the other hand, are never visible as such. Before we ascribe sovereignty to the people we have to imagine that there is such a thing, something we personify as though it were a single body, capable of thinking, of acting, of making decisions and carrying them out ...' Morgan, *Inventing the People*, 153.

[7] A.M. Bernal, *Beyond Origins: Rethinking Founding in a Time of Constitutional Democracy* (Oxford: Oxford University Press, 2017), 85.

[8] H. Lindahl, 'Constituent Power and Reflexive Identity: Towards an Ontology of Collective Selfhood', in M. Loughlin and N. Walker, *The Paradox of Constitutionalism* (Oxford: Oxford University Press, 2008), 9–24, 18. This notion of founding as contingency, only explicable in its final form, echoes Rousseau, who alluded to the paradox of people coming together to form a constitution for the good of all, unaware of what that good might be: 'the effect would have to become the cause'. J.-J. Rousseau (1762) 'The Social Contract', in *The Social Contract and Other Later Political Writings* V. Gourevitch (trans.) (Cambridge: Cambridge University Press, 1997), 39–152, 71.

[9] J. Colon Rios, *Constituent Power and the Law* (Oxford: OUP, 2020); M. Loughlin, 'The Concept of Constituent Power' (2013) *European Journal of Political Theory* 218–237; A. Somek and M.A. Wilkinson,

turns the inchoate and somewhat amorphous idea of the people into a more tightly defined collective political agent: the association, whether conceptual or real, of a self-determining people, acting self-consciously to create a system of rule and in so doing transforming itself from a contingent constituent people into an authority-generating constitutional people.[10]

Even if the conception of its agency remains contingent and open, the foundational act of constitution-making is very much real. It is this act that defines 'the essential form of the political bond between the people (the citizens of the state) and its governing authorities'.[11] The specificity of constitutional theory as a discipline is characterised by the symbiotic interplay of theory and practice, as we explored in the last chapter. Constitutional theory is not an excursion into abstraction; its central function is to explain the normative authority of constitutions. Therefore, the constitutional theorist must make sense of how the real act of constitutional creation, which is so salient to the constitution's validity and normative future, can hinge upon a figurative or imagined 'people' or 'constituent power': per Schmitt, that 'political will, whose power or authority is capable of making the concrete, comprehensive decision over the type and form of its own political existence'.[12] The practical challenge for constitutional theory is clear: popular endorsement is central to conferring legitimacy upon the foundational act of a modern constitution, but is this endorsement borne out by reality if the constitution is in fact made by elites through an act in which the role of the people is marginalised or—in reality—non-existent?[13]

'Unpopular Sovereignty?' (2020) *Modern Law Review* 955–978; M. Patberg, *Constituent Power in the European Union* (Oxford: Oxford University Press, 2020); R. Gargarella, 'Constituent Power in a "Community of Equals"' (2020) 41 *Revus: Journal for Constitutional Theory and Philosophy of Law* [online] <http://journals.openedition.org/revus/6436>; M. Wenman, *Agonistic Democracy: Constituent Power in the era of Globalisation* (New York: Cambridge University Press, 2013).

[10] Or as Arendt put it: 'It is in the very nature of a beginning to carry with itself a measure of complete arbitrariness ... the beginning has, as it were, nothing whatsoever to hold on to.' H. Arendt, *On Revolution* (New York: Viking, 1963), 207. But that is not to underestimate its normative heft in creating a legal normative path. In his recent monograph Colón Ríos takes constituent power to be 'an eminently juridical concept, one that has legal and institutional implications and that can play a role in determinations of legal validity'. Colon Rios, *Constituent Power*, 295. See also Hermann Heller's notion of the 'power-forming quality of law'. M. Loughlin, 'The Concept of Constituent Power' (2013) 13 *European Journal of Political Theory* 218–237, 230.

[11] M. Loughlin and N. Walker, 'Introduction', in Loughlin and Walker, *The Paradox of Constitutionalism*, 1–8, 3.

[12] C. Schmitt, *Constitutional Theory* J. Seitzer (trans. and ed.) (Durham and London: Duke University Press, 2008), 125.

[13] Colón-Ríos poses this problem in his assessment of Arato's account of constituent power: J. Colón-Ríos, 'Arato's Adventures: Between Sovereignty and Constituent Power', (2020) 41 *Revus: Journal for Constitutional Theory and Philosophy of Law* [online] <https://journals.openedition.org/revus/6257>. Bruce Ackerman is currently engaged in an empirical review of the origins of constitutions, as either revolutionary constitutions, establishment constitutions, or elite constitutions. This serves to emphasise the disconnect between legitimacy claims and the notion of active demotic consent upon which these so often rest. B. Ackerman, *Revolutionary Constitutions: Charismatic Leadership and the Rule of Law* (Cambridge MA: Harvard University of Press, 2019).

Constitutional theory surmounts this validation problem in the idea of representation. The people may not be directly engaged in the act of constitution-making, but those elites who make the constitution do so in the name of the people. While the latter may only be tangentially involved, the symbolism of that role is crucial to warrant the constitutional outcome it produces. Furthermore, it is in this very act of representation that the pre-constitutional multitude takes form as constitutional people. The image of the founding people therefore remains a powerful totem in modern constitutional construction, connecting the foundational act to the identity of its subjects, albeit through the abstraction of representation.[14] The relationship between the people as constituent power and the act of constitutional foundations is therefore symbiotic—the former offers validity to the latter, while the latter helps constitute the former by instantiating the people as represented if not (yet) truly present in that foundational act. In other words, the central issue from a validation perspective is less about who performs the foundational act and more about *in whose name* it is performed. As Loughlin puts it: 'Without this dimension of symbolic representation, there is no constituent power.'[15]

(ii) Constituent power: the monist default

What is implicit in the discussion so far is the extent to which constitutional theory has tended to conceive of the demotic dimension of constitutional foundations in monist terms. Constituent power emerges as the key source of legitimacy for the constitution, but it is almost universally assumed that constituent power vests in one undifferentiated group of individuals—'the people'. This default presupposition runs through almost all modern political theory. This is perhaps unsurprising since constituent power has also played another important role—as a vital instrumental resource in the great social-architectural story of the last 200 years, nation-building. The drive to construct large, coherent, and centralised polities is one which was bolstered by fostering a unitary people who would identify with and offer loyalty to the nascent state.[16] This role—and the monist conception that underpins it—has been theorised in a number of ways. One approach is to see 'the nation' in organic terms, as a unified pre-constitutional reality, in which constituent power and nationhood emerge as synonyms—the natural unity of a people coalescing around the inevitability of state creation.[17] Rousseau's approach is less

[14] 'the "people" may not necessarily be the "authors" or "creators" of the new constitution, yet they remain the originators of the ultimate source of legitimacy'. Jacobsohn and Roznai, *Constitutional Revolution*, 14.

[15] M. Loughlin, 'The Concept of Constituent Power' (2013) *European Journal of Political Theory* 1–20, 15.

[16] B. Anderson, *Imagined Communities: Reflections on the Origin and Spread of Nationalism* (London and New York: Verso, revised edn, 1991 [1983]).

[17] E.-J. Sieyes (1789) *What is the Third Estate?* M. Blondel (trans.) (London: Pall Mall Press, 1963), 126.

primordial than that of Sieyes, but he also defines the people, state, and nation in singular terms, rooted in the conception of one indivisible collective of individuals; and again this elision takes on an implicit, almost natural, dimension.[18] Locke's theory of social contract, while largely abjuring the metaphysics of nationhood, nonetheless also has room for only one binary relationship between individuals and the contractually formed government. The language of peoplehood—albeit the modern, rational, and republican conception with which constitutionalism is now more familiar—is still conceived inherently in singular terms.[19] Moving to the twentieth century, the apotheosis of the monist account, unifying people, nation, and state, is to be found in the work of Carl Schmitt. He combines the ontology of early French modernity with the rationalism of the Enlightenment in his conclusion that the state is the inevitable product of history. The state is unified, but this unity rests upon the social fact of popular homogeneity, and the constitution serves to represent or 'positivise' the unified will of the (national) people.[20]

In this long tradition which unifies, and indeed singularises, conceptions of people, nation, and state, demotic monism has become deeply ingrained in the very idea of constitutional foundations.[21] There is and can be no constitutionally meaningful intermediary between the people as individuals and the people as one collective person, synonymous with nation, polity, and state. Leaving aside the issue of whether the foundational constituent act is really performed by 'the people' or by those claiming to represent the people, the crucial point in terms of legitimation through representation is that the constituent act of constitutional foundation is performed exclusively *in the name of* one collective, popular 'self'.

The three dimensions of foundational legitimacy—agency, the nature of the foundational act, and how its validation is articulated—each remain challenges for constitutional theorists, but these challenges have at least been simplified by subsuming them generically within this individualised and homogenised construction of constituent power, and then categorising them as a universalisable set of validatory criteria, applicable to every instance of democratic constitution-making. Across these three dimensions constitutional theorists have tended to take this one underpinning assumption for granted: in the foundation of any constitutional polity, constituent power is always and only conceivable through a singular lens. There is but one collective constituent power, from which derives the

[18] J.-J. Rousseau (1762) 'The Social Contract' in *The Social Contract and Other Later Political Writings* V. Gourevitch (trans.) (Cambridge: Cambridge University Press (1997), 39–152.

[19] J. Locke, *The Second Treatise of Civil Government and A Letter Concerning Toleration* (Oxford: Blackwell, 1948).

[20] 'The constitution-making power presupposes the people as a politically existing entity. The word "nation" denotes in a clear sense a people brought to political consciousness and capable of acting.' C. Schmitt, *Constitutional Theory* J. Seitzer (trans. and ed.) (Durham & London: Duke University Press, 2008), 101. See also P.C. Caldwell, *Popular Sovereignty and the Crisis of German Constitutional Law: The Theory and Practice of Weimar Constitutionalism* (Durham NC: Duke University Press, 1997), 115.

[21] In Chapter 4 I discuss how constitutional monism extends beyond foundations to form the central characteristic of modern constitutional authority more broadly.

constitution's foundational legitimacy as the order of rule for one constitutional people.

(iii) The issue of legitimacy in federal foundations

The foundation of a federal constitution challenges the universalisability of this account of the constituent act by positing a radically different, pluralised alternative. What characterises the federal constitutional moment is the union not of one undifferentiated group of individuals but of territories. And it is the very salience of territories to the foundational constitutional moment that gives federalism its initial—and thereafter path-determining—orientation as a distinct model of constitutionalism. We should be clear as to the radical and dramatic fork in the road which this marks and the nature of the conceptual challenge such a divergence poses to constitutional theory. The categorically distinct constitutional purpose which federalism serves demands nothing less than a conceptual re-routing *ab initio* from the monist default, beginning with a fundamentally divergent account of constitutional foundations.

The first and most fundamental test for the constitutional theorist of federalism is to extract and explain a specifically federal conception of constituent power: a conception that inheres in the nascent polity's constituent territories rather than simply in the individuals of whom these territories comprise. This is a dramatic step for constitutional theory: recognising that 'territorial constituent power' is the essential idea, and hence source of legitimacy, that underpins a discrete 'federal constitutional moment'.[22] The initial drama rests not so much in what federal constituent power consists of, but in the very fact of its discrete existence as a rival to the purportedly universal account of modern constitutionalism.

When we turn to consider constitutionalism's trinity of legitimising factors—agency, the foundational act, and validation—from a federal perspective, the key point of departure is therefore the very identity of the authors upon whom the notion of federal peoplehood and constituent power is built. The agents who come together to found the new constitution are not one undifferentiated constituent body of individuals, rather they are the constitution's 'constituent territories'.[23] By this formulation, *federal constituent power* can be explained as the foundational authority of the constituent territories of a nascent polity to form together a federal

[22] Indeed it continues to be resisted: 'States can move from a unitary structure towards a form of federal settlement without any formal constitutional change; there need not be any grand "constitutional moment"'. N.W. Barber, *The Principles of Constitutionalism* (Oxford: Oxford University Press, 2018), 206.

[23] The name given to constituent territories varies from constitution to constitution: states, provinces, länder, cantons, autonomous communities, etc. See R.L. Watts, *Comparing Federal Systems*, 3rd edn (Montreal, QC, Canada: McGill-Queen's University Press, 2008), 71. I will generally use the term 'constituent territories' to emphasise the foundational constitutional salience of these constitutional subjects.

constitution for that polity. The implications for constitutional theory of this fundamentally different conception of constituent agency lie largely unexplored. This has particular implications for the debate concerning the inchoate nature of the pre-constitutional people and their relationship to the constitution's legal authority, an issue we return to in Section III of the chapter when I address the normative implications of the foundational moment.

Turning to the foundational act, the notion of territorial constituent power also affects how we understand the nature and hence the legitimacy of the moment of constitutional creation. If the 'founding act' of constitution-making does indeed define the political bond between 'the people' and its new system of government, the political bond that is created (and thereby constitutionalised) in a federal foundation cannot be—although it often is—cast in such conceptually unitary terms. Such a bond must be understood as uniting the founding territories—as a plurality—both to one another and to the governing system of constitutional authority created by these territories.[24] For Beaud, the foundation of a federation 'stems from an agreement between Federated States'.[25] The notion of 'the people' is significant for federal constitutionalism, but its meaning demands to be heavily nuanced and possibly varied from polity to polity.[26]

An important particularity of the federal foundational act is that the connection between this act and its constituents is always real rather than symbolic. The nature of the federal moment is the binding together of territories which are at that point, by definition, collective political bodies, representative of their own members. To say 'by definition' is to make a *conceptual* claim. There are in practice different ways in which a federal constitution can emerge—for example, the coming together/holding together alternatives commonly discussed in the federalism literature.[27]

[24] As Madison, put it: 'Each State, in ratifying the Constitution, is considered as a sovereign body, independent of all others, and only to be bound by its own voluntary act . . .' James Madison, Federalist No. 39, C. Rossiter (ed.), *The Federalist Papers* (New York: New American Library, 1961), 240–246. As I will explore in later chapters, Madison's wider political purpose for the US constitution belied the implications of these words; but they are notable as an early articulation of the implications of federal constituent power. In another context Canadian Justices Martland and Ritchie, in dissenting judgments issued in the seminal *Patriation Reference* case, took federalism to be 'the dominant principle of Canadian constitutional law' *Reference Re Resolution to amend the Constitution* (1981) 1 SCR753, 821.

[25] O. Beaud, 'The Founding Constitution: Reflections on the Constitution of a Federation and its Peculiarity' (2017) *Jus Politicum; Revue de Droit Politique* 33–63, 48.

[26] S. Tierney, '"We, the Peoples": Constituent Power and Constitutionalism in Plurinational States', in Loughlin and Walker, *The Paradox of Constitutionalism*, 229–245.

[27] Respectively, whether federations were established by bringing independent territories together (state and constitution being created at the same time albeit in discrete acts—as discussed in Chapters 4 and 5), or by a constitutional reordering within already created states: C.J. Friedrich, *Trends of Federalism in Theory and Practice* (London: Frederick A. Praeger Publishers, 1968). This was characterised by Alfred Stepan as 'coming together' versus 'holding together' origins—A. Stepan, 'Federalism and Democracy: Beyond the U.S. Model' (1999) 10 *Journal of Democracy* 19–33, 21–22. This is essentially a focus upon political origins rather than constitutional foundations: a distinction that is 'only historical, not legal, in nature'. F. Palermo and K. Kössler, *Comparative Federalism: Constitutional Arrangements and Case Law* (Oxford: Hart Publishing, 2017), 40. It is possible certainly to discern that each of these paths can lead to distinct institutional forms within the genus of federal constitutionalism—N. Aroney,

The former may be a more clear-cut example of an act of contracting together, done by already politically formed entities, but the latter also fits this description.[28] The point is that in either case, at the foundational moment, it is the territories of the polity that act as both representatives of their members and as the constituents who form or transform the constitution and in whose name it is made or re-made.[29]

It is notable that the term 'contract' has been co-opted by political theory to explain constitutional origins,[30] and that monist constitutionalism has tended to elide this idea with the notion of popular consent to constitutional foundations.[31] It is, in methodological terms, misconceived to run political and constitutional theory together in this way; but it is also particularly fictitious when we consider the lack of direct individual consent or even active involvement in the birth of

'The Federal Condition: Towards a Normative Theory' (2016) 61 *The American Journal of Jurisprudence* 13–31. But whatever circumstances led to a federal constitution's promulgation, the crucial fact for the constitutionalist is the establishment of 'a compound polity in which each of the different orders of government derives its authority from a supreme constitution rather than from another level of government.' Watts, *Comparing Federal Systems*, 3rd edn, 65. The normative significance of the federal foundation remains equally fundamental regardless of the pre-constitutional legal order from which it emerged.

[28] While some commentators consider that the distinction between aggregative and devolutionary processes leads to very different conceptions of federalism (e.g. Beaud, 'The Founding Constitution: Reflections on the Constitution of a Federation and its Peculiarity', 50), Aroney points out that federal constitutions which emerge in a more 'devolved' way within existing states, such as Canada, Spain, and Belgium do so in recognition that 'nascent local communities' already exist, pushing for recognition of their discrete identity. 'Each federation is thus a unique product of its particular history.' Aroney, 'The Federal Condition: Towards a Normative Theory', 25–26. See also M.G. Breen, 'The Origins of Holding-Together Federalism: Nepal, Myanmar, and Sri Lanka' (2018) 48 *Publius* 26–50. On the other hand, those who take a nationalistic approach to federalism can argue that the very identity of constituent territories is fully subsumed by the act of union. Abraham Lincoln declared, in relation to 1787, 'The Union is older than any of the States; and, in fact, it created them as States.' A. Lincoln, 'Message to Congress in Special Session', in R. Basler (ed.) (1953), *The Collected Works of Abraham Lincoln* (New Brunswick, N.J.: Rutgers University Press for the Abraham Lincoln Association, Springfield, Ill., 1953), 421–441, 433–434, cited by A.R. Amar, 'Of Sovereignty and Federalism' (1987) 96 *Yale Law Journal* 1425–1520, 1460. These accounts emphasise how imperative it is, from the perspective of legal science, to distinguish the historical and political conditions which lead to a federal constitutional founding from the legal-normative consequence of that founding itself.

[29] As James Bryce put it more than a century ago: 'Federalism is an equally legitimate resource whether it is adopted for the sake of tightening or for the sake of loosening a pre-existing bond.' J. Bryce, *The American Commonwealth, 3 vols* (London: MacMillan, 1888), vol. I, 350–351. More fundamentally, each of these paths to federation is, at the level of constitutional validation, underpinned by the same concept of territorially-pluralised constituent power.

[30] G. Wood, *The Creation of the American Republic, 1776–1787* (Chapel Hill: University of North Carolina Press, 1969), 259–305; J.F. Dienstag, 'Between History and Nature: Social Contract Theory in Locke and the Founders' (1996) 58 *Journal of Politics* 985. See also Alexander Hamilton, Federalist No. 33, Rossiter (ed.), *The Federalist Papers* , 201–205, which echoes Locke's notion of a polity as a legally limited contract and also characterises, as did a number of the American founders, the ratification documents of the states in 1787 through the language of 'social compact': A.R. Amar, 'Of Sovereignty and Federalism' (1987) 96 *Yale Law Journal* 1425–1520, 1461, fn 156. In wider context see also M. Loughlin, *Foundations of Public Law* (Oxford: OUP, 2010), 275–311.

[31] 'The fabric of American empire ought to rest on the solid basis of *the consent of the people*.' A. Hamilton, Federalist No. 22, Rossiter (ed.), *The Federalist Papers*, 152.

many constitutions.[32] As I will discuss further in Section III however, the notion of contract or pact is very much applicable to federal foundations and highly salient when we think through its (legal) normative implications.[33]

It is of course on account of the reality gap between the story of popular agency on the one hand and the mythical symbolism of popular deliberation in the foundational act on the other, that representation has played a key role within the default story of monist constitutionalism, providing the foundational act with final validation and at the same time transforming the nebulous concept of the pre-constitutional multitude into the constitutional people. In federal foundations representation plays a very different role. Representation is less significant at the moment of the foundational act because the reality is one of intentional polity formation by territories that already exist as political collectives. The constitutional moment is in this deeper sense non-representational, making territorial constituent power very much real and present.

The territories together form the constitution actively and directly—no other actor does it on their behalf, and therefore symbolic representation is not needed to bridge a conceptual gap between mythical constituents and real act. Secondly, insofar as actual representation is present in a pragmatic rather than conceptual sense in the federal foundational act, elites who perform the representative role do not contract together only in the name of 'the people' as one demotic entity. They stand as representatives of their respective territories, and by extension of the discrete 'territorial peoples' of these territories. In this way territories are the foundational subjects of the constitution and individual entry into the constitutional contract is, at least in part, conditioned by membership of these territories. To take an example from the American foundation, at the Virginia Ratifying Convention in 1788 Patrick Henry argued that the construction of the constitution in the name

[32] Buchanan discusses how the very idea of consent is highly idealised and not a realistic descriptor for the relationship between citizens and political power: A. Buchanan, 'Political Legitimacy and Democracy' (2002) 112 *Ethics* 689–719.

[33] The Swiss and German notion of *Bundesvertrag* or federal treaty goes some way to capture the contractual or compactual essence of federal foundations. It is notable that in the foundation of a number of federal constitutions the active consent of the constituent territories was secured. The Philadelphia process is a prominent example. This came into effect when ratified by nine of the thirteen states, and by 1790 all thirteen had ratified. Article VII of the draft US constitution provided that only those states ratifying the constitution would be bound by it and that they 'could approve or reject as they liked, with no state bound that refused to ratify'. R. Natelson, 'Proposing Constitutional Amendments Through a Convention: Rules Governing the Process' (2011) 78 Tennessee Law Review 693–750, 723. Madison made the same point in Federalist No. 43, Rossiter (ed.), *The Federalist Papers*, 271–280, 272–274. For further discussion see W. Partlett, 'The American Tradition of Constituent Power' (2017) 15 *International Journal of Constitutional Law* 955–987, 966. The importance of territorial consent is also evident from the convoluted ratification process that preceded passage of the British North America Act 1867 (for discussion see *Reference Re Secession of Quebec* [1998] 2 SCR 217, paras 34–41). Another example is the draft Australian constitution which was submitted to referendum in each of the colonies except Western Australia. On 31 July 1900, when the Commonwealth Constitution Bill had already been enacted by the British Parliament, a referendum was held in Western Australia. In all of these processes a majority voted in favour of the federation.

of 'We, the People' was misconceived. 'The people gave them no power to use their name. That they exceeded their power is perfectly clear.'[34] As Bernal puts it: 'For Henry, the issue was not so much whether the people could act rightly or not, but who could represent them best. And the most legitimate and lawfully established body for representing the will of the people was the states. The Framers had thus acted illegitimately in acting as representatives of a national people that did not yet exist.'[35]

When we talk therefore of a federal people in constitutional terms (Chapter 6 Subjects), it must be with a conception of peoplehood very different from the monist account: a conception containing within it collective territorially based pluralism, the nature and strength of which will vary from polity to polity. This has knock-on consequences for how we understand federal constituent power, not only at the founding moment but, as we will now explore, in the normative life of the polity. It also has fundamental implications for the nature of the federal 'nation' and the federal 'state', implications which are so potentially unsettling as to have led ultimately to the enervation of federal constitutionalism and its domestication within one generic account of constitutionalism as conduit for nation- and state-building (explored further in Chapters 4 and 5).

III. Constitutional foundations and legal authority

(i) The monist approach to foundational authority

The way in which constitutional foundations are legitimised has inevitable consequences for the legal authority ascribed to that foundational moment. And here again we see the stark conceptual contrast between the monist conception of the polity and its federal alternative. Whereas the question of legitimacy principally concerns the identity of the constitution's authors (whether real or represented), the 'who' of the constitutional moment as it were, we are now concerned with the 'what' of the constitutional foundation: what is it that is done at that moment and what is its legal-normative significance? The focus moves therefore from authorship to issues surrounding transition and transformation, but it is also the case that the two stages remain intimately connected through the interplay of legitimacy and authority across an inter-temporal setting. Authorship endows legitimacy and hence authority upon the act of making a constitution, but legitimacy remains salient in two ways going forward: one concerns the ongoing authority of

[34] Patrick Henry, 4 June 1788, 'Speech before the Virginia State Ratifying Convention', in *The Anti-Federalist: Writings by the Opponents of the Constitution*, H.J. Storing (ed.) (Chicago: University of Chicago Press, 1985), 296–297.

[35] Bernal, *Beyond Origins*, 85.

the constitution after the moment of creation, the second concerns the extent to which this authority is derived from the pre-constitutional setting from which it emerged. It is through the prism of constituent power that I will explore this interconnection, and just as I have identified a distinction between the default conception of constituent power and the federal alternative at the foundational moment, so too will we see that these different conceptions have the potential to lead to very different ways of understanding the nature and locus of authority within the constituted polity.

I turn first to the authority a constitution acquires in the moment of its creation. In contemporary constitutional practice it is now taken for granted that a constitution comprises a higher order body of law: in Kelsenian terms its authority can only be explained in relation to the basic norm;[36] for Hart, the constitution is the embodiment of second order rules.[37] The common understanding across these accounts is that the constitution is the general referent from which ordinary laws derive their specific authority and to which they are ultimately subordinate.[38]

Although in practice this is now a feature of general acceptance, as a matter of constitutional theory it still presents a conundrum. How is it that the legitimacy to make a constitution, derived from the constituent power of 'the people' (bearing in mind the difficulties we have encountered with this very concept), entails the power to make of this constitution a higher order set of norms that thereafter frame the normative authority of political institutions into the future? This puzzle is encapsulated in the relationship between constituent power (*pouvoir constituant*) on the one hand, and constitutional form (*pouvoir constitué*) on the other, a relationship that has been described as a paradox:[39] how can the unbridled freedom of 'the people' which was sufficiently authoritative—in a sense 'sovereign'—to create a constitutional order, then be subordinated to the very authority it established? How can uninhibited popular sovereignty become constitutionally constrained legal sovereignty?

These challenges have perplexed constitutionalists in the modern era, particularly since the founding of the constitution of the United States which itself emerged with something of a normative breach between the Articles of Confederation and the new constitutional order framed in Philadelphia; in a normative twilight zone

[36] H. Kelsen, *The General Theory of Law and State* (New York: Russell and Russell, 1945), 30.

[37] H.L.A. Hart, *The Concept of Law* (Oxford: Oxford University Press, 1961).

[38] Secondary rules 'specify the ways in which primary rules may be conclusively ascertained, introduced, eliminated, varied, and the fact of their violation conclusively determined'. Hart, The Concept of Law, 92.

[39] 'Modern constitutionalism is underpinned by two fundamental though antagonistic imperatives: that governmental power ultimately is generated from the "consent of the people" and that, to be sustained and effective, such power must be divided, constrained, and exercised through distinctive institutional forms.' Loughlin and Walker, 'Introduction', in *The Paradox of Constitutionalism* 1.

that relied upon, but ultimately supplanted, the legal process of constitutional change operable under the *ancien régime*.[40]

One answer is to be found in a formalistic positivism. One can assert simply that the constitution is a legal order while the process of constitution-making was merely a political act. Hobbes' notion of sovereignty emerges essentially as a political fact that is not dependent for its authority upon its source. As Lev puts it, Hobbes' theory of commonwealth 'offered a way to justify power that did not rely on, indeed excluded reference to, the past possession of it. The terms on which he articulates the alienation of liberty by the individual bar the road to any attempt to contest the legitimacy of power by reference to the means by which he got it.'[41] The temporal dimension of authority that has so vexed constitutional theorists is simply cut off at source: sovereign power exists 'outside history, in a *nunc stans* that can be instantiated at any point in time'.[42] More modern accounts echo this sense that authority emerges from political fact, its validity determined for Kelsen by the very authority of law within a system, or more straightforwardly for Schmitt, through the simple maxim that might makes right.[43] For Schmitt, in fact, the constitution is itself scarcely transformational. The political remains the dominant force. In this sense ultimate power does not really mutate into authority. It remains beholden to the political strength of the sovereign will which is itself unconstrainable, encapsulated in Schmitt's notion of constituent power as the ultimate political power. A more recent approach also moves away from ascribing deep significance to constitutional foundations, but leads to a very different conclusion from Schmitt's. David Dyzenhaus eschews the very idea of the normative salience of constituent power[44] and looks for legal validity in the second order notion of law. In doing so, his account thickens the idea of law itself, giving it substantive content in the notion of the 'rule of law'.[45] In his work Dyzenhaus engages with the idea that law as

[40] James Madison offered a subtle and somewhat opaque assessment of the transition to the new constitution in 1787. On the one hand he seemed to recognise the unlawful and hence revolutionary nature of the new constitution's promulgation: 'in all great changes of established governments, form ought to give way to substance; that a rigid adherence in such cases to the former, would render nominal and nugatory the transcendent and precious right of the people to "abolish or alter their governments as to them shall seem most likely to effect their safety and happiness" ...'. But at the same time he denied that the new constitution emerged from an entirely revolutionary act: the principles of the Confederation were being 'expanded' not usurped; the rules bent not broken. James Madison, Federalist No. 40, Rossiter (ed.), *The Federalist Papers*, 247–255, 252–253. This is discussed by G. Jacobsohn and Y. Roznai, *Constitutional Revolution* (New Haven, CT: Yale University Press, 2020), 46–49; and by A.R. Amar, 'Popular Sovereignty and Constitutional Amendment', in Sanford Levinson (ed.), *Responding to Imperfection: The Theory and Practice of Constitutional Amendment* (Princeton: Princeton University Press, 1995), 89–115, 93–96.

[41] A. Lev, 'Introduction: Federalism and Public Law Theory', in A. Lev (ed.), *The Federal Idea: Public Law between Governance and Political Life* (Oxford: Hart Publishing, 2019), 1–26, 15.

[42] A. Lev, 'Introduction: Federalism and Public Law Theory', 15.

[43] P.J.J. Philips, *The Challenge of Relativism: Its Nature and Limits* (London: Bloomsbury, 2011), 133.

[44] 'the question of constituent power does not arise for normative theory'. D. Dyzenhaus, 'The Politics of the Question of Constituent Power', in Loughlin and Walker, *The Paradox of Constitutionalism*, 129–147, 143.

[45] For an early expression of this idea see D. Dyzenhaus, 'Recrafting the Rule of Law', in D. Dyzenhaus (ed.), *Recrafting the Rule of Law: The Limits of Legal Order* (Oxford: Hart, 1999), 1–14.

order of rule embodies two discrete dimensions. There is the traditional idea of the rule of law as *rule by law*. This, as Trevor Allen also argues, is an inherent characteristic of each particular instance of constitutionalism, whether democratic or otherwise: the constitution provides authority for rule by law and in doing so is the ultimate source and referent for that law.[46] There is, however, also a broader notion of law which encapsulates the principle of legality as a value in itself. This is an externally derived concept which is capable of constraining constitutional authority by way of moral values. Dyzenhaus considers these values to be immanent to the principle of legality and hence to constitutional normativity itself.[47] This approach sees legal authority as detachable from any legitimising moment in time because law's validity rests ultimately upon timeless moral standards. Since the rule of law that underpins constitutional authority is sufficiently supported by its morally informed functional essence, it need not (and indeed should not) derive validation from constituent power or popular sovereignty, both of which can serve to distort its substantive core.

I argue, *contra* these varied approaches, that either a scorched earth approach to the popular underpinnings of constitutional authority or a denial of the salience of the foundational act is unsatisfactory. I have identified legitimacy founded in the consent of its foundational subjects as the very badge of authority in the construction of the modern constitution. The defining characteristic of contemporary constitutionalism is that right in fact makes might, and the task for the constitutional theorist is to identify the source of this right. On this basis, neither the political fact doctrine in the legal tradition of Kelsen and the political tradition of Hobbes and Schmitt, nor an approach founded in moral immanence per Dyzenhaus, accounts adequately for the foundational and ongoing principle of consent that must undergird constitutionalism. In other words, the validity of the constitution's higher authority to act as an ongoing constraint upon political power within a constitution derives in part from the manner of its creation.

That said, there is another answer to the seeming paradox of constitutionalism, namely that while the foundational moment may be deeply significant at the time of constitutional creation, relegating the salience of this moment in the new lived

It is further developed in D. Dyzenhaus, *The Constitution of Law: Legality in a Time of Emergency* (Cambridge: Cambridge University Press, 2006), 6–7.

46 T.R.S. Allen, 'The Rule of Law', in D. Dyzenhaus and M. Thorburn (eds), *The Philosophical Foundations of Constitutional Law* (Oxford: Oxford University Press, 2016), 201–220, 208.

47 'the operation of the rule of law is not confined to limiting public power. The rule of law is also constitutive of a certain kind of power—of legal authority'. Furthermore, 'principles are inherent in the constitution of law itself.' D. Dyzenhaus, *The Constitution of Law*, 7. These principles are not merely procedural, concerning how decisions are made. They 'constrain the decisions of those who wield public power in a way that protects the interests of the individuals subject to those decisions'. *The Constitution of Law*, 2–3. For further explanation of the ontological underpinnings of Dyzenhaus' theory see D. Dyzenhaus, 'The Idea of a Constitution: A Plea for Staatsrechtslehre', in D. Dyzenhaus and M. Thorburn (eds), *The Philosophical Foundations of Constitutional Law* (Oxford: Oxford University Press, 2016), 9–32.

constitution is both necessary and feasible. It is necessary in practical terms, otherwise entrenchment would be impossible and constitutional decision-making would become an everyday plebiscite. It is feasible because of the level of abstraction in the very idea of 'the people'. The 'constitutional people' created by the constitution is understood to be conceptually different from the constituent people who formed it; the act of creating a constitution is transformative not only of the legal order but also of the constitutional subjects who become bound by it. The result of the constitution as 'zero hour' is that the created constitutional people are conceptually distinguishable from the foundational constituent people; the latter being the chrysalis that falls away as the former is born and spreads its wings within the new constitutional world.[48] Therefore, no matter how the constitution was founded, it is the lived consent of its new subjects, understood in individual terms, which really matters; and crucially these subjects are constantly replaced by other individuals by virtue of mortality.[49] Locke's solution to the mortality dilemma is to look to the tacit consent of successive generations,[50] a variation of which remains a working assumption of many theories of constitutional authority.[51] Ultimately however these approaches also fail to explain why a later generation of people should accept the model of constitutionalism bequeathed to them by an earlier.[52]

[48] An approach that seems to rely upon such a conception of normative transition is that which sees legitimacy derive from the everyday deliberation of constitutional life; a notion that purports to replace the redundant and even dangerous notion of constituent power. This deliberative turn looks for constitutional legitimacy not in a constitution's creation but in how the constitutional people, within the created polity, then engages internally, among its constitutive individual members, in an iterative process of constitutional commitment over time. J. Habermas, *Between Facts and Norms: Contributions to a Discourse Theory of Law and Democracy* (Cambridge: Polity Press, 1996), Chapter 7. Hannah Arendt was an earlier sceptic of largely symbolic accounts of 'the people', preferring to find legitimacy in the daily workings of democracy. See e.g. H. Arendt, *On Revolution* (London: Penguin, 2009), 166–169.

[49] As Tuck puts it, one of the major reasons for the 'modern disinclination to accept the radical seventeenth- or eighteenth century view' (R. Tuck, *The Sleeping Sovereign: The Invention of Modern Democracy* (Cambridge: Cambridge University Press, 2016), 257) that a sovereign people remains alive and sovereign through majority voting is that: 'The members of that set change (in a large modern state) every minute or so as people die off and are replaced, so the "people" will have no stable existence. It has therefore to be a kind of imaginary construct, best understood as an entity represented by some set of institutions with a continuous existence.' *Tuck, Sleeping Sovereign*, 259.

[50] J. Locke, *The Second Treatise of Civil Government and A Letter Concerning Toleration* (Buffalo: Prometheus Books, 1986), Second Treatise, 2.120, ch. VI, sec. 74.

[51] Indeed the dominant approach within contemporary constitutional theory no longer turns to lineage as an important referent for constitutional authority. As Tuck puts it: 'Modern jurists almost without exception reject the old view that old laws are tacitly renewed by an existing sovereign when it fails to repeal them, and as a consequence they usually take the authority of pre-existing law to rest on a set of conventions about what we as a society recognise as authoritative, which once again allow a multiplicity of sites of authority.' Tuck, *Sleeping Sovereign*, 259.

[52] The integrity of the tacit consent theory is not strengthened by the casuistic motivation that prompted its formulation and which in fact called into question its legitimacy. As Tuck reminds us: 'the well-known distinction in Locke between "express" and "tacit" consent, with only the former implying citizenship, was primarily intended to justify the exclusion from public life of Catholics, who would not take the oath of allegiance in the form in which it had been phrased since its introduction in 1606, which required them to abjure the authority of the Pope.' Tuck, *Sleeping Sovereign*, 263, fn 13.

Recently theorists have developed innovative approaches which help us overcome the impasse or paradox of constitutionalism. Martin Loughlin and Hans Lindahl, in distinct but complementary writings on the relationship between constituent power and constitutional form, each question whether modern constitutional theory can simply dispense with the idea of constituent power and in so doing supplant the constitution's foundations with a normative *tabula rasa*, focusing only upon the here and now legal (Kelsen), political (Hobbes and Schmitt), deliberative (Habermas), or moral-normative (Dyzenhaus) legitimacy of the constitutional order. In doing so, this work also seeks to offer more nuanced approaches to the inter-temporal dimension of the legitimacy-authority interface; it moves beyond the sticking plaster of tacit consent to offer a more viable account of the link between original and ongoing popular commitment to constitutional authority. In this work we are drawn directly to our second (inter-temporal) query about the extent to which constitutional authority is derived from the pre-constitutional setting from which it emerged: whether a legal-normative relationship survives, linking the act of constitutional creation and the normative authority of the constitution itself.

What is intriguing in the work of Loughlin and Lindahl is that each advances the symbolic or totemic significance of constituent power as an ongoing normative resource for a living constitution, rather than consigning it to an instrumental role in the constitution-making process and hence to ultimate expiration in that original act. In this way, Loughlin's relational theory of sovereignty[53] and Lindahl's reflexivity thesis[54] each attempt to bridge what has often seemed to be an incommensurable gap between constituent power as source of legitimacy and constitutional form as self-standing source of authority. These scholars do not purport to offer a resolution to the inter-temporal conundrum, but seem to suggest that it is in fact not a conundrum at all; constitutional authority plays out in complex and inter-woven ways over time—between past and present—and cannot be conceived in linear terms from politically inchoate origin to constitutionally settled telos.

For Loughlin, as for many theorists of constitutional foundations, the essence of the higher order competence which constitutions have come to acquire is encapsulated in the term sovereignty. But as he explains, sovereignty is not simply the legal-normative power of the constitution, it is a broader concept that unites the normative or institutional question (the legal sovereignty of constitutional form) with the legitimacy question (the political sovereignty of constituent power) in an

53 Expounded in various works: *The Idea of Public Law* (Oxford: Oxford University Press, 2003); *Foundations of Public Law* (Oxford: Oxford University Press, 2010); 'The Concept of Constituent Power'.

54 See H. Lindahl, 'Constituent Power and Reflexive Identity: Towards an Ontology of Collective Selfhood'; 'Constituent Power and the Constitution', in D. Dyzenhaus and M. Thorburn (eds), *The Philosophical Foundations of Constitutional Law*; and *Fault Lines of Globalization: Legal Order and the Politics of A-Legality* (Oxford: Oxford University Press, 2013), 141–159.

ongoing relationship. The source of sovereign power in the constitution is to be found in the relationship between government on the one hand, which encapsulates the institutional fact of the authority of the constitution, and the governed on the other, who provide government with ongoing as well as original validity. In this way, the social dimension of sovereign authority exists in an inextricable and lasting relationship with its institutional dimension.

Continuity is key to this conception of sovereignty in which authority (competence) is tied to legitimacy (capacity) in the lived experience of democratic constitutionalism. The authority of constitutional supremacy does not hinge only upon the authenticity that derives from the original authorship of the constitution by 'the people', it also requires, as its authority continues to play out as an institutional fact, the ongoing sustenance that derives from the continuing consent of those subject to it. In this way 'the people' continues to exist as a vital conceptual resource for the constitution; it is the relationship between the people and the constitution from which the latter derives the source of its ultimate authority. The legal constitution is in a sense the 'power-distributive' component of sovereignty. But this exists in relation to the political dimension, or 'power-generative' component of sovereignty, which rests in the people.[55]

Lindahl's account is, on this inter-temporal issue, strikingly similar. He also considers constitutional authority to be dynamic; an ongoing engagement between the constitution as normative form and the evolving social reality of 'the people' as the ultimate source—and their interests, the ultimate purpose—of the constitution. Lindahl explains this in his reflexive account of constituent power. Constituent power remains important in the transition to, and lived experience of, constitutional rule because the normative turn to constitutional rule itself transforms how the very concept of a people as the collective agent of constitutionalism is understood. The collective self—the constitutional people—is fully shaped by the very act which, in its inchoate form, the pre-constitutional people itself performs: 'the paradox of constituent power indicates that self-constitution begins as the constitution of a political unity through a legal order, not as the constitution of a legal order by a political unity'.[56] For Lindahl, the relationship between the pre-constitutional and the constitutional is traceable looking both forward and backward in time, because it is inherently symbiotic. The constitutional act shapes the constitution and gives it authority, but it is only in the constitution's emergence as a legal order for a people that we can see fully, and not through a glass darkly, the real meaning and purpose of the pre-constitutional act and the real political identity of its agents: both the constituent act and the constituent actors remain embryonic

[55] M. Loughlin and S. Tierney, 'The Shibboleth of Sovereignty' (2018) 81 *Modern Law Review* 989–1016.

[56] H. Lindahl, 'Constituent Power and Reflexive Identity: Towards an Ontology of Collective Selfhood', in Loughlin and Walker, *The Paradox of Constitutionalism*, 9–24, 22.

until their full realisation in the actuality of the constitution. Constitutional authority cannot therefore be understood in temporal terms as linear; it is always circular or dialectical—the act of constitution-making serving to legitimise constitutional authority, and constitutional authority in turn giving meaning to the constitution-making act and ascribing ongoing and potentially changing political identity to its makers.[57] This non-linear account also thereby retrieves the constitutional reality of popular power from conceptual attempts to sideline it to the realm of theoretical abstraction as a mythical flying buttress, supporting the foundational moment but hanging in conceptual thin air.

Building upon the insights of Loughlin and Lindahl in attempting to conceptualise the role of 'the people' in the normative dimension of constitutional foundations, it is clearer to distinguish two manifestations of constituent power in recognition of how this concept changes over time: pre-constitutional, 'foundational constituent power' on the one hand, which is transformed through constitutionalisation into 'constitutional constituent authority' on the other. This helps capture the idea that the meaning of 'the people' is tied inextricably to the role the people performs: the people as 'foundational constituent power' is the active (and collective) agent in the creation of the constitution and—crucially—remains the active (and collective) agent ('constitutional constituent authority') in continuing to authorise the ongoing supremacy of the constitution.

The step forward taken by Loughlin and Lindahl posits the people as a living resource within the normative structure of the constitution, vital not only to the very concept of the constitution's foundational legitimacy but in a very real way to its ongoing authority. But in doing so they emphasise that the constituent moment is significant. The reflexive model offered by Lindahl helps to conceptualise the normative framework of relationality articulated by Loughlin. It is the reflexivity of the constitutional moment—the symbiotic interaction of actors and action—that explains the power-generational sovereignty which in turn defines that moment and which continues to sustain the power-distributive order of rule which it produces. Since the outcome of this process is *constitutional* validity, I will instead conceptualise this inter-temporal connection as *authority*-generation and *authority*-distribution.

The full significance of the interventions made by Loughlin and Lindahl is therefore a reconciliation between the legitimacy and legal-normative dimensions

[57] It is notable that Habermas' deliberative account of constitutional authority is also dialectical and inter-temporal: 'The allegedly paradoxical relation between democracy and the rule of law resolves itself in the dimension of historical time, provided one conceives the constitution as a project that makes the founding act into an ongoing process of constitution-making that continues across generations.' J. Habermas, 'Constitutional Democracy: A Paradoxical Union of Contradictory Principles?' (2001) 29 *Political Theory* 766–781, 768. However, for him there is no vital link between the constitutional people and the pre-constitutional constituent people as there is for Lindahl. In Habermas' account, only the now present constitutional people, as ongoing constitution-makers, are significant both conceptually and in moral-normative terms as the legitimisers of authority.

of constitutional foundations: the relationship between constituent power and constitutional form is not a paradox, it is merely one of complexity. And central to this relationship is the notion of agency—the active agency of a constitutional people. But it is in recognition of this step forward that we must also pause to recall the deep assumption regarding the nature of 'the people' which we explored in modern political thought from Sieyes to Schmitt, and which is in fact shared by Loughlin, Lindahl, and modern constitutional theory in general—namely a notion of the people conceived in singular terms. Even accounts as sophisticated and demotically nuanced as Loughlin's and Lindahl's are rooted in an approach to agency which is monist in nature and universalising in orientation.[58] Loughlin and Lindahl demand of us a conceptually deeper and sociologically sensitive understanding of the nature of 'the people', and of foundational constituent power and its transition into constituent authority. At the same time, both ground their theories in a default, unitary approach to the demos that envisages one pre-constitutional constitutive group (monist foundational constituent power) becoming (or remaining) one constitutive constitutional people (monist constitutional constituent authority).

What I will now seek to do is to build upon these accounts, opening them up to the pluralised sources of constitutive power that characterise federal foundations. I adopt the illuminating insights on the ongoing relationship between contingent/foundational constituent power and constitutional constituent authority developed by Loughlin and Lindahl, but adapt the relational methodology to the radically different conception of the structure of constitutional authority that characterises the idea of the federal constitution.

(ii) Federalism, foundations, and constitutional authority

Despite the theoretical insights they offer, both Loughlin and Lindahl seem to leave open how, respectively, the relational and reflexive accounts translate into constitutional institutionalisation. Each writer is, after all, primarily concerned with conceptual rather than institutional frameworks. But it would appear that their accounts are intended to be explanatory of contemporary constitutionalism rather than irritants against it. They are not political manifestos seeking to undermine the notion that the created constitution enjoys higher order authority. A seemingly implicit understanding for both Loughlin and Lindahl is that constituent power, insofar as it remains salient within constitutional settings, does so in a largely

[58] Loughlin: 'constituent power vests in the people . . . [and] . . . expresses a virtual equality of citizens', Loughlin, 'The Concept of Constituent Power', 229. Lindahl interrogates 'the kind of collective agency implied in the evocation of the "we" that enacts a constitution', but this does not extend to considering the possibility that it might contain a plurality of collective "we's"'. Lindahl, 'Constituent Power and Reflexive Identity: Towards an Ontology of Collective Selfhood', 14.

symbolic sense, and not by way of clear institutional instantiation, and certainly not as a form of *plébiscite de tous les jours*, destabilising constitutional entrenchment. For Lindahl, constituent power survives conceptually, helping to make sense of the very idea of a constitutional people; rooting that idea in its source, and hence giving it an identity that can transcend the constitutional moment. For Loughlin, it survives as political sovereignty or capacity, constraining the legal competence of the government of the polity by conditioning political behaviour, rather than positioning itself institutionally as a legal-normative rival to the legal supremacy of the constitution itself.[59]

These approaches make sense when we consider how difficult it is to give institutional meaning to the idea of constitutional constituent authority without supplanting the very idea of constitutional hierarchy. Agents and constitution exist in a symbiotic relationship, each defined by the other: the people generate authority for the constitution but the constitution in the same way, as Lindahl explains, creates the people, or, as this idea was expressed in a paper I wrote with Martin Loughlin, 'the people exist qua people—that is, as the bearers of sovereignty—only once governing arrangements have been established'.[60] That is why a conceptual distinction between 'contingent or foundational constituent power' (the constituent people as *pouvoir constituant*) and 'constitutional constituent authority' (the constituted people as *pouvoir constitué*) is required. For constituent power to emerge/re-emerge in a fully sovereign sense within a unitary constitutional setting it can, therefore, only do so through revolution: by a new contingent constituent power asserting itself against both the constitution and the identity the constitution has given the people as constituted (constitutional) constituent authority. In effect, a new pre-constitutional constituent power throwing off the identity ascribed to it by the existing constitution in order to begin to make a new polity. What we can take from these accounts is that popular identity is not just *transformed* by the constitution, it is ultimately *formed* by the constitution. The notion of 'the people', as a concept understood within constitutional theory, makes no sense absent the constitution. And therefore a popular challenge to the authority of the constitution cannot be framed within its terms. It can only emerge externally by the people removing themselves from the constitution both authoritatively and conceptually and declaring themselves to be the contingent or foundational constituent power of a new, incipient legal order, yet to be made.

It is when we turn to federal constitutions that we see the possibility of a truly radical alternative to this narrative of the relationship between constituent power and constitutional authority. The move from pre-constitutional moment to constitutional transformation is arguably very different in the federal context,

[59] M. Loughlin, *The Idea of Public Law* (Oxford: Oxford University Press, 2003), ch. 5. Loughlin, 'The Concept of Constituent power', 14.

[60] Loughlin and Tierney, 'The Shibboleth of Sovereignty', 999.

with potentially explosive implications for the notion of federal constitutional sovereignty.

To make this case it is necessary to recall that a constitution's normative authority is tied intrinsically to the nature of its foundational legitimacy. I have addressed how federal foundations take on their own form of legitimacy through the registers of agency, the foundational act, and validation. In terms of agency, I have argued that the federal foundational moment involves a specific 'territorial constituent power': the foundational authority of the constituent territories of a nascent polity to form, together, the federal constitution for that polity. This is a conception of constituent power that is inherently pluralised. In turn, the normative constitutional bond created by the federal idea is conceptualised as one between territories rather than individuals. The most dramatic consequence of this is that federal foundations avoid the reflexive paradox which I have suggested afflicts default, unitary constitutionalism. In the unitary or monist account of foundations, which imagines an amorphous group of individuals as bearers of constituent power, it is only realistic to think of them as a cohesive collective political entity once they have been conceptually formed/transformed into such an entity by the constitution itself: in this way the constitutional theory of unitary constitutionalism must always live with a conceptual impasse, whereby the pre-constitutional constituents and post-foundational citizens each derive meaning only in a state of reflection, one with the other. In a sense Lindahl's reflexivity is a sociological necessity; it is only in the formation of the constitution that the people takes real collective form as a coherent unified entity. The conundrum of whether the people shape the constitution or *vice versa* is therefore an irresoluble enigma inherent in a monistic conception of the demos as one collective entity made whole by the act of constitutionalisation. As Bernal puts it: 'The moment of founding a constitutional democracy poses a paradox in that it requires, for its legitimate constitution, that which is not yet.'[61]

But does the same conceptual or sociological puzzle necessarily apply in relation to territories as founders of the federal polity? In fact, territories which contract to form the constitution must exist as political entities at the time of the foundational act for the constitutional pact to make conceptual sense. The constitution may demarcate territories which had no previous discrete constitutional existence in this foundational moment, but in doing so, these territories become its foundational subjects. Certainly, if the constitution is to have any meaning as a new system of rule, the identities of these territories are normatively transformed, giving them a new constitutional identity (a point discussed further in Chapters 5 and 6). However, the possibility exists that this transformation is more contingent than it is for the far more inchoate concept of 'the people' in the foundation of

[61] Bernal, *Beyond Origins*, 87.

a unitary constitution. Federalism offers a more tangible notion of foundational constituent power, manifest in a plurality of already formed political collectivities, and hence one that is capable of transcending the foundational moment and of retaining more than merely conceptual reality in the post-foundational period; if the territories before the constitution is made are already coherent political entities, then the conceptual gap between foundational constituent power and constitutional constituent authority is far less pronounced than it is with the individualised conception of constituent power; when we think about agency at the moment of federal foundation, the fact of territorial constituent power is different from the default account not simply because the relevant actors are themselves pluralities rather than individuals, but because of what this implies about the maturity of pre-constitutional collective political identities and the impact these can have in due course upon the normative connection between pre-constitutional subject and post-constitutional 'citizen'. As I will explore throughout the rest of the book, the normative fact of federal foundations has constitutional resonance not only on the register of authority distribution within the constitution but far more fundamentally in the very generation of that authority and in the inter-temporal salience of the link between the generation and the distribution of constitutional authority.

One reason why the constitution is, in theoretical accounts, so transformative of unitary constituent power is practical as much as conceptual; associated with mortality itself. The constitutional people are within a generation very different in real as well as normative terms from the people who founded the constitution. This is why the term 'the people', to make sense over time, can only do so by way of representation. It is an expression that represents each generation of citizens at any moment.[62] A related point is that it is difficult for theory to make sense of a large, undifferentiated group of individuals as a direct decision-maker. Even Schmitt, who reifies constituent power as still salient within the constitutional order, conceptualises the people only in a representational way, personified by those who act in their name.[63]

This gap between the real and the fictive constituent power need not arise in the federal context. The territories which found the constitution remain in existence as subjects of the constitution.[64] The constitution's subjects of course do undergo

[62] As Maistre put it: 'the people which *command* are not the people which *obey*'. Joseph de Maistre (1795), 'Study on Sovereignty', in J. Lively, *The Works of Joseph de Maistre* (London: Allen & Unwin, 1965), 93–129. In this way Maistre sees sovereignty of the people as moving to the realm of representation, a trope that has continued to inform all accounts of modern democracy and constituent power, provoking Jefferson's famous question concerning constitutional entrenchment: 'whether one generation of men has a right to bind another'. Letter, Thomas Jefferson to James Madison, 6 September 1789, Papers 15:392–397.

[63] W. Rasch, 'Carl Schmitt's Defense of Democracy', in J. Meierhenrich and O. Simons (eds), *The Oxford Handbook of Carl Schmitt* (New York: Oxford University Press, 2016), 312–335.

[64] There are numerous instances within federal constitutions of how the constituent territories are considered to retain subjecthood within the new constitutional order. For example, the Australian constitution expressly provides that the constitutions of the states continue into the new constitutional

normative transformation, and the number of constituent territories can indeed grow or diminish.[65] The crucial point for constitutional theory however is that in conceptualising the foundations of the federal constitution, it is territories not individuals which pact together to form the constitution; the territories are its constitutional constituents, and these territories have the capacity to maintain their collective identities in a conceptually coherent way into the new constitutional polity, while others may be admitted to the federal contract with the same constitutional status. The reality of this pact is validated not only by the foundational process but also by the ongoing practice of mutual recognition among the polity's constitutive territories: with scope for acknowledgment (horizontally among themselves) that these territories have, in identity terms, transcended the founding moment to establish a crucial normative bond between constituent power and constituted authority.[66] Territorial pluralism is therefore not merely a characteristic of federalising constitutionally, it is *the* definitive characteristic of this foundational act, and in this way the foundational act of federal constitutionalism brings to the table a radically different conception of authorship—and hence process of constitutional validation—than we find in unitary constitutionalism.

These are key empirical points of departure in the foundations of, respectively, unitary and federal constitutionalism. But the legal-normative implications of them have largely been lost by the subsumption of federal foundations within a conceptually monist account of the constitutional demos.[67] In fact, the relational and reflexive accounts of constitutional authority proffered by Loughlin and Lindahl tell us that constitutional authority is shaped by the demotic specificity of the demos, and not vice versa. On that basis we need to start from the fundamental character of any constitution, and from this sociological as well as normative fact assess its legal-normative implications, rather than assume one standard approach to normative hierarchy across all constitutional models.

A federal constitution, as I have suggested, must still be prescriptively transformative, or it would be of no legal-normative consequence. *Constituent* territories become *constitutional* territories by virtue of the constitution. But in societal

order as do the powers of the states unless altered by the constitution itself. Constitution of the Commonwealth of Australia (1901), ss 106 and 107.

[65] Allowing also for the emergence of new territories through state expansion, the splitting of original territories, and the merging of territories. The British North America Act 1867 was declared in its long title to be 'An Act for the Union of Canada, Nova Scotia, and New Brunswick'. Its preamble also stated however that it was 'expedient that Provision be made for the eventual Admission into the Union of other Parts of British North America . . .'.

[66] The BNA Act is in fact an example of how preambles to federal constitutions often refer to the founding of the constitution by the territories: 'Whereas the Provinces of Canada, Nova Scotia, and New Brunswick have expressed their Desire to be federally united into One Dominion . . .'.

[67] This obfuscation is in part due to the American precedent. Although founded as a federal polity, the demotic narrative at the moment of constitutional creation was largely monist in nature, framed in the language of 'We, the People' and overlain with the language of '*the* republic' and '*the* nation'. This is explored in later chapters.

terms this need not be accompanied by the same transformation that affects 'the people' in a unitary constitution. Furthermore, real world deliberation and direct decision-making is entirely feasible among a small number of territories both at the moment of foundation and in the constitutional life of the polity, whereas it is not in relation to millions of citizens, except through representation.[68]

Another logical outcome of territorial constituent power is that the authority allocation between central and territorial government in any constitution is open to a wide range of normative architectures. For example, these territories may seek to establish authority for the constitution which is explicitly contingent upon their own ongoing constitutional constituent authority, exercisable in particular in relation to constitutional amendment, requiring in certain situations the unanimous approval of all constituent territories for certain decisions.[69]

The implications of this are very challenging for constitutional theory, opening up a debate about whether territorial constituent power has the potential to survive into a federal constitution in a real rather than symbolic sense, as a feature that in effect conditions the idea of constitutional supremacy itself, in the way that constitutional constituent power in a unitary constitution does not. I take this argument forward in Chapter 5 where I explore the nature of constitutional constituent authority in a federal constitution, building upon the account of Chapter 4 of how the concept of constitutional sovereignty has been developed within a default monist mentality.

[68] This opens up space for active constituent politics in an era or representation, yearned for now by commentators on constituent power. See e.g. Roberto Gargarella, 'Constituent Power in a "Community of Equals"'.

[69] The role of constituent territories in constitutional amendment processes is discussed in Chapter 10.

4

Sovereignty and the Monist Constitution

I. Introduction

In Chapter 3 we addressed the legitimacy that underpins constitutional foundations and traced the relationship between this legitimacy and the foundational normative authority of the new polity. We now turn to the next stage in the story of constitutional rule: the enduring legal authority of the living constitution. Our focus in this chapter and the next centres upon sovereignty, the much discussed but often confused theoretical totem that undergirds the efficacy of constitutional government in the modern state.

In addressing the link between the legitimacy of a constitution and its normative authority I have emphasised the significance of constituent power, adapting the classical distinction between *pouvoir constituant* and *pouvoir constitué*, and reconceiving this—in recognition of its social-legal as well as its conceptual-legal salience—as an inter-temporal relationship between a contingent 'foundational constituent power' on the one hand, and reflexive 'constitutional constituent authority' into which it is transformed, on the other; the former providing initial legitimacy to the foundational act, the latter conjoining with the former in continuing to validate the ongoing supremacy of the constitution through enduring demotic consent: its iterative nature making of sovereignty a sociological as much as an ontological concept.

In this chapter and the next I further pursue the key theme of the book: how the specific nature of federal constitutionalism complicates and pluralises what has largely been a generic theoretical debate about the nature of constitutional authority within the modern state. Here I lay the ground for a consideration of federal constitutional constituent authority in Chapter 5 by tracing how the default monist account of constitutional sovereignty developed within modern constitutional theory. I begin by outlining the emergence of the constitutional theory of sovereignty in the early modern period. I then explore the link between sovereignty, state, and nation in which we see how the modern concept of constitutional sovereignty is tied ineluctably to statehood. A key role in the construction of sovereignty as the totemic apex of constitutional rule is played by 'the people'. I discuss the popular underpinnings of sovereignty; how its legitimacy rests upon its foundation in popular consent, which in turn brings us back to the idea explored in Chapter 3, of sovereignty as relational or reflexive. This link between authority and popular legitimacy also remains central to understanding constitutional

The Federal Contract. Stephen Tierney, Oxford University Press. © Stephen Tierney 2022.
DOI: 10.1093/oso/9780198806745.003.0004

constituent authority. Within modern constitutional theory one dominant story of constitutionalism emerged to support the consolidation of the modern state. And a singular conception of statehood found a political mirror in an exclusively monist conception of the constitution: one site of ultimate authority legitimised by a unified sovereign people whose political identity was moulded to the task of state-building through the ideology of nationhood.

Since the key point that emerged from Chapter 3 was the salience of ongoing as well as original popular legitimacy for any constitution, a key argument in this chapter and the next is that sovereignty is best conceived not only in terms of relations of authority *within* the constitution but also in the relations of authority *to* the constitution: the legitimacy of the constitution is not self-contained but derives from the consent of its subjects, and while the constitution might refashion the legal status of its subjects, its own authority is, on the register of representation, always the product of their original and continuing sanction. In this sense sovereignty remains a dynamic political resource for any set of constitutional subjects, and any constitutional form depends for its ongoing legitimacy upon the active sovereign agency of these subjects. In this chapter we see how this conception of sovereignty as a vibrant political emblem, invigorating constitutional life, has largely been lost within the dominant story of modernity that has chained sovereignty and constitutionalism to the service of state-building. This elision of sovereignty and state has come to assume an almost metaphysical expression which has in turn co-opted and reified the constitution as a proxy for the nation-state. The upshot has been the foreclosure of the constitution's active political potential. I seek to explain this story and recover theoretically the political potential immanent within the legitimacy/authority nexus. In doing so I seek to draw out the real and vivid political capacity of constitutional sovereignty which paves the way for a particularly radical re-articulation of the nature of constitutional authority within a federal setting, this last task being the focus of Chapter 5.

II. Constitutional theories of sovereignty

Sovereignty took on particular normative significance with the emergence of the modern state. Beginning in the seventeenth century this concept came to embody the 'autonomy of the political',[1] through the establishment of 'a specialized, institutionalized form of territorial government'.[2] The intimate and crucial link between sovereignty and territory reflected the emergence of the state in modern Europe

[1] M. Loughlin, 'Ten Tenets of Sovereignty', in N. Walker (ed.), *Sovereignty in Transition* (Oxford: Hart, 2003), 55–86, 56; 'Political Jurisprudence', in M.A. Wilkinson and M.W. Dowdle (eds), *Questioning the Foundations of Public Law* (Oxford: Hart Publishing, 2018), 15–31, 21.

[2] G. Nootens, *Popular Sovereignty in the West: Polities, Contention, and Ideas* (London: Routledge, 2013), 44.

as the primary site of political power and legal authority: 'the general assumption that having rights over territory is part of what it means to be "sovereign", and sovereignty, especially state sovereignty, is assumed to range across a geographic domain'.[3] As singular sources of authority consolidated within particular territorial spaces, sovereignty came to encapsulate the autonomous nature of political control in both its external and internal dimensions. In an outward-facing way, a state was sovereign in relation to other states, enjoying both untrammelled autonomy in relation to them and security from interference in its internal affairs. In its other dimension, internal or constitutional sovereignty came to encapsulate the source and nature of ultimate rule within the boundaries of the territory.[4] It is the latter feature with which we are principally concerned in this chapter.

The contemporary idea of sovereignty first stirred in the work of early modern thinkers, principally Jean Bodin (1530–1596) and Thomas Hobbes (1588–1679), before the modern state as we understand it had fully developed. Each had a clear sense of the link between sovereignty, territory, and bounded community. In this respect the new turn in conceptualising sovereignty in the sixteenth and seventeenth centuries took on a number of important differences from medieval understandings of the term, and in doing so paved the way for the normative structure of the nation-state. Sovereignty theory developed in tune with shifting political realities. The Peace of Westphalia (1648) transformed the much looser and wider matrix of constitutional authority of the pre-modern era—the corporatist world described by Althusius (1557–1638), with its diverse and pluralised patterns of authority[5]—into an idea of indivisible sovereignty applicable to a self-enclosed territorial space. Sovereignty in this way came to represent the ultimate attribute of government within fixed boundaries, positivising constitutional authority by tying it concretely to a particular territory through the internal constitutional arrangements of that polity.

In short, even in a period when the state had not yet fully emerged as the standard site of ultimate rule in Europe, the crucial methodological move that characterises modern public law was being conceptualised—linking ultimate authority to the government of a particular community through the register of territory. The vital developmental step therefore was not so much statehood itself, but rather the anterior notion that sovereignty derives from a territorially bounded political community. The next stage, through which the state comes to embody and represent

[3] M. Moore, *A Political Theory of Territory* (Oxford: Oxford University Press, 2015), 3.

[4] Through this dual function the link between sovereignty and territory inevitably leads to boundaries. Sovereignty is in this sense 'the double-claim to ultimate authority over where the boundary between the inside and outside lies and to ultimate authority, to final power of decision which defeats any claim of "external" encroachment, within that self-defined boundary'. N. Walker, 'Late Sovereignty in the European Union', in *Sovereignty in Transition* (Oxford: Hart, 2003), 22.

[5] J. Althusius, *Politica Methodice Digesta, Atque Exemplis Sacris et Profanis Illustrata*, [1603], F.S. Carney (ed. and trans.) (Indianapolis: Liberty Fund, 1995).

this community, was a logical, even an inevitable, consequence of the conceptual nexus of territory, people, and authority.

The longer-term consequence of this interconnection is a reification of the idea of the state itself, and just as significantly, a tendency to merge conceptually the state as a territorial entity and the way in which it is governed. While the state in its outward-facing character does indeed take on a monolithic quality, bolstered by sovereign power vis-à-vis other states, this need not map onto how sovereignty is conceived in its internal dimension—as the way in which the constitution orders power lawfully within the state. Even Bodin, who brought a rigidly monist conception to authority within the polity, embraced a category distinction between internal and external sovereignty, observing that there is a 'great difference between the state and the government of the state',[6] and warning that unless this be maintained we will be thrown 'headlong into an infinite labyrinth of errors'.[7] Bodin conceived of this category difference but, theorising before the age of modern popular government, did not follow through on its implications for how relations of authority between people and government—the internal dimension of sovereignty—might manifest themselves in a range of different ways. It is my ultimate contention that the constitutional dimension of sovereignty, being inherently relational and reflexive, is open to variegated institutional instantiations, including that of federalism, making of it a far more capacious concept than that of external, state sovereignty. I will return to this argument in Chapter 5. In this chapter however I must complete an initial task: to explain how a monistic idea of the state came to impose upon constitutional thought a monistic idea of government and of the relations of sovereignty within the state.

What is clear is that this elision of the two dimensions of sovereignty—that of the government of a territorially bounded community and that of the state which was taken to embody this community in its external capacity—became an established motif of modern sovereignty theory. Indeed, it is in the comprehensiveness of this nexus that we can say not only that there is a modern conception of sovereignty, but that in any meaningful sense there is *only* a modern conception of sovereignty[8] and that this idea is encapsulated in the role sovereignty plays in making meaningful the very idea of the modern state.[9]

[6] J. Bodin, *The Six Bookes of a Commonweale* [1576] R. Knolles (trans.) 1606, K.D. McRae (ed.) (Cambridge MA: Harvard University Press, 1962), 199.

[7] Bodin, The Six Bookes of a Commonweale, 249–250. For discussion see M. Loughlin. 'Why Sovereignty?', in R. Rawlings, P. Leyland, and A. Young (eds), *Sovereignty and Law: Domestic, Regional & Global Perspectives* (Oxford: Oxford University Press, 2013), 34–49.

[8] H.A. Lloyd, 'Sovereignty: Bodin, Hobbes, Rousseau' (1991) 4 *Revue Internationale de Philosophie* 353–379, 354.

[9] M. Loughlin, *The Idea of Public Law* (Oxford: Oxford University Press, 2003), 74–75.

(i) Popular sovereignty

The development of the modern idea of sovereignty was implicitly tied to territory (and in time more specifically to the state), but another central feature of it was the concept of political community within that bounded space. Bodin, in the 'absolute and perpetual power' of the commonwealth or '*majestas*',[10] and later Hobbes, through the absolute power of the sovereign Leviathan,[11] each located internal sovereignty in a form of rule exercised by government. In this way sovereignty was positivised and institutionalised in addition to being territorialised.[12] However, what is clear from the concepts of *majestas* and *Leviathan* is that the political community came to play a central role in the matrix of sovereignty by imbuing power with validity; supplementing the political power of sovereignty and its institutional manifestation through government with its other essential feature, legal authority. In the modern turn, the authority that comes with sovereignty cannot be detached from the legitimate source of that authority. What then ties together territory and ultimate rule in a bond of legitimacy? In Chapter 3 we explored how 'the people' became instrumentally important to constitutional foundations; sovereignty over a territory being legitimised by an authorising people. And the story of modern constitutionalism is one in which the legitimacy dimension of sovereignty has grown in significance as political theory has evolved to reflect the deep interconnection between sovereignty and popular consent, leading to the central relationship between democracy and constitutionalism within the contemporary state.[13]

Although the juxtaposition of sovereignty, territory, and political authority is the essential characteristic of modern sovereignty, and although 'the people' is central in binding these three dimensions of the modern constitutional state together, in fact the idea of the people—the demotic dimension of sovereignty—is of considerably deeper provenance. The relationship between people and sovereignty stretches back to early modern Europe[14] and arguably to republican Rome,[15] well

[10] Bodin, The Six Bookes of a Commonweale, Book 1, ch. VIII, para. 1, 84–86.

[11] T. Hobbes, *Leviathan* [1651] (Cambridge: Cambridge University Press, 1991), XVII, para. 12 and XVIII.

[12] Leviathan is all powerful, but this power is tied in an intrinsic relationship with the subjects of that power. Leviathan is the omnipotent saviour of constitutional subjects from the war of each against another, a 'mortal god' to guarantee 'our peace and defence'. Ibid.

[13] See the discussion in Chapter 3 of J.I. Colón Ríos, *Weak Constitutionalism: Democratic Legitimacy and the Question of Constituent Power* (Oxford: Routledge, 2012), 102. See also N. Walker, 'Constitutionalism and the Incompleteness of Democracy: An Iterative Relationship' (2010) 39 *Netherlands Journal of Legal Philosophy* 206–233; M. Wenman, *Agonistic Democracy: Constituent Power in the Era of Globalisation* (New York: Cambridge University Press, 2013).

[14] D. Lee, *Popular Sovereignty in Early Modern Constitutional Thought* (Oxford: Oxford University Press, 2016).

[15] V. Arena, 'Popular Sovereignty in the Late Roman Republic', in R. Bourke and Q. Skinner (eds), *Popular Sovereignty in Historical Perspective* (Cambridge: Cambridge University Press, 2016), 73–95.

before modern contract theory tied the popular dimension of rule exclusively to statehood.[16]

It follows that the idea of the people is another register through which the external and internal dimensions of sovereignty must be distinguished. While the link between state and sovereignty in its external dimension is one in which sovereignty is conceptually unified, the notion of the people as the source of sovereignty's internal, constitutional legitimacy opens up this dimension of sovereignty through the two facets of constituent power (foundational constituent power and constitutional constituent authority) to different understandings, depending upon how constitutional subjecthood is conceived. In turn it also suggests that internal sovereignty can accommodate a capacious range of different constitutional instantiations.

It is indeed correct that sovereignty as it applies to the state—the ultimate site of authority for a bounded and internationally recognised territory—is an essentially modern concept. However, the notion of 'the people' that underpins its legitimacy is not only older than the idea of the state, it has always carried with it a radical potential; a tendency to act as an irritant against attempts to positivise power institutionally. This was apparent to early-modern theorists, particularly during the Reformation, where theories of resistance to 'illegitimate' monarchs were developed.[17] In this, we see a tapping of the potentially radical, disruptive, and revolutionary nature of 'the people' that would fuel the revolutions of the eighteenth and nineteenth centuries.[18] This popular threat to settled patterns of authority was clear to those attempting to construct modern states and endow them with stable and authoritative institutions of government. What we see therefore in the modern turn to statehood, and the subsequent elision of the idea of the people with that of the subjects of state sovereignty, is an endeavour as much to contain the political potential of the people *internally* as to bolster the authority of the state *externally*.

Bodin and Hobbes were instrumental in this move. In the positivisation of sovereignty which they pioneered, the notion of popular sovereignty found itself confined effectively to the foundational moment of the constitution. The idea of 'the people' acted as an initial source of legitimacy for the nascent polity but was then conceptually subsumed within the constitution through the act of polity creation. In Chapter 3 I discussed one possible paradox of constitutionalism—that between

[16] Skinner, in reviewing the medieval theory of writers such as Marsilius of Padua and Bartolus of Saxoferrato, offers an account of their conceptions of popular sovereignty that seems to anticipate the contract theory of early modernity. They took the view 'that the citizens do not alienate their original sovereign authority ... [which] ... must remain at all times in the hands of the people themselves'. Q. Skinner, *The Foundations of Modern Political Thought, vol. I: The Renaissance* (Cambridge: Cambridge University Press, 1978), 62–63.

[17] Skinner, *The Foundations of Modern Political Thought, vol. I: The Renaissance*, 121–126.

[18] Morgan argues that as early as the sixteenth century 'the people' were emerging as the highest source of political authority. E.S. Morgan, *Inventing the People: The Rise of Popular Sovereignty in England and America* (New York: Norton, 1988), 52.

foundational constituent power and constitutional authority. But another apparent paradox is also present in the connection between the people and the idea of sovereignty. Just as the role of the people, as the legitimising sustenance for the sovereignty of the state's order of rule in an age of gradual democratisation grew in importance, so did sovereignty theory seek to negate one logical consequence of this move: the real power of the people stretching beyond foundational constituent power and taking on meaningful life as constitutional constituent authority.

And it was constitutionalism itself that fulfilled the function of emasculating constitutional constituent authority, subsuming it within a narrow legal positivism. Modern constitutionalism accepted, indeed needed, the role of the people to validate the new order of rule, but at the same time the normative positivisation of that order of rule through constitutionalism served to divest the people of much of its political force. In this way 'the people' became a figurative concept with no real political instantiation. A necessary concomitant to the concept of the people was, therefore, the idea of 'representation', which, as was discussed in the last chapter, led to the active agency of the people being supplanted by the representational role of the constitution as collective embodiment of their foundational political role.[19] This is very much the sense in which Hobbes envisaged Leviathan: displacing, and in so doing taking on the identity of, the constitutional people: 'A multitude of men are made one person, when they are by one man, or one person, represented so that it be done with the consent of every one of that multitude in particular. For it is the unity of the representer, not the unity of the represented, that maketh the person one.'[20] As Grimm puts it, although sovereignty came in effect to mean 'popular sovereignty', the people 'were not capable of acting politically ... Sovereignty therefore found expression only in the act of constitution-making. The powers connected with sovereignty were exercised by delegates or representatives as derived powers. This made it easier to reconcile sovereignty with limitations of power, because the limitation took place only below the level of sovereignty, at the level of its exercise.'[21] In this way the idea of the people is consigned to abstraction, while the notion of its 'sovereignty' becomes merely a symbolic totem whose real force is displaced by an order of legal rule. The people's democratic strength is subordinated to institutional normativity; constitutional sovereignty becomes representative, embodied in the institutions of government rather than in the people who ultimately legitimise this supposedly contingent and dependent institutional authority.[22]

[19] S. Tierney, 'Sovereignty and the Idea of Public Law', in E. Christodoulidis and S. Tierney (eds), *Public Law and Politics: Definitions, Debates and Critiques* (Farnham: Ashgate Law Publishers, 2008), 15–26, 17.

[20] Hobbes, *Leviathan*, 16.13.

[21] D. Grimm, *Sovereignty: The Origin and Future of a Political and Legal Concept* Belinda Cooper (trans.) (New York: Columbia University Press, 2015), 106.

[22] 'The volition of the people exhausts itself in the act whereby it wills itself into being. Its genesis coincides with its eclipse as a political agent which means that the people is never properly present within constitutional order but only intersects with it.' A. Lev, 'Sovereignty and Federalism: Inventing and Reinventing Public Law' (2017) *Jus Politicum* 191–208, 194–195.

When we turn to later contract theorists, the picture becomes more complex but the notion of representation remains the essential prism through which 'the people' and its sovereignty is conceived. In Locke's work for example, constituent power as popular sovereignty retains salience in an extra-constitutional sense through the right of resistance or revolution.[23] But again we are left with a significant gap between the rhetoric of popular sovereignty as a political principle and the hard-headed legal-normative reality of constitutionalism. The relationship between constitution and people eventually reduces for Locke, as it does for Hobbes, to institutionalisation. The representative nature of Hobbes' sovereignty is unequivocal, resting in the institutional bearer of essentially uninhibited central rule. Locke's concept of popular sovereignty is less obviously consigned to the political imaginary but it is also ultimately a confining one. Although *individuals* retain natural rights within the state, the collective political power of 'the people' is inhibited by a constitution that takes on the role of representing this intangible and essentially figurative collective concept, while giving actual legal recognition to the people only once this concept has been subjectively individualised.[24] What remains is an ongoing area of uncertainty in constitutional theory stemming from the narration of the consent-authority chain that flows in an ontologically linear way from Bodin to Hobbes and ultimately to Locke. The constitution rests on popular consent, but it is also an institutional apparatus that not only claims to represent the holders of this consent—the people—but at the same time displaces the people's power of ultimate rule through processes of representation, institutionalisation, and individualisation.[25]

[23] J. Locke, *The Second Treatise of Civil Government and A Letter Concerning Toleration* (Oxford: Blackwell, 1948), Second Treatise on Government, § 208. We see an earlier, similar account in G. Lawson, *Politica sacra et civilis*, C. Condren (ed.) (Cambridge: Cambridge University Press, 2012). In these justifications for the seventeenth- and eighteenth-century revolutions, Lawson and Locke in effect both conceptualise constituent power and point to its survival within constitutional systems. See also M. Canovan, *The People* (Cambridge: Polity Press, 2005), 130–137.

[24] As Falk puts it, the locus of sovereignty for Locke is 'suspended somewhere between the state and society, a constitutionalist nexus that has become associated with the inner nature of legitimate government at the level of the sovereign state'. R. Falk, 'Sovereignty', in J. Krieger (ed.), *The Oxford Companion to Politics of the World* (Oxford: Oxford University Press, 1993), 852. Rousseau's conception of representation is complex and somewhat opaque but does, at least at times, seem to free the people from institutional representation. Despite aligning the very idea of the people closely with the legislative body within a constitutional structure, his theory is largely built upon freeing 'the people' from the confines of political representation. For a discussion of this see J.I. Colón-Ríos, 'Rousseau, Theorist of Constituent Power' (2016) 36 *Oxford Journal of Legal Studies* 885–908.

[25] As Tuck puts it: 'the appearance of a clear conceptual distinction between sovereignty and government was a necessary precondition for the emergence of a distinctively modern idea of democracy'. R. Tuck, *Sleeping Sovereign* (Cambridge: Cambridge University Press, 2016), 249. The process of abstracting the people was also informed by an elitism that was both dismissive of the ability of citizens to govern themselves and wary of the consequences for those with vested property interests. We see each of these tendencies in the origins of the US constitution; e.g. in the work of John Adams and Alexander Hamilton respectively. J. Adams, 'A Defence of the Constitutions of Government (1787)', in *American Political Thought: A Norton Anthology* I. Kramnick and T.J. Lowi (eds), (New York: W. W. Norton, 2009), 181–191; A. Hamilton, Federalist No. 9, C Rossiter (ed.), *The Federalist Papers* (New York: North American Library 1961), 71–76. As Bernal observes, through this process of abstraction, the 'normative' people supplant the 'empirical' people whose real democratic presence would threaten the model of

These various processes of both abstracting and positivising internal sovereignty leave us with different images of the modern 'state people' as sovereign. For Grimm, the people's role can be described by way of 'latent sovereignty': sovereignty is popular but is so transfigured by the constitution as to be effectively withdrawn from the field of political agency; what remains is some vague allusion to a popular longstop.[26] Grimm states that: 'Sovereignty in the fully formed constitutional state is popular sovereignty.'[27] However, the constitutional state creates institutions of government which are not themselves sovereign. 'It follows from this that there is no sovereignty in a constitutional state, but only powers. Sovereignty withdraws into the constituent power and expresses itself only in the act of constitution making. As long as the constitution is in force, it remains latent.'[28]

Tuck meanwhile talks of the people as a 'sleeping sovereign.'[29] Therefore, so institutionalised is the people's status within the constitution, that the only outlet for popular sovereignty (what I have called constitutional constituent authority) is in fact *extra-constitutional*: for example, in Locke's power of revolt—a rebellion *against* the constitution itself rather than a manifestation or real popular will *within* it. Rather than a manifestation of constitutional constituent authority, it is in fact a rebooting of popular sovereignty *ab initio*; the generation of a new, foundational constituent power, an issue I began to consider in Chapter 3. It is consequently more accurate to describe popular sovereignty not as latent within the constitution but as alienated to it; not as the manifestation of real constitutional authority but as a potential irritant against it. It is a device which, as rhetorical or symbolic mythology, serves to sustain the validity of the constitution but which, if emerging as real political force, is considered to endanger it.[30] In this way, for modern contract theory, the legal and the political dimensions of constitutional sovereignty are quarantined, one from the other. The constitution comes to overwhelm internal sovereignty with all-encompassing legal authority; the people, should they seek

representation designed to protect vested interests. A.M. Bernal, *Beyond Origins: Rethinking Founding in a Time of Constitutional Democracy* (Oxford: Oxford University Press, 2017), 84–85. John Adams also explained representation in the constitution as a way of displacing the actual diffuse people with a conceptualised abstraction of 'the people', the latter then able to assume the (fictional) performative roles of a collective, rational body exercising a common will. For discussion see Bernal, *Beyond Origins*, 85; E.S. Morgan, *Inventing the People: The Rise of Popular Sovereignty in England and America* (New York: Norton, 1988). 130–137.

[26] Grimm, *Sovereignty*, 67–75.

[27] Grimm, *Sovereignty*, 69.

[28] Grimm, *Sovereignty*, 71.

[29] Embodied through representation in the sovereign legislator that has an institutional shape 'but is usually dormant'. Tuck, *Sleeping Sovereign*, 252. Tuck argues that once governing powers are allocated through a constitution, the sovereign is generally set aside and forgotten about, effectively supplanted by the political life of the constitution. See also R. Douglass, 'Tuck, Rousseau and the Sovereignty of the People' (2016) 42 *History of European Ideas* 1111–1114.

[30] C. Möllers, '"We Are (Afraid of) the People": Constituent Power in German Constitutionalism', in M. Loughlin and N. Walker (eds), *The Paradox of Constitutionalism: Constituent Power and Constitutional Form* (Oxford: Oxford University Press, 2008), 87–106.

to assert constitutional constituent power, can do so only by resort to unconstitutional political revolt which must find for itself a source of legitimacy apart from, and in opposition to, the constitution itself.

(ii) The nation: abstracting and enfeebling the people

How then was the people's conceptual enfeeblement accomplished in an era where the very idea of the people grew in salience as the validator of constitutional authority? The task for the theorists and practitioners of state-building was clear: the idea of popular sovereignty was crucial to the modern project, but it had to be husbanded in a way that would serve to sustain, rather than menace, the stability of both the state (for Hobbes) and the constitution (for Locke). This required a conceptual or ideological as much as an institutional move because it needed the consent—whether real or contrived—of the very 'people' whose political power was being domesticated. The vital step which completed the sapping of popular agency as political force came with the transformation of 'the people' into 'the nation'.[31] It is in the nation that we see the idea of the people as 'collective political agent'[32] become wedded ineluctably to the state; the source of internal sovereignty becoming also the essential bolster of its external orientation. The nation in this way assumes the demotic representation of state sovereignty as well as that of constitutional sovereignty, turning the people's face outwards, declaring the state to be 'ours', and distinguishing we from they.[33] It is in the nineteenth century that we see the development of the theoretical underpinnings which tie the real sovereign authority of the state to the abstract sovereignty of the nation. As Merriman puts it in the German context, Hegel 'made explicit the close relationship between the development of German nationalism and the reverence for a strong state as the embodiment of national sovereignty, which characterised German liberal thought'.[34]

Hence we arrive at a conception of the people that maps neatly onto the abstraction of the state. This move was able to overcome the troubling paradox faced by the contract theorists, whereby the legitimising agent of state and constitutional unity was also potentially a menace to this solid inter-relationship; the politically active people a brooding irritant, always threatening settled constitutionalism. The

[31] The vital conceptual move made by Sieyes: 'The Nation is prior to everything. It is the source of everything. Its will is always legal; indeed it is the law itself.' E.J. Sieyes, *What Is the Third Estate?* (London: Pall Mall Press, 163). For discussion see D. Miller, *On Nationality* (Oxford: Oxford University Press, 1995), 29–30.

[32] Nootens, *Popular Sovereignty*, 56.

[33] 'What was new was the belief that nations could be regarded as … the bearers of the ultimate powers of sovereignty.' Miller, *On Nationality*, 31. See also B. Anderson, *Imagined Communities* (London: Verso, 1991).

[34] J. Merriman, *A History of Modern Europe: From the Renaissance to the Present*, 3rd edn (London: Norton, 2010), 605.

nation, as unified embodiment of the state's international personality, could however be harnessed internally by the constitution to build a nexus between nation, state, and constitution as an unbreakable bond which together represented, and in so doing enervated, the real political manifestation of the people.[35] In this way the unitary, monolithic nature of external sovereignty is conceptually reproduced in a unitary, monolithic internal characterisation: the external state and internal nation mapping neatly onto one another as demotically monistic synonyms.[36]

This process of elision of nation, state, and constitution[37] which turns both the dynamic, constitution-making process and the potentially politically powerful people into the abstraction of the symbolic nation, serves another instrumental purpose. In addition to legitimising the polity by embedding the people in the very concept of that polity, it also helps overcome the mortality problem we encountered in Chapter 3. Transforming the temporal and corporeal people into the infinite and metaphysical nation sustains a concept of the collective popular self in a viable way over time. In this way the gap can close between foundational constituent power—the real generation of a new constitutional regime by an actual people—and constitutional constituent authority; the latter, now in reality embodied in 'the nation' of the state, becoming a vague, inter-temporal, and politically deracinated notion of 'the national people' represented by the national constitution. The nation as a concept effects this move towards constitutional representation, and in this further process of abstraction from people to constitutional subjects to nation, we see again the stripping of the people's radical political potential. The revolutionary promise that was inherent in foundational constituent power, that legitimised the people's power to give birth to an authoritative constitution, is not empowered by, but shackled to, institutionalisation. Therefore, in this account of modern 'national' constitutionalism, constitutional constituent authority cannot possess independent political salience as a potential irritant against institutional instantiation of the people's sovereignty because it is embodied through a collective sense of constitution, nation, and state in a unity that is itself institutionalised. Just as the nation and the state are, in effect, synonyms, so too the constitutional people and the national people are one and the same. Therefore, the people cannot meaningfully challenge the authority of the constitution *politically* without also undermining the nation and the state as *identity-holders*, for it is in the merging of all of these

[35] In the French revolutionary period the nation took on a secular metaphysical presence. As Arendt explains: 'Like the absolute prince, the nation, in terms of public law, could do no wrong because it was the new vicar of God on earth.' H. Arendt, *On Revolution* (London: Penguin Books 1963), 190. And it was in this way that 'the people' as active agent was no longer needed—see Lev above n. 22.

[36] Thus the community and state come together—the former as source of sovereignty, and the state 'as the sole instrument which exercised it'. F. Hinsley, *Sovereignty*, 2nd edn (Cambridge: Cambridge University Press, 1986), 222.

[37] Signe Larsen describes the authority of the state as embodying 'the triadic unity' of one people, one territory, and one ruling authority: S.R. Larsen, *The Constitutional Theory of the Federation and the European Union* (Oxford: Oxford University Press, 2021), 41.

constructions that 'the people' are represented, and it is through this symbiosis that the modern idea of 'the people' finds not only its enduring meaning but also, ultimately, its political debilitation.[38]

There is in all of this a further, implicit step. The people becomes an instrumental device in supporting nation and state, but in order to serve this purpose it must itself be conceptually unified. The reductive move that transported the idea of popular sovereignty as active foundational constituent power to the realm of metaphysics in the abstract embodiment of nation and state brought with it a further layer of representation: the fostering of popular homogeneity in the service of the state-nation relationship. Societal or ethnic differences among the people could and must be acculturated by a process of integration, subsuming them within the idea of the nation as the ultimate locus of meaningful political identity for all. There are many reasons why such a homogenised notion of a singular people was so conducive to the modern project: the fostering of a strong state with a clear externally facing identity that emphasised the state's unity, a cohesive commitment to the state's security and defence, and the building of a state-wide economy and a community of solidarity through which this economy would operate effectively. In this way the state acquired its incorporeal foundations, controlling, as Cynthia Webber puts it, 'the meanings of its mystical source of authority'.[39] But it also served a more practical function. The supplanting of the idea of the people by the nation was in turn crucial to the legitimacy of the state: 'Only by maintaining control over the depiction of its people can the state authoritatively claim to be the agent of its people.'[40] The overall goal was of course central governmental authority. In controlling the definition of the people, one also circumscribes the locus and meaning of sovereignty as a metaphysical construct. And it was the nation as homogenising agent that denuded the people of real political existence, thereby tying this concept to the unquestionable validity of the state.

But this elaborate process of producing a unified people—transformed into nation—was not achieved without cost to the heterogeneous collective identities that preceded it and from which it was forged.[41] The modern state brought with it of course a monopoly on the use of force;[42] and in this way the elision of state and nation came to play not only an instrumental and a homogenising, but also an inherently hegemonic, role: 'it was designed for the very practical purpose of setting

[38] Grimm, *Sovereignty*, 106.

[39] C. Webber, *Simulating Sovereignty: Intervention, the State, and Symbolic Change* (Cambridge: Cambridge University Press, 1995), 28.

[40] Webber, *Simulating Sovereignty: Intervention, the State and Symbolic Exchange*, 28.

[41] L. Colley, *Britons: Forging the Nation 1707–1837* (New Haven: Yale University Press, 2005); E. Weber, *Peasants Into Frenchmen: The Modernization of Rural France, 1870–1914* (Stanford: Stanford University Press, 1976).

[42] For Weber, the state is 'a compulsory political organization with continuous operations ... [that] successfully upholds the claim to the *monopoly* of the *legitimate* use of physical force in the enforcement of its order'. M. Weber, *Economy and Society* (Berkeley: Berkeley University of California Press, 1978), 54.

up the sovereign as an agent of legitimate coercion in the name of the imagined unitary popular state'.[43]

The upshot of this elaborate process of identity construction and co-option was the further bolstering of the essential monism that characterised the modern state project. The bounded complementarity of state, nation, constitution, and people, the latter taking on a singular personality in service of the monistically conceived territorial polity it was fashioned to legitimise and ultimately to serve. But in the end this move of co-opting the people to this project by bringing to constitutionalism the same homogenising approach it brought to the conception of the nation is unconvincing. The nation and the state may become synonyms, but the nation and the constitution cannot. The role of the people in relation to each of the latter two registers of belonging is categorically different *inter se*. The people as nation may be domesticated as the passive or abstracted embodiment of the state but such a move is not possible in relation to the constitution. The constitution is a self-conscious establishment of legal authority which, in the modern turn, depends for both its foundational and *ongoing* legitimacy upon the people as *active political agent* rather than merely as ethereal symbol.

A sense of the divergent political path taken by constitutionalism is evident in how constitutional theory has had to construct the idea of constituent power to explain and legitimise the significance of active popular agency. Constituent power in both its foundational and constitutional dimensions embodies the idea of people as an independent, active, and potentially unconstrainable constitutional agent: in its foundational position, as creative agent; in its constitutional manifestation, as life-sustaining agent. The very idea of constituent power is one that alights upon the political dynamism of the people as, initially, authors and, subsequently, subjects, of a constitutional order; the constitutional people is not simply a passive collective canvas upon which is painted a pastoral idyll of identity and loyalty to the nation and the state; rather, as an expression of the general will it is in 'perpetual motion'.[44] The political life of the people is dynamic not latent. In this light, the move from 'the people' to 'the nation' as embodiment of popular sovereignty is inadequate because, as Margaret Canovan reminds us, the idea of the nation is primordial and figurative: 'The problem with popular sovereignty is therefore the attribution of ultimate political authority to a "people" that manages somehow to be both a set of concrete individuals, taking action in a particular place at a particular time, *and* an abstract collective entity with a life beyond such limitations.'[45] 'The people' is a

[43] I. Hont, 'The Permanent Crisis of a Divided Mankind: "Contemporary Crisis of the Nation State" in Historical Perspective' (1994) 42 *Political Studies* 166–231, 187, cited by Nootens, *Popular Sovereignty*, 69.

[44] Urbinati claims that, since representative democracy establishes a system of government that must be responsive to popular will, it 'has the power of keeping the sovereign in perpetual motion'. N. Urbinati, *Representative Democracy: Principles and Genealogy* (Chicago: Chicago University Press, 2006), 5.

[45] M. Canovan, *The People* (Cambridge: Polity Press, 2005), 91–92.

coherent account of an active constituent power capable of independent political agency. Any constitutional conception of the people serves to acknowledge it as a normatively empowered political actor, in contrast to the politically intangible idea of nation. The latter instead embodies an incorporeal account of inter-temporal collective belonging rather than substantiated and active political energy. In this way the concept of the nation does not in fact close the gap between contingent constituent power and constitutional constituent authority; instead the concept of the nation can be deployed to negate the very idea that constituent power remains a meaningful concept within constitutionalism at all. Through instrumental reductionism it fillets out the political vitality of the people, leaving a mythical collective shell disembodied from its lived reality and its own collective political self. Having performed the state-driven task of supplanting the people, the nation is then well suited to play the role of demotic sedative, supplementing the institutional anaesthetic of constitutionalism: each in their own way abstracting and suppressing the political potential of the people.

Therefore, when in modern political theory we trace the conceptual move from *pouvoir constituant* to *pouvoir constitué* what we find is a theoretical schizophrenia. The former is envisaged as embodying active and radical political promise; the latter is domesticated and essentially denuded of even potential political animation. Grimm, for example, offers a blunt assessment of the American founding: 'the enactment of the constitution was also the end of the constituent power'.[46] In conceptual—or rather, symbolic terms—the people in the American formulation are still envisaged as the masters of the constitution, but popular sovereignty is now, after the constitutional move, essentially an abstraction, consigned to the relationship between constitution and nation which as we have seen is indivisible; for Malberg, a hard-headed distinction is therefore required between *pouvoir constituant* as a 'realistic' conception of sovereignty, and *pouvoir constitué* as an 'unrealistic' conception.[47]

While this instrumental move is understandable, given the material and other demands of modern state-building, this does not mean that it is theoretically coherent. Foundational constituent power, as legitimiser of the constitution, must remain as an active force in relation to the positive legal supremacy which it underpins; that is the logic of the relational and reflexive theories of sovereignty we addressed in Chapter 3. If the people are not in fact this active political force then, rather than the people supplying legitimacy to the constitution, the constitution supplies legitimacy to the people, denying *ab initio* that the people as a concept

[46] Grimm, *Sovereignty*, 40.

[47] Malberg contrasted popular sovereignty (*souveraineté du people*), the sovereignty of living individuals, with national sovereignty (*la souveraineté nationale*), a more symbolic sovereignty that lasted over time, from generation to generation. R. Carre de Malberg, *Contribution à la théorie générale de l'Etat, 2 vols* (Paris: Librairie de la Société du recueil Sirey, 1920), vol. 1, 69.

even exists without its institutional instantiation.[48] This cannot be true if the idea of the people is to survive as the meaningful source of legitimacy—constitutional constituent authority—for the constitution. The idea of the nation is not of course incompatible with a constitution as site of democratic agency, but to be constitutionally relevant it must embody, rather than traduce, active constitutional constituent authority; it must feed off the legitimacy of consent in the same way as does a modern constitution if it is to be a consequential player within a democratic order of rule rather than an *a priori* constraint upon republicanism's inherent promise. The radical meaning of popular sovereignty means that not only the constitution but also the idea of the nation, including the monism that has so characterised it, must be open to ongoing political interrogation and potential reshaping in the life of the democratic polity.

III. Concluding remarks

The move within modern public law towards a constitutional state depended upon popular legitimacy. And for the state and its instrument of internal authority—the constitution—to acquire legitimacy, a conception of a constitutional people was essential to underpin it. At the same time 'the people' proved itself to be a volatile instrument, as capable of overthrowing as underpinning constituted power. It became necessary in the interests of a viable and stable international system of states to contain the people, and this was done by stripping the idea of constituent power, and hence the people, of meaningful constitutional agency within the state. The people was instead transformed into one unified, homogeneous, and inter-temporal source of legitimacy—the nation—that would reinforce the constituted order of rule for the state. Through this metaphysical turn, one national people became the only conceivable demotic construction within states. In this way state-building, nation-building, and (national) popular sovereignty coalesced in a mutually supportive relationship, creating a default constitutionalist mentality that was and remains normatively monist, governmentally centralist, and demotically uniform.[49]

As a result, internal sovereignty came to take on a similar monolithic appearance to external sovereignty. The externally facing unified sovereignty of the state found a mirror in the unified sovereignty of the nation. Constitutional sovereignty

[48] P. Mair, *Ruling the Void: The Hollowing of Western Democracy* (London: Verso, 2013). Joel Colón Rios makes a similar point in his discussion of how sovereignty has been used to supplant the very idea of constituent power: J.I. Colón Rios, *Constituent Power and the Law* (Oxford: Oxford University Press, 2020), ch. 5.

[49] The homogenising effect of sovereignty theory continues to prove challenging to those who try to conceptualise constituent power in the international context. R. Bellamy, *A Republican Europe of States: Cosmopolitan, Intergovernmentalism and Democracy in the EU* (Cambridge: Cambridge University Press, 2019); M. Patberg, *Constituent Power in the European Union* (Oxford: Oxford University Press, 2020).

depended upon the legitimacy of popular consent but this was to be both unified and abstracted in the idea of the nation. This was a pragmatic and instrumental move but ultimately one that over-reached in attempting to elide the concept of nation and constituent power. The latter, to be meaningful, is active, not passive; real, not symbolic. In a democratic conception of the constitution, the concept of constituent power remains alive in its vital and unbreakable role as legitimiser of any modern order of rule.[50] Constitutional constituent authority, as the inheritor of foundational constituent power, is the motor that operates the engine of modern constitutional government. In this way internal sovereignty as a constitutional concept always asks the question, who is the people to whom the constitution belongs, and what is the character of that constitution to which the people provide legitimacy?[51] In this way, a crucial task for the constitutionalist is to distinguish the idea of the constitutional people (or, more particularly, the constitutional subjects) within any polity from the abstract and non-constitutional concept of the nation; to understand that the foundational people who imbued the constitution with original authority are transformed into the constitution's subjects, who in turn transform the political agency of the founding people (foundational constituent power) into constitutional constituent authority; and that any constitutional order of rule depends upon the legitimacy provided by these subjects, however they manifest themselves demotically, in an ongoing symbiotic relationship between people and authority. The search for sovereignty in any constitution therefore, is ultimately the search for the people who created it, in whose name it finds legitimacy, and by whose act were formed the constitutional subjects who sustain its validity through their ongoing political agency; it is the search for the relationship between foundational constituent power and constitutional constituent authority that was imagined in the creation of the constitution, which may have taken life at that moment in unforeseen ways and which remains the source of legitimacy that gives valid public vitality to the polity.

As we explored in Chapter 3 federalism, as a distinctive form of constitutionalism, complicates the relationship between foundational constituent power and constitutional constituent authority. In particular, it introduces territorially situated demotic pluralism to a narrative that links territory, authority, and subjecthood in a nexus of monism founded epistemologically upon assumptions of

[50] Notably a recent strand of radical democratic theory focuses not upon any dangers associated with constituent power but with its 'emancipatory telos'—M. Wilkinson and A. Somek, 'Unpopular Sovereignty?' (2020) 83 *Modern Law Review* 955–978. See also J. Tully, 'The Imperialism of Modern Constitutional Democracy', in M. Loughlin and N. Walker (eds), *The Paradox of Constitutionalism: Constituent Power and Constitutional Form* (Oxford: Oxford University Press, 2007), 315–338.

[51] H. Lindahl, *Fault Lines of Globalization: Legal Order and the Politics of A-Legality* (Oxford: Oxford University Press, 2013), 141–159, 141–142. See also H. Lindahl, 'Constituent Power and Reflexive Identity: Towards an Ontology of Collective Selfhood'; and 'Constituent Power and the Constitution', in D. Dyzenhaus and M. Thorburn (eds), *The Philosophical Foundations of Constitutional Law* (Oxford: Oxford University Press, 2016);.

individualised citizenship. But it also calls into question even more starkly the notion that constituent power falls into desuetude with the advent of a constitution. The constitutional innovation of federalism lies not so much in the social reality of territorial pluralism as in how it exposes the normative impossibility of stilling the political dynamism of the pluralised constituent power which it embodies. In Chapter 5 we will explore further the extent to which this federal reality poses a challenge to the orthodox construction of constitutional constituent authority.

5

Authority and the Federal Constitution

I. Introduction

In Chapter 3 I argued that federalism, through foundational constituent power at the germinating moment of the constitution, takes a divergent path from monist constitutionalism in terms of agency, foundational act and validation, and that the particularities of normative authority within the federal polity, continually rooted in constitutional constituent authority, derive from the territorial essence of the constitutional contract. The central point of contrast which I drew out in addressing constitutional foundations is that the nature of constituent power in monist constitutionalism is conceived in demotically singular terms. I therefore counterpoised the idea of federal constituent power, characterised by territorial pluralism, as a radically alternative account of the concept of agency underpinning the legitimacy-normative link. Several arguments flowed from this: that the federal contract as foundational act is more real in federal constitutionalism than the fictional constitutional contract imagined within monist political theory, where 'the people' has to be conceptually collectivised; that federalism does not suffer from the mortality problem: the territories which possess foundational constituent power remain alive in the constitution as the active agents of constitutional constituent authority even after its constitutional transformation (the radical conceptual alienation that occurs in unitary constitutionalism from pre-constitutional subject into constitutional citizen does not find an easy analogy in federal constitutionalism); that, flowing from this, the paradox of constitutionalism (that those who generate its authority are thereupon disempowered by it) does not translate so obviously, if at all, to a federal polity: in terms of agency, the constituent territories are actually instantiated constitutional actors at the foundational moment in contrast with the more ephemeral pre-constitutional 'people' within monist constitutionalism; and therefore that federal constitutionalism complicates the conceptual and actual supplanting of foundational constituent power by constitutional authority. As a consequence, the distinction between 'foundational constituent power' and 'constitutional constituent authority' takes on a highly particular form within federal constitutional theory, given that the subjects of each overlap far more substantially than they do within monist constitutional theory.

In Chapter 4 I turned to the idea of constitutional authority itself and discussed how the notion of constituent power has been so stripped of political life within monist constitutionalism as to be left with little real meaning. The idea of 'the

The Federal Contract. Stephen Tierney, Oxford University Press. © Stephen Tierney 2022.
DOI: 10.1093/oso/9780198806745.003.0005

people' has, in effect, been consigned to normative abstraction by way of the representation and institutionalisation that links the nation to the constitution. Insofar as the abstraction of 'the people' survives as a potential source of legitimate political power, its manifestation can only be extra-constitutional; an act of revolution. Popular sovereignty, as a constitutional rather than political concept, is thereby effectively supplanted by constitutionalism conceived of as inhibitor rather than facilitator of political action; it concerns relationships of authority *within* the constitution, not *to* the constitution; the people do not in any way retain authority over the constitution itself; only the raw power of rebellion remains—an act that is by definition outside, and hence not consistent with, the idea of constitutional rule.

It is in this context that we now turn to the federal constitution as a fundamentally distinctive form of polity. The federal constitution, through its recognition *a priori* of territorial pluralism as so essentially salient to the polity, fundamentally challenges both the homogenising and enervating approach of default constitutionalism towards the people and the instinctive elision of the people with 'the nation'. The constitution is not, on its face, co-opted automatically to the service of an exclusive and singular national uniformity; its foundation on the basis of discrete, constitutionally salient territories and their governments challenges this very characterisation of the state. In short, federalism does not allow for the easy elision of the concepts of nation and people; it is founded in recognition of a plurality of territorial publics. As Hueglin and Fenna put it, federalism emerges to meet 'the mismatch between the complexities and threats of real social life and the simplicity of the modern state construction imposed upon it'.[1] Any 'federal nation' that emerges is one that must take account of, and be both demotically and normatively conditioned by, a very specific conception of constitutional constituent authority.

In this chapter I return therefore to the issue of constitutional sovereignty. I explore in the next section of the chapter how this has been a confusing and frustrating concept for federalist scholars, and how they have sought to interpret sovereignty in different ways, or indeed bypass sovereignty altogether, in constructing federal theory. I argue however that constitutional sovereignty as constitutional constituent authority is in fact an essential register through which to understand federal legality: as pertinent to federalism as it is to any form of government for the modern state; and that by addressing sovereignty through the prisms of relationality and reflexivity introduced in Chapter 3, we can arrive at a nuanced approach that takes account of how federalism's particularity centres around its inherent territorial pluralism. The task in the latter sections of the chapter is therefore to unpack constitutional sovereignty in federal context, exploring the highly specific iterative relationship between constitutional constituent authority and foundational constituent power in the lived federal constitution. In this way we can

[1] T.O. Hueglin and A. Fenna, *Comparative Federalism: A Systematic Inquiry*, 2nd edn (Toronto: University of Toronto Press, 2015), 98.

better appreciate how a federal conception of sovereignty posits a radical challenge to the narrow normative confines within which default modern constitutionalism has been conceptually constrained.

II. Federalism and sovereignty: an uneasy relationship

There are two common approaches within federal theory to the relationship between federalism and sovereignty. One, familiar within political studies, is to argue that the concept of sovereignty can and must be accommodated within the idea of federalism, but that it needs to be understood as conceptually divisible. An alternative approach insists that conceptual indivisibility underpins the very idea of sovereignty but that this essential characteristic is so ill-fitting with the inherent governmental pluralism of federalism that either the 'federal state' must be categorised as a particular type of state different from 'unitary states', or that the idea of sovereignty must be jettisoned altogether from any meaningful account of federal constitutionalism. I address these different approaches in turn. In doing so I contest the plausibility of each, arguing that the divisibility thesis is conceptually misconceived and that the move to side-step sovereignty altogether stems either from a mistaken elision of state and constitution (the external and internal dimensions of sovereignty), or from an unduly narrow, positivist understanding of constitutional sovereignty itself. In fact, sovereignty remains a vital register through which to understand the nature of federal constitutional authority.

(i) Political studies and the divisibility thesis

It is a trope of the political studies literature on federalism that sovereignty is 'divided'. Scholars who advance the divisibility thesis make one of two moves: the first is a conceptual claim that sovereignty need not be conceived in unitary terms; the second parks the conceptual argument and simply rejects the real world salience of sovereignty as a meaningful account of how political power works in a federal system. I will discuss each in turn.

A number of federal theorists confront the relevance to federalism of a unitary conception of sovereignty in the tradition of Bodin and Hobbes. Elazar, for example, expressly rejects the notion of a unified 'last word' within the very idea of federalism: 'Federal polities are characteristically non-centralized; that is, the powers of government within them are diffused among many centers, whose existence of authority are guaranteed by the general constitution, rather than being concentrated in a single center.'[2] Despite its initial appearance as a theoretical

[2] D. Elazar, *Exploring Federalism* (Tuscaloosa: The University of Alabama Press, 1987), 34. From here he attempts to extricate federalism from the modernist project of sovereignty altogether, arguing that 'the

challenge, in fact this argument barely engages with the concept of sovereignty as the register of ultimate constitutional authority. In work I have done with Martin Loughlin I contend that sovereignty should be categorised in relational terms across two dimensions: 'authority generation', through which we understand how a constitution's claim to authority is validated by the legitimacy given to it by its subjects, and 'authority distribution', whereby the authority of any constitutional order, once created and legitimised, authorises the creation of constitutional institutions and their operation by public actors. Constitutional sovereignty is, in essence, the interplay of these two dimensions.[3] When we turn to the divisibility thesis within federal theory we find however that the 'authority distributive' dimension of sovereignty is taken to encapsulate the idea of sovereignty in its entirety. The distribution of authority between central and territorial governments within a federal constitution is considered to be a division *of sovereignty* rather than merely an internal constitutional allocation of institutional authority generated *by sovereignty*. Elazar focuses explicitly upon the powers of government within federal polities rather than the authority of the federal constitution, and in doing so confuses these with the broader concept of sovereignty. Palermo and Kössler offer a similar account: 'it is theoretically conceivable ... that each level of government has ultimate authority within distinct areas and is thus sovereign, in a more limited and relative sense, regarding these jurisdictions'.[4] Authority generated by a constitution is certainly distributed, but the constitution itself is a manifestation of the sovereignty of those who created it and from whom it continues to derive its authority; sovereignty is therefore a holistic account of ultimate authority and cannot be conceived merely in institutional terms.

An additional, or alternative, step taken by the divisibility thesis within political studies does not engage with constitutional theory at all but instead focuses upon what are taken to be salient political realities which supervene over constitutionalism. In a federal system the division of 'power' among different governments is a political fact. Since power is treated as a proxy for sovereignty, sovereignty is itself therefore divided.[5] From a constitutionalist perspective this move is, by definition, misconceived. Political power is certainly dispersed within a federal constitution, as it is within any constitutional system, but this does not mean that 'sovereignty' is divided. Sovereignty as a relationship between the legal and political bases of

federal principle represents an alternative to (and a radical attack upon) the modern idea of sovereignty'. Elazar, *Exploring Federalism*, 109. See also D.J. Elazar, 'The United States and Europe: Models for Their Epochs', in K. Nicolaidis and R. Howse (eds), *The Federal Vision: Legitimacy and Levels of Governance in the United States and the European Union* (Oxford: Oxford University Press, 2001), 31–53, 34.

[3] M. Loughlin and S. Tierney, 'The Shibboleth of Sovereignty' (2018) 81 *Modern Law Review* 989–1016, 999.

[4] F. Palermo and K. Kössler, *Comparative Federalism: Constitutional Arrangements and Case Law* (Oxford: Hart Publishing, 2017), 88.

[5] R.H. Leach, *American Federalism* (New York: WW Norton, 1970), 1.

authority does not lead to the subsumption of the former by the latter. As Walker puts it, 'the legal and the political are mutually constitutive or symbiotic. The political requires a legal frame, most evidently in the case of the basic underlying legal order itself but also in the normative articulation of the specialized system of political rule and in the recognition and channelling of constituent power. But the legal also requires political imagination—the very idea of reflexivity of political community, as well as political will—punctual or retrospective popular support or initiative.'[6] It is important to observe that the application of constitutional theory as I have presented it in this book does not tie constitutionalists didactically to legal positivism; fundamental law exists within, and draws its sustenance from, a political context, occupying 'the space where the relationship between the deep culture of political power and authority which is a necessary support of any effective legal system and the normative structure of that legal system is worked out'.[7] But a constitution is not reducible to a mere instrument of political power. It serves to institutionalise political power, turning it into legitimate authority and thereby both, and at once, validating and constraining its exercise. This exposes the fatal flaw within the divisibility thesis. If the *realpolitik* conception of divided sovereignty is simply concerned with political power then it says nothing about the role or significance of constitutionalism as legitimiser; if it serves in fact to roll together political power and constitutional *powers* (i.e. authority) within a constitutional system, then, in arguing that these are together divided, the argument suffers from the same problem as the first 'conceptual' strand of the divisibility thesis; it focuses only upon the authority distributive dimension of sovereignty and not also upon the authority generational aspect which gives sovereign authority its political legitimacy.

(ii) Federal constitutionalism: side-stepping the sovereignty dilemma

The missteps taken within the divisibility thesis are problematic but they are certainly understandable. Constitutional theorists in addressing the normativity of federal constitutionalism are also confronted by an apparent paradox. We address sovereignty through a legal-normative register that insists upon its indivisibility, but how can we square a constitutional concept that is presented as ineluctably unified on the one hand with its constitutional manifestation in the form of multiple and divided *loci* of territorial government on the other? Hobbes' conception

[6] N. Walker, 'European Constitutionalism in the State Constitutional Tradition' (2006) 59 *Current Legal Problems* 51–89, 67.

[7] N. Walker, 'Fundamental Law', in *The Laws of Scotland: Stair Memorial Encyclopaedia* (Edinburgh: Butterworths, 2002), 29–82, para. 50.

of territorially unified sovereignty had no room for what has been called, in reference to the fluid and pluralised patterns of authority that characterised the late Middle Ages, *imperium in imperio*.[8] The threat that federalism seemingly posed to coherent constitutional rule cast a shadow over the emergence of modern constitutionalism. Alexander Hamilton in fact described the idea of *imperium in imperio* as a 'political monster' in his account of the Articles of Confederation.[9] And more than two centuries later, the doctrine of sovereignty is still described as 'the main obstacle to federalism's development'.[10]

Although accepting Hobbes' premise that the concept of sovereignty encapsulates an inherently unified order of rule, constitutional theory has tended to take two wrong turns in explaining its function in relation to a federal constitution: the elision of the external and internal dimensions of sovereignty and/or a narrow positivist approach to the latter. The consequent conclusion for many is that sovereignty should simply be dispensed with as a register through which to explain federal authority.[11]

Constitutional theory has often tended to elide sovereignty in its external context, 'state sovereignty', with internal 'constitutional sovereignty'. Consequently, one problematic concept that has emerged is that of the 'federation' as a distinct category of 'federal statehood', distinguishable from a unitary state.[12] The distinction in fact tends to treat 'federations' as incomplete or 'hybrid' states; a poor cousin lying in some grey zone between a league of independent states and a fully

[8] P. Downes, *Hobbes, Sovereignty, and Early American Literature* (Cambridge: Cambridge University Press, 2015), ch. 6. Hobbes considered the very idea of dividing sovereignty to be a political threat to a successful polity as well as a conceptual absurdity. He derided the idea of 'the immoderate greatnesse of a Town' or a 'great number of Corporations'. These would be 'as it were many lesser Commonwealths in the bowels of a greater, like wormes in the entrayles of a naturall man'. T. Hobbes, *Leviathan* (New York: J.M. Dent & Sons, Ltd Publishing, 1914), 177. See also J.A.W. Gunn, *Beyond Liberty and Property* (Montreal and Kingston: McGill-Queen's University Press, 1983), Chapter 2.

[9] A. Hamilton, Federalist No. 15, C. Rossiter (ed.), *The Federalist Papers* (New York: North American Library 1961), 105–113, 108. For a similarly dystopian assessment of the pre-Philadelphia union see J. Madison, Federalist No. 44, Rossiter (ed.), *The Federalist Papers*, 280–288; and further discussion: G. Wood, *The Creation of the American Republic, 1776–1787* (Chapel Hill: The University of North Carolina Press, 1969), 344–354; Alison LaCroix, 'Drawing and Redrawing the Line: The Pre-Revolutionary Origins of Federal Ideas of Sovereignty', University of Chicago Law Occasional Paper, No. 47 (2008); P. Downes, *Hobbes, Sovereignty, and Early American Literature* (New York: Cambridge University Press, 2015).

[10] A. Lev, 'Introduction: Federalism and Public Law Theory', in A. Lev (ed.), *The Federal Idea: Public Law between Governance and Political Life* (Oxford: Hart Publishing, 2019), 1–26, 1. Neil MacCormick was also famously sceptical of the continued utility of the very concept of sovereignty in the context of the territorial layering of government. N. MacCormick, *Questioning Sovereignty: Law, State, and Nation in the European Commonwealth* (Oxford: Oxford University Press, 2002), esp. 122–136.

[11] There is also within the contemporary literature a wider, and often ideologically infused, disaffection with sovereignty altogether as an explanation of modern government, e.g. D. Herzog, *Sovereignty RIP* (New Haven: Yale University Press, 2020), and a sense that it is out-moded within a purportedly more cosmopolitan climate: C. Barbour and G. Pavlich (eds), *After Sovereignty: On the Question of Political Beginnings* (London: Routledge, 2010); M. Avbel and J. Komárek, *Constitutional Pluralism in the European Union and Beyond* (Oxford: Hart, 2012).

[12] O. Beaud, *Théorie de la Fédération* (Paris: Presses Universitaires de France, 2009), 434.

modern state, the latter characterised axiomatically as the home for unitary constitutions or for 'federal constitutions' that, although institutionally distinctive, are in legal-normative terms conceptually indistinguishable from unitary constitutions. In this way, 'federations' are not quite states at all, and in order to become 'states' proper, conforming to a monist conception of constitutional sovereignty, federal constitutions must be denuded of any deep normative particularity. Olivier Beaud has done much to advance the argument that a 'federation' represents a different category of state. He does so by situating it between a 'federative constitution' (that is indistinguishable in any meaningful legal way from a unitary constitution) on the one hand, and a confederacy of independent territories on the other: 'in the context of the federal State, the federative constitution is most often assimilated to the unitary constitution, and therefore has no specific nature in jurists' eyes, while the act founding a confederacy is considered to be a treaty and therefore falls outside the ambit of the constitution'.[13]

The elision of state sovereignty and constitutional sovereignty within federal theory flows from the purported distinction within constitutional theory between a confederation and a federation. This was a core differentiation (although not articulated in these terms) that did so much to shape the debate leading to the promulgation of the United States constitution. Under the Articles of Confederation, the union of the American states had an unclear international status; a union for certain purposes, but one in which each of the states still enjoyed a distinctive international personality.[14] A confederation (for which, confusingly, the term 'federation' tended to be used in the Federalist debates[15]), has therefore come to be characterised by Beaud and other theorists[16] not simply as a different type of constitutional arrangement, but as a specific form of international actor; as a third category of polity between a loose union of independent states on the one hand

[13] O. Beaud, 'The Founding Constitution: Reflections on the Constitution of a Federation and its Peculiarity' (2017) *Jus Politicum; Revue de Droit Politique* 33–63, 39. We find an earlier instance of this 'spectrum' approach, which elides state and constitution, in the work of Edward Freeman, *History of Federal Government in Greece and Italy*—the first grand historical review of federal thinking. For Freeman, 'A federal government . . . is a mean between the system of large states and the system of small states.' E.A. Freeman, *History of Federal Government in Greece and Italy* J.E. Bury (ed.) (Freeport: Books For Libraries Press, 1972), 13.

[14] Madison was concerned by the uncertain international status of the United States under the Articles: 'A compact between independent sovereigns, founded on ordinary acts of legislative authority, can pretend to no higher validity than a league or treaty between the parties.' Federalist, No. 43, Rossiter (ed.), *The Federalist Papers*, 271–280, 280. See also F.W. Marks III, *Independence on Trial: Foreign Affairs and the Making of the Constitution*, 2nd edn (Baton Rouge: Rowman and Littlefield, 1993).

[15] M. Diamond, 'The Federalist's View of Federalism', in G.C.S. Benson (ed.), *Essays in Federalism* (Claremont: Claremont Men's College, 1961); J. Yarbrough, 'Rethinking "The Federalist's View of Federalism"' (1985) 45 *Publius* 31–53. LaCroix notes how the attempt to conceptualise plural sources of authority posed problems for the American founders with the 'Continental notion of divisible sovereignty' jostling 'against the common-law version of unitary sovereignty in the middle decades of the eighteenth century'. A.L. LaCroix, *The Ideological Origins of American Federalism* (Cambridge MA: Harvard University Press, 2011), 18.

[16] M. Forsyth, *Unions of States: The Theory and Practice of Confederations* (New York: Leicester University Press, 1981), 15.

and a fully formed modern state on the other.[17] However, given that sovereignty has two dimensions—external and internal—it is an error to elide state and constitution. The external or outward-facing perspective of sovereignty *vis-à-vis* other states and the international community is a singular concept that imbues the sovereign 'federal state' with a singular international personality of the same nature as that of the 'unitary state'. The state is the universal political construction of modernity. Its singularity is the key dimension that grants it equal subjecthood upon the international plane with other states, and it is exemplified by international law's refusal to accept a state's internal constitutional arrangements, including federalism, as in any way qualifying a sovereign state's duty to perform its international obligations.[18] It therefore makes no sense from the perspective of constitutional theory to attempt to draw any meaningful distinction between federal 'states' and unitary 'states'. It follows that the federal or unitary nature of a polity are features of *constitutional law*, not of *statehood*. That is not to say that the birth of both state and constitution cannot occur at similar points in time, nor that issues of consent and legitimacy in relation to the nature of the state itself cannot arise; it is simply to observe that legitimacy questions concerning the state operate upon a different register, which involve the state's external as well as its internal manifestation, than do those concerning the constitution, which is solely an internal issue.

Federal constitutionalism is a distinct form of government but this does not imply that it maps onto a distinct form of statehood. In order to understand the federal idea as a coherent concept of constitutional rule since 1787 we must view it squarely within the context of the modern state.[19]

[17] In this way, Beaud's category of 'federation' is presented as a *sui generis*, non-state form of rule, while for him, a federal state fits neatly into the modern paradigm of monist constitutional sovereignty. Although Beaud attempts to differentiate 'federation' from the older term 'confederation', in fact the two bear strong similarities: 'A Federation arises from the agreement between States that confederate to create a new political entity.' Beaud, 'The Founding Constitution Reflections on the Constitution of a Federation and its Peculiarity', 35. His categorisation echoes that of the *fin de siècle* scholar Henry Sidgwick, who discussed the 'confederation of states' and the 'federal state' as representing two stages in the development of a constitutional mentality he termed 'federality'. H. Sidgwick, *The Development of the European Polity* (London: MacMillan, 1903), 433. See also Hugues Dumont who argues that the idea of confederation has been 'revised and corrected by Olivier Beaud under the name "federation"'. H. Dumont, 'The European Union, a Plurinational Federation in Sensu Cosmopolitico', in A.-G. Gagnon and M. Seymour (eds), *Multinational Federalism: Problems and Prospects* (UK: Palgrave MacMillan, 2012), 83–106, 103. The federal/confederal distinction is also core to Forsyth's analysis: Forsyth, *Unions of States: The Theory and Practice of Confederations*, 15.

[18] Vienna Convention on the Law of Treaties (opened for signature 23 May 1969, entered into force 27 January 1980) 1155 UNTS 331, art. 27.

[19] This was recognised by Woodrow Wilson, who saw federal systems of government as entirely the 'creation of modern politics' [W. Wilson, *The State* (Boston: DC Heath &Co, 1918), 544], by which, according to Duncan Kelly, he 'really meant the modern state'. D. Kelly, 'Woodrow Wilson and the Challenge of Federalism in World War One', in A. Lev, *The Federal Idea: Public Law Between Governance and Political Life* (Oxford: Hart, 2017), 167–188, 174–175. It is worth noting that my concern in this book is with the constitutional arrangements *within* states. I leave to one side efforts to conceptualise sovereignty within the multi-state European Union. See R. Bellamy, *A Republican Europe of States: Cosmopolitan, Intergovernmentalism and Democracy in the EU* (Cambridge: Cambridge University Press, 2019). Whatever legal form this body is deemed to have

Another reason why the notions of state and constitution have come to be elided in constitutional theory is that, as the prototype for modern federalism, the inauguration of the United States constitution also served to position the United States internationally as a unified international state, overcoming any debate concerning the more inchoate international status of the preceding territorial arrangement.[20] But the two acts—state-making and constitution-making—are conceptually and materially distinct. For example, a new constitution may not be promulgated for a new state until some time after the state is established and recognised by other states. Furthermore, this constitution can be entirely replaced at a later point in time and such an act of new constitution-making, even if it introduces a federal constitution in place of a unitary constitution or *vice versa*, does not detract from the territory's status as a state. The state/constitution distinction is also clear when we consider how international law disaggregates the issue of international recognition of states from international recognition of governments.[21] The conceptual distinction between a state and any order of rule within it also points us to the fact that state-making and constitution-making each has its own distinct source of legitimacy, evident from the different ways in which the validity of each is recognised. A state's legitimacy and hence authority comes from the international order of rule and from recognition by other states; a constitution's legitimacy and hence authority stems from the recognition of this authority by those subject to it.

From all of this it follows that the creation of a federal system is a constitutional act, not a state-making act. Constitutionalists therefore should not conceive of federalism as some form of 'hybrid state' and should not attempt to remove federalism from the framework of constitutional sovereignty that has come to define the modern state, and which remains the essential source of validity for the rule of modern public law. The challenge facing federal constitutional theory is to move on from the distraction of statehood to explain how the internal, constitutional scale of sovereignty resonates in a unique way when played in a federal key.

III. Constitutional positivism in federal theory

The elision of state and constitution leads to a second error within federal constitutional theory. This is a tendency to define internal or constitutional sovereignty within 'federal states' by way of a narrow positivism, focusing only upon its

acquired over time it is founded upon international treaties that should not be conflated with a state federal constitution.

[20] In Madison's view the transition at Philadelphia moved the United States from 'a league of sovereign powers' to a 'political constitution by virtue of which they are become one sovereign power'. J. Madison, 'Vices of the Political System', in G. Hunt (ed.), *The Writings of James Madison* (New York: The Knickerbocker Press, 1901), 361–369, 365.

[21] M. Shaw, *International Law*, 8th edn (Cambridge: Cambridge University Press, 2017), 329–360.

institutional manifestation; what is often termed 'legal sovereignty'.[22] In this way, the register of analysis within constitutionalism tends to mirror that predominating within political studies in concentrating squarely upon the authority-distributive dimension of constitutional sovereignty—albeit that the constitutionalist's focus is more clearly upon constitutional authority than the vague notion of 'power' or 'powers'.

We see how the insistence that the federal polity is a discrete category of state informs a positivist approach to the internal dimension of sovereignty in Hans Kelsen's work. By the time Kelsen was writing it was clear that the USA was a state for international purposes, as were other polities with federal constitutions. Kelsen was a key player in categorising the United States, and in due course other federal polities, as 'hybrid states'. The broader drive of his work was of course an attempt to explain the external and internal dimensions of sovereignty through one, holistic account of normative hierarchy.[23] In this endeavour, federalism posed a problem. For Kelsen, so great was federalism's disjuncture with the default monism of the modern constitutionalism-statehood nexus, that it required its own account not only within the theory of constitutionalism but also of the state. The category of hybrid state was therefore necessary to capture the extent to which territorial pluralism was institutionalised within, and served to decentralise, the federal polity; distinguishing it from those systems where a unified conception of sovereignty's external dimension mapped neatly onto a monist account of its internal manifestation.

Kelsen encapsulated this bespoke approach to the external/internal sovereignty fusion in the idea of the 'three-branch federal state'. He took the view that within a federal polity there are three levels of rule: sub-state territorial governments and the central government, and beyond these 'the federal state' itself, which ought not to be confused with the central institutions of the state. As Grimm puts it: 'above them [the sub state territorial governments and the central government] existed the common state, which was the actual federal state and an expression of the unity of the whole'.[24] For Kelsen, *kompetenz-kompetenz* rested in this third level: the federal state itself.

Kelsen's articulation of a third order of authority within a federal system is a powerful one which, as we will discuss later in this chapter and in later chapters, helps us to conceptualise the specific nature of authority distribution within a federal constitution. However, ultimately, in fusing the third level of rule with that of the state, he merges, and in so doing confuses, constitution with state. In fact, all three branches of rule within Kelsen's schema are manifestations of internal,

[22] Palermo and Kössler, *Comparative Federalism*, 84.

[23] H. Kelsen, *Allgemeine Staatslehre* (Berlin: Springer, 1925).

[24] Cited by D. Grimm, *Sovereignty: The Origin and Future of a Political and Legal Concept* B. Cooper (trans.) (New York: Columbia University Press, 2015), 66. And see Kelsen, *Allgemeine Staatslehre*, 198.

constitutional authority, rather than of statehood, which operates on the international plane of authority-recognition. The nature of a state's external sovereignty is no different whether internally it is characterised by these three dimensions of rule or not; Kelsen's three orders of authority are squarely jurisdictional issues arising from the internal constitutional order of rule.

The problem with a positivistic attempt to overcome the distinction between the external and internal dimensions of sovereignty is that it underplays the significance of the constitution itself, conceiving it only as a vehicle for the distribution of authority and hence as the last word on the validity of that distribution; the bearer of *kompetenz-kompetenz*. But, as I have argued in Chapters 3 and 4, a constitution must also explain and justify the legitimacy of these allocation and arbitration functions. Kelsen's third level of rule within a federal system is illuminating, but ultimately it does not take us from the distributional to the generational dimension of normative authority. As such, it offers only a partial account of the function of constitutional authority.

The conceptual problem that arises when the authority distributive dimension of sovereignty comes to be equated with sovereignty itself is evident in the work of Dieter Grimm. Grimm co-opts Kelsen's approach to explain the specific nature of the federal constitution, focusing upon sovereignty within the federal polity, in positivist terms, as the last word: 'What is crucial for sovereignty in a federal state is not the extent of state power, but only who determines its distribution. One who establishes one's own powers oneself, and therefore determines the powers of the other side, is sovereign. In other words, what is crucial for sovereignty in a federal state is *kompetenz-kompetenz* (the power to distribute powers).'[25] Grimm takes an important step in recognising that the federal polity's distinctiveness must be conceived in terms of constitutional rather than state theory. However, while distancing himself from the aspect of Kelsen's *grundnorm* which elides state and constitution, he himself fails to distinguish the authority distributive from the authority generational dimension of sovereignty, focusing exclusively upon the former within the federal constitution.

It is indeed important to differentiate the federal constitution from the two levels of government that operate within it and by which they are given lawful authority: this is the particular institutional framework within which we must understand the distribution of authority in a federal system as I discuss in Chapters 8 and 9. However, this approach does not take us to how sovereignty within a federal constitution is generated. Within the positivist account offered by Kelsen and his followers, this ultimately is not a question that matters to legal analysis. For Kelsen, the legitimacy of the federal hybrid state is tied up in the third branch of

[25] Grimm, *Sovereignty*, 65.

rule; for Grimm, it similarly stems from the *kompetenz-kompetenz* of the federal constitution.

To conclude, attempts within constitutional theory to articulate the nature of ultimate authority within a federal system through the classical lens of modernist sovereignty theory are, in effect, attempts to square a circle. By one approach, the sovereign state is a unified entity that is characterised by the close fusion of the internal and external dimensions of its own sovereignty, each taking on a monist personality. It follows that constitutional sovereignty as the internal mirror of external sovereign statehood must be located in a single and unified source, be that the people or the nation. Federalism complicates this picture, founded as federal constitutions are upon the *a priori* salience of plural territories within one polity and operating through a plurality of governments. This is so unsettling to the simple and holistic vision of modern sovereignty that federalism must be cast out from the very galaxy of statehood as a hybrid category.

An alternative approach is to recognise that federal arrangements do operate within modern states, but that they are not in fact a particularly distinctive form of constitutional arrangement. Federalism is thus packaged by way of legal positivism to fit within one default account of constitutional sovereignty; the internal dimension of constitutional sovereignty being articulated through an authority distributive register that views federalism as just another way of dividing unified, internal authority under a constitutional umbrella. In this way, the state and constitution are still united within a monist frame, the function of the latter is simply to distribute internal legal authority among different governments; constitutional sovereignty, regardless of the territorial pluralism that brought the federal constitution into being, is explained by way of the same positivist state-constitution nexus that explains the unitary constitution.

These two attempts to fit federalism within modern sovereignty theory are ultimately unconvincing. It is therefore no surprise that these moves have led constitutional scholars to conclude that sovereignty is such a deeply problematic register through which to explain authority in federal context that it serves no utility.[26] As Leach put it half a century ago in his assessment of federal authority: 'Sovereignty, in the classic sense, has no meaning: divided as power is, the element of absoluteness which is essential to the concept of sovereignty is not present.'[27] Lev also presents a fundamental challenge to federal theory: 'the critique of sovereignty consists in pointing out that power never actually inheres in a single locus, from

[26] Beaud argues that it is necessary to 'play down' the notion of sovereignty 'to help understand the federal phenomenon' and to exclude 'the *summa divisio* between the Federal State and the confederacy of States which seems to be more an obstacle than a way of thinking federalism in terms of law'. O. Beaud, 'The Founding Constitution Reflections on the Constitution of a Federation and its Peculiarity' (2017) *Jus Politicum; Revue de Droit Politique* 33–63, 34. This argument is also a central thesis of *Théorie de la Fédération* (Paris: Presses Universitaires de France, 2009), where (at 56) Beaud discusses sovereignty as 'inadequate to think through the federal phenomena'.

[27] R.H. Leach, *American Federalism* (New York: WW Norton, 1970), 1.

which the untruth of sovereignty as a theory about how to organize political life is taken to follow'.[28] In the end, the doctrine of sovereignty presents nothing less than an existential crisis for the very idea of federalism as a discrete order of rule for the modern state.

IV. Towards a relational account of federal constitutional sovereignty

Such a rejection of sovereignty theory however will not serve. Federal constitutionalism is an order of rule for the modern state. Therefore, it is party to, and must account for, the modern doctrine of sovereignty that characterises constitutional authority within the state. In order to move past the confusion which has beset this question two steps are necessary. The first is to focus squarely upon the internal dimension of sovereignty as categorically distinct from the external. The second is to bring to the former a relational approach that explains internal federal constitutional sovereignty through a legitimacy-authority nexus—addressing, respectively, its authority generational and authority distributive dimensions, and explaining the relationship between the two. It follows that the authority of a federal constitution cannot be understood without reference to the constitution's demotic underpinnings; as we saw in Chapter 3 the 'who' of sovereignty is an essential dimension of the 'what' of sovereignty.

Of course, positivism is but one tradition within constitutional theory. Carl Schmitt, unlike the positivist-institutionalists, did look for a sociologically informed conception of sovereignty that tied it to the legitimacy of popular rule. But, in common with constitutional positivists in the modern period, his idea of the people was entirely monist in construction, connected inescapably to that of the nation and hence to the state, a construction that fed into, and was in turn supported by, a unified popular validation. In this intimate relationship connecting territory, popular sovereignty, and nation, Schmitt also shared with other modernist constitutionalists an inclination to elide the notions of state and constitution. It follows from Schmitt's holistic approach that he had no more room for the demotic pluralism that seemed to be implied by a federal constitution than had Hobbes or Hamilton before him. A '*Bund*' as a union of territories could only survive if it left the question of the sovereign in abeyance, given the monist vision which Schmitt attributed to sovereignty's very source: for Schmitt, within federal constitutions, the question of sovereignty 'always remains open' or 'suspended'[29]

[28] A. Lev, 'Sovereignty and Federalism: Inventing and Reinventing Public Law' (2017) 17 *Jus Politicum* 191–208, 191.

[29] C. Schmitt, *Constitutional Theory* J. Seitzer (trans.) (Durham NC: Duke University Press, 2008), 390.

and hence unsettled. If the sovereignty question is seriously confronted, the *Bund* must collapse into either a single sovereign state or separate states because only one unified popular receptacle of sovereignty is comprehensible within the logic of the holistic state envisaged by Schmitt.[30]

Schmitt's approach emphasises the extent to which the move from constitutional people to metaphysical nation, made institutionally manifest through the state, took hold upon modern constitutional theory.[31] It also illustrates the homogenising effect of this account upon how the demotic base that characterises relations of authority came to be understood within both foundational constituent power and constitutional constituent authority. As Aroney puts it: 'the sovereignty of the state has a tendency to absoluteness: it tends to assert a claim to authority over persons that supervenes on any competing loyalty or allegiance and it purports, in its extreme form, to possess the power and authority to reconstruct the entire ensemble of human relationships if it so wishes'.[32] The state becomes, within Schmitt's modernity, the real Leviathan; the constitution its mere functional appendage. Although Schmitt's account is not narrowly positivist, his reinforcement of the monistic demos thesis serves to bolster positivist accounts of internal constitutional sovereignty by confirming that in both its authority generational and authority distributive dimensions sovereignty can only be conceived in singular terms.

In Chapter 4 I argued that the elision of state and constitution is a category mistake in relation to unitary constitutionalism, but that since unitary constitutionalism is supported by a monistic conception of the demos, it is much easier to understand how the melding of people, nation, and constitutional subjects works to sustain a coalescence of monist state and unitary constitution. This monistic coincidence, and hence serendipity, does not occur with federalism. Federal constitutions are created to govern states but while the external dimension of state sovereignty is a simple story, the internal dimension by which federal government is created and validated is not. Internal sovereignty can only be explained constitutionally through the relationship between constitutional authority and the social fact of the constitution's subjects. It is in this search that federalism complicates modern constitutional sovereignty.

The crucial task then is to explain the distinctive nature of constitutional constituent authority in federal context. Constitutional sovereignty, ultimately, is not about relations of authority *within* the constitution; it is about relations of authority *to* the constitution; and these relations are contingent upon the demotic nature of the polity. The foundational federal constitutional subjects are territorial; it is this

30 For discussion see Grimm, *Sovereignty*, 67.

31 D. Kelly, 'Carl Schmitt's Political Theory of Representation' (2004) 65 *Journal of the History of Ideas* 113–134.

32 N. Aroney, 'The Federal Condition: Towards a Normative Theory' (2016) 61 *The American Journal of Jurisprudence* 13–31, 21.

social and legal-normative reality that distinguishes federalism as a discrete order of rule within the register of constitutionalism. Territory has been neglected within political and constitutional theory,[33] but its salience is crucial if we are to understand constitutional sovereignty in federal context. In this section of the chapter I will explore how the specificity of federal subjecthood informs constitutional sovereignty in a federal constitution. There are two dimensions to this. The first is 'popular sovereignty' itself which is a vital legitimising and validatory resource within federal constitutionalism as it is for any modern constitutional form. The second is the normatively transformative effect of the federal constitution as a sovereign, authoritative regime of government.

V. Federalism and popular sovereignty

In Chapters 3 and 4 we explored how an essential move within modern constitutionalism is to build a category distinction between *pouvior constituant* and *pouvoir constitué*. While the former is conceived as the active agency of the people, the latter is represented, contained, and abstracted into the concept of the nation. Through the nation it is sublimated to the state and its constitution, and hence to the institutions of representation which the national constitution creates and by which its political energy is depleted.

The key question for federal constitutional theory is whether the same demotic move necessarily occurs within federal constitutionalism. In Chapter 4 we saw how, in the modern conception of the state, sovereignty is underpinned by popular legitimacy, and how this connection is conceived through the portal of a monistic demos. Federalism was, from the beginning, caught up in this homogenising story, given the circumstances surrounding the origin of the United States constitution. The USA emerged as a modern state at the same time as it framed the legitimacy of its federal constitution in the name of *We, the People*. In Chapter 6 I will discuss how popular sovereignty was conceptually packaged by a number of influential American founders in a monist and ultimately confining way.[34] The fact that this conceptual move took place while establishing a federal constitution seems to

[33] M. Moore, *A Political Theory of Territory* (Oxford: Oxford University Press, 2015), 3.

[34] S. Beer, *To Make a Nation: The Rediscovery of American Federalism* (Cambridge MA: Harvard University Press, 1993), 279–280. As Hueglin and Fenna put it: 'Overall, the Federalists were much more concerned with *republicanism* than with federalism, and therefore with the rights and liberties of people rather than those of states.' Hueglin and Fenna, *Comparative Federalism*, 90. The focus upon republicanism rather than democracy also served to suppress the radical democratic potential of federalism: I. Hampsher-Monk, 'Democracy and Federation in the Federalist Papers', in A.-G. Gagnon and M. Burgess (eds), *Federal Democracies* (London: Taylor and Francis, 2010), 29–45. Republicanism, as highly conditioned democracy, was to be secured through a strong central government and also by the separation of powers and by federalism. See also J. McGarry and B. O'Leary, 'Federations and Managing Nations', in M. Burgess and J. Pinder (eds), *Multinational Federations* (London: Routledge, 2007), 180–211.

emphasise the universality of demotic monism within modern constitutionalism. In this way, it is no surprise that a positivist account of federalism emerged that was able to subsume 'federal states' within a wider story of demotically monist constitutionalism, thus denying federal constitutionalism any real distinctiveness.[35] A 'federal state' came to be characterised simply as one that institutionalises a plurality of territorial governments. These plural governments were not perceived to represent discrete demotic bases. Rather, the demos of the federal polity was conceived in singular terms, underscoring monist nation-building in the same way as a unitary constitution. In short, categorising federal systems through the register of statehood rather than constitutionalism helped avoid the real interrogation which the federal contract poses for a universalising account of modern constitutional theory.

Nonetheless, and despite attempts to undercut its significance, this move requires conceptual justification from a constitutional perspective. Different accounts have been offered of how a foundational constituent power, characterised by a plurality of territories, could lead to a constitutional constituent authority that was essentially monist in form. One is the idea of a 'transference' of sovereignty. This is perceived to occur not only in the legal positive sense—whereby the holders of constituent power transfer ultimate lawful authority to the constitution—but also through a transformation in the very character of the constituents themselves in the act of constitution-making: from the plural to the singular. As Grimm puts it: 'A solution was offered in the form of a transfer of sovereignty from the people of the individual states to the people of the United States.'[36] The process is therefore one of demotic alchemy. In the moment of ratification by the American states of the constitution, the 'peoples' of these states ceased to exist and became one people of the United States.[37]

This historiographical story of American foundations which elides federalism and republicanism through an implicit demotic monism came in time to plant its impression strongly upon modern constitutionalism, even in federal systems with monarchical forms.[38] Popular sovereignty emerges as a fundamental source of legitimacy for a federal constitution, but no attempt is made to conceive of its demotic underpinnings in a pluralistic way. The move to demotic unification is however unconvincing from the perspective of constitutional theory. We have

[35] Olivier Beaud, *Théorie de la Fédération*.

[36] Grimm, *Sovereignty*, 38.

[37] A.R. Amar, 'Of Sovereignty and Federalism' (1987) 96 *Yale Law Journal* 1425–1520, 1446–1466, esp. 1460. This is discussed in detail in Chapter 6.

[38] Aroney in discussing constitutional systems such as Australia and Canada, as well as the USA and Switzerland, observes: 'the idea that each constitution is essentially a "compact" between "sovereign states" has generally been supplanted by the view that the constitution derives its legal force from "the People"'. N. Aroney, 'Formation, Representation and Amendment in Federal Constitutions' (2006) 54 *American Journal of Comparative Law* 277–336, 285–286. And while it can be argued that this leaves open a debate as to whether 'the people' should be conceived in plural rather than singular terms, typically that has not been the case.

traced how the authority distributive dimension of sovereignty depends for its legitimacy upon how that authority is generated. The picture painted of American constitutional foundations by the nationalist account is that, while the former dimension may have been characterised by its plural demotic source at the moment of constitution-making, this plural source disappeared in the moment of constitution-making. This is however belied by the form of constitution that was created. A pluralised model of government was formed by the constitution precisely to reflect the territorial nature of the polity's constituent power. The territorial constituents entered into the new constitution as constitutional subjects, endowed with strong governmental autonomy and a central role in the federal government itself. In the revisionist account, which retrospectively accords to the foundational moment the process of nationalisation that did occur over time within the American polity, a monist conception of the demos emerges not only as a matter of historical development but as the foundational source of authority itself. Territorial pluralism within the new constitution manifests itself only in institutional terms, stripped of any real demotic salience: the distribution of governmental authority on a territorial basis as equivalent to other forms of authority distribution such as separation of powers and checks and balances, all of which allocate authority in the name of one singular constituent power.

Such a conceptualisation does not work as a way of explaining constitutional authority within a federal constitution. The authority distribution dimension within a federal constitution is certainly distinctive—as recognised by Kelsen. The constitution recognises its territorial pluralism partly by constitutionally demarcating the powers of each level of government and among the constituent territories themselves, while also preventing the encroachment by one branch of government upon the constitutionally guaranteed powers of the other branch, or by one constituent territory upon the powers of any other. However, federalism is about more than the demarcation of institutional competence. We see this by drawing an analogy with a unitary constitution. In a unitary constitution, authority is allocated to branches of government—legislature, executive, judiciary, etc. Nonetheless, constitutional sovereignty is a larger concept that embraces also the legitimacy dimension, encapsulated in the people—those who generate that authority. The constitution allocates authority but does not by itself embody it.[39]

In a federal constitution, authority distribution is characterised by two levels of government, one of these defined by territorial jurisdiction. This reflects foundational constituent power. The constitution-creating act recognises not only the foundational salience of the state's territories but also the ongoing significance of these territories and their governments to the polity's order of rule: (territorial) constitutional constituent authority. In a federal polity the authors of the constitution,

[39] Constitutions are bearers of identity as well as conveyors of rules. G.J. Jacobsohn, *Constitutional Identity* (Cambridge MA: Harvard University Press, 2010).

the generators of its authority, are institutionalised as active players in the state's governance. The authority of a federal constitution finds not only its initial, but also its ongoing, legitimacy in the vital political salience of plural territories.[40]

A constitution's authority always depends upon the underpinning nourishment of the subjects in whose name it is founded and who it then 'represents'. In order to understand constitutional authority we must also understand and take seriously the nature of those subjects. If they are in fact collective territorial subjects, and if this collective subjecthood is so salient that it is the foundational marker of the constitution's legitimacy and agency, this must continue to be fully accounted for in the constitutional theory of constitutional constituent authority. In relational or reflexive terms, the dimensions of legitimacy and agency always remain, in any constitutional system, in a symbiotic interplay; they are not reducible to a Kelsenian positivism.[41] The fundamental allocation of authority on the basis of constituent territories is tied inseparably to the recognition of demotic plurality, otherwise the foundation of a constitution as federal makes no sense and would be in no way significantly different from a unitary constitution, except in institutional form. In this context, it is remarkable that the pluralisation of popular sovereignty within federal polities has rarely been addressed by theorists. As Nootens puts it: 'State sovereignty has been widely debated, for example in discussions on legal and constitutional pluralism, in which states are challenged as the sole locus of constitutional authority. Such a challenge has not yet had any significant counterpart in reflections on popular sovereignty.'[42]

The salience of constituent territories for the agency and validation that underpin the federal constitution cannot therefore be conceived merely through the register of power distribution. In establishing an autonomous territorial level of government, and in giving that level of government a significant role in the government of the entire polity, the constitution embodies and institutionalises the inherent significance of its territorial constituents as its authority generators. In this way constituent territories remain the vital subjects of the constitution just as they were the vital bearers of foundational constituent power. Furthermore, unlike 'the people' within monist constitutionalism, territories are not conceptual abstractions, they are real entities. They survive inter-temporally as demotically representative entities. In this way, the establishment and maintenance of territorial

[40] It is notable that the Supreme Court of Canada in a seminal opinion concerning the legality of secession laid out federalism as a fundamental principle of the constitution, asserting: 'In our constitutional tradition, legality and legitimacy are linked.' Reference Re Secession of Quebec [1998] 2 SCR 217, para. 33. This case is discussed in detail in the next chapter.

[41] I have noted that Kelsen is correct to identify that federalism is a challenge to how we must conceive of internal, constitutional sovereignty. But his positivist analysis misses how radical this challenge is, and that it in fact stems from a need to reconceive federal constitutionalism through the lens of popular sovereignty; to arrive at an understanding of how different constitutional authority is when it rests upon the authority generated by territorial as opposed to individualised subjects.

[42] G. Nootens, *Popular Sovereignty in the West: Polities, Contention, and Ideas* (London: Routledge, 2013), 45.

government is not in itself the encapsulation of constitutional sovereignty, but rather the institutional and governmental bridge between the generators and the active bearers of sovereignty in the federal constitution.

VI. Federal constitutional sovereignty: legitimacy and authority

Federalism therefore introduces an issue of considerable potential tension. Constitutional constituent authority seems to suggest the real survival of meaningful constituent power into the constitution. However, a constitution is by definition normatively transformative, turning political power into legal authority. A federal constitution, like any modern constitution, creates a new legal order and in so doing refashions the rights and obligations of its constituent subjects. It is a constitutional contract through which the constituent territories agree to pool their authority and recognise the validity of the constitution as a third level of rule,[43] regulating the distribution of authority between the territorial and central governments.

One argument therefore, which we encountered early in this chapter, is that sovereignty is in the end a matter of authority distribution. The constitution encapsulates sovereignty itself, providing it with a locus and in doing so supplanting the sovereignty of its constituents: 'The federal big bang turns the original sovereignty of member units into autonomy, due to the primacy of the federal constitution.'[44] What are sometimes called 'homogeneity clauses' are called upon in support of the thesis that a federal constitution automatically assumes a unitary demos: for example, a constitutional commitment to the rule of law in Switzerland,[45] the United States constitution's guarantee to every state in the Union of 'a Republican Form of Government',[46] and a commitment that the government of the German *Länder* 'must conform to the principles of a republican, democratic, and social state governed by the rule of law'.[47] These clauses are however concerned with a far more limited issue than sovereignty: namely a shared commitment by all constituents to

[43] For example, the US constitution declares itself to be 'the Supreme law of the land': Constitution of the United States, (1776), art. VI, cl. 2. For Hamilton, this was a crucial distinction between the new constitution and the Articles of Confederation. 'If individuals enter into a state of society, the laws of that society must be the supreme regulator of their conduct. If a number of [pre-existing] political societies enter into a larger political society, the laws which the latter may enact, pursuant to the powers intrusted to it by its constitution, must necessarily be supreme over those societies and the individuals of whom they are composed. It would otherwise be a mere treaty, dependent on the good faith of the parties, and not a government . . .' A. Hamilton, Federalist No. 33, Rossiter (ed.), *The Federalist Papers*, 201–205, 204.

[44] Palermo and Kössler, Comparative Federalism, 40; see also 130–136.

[45] Constitution of Switzerland 1999 (rev. 2014), art. 5.

[46] Constitution of the United States, art. IV, s. 4.

[47] Basic Law for the Federal Republic of Germany (1948), art. 28(1).

abide by the constitution and to practise a democratic form of government, essential practical requirements for any constitution concerned with popular legitimacy to operate coherently as a joint enterprise. None of these provisions touch upon the deeper question of the constitutional constituent authority underpinning the constitution itself: the relationship of the constituent territories themselves *to* the constitution rather than the nature of political organisation *within* the constitution.

In fact, federal constitutions can and often do recognise in a range of ways how the constituent constitutional authority of the constituent territories remains alive conceptually as well as institutionally. We will explore these in detail in Chapters 8–10 but examples include the express recognition of the constitutional subjecthood of the constituent territories, particular constitutional protection for the existence, status and territorial boundaries of constituent territories, the recognition that residual, non-allocated authority of the constitution rests with its constituent territories, and the significant role for constituent territories in processes of constitutional change, including veto powers.

Federal constitutions are therefore normatively transformative but they are so in nuanced and conditioned ways, ways that continue to recognise the fundamentality of constituent territories to the identity and government of the federal constitution and to its normative evolution. The relationship between the settled authority of the constitution and the active constitutional constituent authority that empowers the constituent territories as bearers of constitutional sovereignty is an uneasy one. It is also one that can vary from one constitution to another, depending upon the terms of the original contract and amendments to it. The crucial issue is how any federal constitution manages the relationship between its constitutional form and the retained constitutional constituent authority of its subjects. This serves to overcome the positivist distinction between confederal and federal constitutions. The former, which might require territorial unanimity for a range of constitutional decisions and which may offer a constitutional right of secession, can be accommodated within the contract theory of federalism. As Larry Backer puts it:

> the notion of federalism ought not invariably lead to the certain conclusion that the actions of the most general jurisdiction ought to be supreme within its areas of competence. There is nothing within a general theory of federalism, other than the historical practices of generally recognized federations *to date*, which decrees that the actions of the general government ought invariably to be supreme. Thus, for example, a federal system could be constructed in which all of the acts of the general government must meet the basic constitutional requirements of *each* of the member states thereof.[48]

[48] L. Backer, 'Critical Turnings in Federalism', unpublished paper, ECSA Conference, 1999, 14. See also L. Backer, 'The Extra-National State: American Confederation Federalism and the European Union' (2001) 7 *Columbia Journal of European Law* 173–240. For example, the Constitution of Iraq of 2005 provides that the supremacy of federal law only extends to areas falling within the exclusive

Federalism is in design terms very capacious, not just in its institutional framework but at the deepest level of constituent power-constitutional form relationships. In this way the form of government called confederalism fits on a spectrum of federal government that extends from relatively centralised to relatively decentralised institutional arrangements.

VII. Concluding remarks

Sovereignty has been largely misunderstood within the political studies and constitutional law scholarship on federalism. One reason for this has been confusion over the distinction between its respectively internal and external manifestations. Another is the way in which the former has been co-opted within modern constitutionalism to support a nexus between territory, people, and nation. This has presented a stern challenge to constitutional theorists to explain how federalism can accommodate plural governments within one constitutional system. It is no surprise that many conclude that sovereignty is either divisible or dispensable within constitutional theory. In fact, however, it is neither. Sovereignty is the essential register through which we must explain authority within any constitutional system. In its internal constitutional form, sovereignty is the expression of a foundational political bond between a group of constitutional subjects and their agreed mode of government. When a constitution is founded through the constituent act of a plurality of collective territorial subjects, and when the modes of governance created by the constitution are also pluralised to reflect this sociological reality, then so too constitutionalism must respond by accommodating within the concept of constitutional sovereignty ways of explaining the particular political bond that is represented by this collective territorial subjecthood both foundationally and in the life of the constitution. Federal constitutions assimilate this different conception of the interface between foundational constituent power and constitutional constituent authority in varying ways. In the next chapter we discuss further the centrality of territorial subjecthood to federal constitutional sovereignty, and in the chapters that follow we explore how the institutional manifestation of federal subjecthood, and the sovereignty it represents, varies from one federal constitution to another.

powers of the federation; in areas where powers are shared, regional law prevails. V. Ferreres Comella and P. Bossacoma Busquet, 'Case Studies in Forms of Self-Determination: A Comparison of the Åland Islands, South Tyrol, the Kurds In Iraq, and Catalonia', Social Science Research Council Working Papers, March 2017 <http://webarchive.ssrc.org/working-papers/CPPF_Models%20of%20Autonomy_3_Ferreres%20and%20Bossacoma.pdf> (ssrc.org).

6
The Subjects of Federalism

I. Introduction

We now turn to another dimension of the foundational constituent power/constitutional constituent authority interface: subjecthood within the federal constitution. In unitary constitutionalism, the notion of the constitutional subject is encapsulated in the idea of individual citizenship. While there are debates around issues of birth and residence as to who qualifies as a citizen, the concept of citizenship itself is at root a fairly straightforward idea; it is an ascription of belonging to, or membership of, the polity, including the attribution of obligations and rights—designated invariably on an equal basis—to each individual who qualifies for this status by the law of the constitution. In short, citizenship within the unitary constitution is characterised by the markers of individual membership and equality.

In this chapter I contend that the notion of subjecthood is a more capacious concept than—and within a federal constitution is not exhausted simply by an account of—individual citizenship. Since the territories which bring the federal constitution into being are its foundational constituents, and given that the overarching purpose of the federal constitution is to recognise their centrality to the constitution's identity and design, it follows that these territories must themselves be conceived of as constitutional subjects. This in turn has implications for the concept of federal citizenship, to which the seemingly intuitive principles of individuality and equality cannot be so readily assigned; citizenship in a federal system is, by definition, conditioned by territory, which mediates the ways in which individuals relate to the constitution and to the state.

Citizenship is a pre-eminent point of focus within modern political and constitutional theory;[1] and it is a growing one, as its meaning and manifestation adapt to the context of ever more intricate developments in territorial government.[2] It is therefore surprising that theorists have not given more attention to

[1] J.-T. Arrighi and D. Stjepanović, 'Introduction: The Rescaling of Territory and Citizenship in Europe' (2019) 18 *Ethnopolitics* 219–226; C. Wiesner, A. Björk, H.-M. Kivistö, and K. Mäkinen, *Shaping Citizenship: A Political Concept in Theory, Debate and Practice* (UK: Routledge, 2019); J. Shaw, *The People in Question: Citizens and Constitutions in Uncertain Times* (Bristol: Bristol University Press, 2020).

[2] J.-T. Arrighi and D. Stjepanović, *Migrating Borders: Territorial Rescaling and Citizenship Realignment in Europe* (UK: Routledge, 2019).

The Federal Contract. Stephen Tierney, Oxford University Press. © Stephen Tierney 2022.
DOI: 10.1093/oso/9780198806745.003.0006

the implications of federalism for the idea of citizenship, particularly since federalism is today proving to be so institutionally malleable in response to demotic complexity.[3] As a result, it is necessary to explore how the elaborate framework of federal subjecthood—combining an intricate interplay between collective and individuals subjects—greatly complicates the standard constitutional concept of citizenship as simply a binary relationship between individual and state.

The chapter begins by considering the link that unites pre-constitutional agency and subjecthood with democracy. Democracy is an inherent feature of modern constitutionalism—stemming from its very function in imbuing authority with the legitimacy that stems from popular participation—and yet the concept of the demos upon which democracy rests is often taken for granted, both in terms of the political space in which it operates and the identity of the constituents who together constitute that space. I will set the scene for how federalism, with a different conception of relevant political space and constitutional subjecthood, challenges the default account of the demos within modern constitutionalism. I then move to address territories as constitutional subjects. This is a deeply unsettling idea when set against default monist constitutionalism with its conception of the individual citizen as the only salient constitutional subject. So overwhelming has been the assumed individualisation of constitutional subjecthood that federal practice has often not reflected the rich demotic potential of federalism as an idea. In the final section of the chapter I explore how the very idea of territorial subjecthood within federal systems has been so troubling for both constitutional theory and practice. Taking the USA as a case study, I explore how modern federalism emerged in the era of nation-building. In the evolution of the American polity we see the strain between a monist conception of the demos and the federal promise of territorial pluralism. Then, turning to a second case study, I examine how the ongoing tensions in the idea of territorial subjecthood fuelled a long and fraught period in Canadian constitutional history. I address the late twentieth-century attempts in Canada to arrive at a settlement of Quebec's constitutional status. This fraught period saw the Quebec National Assembly stage two secession referendums, the latter leading to an important case before the Supreme Court of Canada concerning the legality of secession. In the Court's Opinion we see the coming together of different strands of the demos question and the deep gulf that exists between monist conceptions and a more pluralist approach that characterises the complexity of federal constitutional subjecthood.

[3] For example, Rawls, in arriving at principles of justice took for granted that his framework of 'Original Position' and 'Veil of Ignorance' applied inside 'a self-contained national community'. He made no attempt to elaborate upon how such a community would be brought into being or to address complications arising from deep territorial pluralism within it. See J. Rawls, *A Theory of Justice* (Oxford: Oxford University Press, 1972), 102 and 357.

II. Constitutional subjects: the issue of legitimacy, from consent to democracy

Constitutional subjecthood is the institutional manifestation of what I have called constitutional constituent authority. As we explored in Chapter 3, the relationship between a constitution and its subjects is reflexive: the constitution articulates what it means to be a subject of the constitution, while at the same time the constitution's legitimacy hinges upon the validation of those subjects in whose name the constitution was made. This reflexivity therefore serves two functions. It endows subjects with a public identity by ascribing to them, and constitutionally recognising, markers of belonging. In a complementary way it also provides the constitution with the authenticity that stems from the original and ongoing recognition and consent, manifest in the political participation, of the constitution's subjects. It is this nexus that creates an inextricable relationship between modern constitutional authority and democracy. But despite the centrality of subjecthood to contemporary understandings of its very meaning, it is notable that democracy as an idea does not in itself contain a definition of the subject group—or demos—to which it is the ideological referent. There are two dimensions of democratic practice that require further elaboration: the boundaries of the democratic space and the public or demotic character of the constitutional subjects within it.

It is often observed that democratic theory rarely confronts the 'boundary question'[4] and, in particular, the legitimacy of the nation-state.[5] What is it about states that makes them authentic political spaces for the purposes of authoritative collective decision-making? As Kahn puts it: 'Democratic theory is internally (perhaps, eternally) incomplete: there are no grounds within democratic theory for determining the "rightfulness of the unit itself".'[6] The approach that constitutionalism tends to bring to this fundamental conceptual question is similar to that which attends the link between authorship and foundational legitimacy, explored in Chapter 3—often to ignore it, or treat it as a matter of fact: 'public law theory proceeds on [the] supposition of a good enough fit between people and government'.[7]

[4] Margaret Moore: 'Territory is ... one of the most undertheorized elements in political theory.' M. Moore, *A Political Theory of Territory* (Oxford: Oxford University Press, 2015), 3.

[5] A. Buchanan and M. Moore (eds), *States, Nations, and Borders. The Ethics of Making Boundaries* (Cambridge: Cambridge University Press, 2003).

[6] J. Kahn, *Federalism, Democratization and the Rule of Law in Russia* (Oxford: Oxford University Press, 2002), 45. Or, as Moore states: 'We do not have a clear consensus either about what territory is, or how disputes about territory should be resolved, or the appropriate justice limits of territorial rights.' Moore, *A Political Theory of Territory*, 3. And yet this is key: 'The manner in which we answer questions about the nature of The People affects our attitude towards the scope and limits of government.' D. Ivison, 'Pluralism and the Hobbesian Logic of Negative Constitutionalism' (1999) 47 *Political Studies* 83–99, 98.

[7] A. Lev, 'Introduction: Federalism and Public Law Theory', in A. Lev (ed.), *The Federal Idea: Public Law between Governance and Political Life* (Oxford: Hart Publishing, 2019), 1–26, 15. Modern theorists accept that the very idea of the state refers to its existence 'as a clearly defined, independent territory'. M. Loughlin, *Foundations of Public Law* (Oxford: Oxford University Press, 2010), 192. But how this territory becomes the state and the legitimacy of this move is rarely interrogated. Margaret Moore makes

The democratic unit tends to be taken for granted; it is the outcome of those historical processes that led to the creation of particular nation-states. This pragmatic approach, dependent as it is upon a monist conception of the demos that maps a singular constitutional people neatly onto a territorial nation, is however simply unworkable when we turn to a federal polity.[8] A state with a federal constitution is certainly, in its outward-facing presence, a singular political space; international law ascribes to it the same conception of sovereignty as it does a state with a unitary constitution. However, internally it contains a plurality of territorially located and constitutionally recognised political spaces; a reality which complicates the boundary question for the purposes of constitutional authority.[9]

In pluralising the spaces within which democracy operates, federalism also has the potential, and is in fact designed in order, to accommodate the plural political identities of its collective subjects. In general, as we saw in Chapters 4 and 5, constitutional theory tends to elide the notion of territorial boundary and demotic identity. Just as it takes the notion of the polity as one unified political space for granted, so too it implicitly assumes that one territorial political community occupies this space: one collective set of individual constitutional subjects who together constitute one body of constitutional citizens: 'the people', or its frequently used synonym, 'the nation'. As Carens puts it, there is an assumption that 'the nation-state is the only locus of political community that really matters and citizenship just means membership in a nation-state'.[10]

But in fact this default assumption about the link between the state and the constitution's subjects is historically and ideologically contingent. It is the result of the pragmatics of nation-building which were often deployed to supersede already existing territorial attachments with a new, larger state project to which the communal identity and loyalty of citizens would be entirely transferred. The existing plurality of territorially based communal attachments which might impede such a coalescence of identity around the nationalist project were therefore consigned to history as either insignificant or out-moded. This move has dominated modern

this observation in relation to political science. 'Political scientists operating within the general field of international relations typically begin by noting that it is inherent in state sovereignty that it involves political authority over a territory (a geographical domain), and while they theorize extensively the relations between such sovereign units, the territorial dimension of sovereignty is rarely questioned, or theorized.' Moore, *A Political Theory of Territory*, 3. Legal theorists generally adopt a similar approach. An example is Ronald Dworkin: 'the boundaries created by accidents of history remain the default' and 'we rarely find a persuasive argument for correcting what history has achieved'. R. Dworkin, *Justice for Hedgehogs* (Cambridge MA: Harvard University Press, 2013), 380–382.

[8] 'Rawls and Dworkin, like most post-war political theorists, work with the very simplified model of the nation-state, where the political community is co-terminous with one and only one cultural community'. W. Kymlicka, *Liberalism, Community and Culture* (Oxford: Clarendon Press, 1989), 177.

[9] The Supreme Court of Canada recognised how challenging territorial pluralism can be for federal constitutions in its notion of 'equally legitimate majorities'. *Reference re Secession of Quebec* [1998] 2 SCR 217, para. 66. This is discussed below.

[10] J.H. Carens, *Culture, Citizenship and Community* (Oxford: Oxford University Press, 2000), 161.

political theory to the point that both the spatial and demotic dimensions of the boundary question are usually brushed over to allow supposedly more interesting issues about the practice of democracy to be addressed.

Constitutional theory however must avoid this type of ideological superimposition. The purpose of constitutions is to manage political power in response to the societal specificities of the polity concerned: to take the demos as it finds it. As Carens puts it: 'our conceptions of citizenship and political community should grow out of, rather than determine, the political and social arrangements we choose'.[11] Given the societally contingent nature of constitutions, it is the case that federal constitutionalism as a genus of government emerged precisely because the nation-building story was itself complicated within certain nascent states by the presence of a plurality of territories which brought to the constitution their own discrete political identities. It is my contention therefore that, as a distinct constitutional tradition, federalism offers a specific conceptualisation of constitutional subjecthood, overlaying it with a collective dimension largely neglected by constitutional theory. It is to the very idea of the 'federal constitutional people' and to the 'federal subject' that we now turn.

III. The federal matrix: territories as subjects

Given that the key purpose of federal constitutionalism is the recognition and accommodation of territorial pluralism within one state, federal subjecthood must therefore be understood in all its complexity as a matrix, involving the constitutional polity, the territories which constitute it, and the individuals within them, each interacting through a number of overlapping relationships. It is also the case that this conceptualisation of subjecthood carries consequential implications for how the constitution's subjects relate to the constitution in patterns of identity and loyalty, and hence for how the normative authority of the constitution is legitimised and the concept of sovereignty understood.

The key point of departure for federal rule from the default monist story of modern constitutionalism is that federal territories are themselves constitutional subjects. But what does this mean? It may well be that the default account of subjecthood as synonymous with individual citizenship is both incomplete and

[11] J.H. Carens, *Culture, Citizenship and Community*, 162. It is notable that, among early modern thinkers, Althusius saw the boundary question as logically precedent to the authority question, insisting, as Hueglin puts it, 'that a proper theory of politics must first determine the members of this realm and of cities and provinces, and then proceed to discuss the nature of the universal right of sovereignty these members will establish among themselves'. T.O. Hueglin, *Early Modern Concepts for a Late Modern World: Althusius on Community and Federalism* (Waterloo: WLU Press, 1999), 130. Hueglin also notes that this 'is in stark contrast to Bodin's method of first establishing sovereignty as a universal principle and then deducing from it the nature and status of all members of a commonwealth.' Hueglin, *Early Modern Concepts for a Late Modern World*, 130.

ideologically informed, but this is nonetheless an *idée fixe* within contemporary constitutionalism. A conceptual leap is therefore required to suggest that territories as well as individuals are in fact constitutional subjects.

In this section of the chapter I explore the implications of territorial constitutional subjecthood in historical perspective. It is important to preface the discussion by noting that my primary concern is with a legal rather than a sociological conception of subjecthood: subjects as constitutionally defined 'persons'. It is of course the case that the former framework is conditioned through a relational interaction with political and social factors, but what is of essential significance from a constitutional perspective is the fundamental statement of *constitutional identity* in that foundational moment, when the nature of constitutional subjecthood is articulated and institutionalised. This is particularly significant because of the legally transformative effect the new constitution has upon its subjects. Constitutional theory explains how individual subjects who constitute the foundational constituent power in a unitary constitution are conceptually transformed into citizens. This happens in the act of constitution-making, through the new order of authority to which they are deemed to have consented and are now beholden. In this way, a symbolic link can be made between the founding generation and later generations of citizens. In Chapters 3 and 5 it was argued that the transformative role of a federal constitution is complicated precisely because of the foundational role of constituent territories in establishing the constitution, and because of the recognition of them by the constitution as distinct subjects with autonomous governments. In a similar way as do individual subjects in a unitary constitution, constituent territories of a federal polity accept the binding authority of the constitution, and in doing so change from pre-constitutional territorial subjects to become collective constitutional persons, be that states, provinces, cantons, etc. It is however my contention in this chapter that this latter form of transformation is open to a range of possibilities which do not necessarily lead to the same simple hierarchical pattern that has been taken to characterise unitary constitutionalism in its ordering of individual subjecthood. Territorial subjects—as constitutional persons—enter the constitution as already formed political collectivities; the constitution recognises them as such. Therefore these territorial collectivities can and do survive conceptually, as well as in social reality, over time in a way that a founding generation of individuals does not. The federal constitution is therefore far less a *tabula rasa* than is a unitary constitution which fundamentally fashions the public political identities of individuals.

The relationship between the federal constitution and the state is also more complex. In unitary constitutions the central government has often come to be seen as a proxy for the state,[12] and as such the vital political referent around which public

[12] M. Loughlin and S. Tierney, 'The Shibboleth of Sovereignty' (2018) 81 *Modern Law Review* 989–1016.

identities are formed. However, in a federal constitutional system the territorial level of government offers another potential site of public authority within which collective identities can be shaped, often in combination with those identities which relate to the constitution, the state, or the nation as a whole. This socio-political reality also has legal-normative implications. A state with a federal constitution needs to be conceived as a polity of polities: its foundational territorial pluralism conditions how we understand constitutional authority within it. Federal constituent power can continue to operate within a federal constitution in a far less abstract or represented sense than it does in a unitary constitution by virtue of a more attenuated or conditional normative transformation.

Another feature of federal constitutionalism's specificity is that it may well be asymmetrical in nature. In Chapter 3 we explored how the federal constitution may ascribe recognition and status to its constituent territories in varied ways. But the very fact that it would choose to do so is a consequence of societal differences among the territories themselves. Since there is a plurality of territorial sites within the constitution, each of these can continue to build and develop its own discrete social identity in a specific way, some assimilating within one homogenising national identity, others doing so to a lesser extent, if at all. Since the federal polity is designed to accommodate territorial pluralism in all its shapes and sizes, it needs to respond to such a variegated social map by recognising any deep differences among the territories in terms of history, population, geographical size and, accordingly, relative levels of citizen attachment to the state-national project. In this way, asymmetry rather than sameness may be a defining characteristic of federal subjecthood, a radical departure from unitary constitutional formation which, in orthodox political theory, brings with it the premise of equal citizenship for its only set of constitutional subjects—individuals.[13] Federalism as a constitutional idea therefore challenges the very ideological premise of nation-building, positing as its premise a politics of inter-societal diversity rather than of uni-societal homogeneity. In short, the issue of subjecthood brings to the fore the core tension between the federal idea and the dynamic of nation-building that has characterised modern constitution-making.

As we turn to two of the seminal examples of federal state-building—the USA and Canada—we find that the federal turn in North America ran up against precisely this nation-building dynamic. The story of the origins and subsequent development of federalism in each of these polities is dramatised by a tension between

[13] In fact, it is not necessarily the case that 'equality' is undermined by asymmetry, if the aim of an asymmetrical constitutional approach is to arrive at equal outcomes for different subjects. See M. Sahadžić, *Asymmetry, Multinationalism and Constitutional Law—Managing Legitimacy and Stability in Federalist States* (London: Routledge, 2021); and P. Bossacoma Busquets, 'Asymmetry as a Device for Equal Recognition and Reasonable Accommodation of Majority and Minority Nations', in P. Popelier and M. Sahadzik (eds), Constitutional Asymmetry in Multinational Federalism: Managing Multinationalism in Multi-tiered Systems (London: Palgrave, 2019), 429–460.

the unitary, centralising, and homogenising impetus of state-nation construction on the one hand and the multiple, decentralised, and pluralising dynamics that characterise the federal idea of constitutional rule on the other. It is in these case studies that we also see differing ways in which the federal constitution is normatively transformative. In the case of the USA, despite a federal structure, the constitution served to homogenise territorial subjecthood entirely within a nationalist narrative; in Canada, as certain territorial identities remained distinct and salient, the constitution required to adapt to this through meaningful asymmetry.

(i) The 'nationalisation' of American federalism

It is no surprise that the birth of the American polity in 1787 became, over time, an unparalleled focus for theoretical constitutional scholarship. One reason for this of course is the very endurance of the US constitution and its subsequent influence upon the formation and evolution of other republican polities. But another is that the ideological story which attends this originating moment is one of intellectual fertility nurtured in a period of deep but peaceful political contestation. The struggle between competing ideas that played out before, during, and after the Philadelphia process was not only erudite and eclectic, it was characterised by a spirit of openness and genuine deliberation as ideas evolved and took institutional form in shaping the first modern constitutional system. Such was the sophistication of these debates as they fashioned the new republic that they have continued to provide an evocative reference point for constitutional puzzles elsewhere over the following two and a half centuries.

A seminal intervention in the debate were the papers published by Alexander Hamilton, John Jay, and James Madison as 'Publius'. These articles were polemics (less charitably, 'propaganda'[14]), making the case for the ratification of the constitution drafted at the Philadelphia Constitutional Convention. However, they drew upon extensive learning and comparative constitutional history and it is as much for this intellectual hinterland as their political success that 'the Federalist Papers' bear the test of time. It was largely through this historical experience and the debates which have emanated from it that the modern link between federalism and constitutionalism was drawn, and it was in this moment that federalism emerged as a discrete concept of constitutional rule for the modern state.[15]

[14] T.O. Hueglin and A. Fenna, *Comparative Federalism: A Systematic Enquiry*, 2nd edn (Toronto: University of Toronto Press, 2015), 88.

[15] C. Rossiter (ed.), *The Federalist Papers* (New York: The New American Library, 1961), xii. Although it is important not to overlook European influences upon the founding debates in the United States, for example, Montesquieu. He warmly endorsed early attempts to construct an American federal model: 'It is, therefore, very probable that mankind would have been, at length, obliged to live constantly under the government of a single person, had they not contrived a kind of constitution that has all the internal advantages of a republican, together with the external force of a monarchical, government. I mean a

A number of key tensions were in play in this laboratory of modern constitutional theory, but perhaps the most fundamental involved the nature of the American demos. The development of what we now call federalism in the United States emerged largely from the happenstance of a pre-existing collection of British colonies rather than from any theoretical schema to accommodate strong demotic pluralism. In fact, the association among the American colonies was always characterised by a strong sense of ethnic and cultural homogeneity,[16] and this sense of demotic unity was further consolidated in the common cause of the revolutionary war.[17]

The thirteen colonies were linked by their common history with, and relationship to, the British metropole, and in due course they came together politically in common cause to reframe, and then in time to break from, their relationship to Great Britain. The process of rebellion initially produced a highly contingent constitutional union. The United States' first constitutional move took 'federal' form in a loose union of revolutionary colonies embodied in the Articles of Confederation (1781–1789). This arrangement was widely criticised, principally for its weak and ultimately centrifugal tendencies.[18] The impetus for the ensuing Philadelphia process was therefore, in the eyes of 'the Federalists', to produce a closer union. The key issue became how close the union should be, how its institutions should be framed, and how powers should be allocated across territorial levels.

Although the deliberations before and after Philadelphia concerning the best form of government for the new polity were fraught, one area that was not in fact a source of real tension was the nature of the constitutional people. The arguments over how much power ought to be accorded to or retained by the states vis-à-vis that of the federal government tended not to revolve around claims by the states to discrete vernacular identities, the accommodation of which justified strong

confederate republic ... As this government is composed of petty republics, it enjoys the internal happiness of each; and with respect to its external situation, by means of the association, it possesses all the advantages of large monarchies.' Montesquieu, *The Spirit of Laws, vol. I*, Book IX, ch. I. This passage was heavily influential and forms the backdrop to Hamilton's reflections in The Federalist, No. 9, C Rossiter (ed.), *The Federalist Papers*.

16 'Providence has been pleased to give this one connected country to one united people—a people descended from the same ancestors, speaking the same language, professing the same religion, attached to the same principles of government, very similar in their manners and customs.' J. Jay, Federalist No. 2, Rossiter *The Federalist Papers*, 38.

17 Jay concludes that with a common identity forged through conflict, 'it appears as if it was the design of Providence' that the country and the people were made for each other: 'an inheritance so proper and convenient for a band of brethren, united to each other by the strongest ties, should never be split into a number of unsocial, jealous, and alien sovereignties'. J. Jay, The Federalist No. 2, Rossiter, *The Federalist Papers*, 38.

18 A number of Federalist papers highlight what Hamilton termed the 'insufficiency of the present confederation to the preservation of the union'. J. Jay, Federalist No. 2, , *The Federalist Papers*, 105. A national government was needed that could build foundations 'deeper than in the mere sanction of delegated authority', and issue from the 'pure, original fountain of all legitimate authority', namely, 'the consent of the people'. A. Hamilton, Federalist No. 22, Rossiter, *The Federalist Papers*, 152. For a similar critique and prescription see also J. Madison, Federalist Nos 19 and 20, Rossiter, *The Federalist Papers*, 131–132, 137–138.

self-government. The colonies were a creation of British rule in the Americas and remained separately governed territorial units under the Articles of Confederation, but they were in essence arbitrarily created territories rather than discrete communities deeply rooted in history. The states certainly had developed distinctive identities, in some cases with particular religious characteristics.[19] At the same time however the states were also linked by a strong cultural similarity, their residents largely united by a sense of common British origins. Arguments for federalism as they played out around the Philadelphia convention therefore focused principally upon the utility of pluralised government not for its accommodation of territorial pluralism but rather for the way in which it might divide, and in so doing dilute, the power of government within the polity as a whole, to preserve the liberties of 'the people', conceived monistically.[20] This was the driving normative impetus behind the preamble of the constitution, authored by 'We, the People . . .': emphasising that the founding demos of the new polity was conceived in singular terms.[21] The debate in the Federalist and beyond tended to focus first upon forging a strong central government in the name of a sovereign people to replace the looser Articles of Confederation, and secondly upon how to explain this apparent breach with the amendment process provided for by the Articles themselves.[22] The fact that a federal constitution was being founded by a plurality of states, itself a matter of profound constitutional innovation, received comparatively scant attention. It follows that federal constitutional theory must recognise in the American experience a capricious opposition: a territorially based pluralisation of institutions on the one hand, and a nation-building demotic project on the other, with the reconciliation between these two potentially conflicting goals left to the future.

We must of course approach the Federalist papers as political argument rather than reify them as idealised political or constitutional theory. The authors' task was as much one of persuasion as explication, with rhetoric at times supplanting evidence and sophistry deployed to disguise real intention. It is inevitable from the competing goals that characterised the American founding that elements of self-contradiction crept into these papers, and that in places they offer opaque assertions that are open to different interpretations, including those that may hint at a more demotically pluralist vision than in the end played out in American constitutional life.[23] But often the rhetoric is unambiguously nationalistic, for example John

[19] J.T. Levy, Federalism, Liberalism, and the Separation of Loyalties' (2007) 101 *American Political Science Review* 459–477, 466.

[20] N. Aroney, 'Formation, Representation and Amendment in Federal Constitutions' (2006) 54 *American Journal of Comparative Law* 277–336, 307–308.

[21] As Rakove puts it, by 1787, 'Americans had ... become a people who defined themselves by the constitutions they framed.' J. Rakove, *Revolutionaries: A New History of the Invention of America* (Boston: Houghton Mifflin Harcourt, 2010), 159.

[22] A.M. Bernal, *Beyond Origins: Rethinking Founding in a Time of Constitutional Democracy* (Oxford: Oxford University Press, 2017), 86–88.

[23] Jean Yarborough argues that in the Federalist Hamilton and Madison mask their true opinion of federalism. In fact, 'The Federalist secretly opposed the federal aspects of the Constitution.' J. Yarbrough, 'Rethinking "The Federalist's View of Federalism"' (1985) 15 *Publius* 31–53, 32. Peter Onuf

Jay in the Federalist No. 2 presented the task at hand as follows: 'whether it would conduce more to the interest of the people of America that they should, to all general purposes, be one nation, under one federal government, or that they should divide themselves into separate confederacies, and give to the head of each the same kind of powers which they are advised to place in one national government'.[24]

Madison's approach was more subtle but the legerdemain at work in his account of the normative process by which the constitution was to be ratified merely adds a veneer to the same point:

> on one hand ... the Constitution is to be founded on the assent and ratification of the people of America, given by deputies elected for the special purpose; but, on the other ... this assent and ratification is to be given by the people, not as individuals composing one entire nation, but as composing the distinct and independent States to which they respectively belong. It is to be the assent and ratification of the several States, derived from the supreme authority in each State, the authority of the people themselves. The act, therefore, establishing the Constitution, will not be a *national*, but a *federal* act.[25]

This can certainly be read as a pluralist vision; the popular underpinnings of the new republic manifest in multiple demoi— 'the distinct and independent States'— rather than a singular demos. But any such interpretation should be taken with three points of considerable qualification. The first is the immediate purpose behind this paper. Madison and the other authors of the Federalists were trying to appease those in New York who feared that the constitution would effectively destroy the powers of the states.[26] Although here, as at other points in his contributions to the Federalist, Madison appears to defend the significance of the states, this is at least in part for strategic reasons and must be read in the context of his overall vision which was a nationalising one.[27]

and Nicholas Onuf suggest that Hamilton's apparent support for a new form of federal government was disingenuous: 'manipulation to the point of obfuscation', while weakening the idea of federalism in stark contrast to the strongly confederal meaning it had at that time. P. Onuf and N. Onuf, *Federal Union, Modern World: The Law of Nations in an Age of Revolutions 1776–1814* (Madison, Wisconsin: Madison House, 1993), 56. Hueglin and Fenna also accuse Hamilton of 'disingenuousness'. Hueglin and Fenna, *Comparative Federalism*, 2nd edn, 90. See also M. Klarman, *The Framers' Coup: The Making of the United States* Constitution (Oxford: Oxford University Press, 2016), ch. 1.

[24] J. Jay, Federalist No. 2, Rossiter, *The Federalist Papers*, 37.

[25] Federalist No. 39, Rossiter, *The Federalist Papers*, 243.

[26] N. Feldman, *The Three Lives of James Madison: Genius, Partisan, President* (New York: Random House, 2017), 179–180.

[27] For example: '*the people* are the only legitimate fountain of power'. (emphasis added) J. Madison, Federalist No. 49, Rossiter, *The Federalist Papers*. This is not to say that it was an institutionally centralising one. It is clear that Madison saw strength in federalism precisely because it weakened the power of the central branch. Bruce Ackerman observes how Madison's commitment to the constitutional authority of the states in fact grew later in his working life, in particular during his period as president. B. Ackerman, 'The Race Against Time', in R. Albert (ed.), *Revolutionary Constitutionalism: Law, Legitimacy, Power* (Oxford: Hart, 2020) 377–399, 390. For discussion see also

The second point is that even in Madison's vision of the ratification process there is no real evidence of deep popular pluralism. Madison acknowledged that ratification and assent was given by the states. But his subtle turn is to present their role as plural representatives of *one people*, a singular national demos. Certainly, in institutional terms the process of ratification was not one in which the people would assent to the constitution directly as individuals composing one nation but 'composing the distinct and independent States to which they respectively belong'. At the level of demotic validation however, the states themselves derive power from 'the [supreme] authority of the people themselves'. Although Madison asserts that ratification is not a 'national' act, this assertion should be understood in institutional rather than demotic terms; in the latter sense it clearly is a national act: the constitution is founded 'on the assent and ratification of *the people* of America' (emphasis added). Throughout this and other Federalist papers which he wrote,[28] 'the people' is expressed in singular terms; at no point does Madison characterise the process of popular endorsement as acts of *the peoples* of the states.[29]

A third point is that, read in the context of his other contributions to the Federalist, and to his approach to the constitution-making process more generally, Madison's agenda was an overtly nationalising one. Throughout the Federalist Papers, his mindset had no space for real territorial pluralism, whereby the states would intervene as discrete and meaningful sources of public identity between the national government and individual citizens. In fact, Madison saw in such a vision a clear threat to the new republic:

> The important truth, which it unequivocally pronounces in the present case, is that a sovereignty over sovereigns, a government over governments, a legislation for communities, as contradistinguished from individuals, as it is a solecism in theory, so in practice it is subversive of the order and ends of civil polity, by substituting violence in place of law, or the destructive coercion of the sword in place of the mild and salutary coercion of the magistracy.[30]

Notably Madison used the monistic demos thesis to counter arguments that the mode of promulgating the new constitution was unlawful under the Articles of Confederation: 'The people were in fact, the fountain of all power, and by resorting to them, all difficulties were got over. They could alter constitutions as they pleased.

B. Ackerman, *Revolutionary Constitutions: Charismatic Leadership and the Rule of Law* (Cambridge MA: Harvard University Press, 2019).

[28] For example, Federalist No. 45, Rossiter, *The Federalist Papers*, 288, and Federalist No. 28 Rossiter, *The Federalist Papers*), 178.

[29] Even on an institutional register, at the Convention Madison and Hamilton 'sought to create a vigorous national government at the expense of the states.' Yarborough, 'Rethinking "The Federalist's View of Federalism"', 35.

[30] J. Madison, Federalist No. 20, Rossiter, *The Federalist Papers*, 138.

It was a principle in the Bill of Rights, that first principles might be resorted to.'[31] As Edmund Morgan puts it: 'Madison was inventing a sovereign American people to overcome the sovereign states.'[32] This view is supported by Grimm: 'Neither the organs of the states nor those of the United States were sovereign; nor were the individual states nor the United States sovereign. The American people alone were sovereign—in the view of the majority.'[33] Madison was not alone in this endeavour. It is an established thesis within the historiography of the period that the foundations of national unity were clearly being laid by the founders. Martin Diamond suggests that the Federalist papers masked an overtly nationalist project.[34] Yarborough agrees: 'despite its ostensible praise of federalism, ['the Federalist'] is a radically nationalist work'.[35]

Madison's views were widely shared and the sense of a nation-building project is evident in other leading figures of the time. In 1776, when discussion was taking place around the Articles of Confederation, Benjamin Rush said: 'I would not have it understood that I am pleading the Cause of Pensilvania. When I entered that door, I considered myself a Citizen of America.'[36] When ten state conventions had ratified the Federalist Constitution, which, under Article VII of the constitution was one more than necessary to bring the constitution into effect, Rush wrote: 'Tis done . . . We have become a nation.'[37] John Adams also suggested that the 1787 constitution marked a category shift from the historical example of confederacies 'in which the federal council was only a diplomatic body'. The 1787 constitution by contrast was much more deeply unifying for the United States, serving to 'unite their wills and forces as a single nation'.[38] This national vision led many to see

[31] M. Farrand (ed.), *The Records of the Federal Convention of 1787* (New Haven: Yale, rev edn, 1937) vol. 2, 475. See also B. Ackerman, 'The Storrs Lectures: Discovering the Constitution' (1984) 93 *Yale Law Journal* 1013–1072, 1020–1024.

[32] E.S. Morgan, *Inventing the People: The Rise of Popular Sovereignty in England and America* (New York: Norton, 1989), 267.

[33] D. Grimm, *Sovereignty: The Origin and Future of a Political and Legal Concept* (New York: Columbia University Press, 2015), 48.

[34] M. Diamond, 'The Federalist's View of Federalism', in G.C.S. Benson (ed.), *Essays in Federalism* (Claremont: Institute for Studies in Federalism, 1962) 21–64. See also A. R. Amar, 'Of Sovereignty and Federalism' (1987) 96 *Yale Law Journal* 1425–1520.

[35] Yarbrough, 'Rethinking "The Federalist's View of Federalism" ', 35. This argument is supported by the early jurisprudence of the US Supreme Court. In one significant early case Wilson J. stated: 'the people of the United States form a nation'. *Chisholm v. Georgia*, 2 U.S. (2 Dall.) 419, 453 (1793). However, for an alternative view that finds in the Federalist the good faith commitment to plural government see V. Ostrom, *The Political Theory of a Compound Republic: Designing the American Experiment*, 2nd edn (Lincoln: University of Nebraska Press, 1987).

[36] Cited by A.L. LaCroix, *The Ideological Origins of American Federalism* (Cambridge MA: Harvard University Press, 2011), 131. LaCroix records James Wilson making a similar point at Philadelphia: 'We must remember the language with wh. we began the Revolution, it was this, Virginia is no more, Massachusetts is no more—we are one in name, let us be one in Truth & Fact . . .'. LaCroix, *The Ideological Origins of American Federalism*, 151.

[37] C.D. Bowen, *Miracle at Philadelphia: The Story of the Constitutional Convention May to September 1787* (New York: Little, Brown and Co., 1986), 310.

[38] J. Adams, 'A Defence of the Constitutions of Government (1787)', in I. Kramnick and T.J. Lowi (eds), *American Political Thought: A Norton Anthology* (New York: W. W. Norton, 2009), vol. 3, 505–506. There is much evidence to suggest that the Anti-Federalists, often with regret, also viewed the process of

federalism as an unfortunate and hopefully temporary step, necessary in light of the very loose constitutional arrangement that preceded the constitution, on the way to an essentially unitary polity.[39]

Akhil Reed Amar, in a series of comprehensive articles surveying the founding debates, has come to similar conclusions about the nation-building role of the constitutional process and does so in a way that attempts to legitimise the constitutional foundation despite its incompatibility with the Articles of Confederation. Referring to the process by which the constitution was ratified by state conventions rather than a national convention, he writes that this process would have 'transcendent consequences':

> It was by these very acts that previously separate state Peoples agreed to 'consolidate' themselves into a single continental People. Before ratification, the People of each state were indeed sovereign—and for that very reason could not be bound by the new Constitution if they chose not to ratify, no matter what any of the other sovereign Peoples chose to do. Thus, although Article VII required only nine states to ratify, it confirmed the pre-existing sovereignty of the People of each state by proclaiming that the Constitution would go into effect only between the nine or more states ratifying. The ratifications themselves thus formed the basic social compact by which formerly distinct sovereign Peoples, each acting in convention, agreed to reconstitute themselves into one common sovereignty. The Gettysburg Address notwithstanding, it was in 1788, and not 1776, that 'a new nation' was legally 'brought forth upon this continent.'[40]

In the work by Amar which I have cited he advances what he calls 'the unitary People thesis', arguing that the constitution was framed in a way that emphasised

ratification as one which both created, and depended for its legal legitimacy upon, a conception of one unified people. Amar, 'Of Sovereignty and Federalism', 1461–1462, fn. 157.

For other accounts of the nation-building effects of the Philadelphia period, see L. Benning, 'James Madison and the Nationalists, 1780–1783' (1983) 40 *The William and Mary Quarterly* 227–255; G.S. Wood, *Creation of the American Republic, 1776–1787* [1969] (University of North Carolina Press, 1998), 128, noting that 'the American Revolution was not simply a war for independence' but of national unity; J.P. Roche, 'The Founding Fathers: A Reform Caucus in Action' (1961) 55 *American Political Science Review* 799–816; A. Taylor, *American Revolutions: A Continental History, 1750–1804* (New York: W.W. Norton & Co, 2016), 373: the founders 'designed a national republic'. See also J.N. Rakove, *The Beginnings of National Politics* (New York: Alfred A. Knopf, 1979), 393, noting how delegates followed Madison's nationalising lead, encapsulated in the Virginia Plan.

[39] It is notable that both Hamilton and Madison were deeply pessimistic about the prospects for the constitution's success. Taylor notes that just before signing the new constitution, Hamilton declared that 'no man's ideas were more remote from the plan than mine were known to be'. Taylor, *American Revolutions: A Continental History*, 176. Madison was also fearful that the lack of a veto power over state legislation 'would ultimately prove fatal'. Ibid. Although I have also noted above how, over time, Madison's view as to the appropriate balance between the constitutional powers of the central government and the states seems to have changed.

[40] Amar, 'Of Sovereignty and Federalism', 1460, and see the full argument:1446–1466.

the existence of one national people. As well as his general interpretation of the founding, he offers various textual arguments in support of his thesis, including important omissions from the constitution: 'we must not neglect the silence roaring between the lines of the preamble: Nowhere is there any reference to the "sovereignty" of the People of "each state" that had been the express animating principle of the Articles'.[41] And in relation to the supremacy clause: 'the implication was continental: one Constitution, one land, one People'.[42] Amar's argument leads him to the ultimate conclusion that while ratifying conventions in each state were a necessary institutional step in the ratification of the constitution, the process of ratification was itself a form of normative alchemy through which a national people was born, and the popular sovereignty at work in the ratification by each state convention should be seen as the act of a wider national popular sovereignty which, in demotic terms, joined these discrete state peoples together.[43]

Scope for disagreement remained of course on account of Madison's elision of institutional and demotic conceptions of 'the nation'. It was common for him to refer to the constitution as an institutional 'compound'. But when he referred to the constitution as 'not forming one aggregate nation', he was referring to the institutionalisation of plural statehood, not of peoplehood. His prioritisation between institutional pluralism and demotic monism was clear: 'As far as the sovereignty of the States cannot be reconciled to the happiness of the people, the voice of every good citizen must be, Let the former be sacrificed to the latter.'[44] From all of this Amar concludes: 'the most important thing that the Constitution constitutes is neither the national government, nor even the supreme law, but one sovereign national People, who may alter their government or supreme law at will.'[45]

This is certainly the narrative which has taken hold within American constitutional historiography since the founding.[46] It was reinforced of course by the outcome of the Civil War, as voiced by Chief Justice Chase, who described how the United States: 'grew out of common origin, mutual sympathies, kindred principles, similar interests, and geographical relations'.[47] Amar also takes the view that the post-Civil War period consolidated the founding vision of one national people. The Reconstruction amendments 'swept aside the formal limitations of Article V

[41] Amar, 'Of Sovereignty and Federalism', 1456; see also 1455–1462.

[42] Amar, 'Of Sovereignty and Federalism' 1458.

[43] A.R. Amar, 'Philadelphia Revisited: Amending the Constitution Outside Article V' (1988) 55 *University of Chicago Law Review* 1043–1104, 1050.

[44] J. Madison, Federalist, No. 45, Rossiter, *The Federalist Papers*, 289. For further detailed accounts of how the federalist arguments focused upon a singular conception of the people see J.N. Rakove and O. Handlin, *James Madison and the Creation of the American Republic* (Glenview: Scott, Foresman/ Little, Brown Higher Education, 1990); M.J. Klarman, *The Framers' Coup: The Making of the United States Constitution* (New York: Oxford University Press, 2016), ch. 1; Q. Taylor, '"A System Without a Precedent": The Federalism of the Federalist Papers', in A. Ward and L. Ward, *Ashgate Research Companion to Federalism* (Aldershot: Ashgate, 2016) 175–192.

[45] Amar, 'Of Sovereignty and Federalism', 1463, fn. 163.

[46] H. Sidgwick, *The Elements of Politics* (London: Macmillan & Co., 1891), 513–514.

[47] *Texas v. White* [1868] 74 U.S. 700, 725.

in order to vindicate the American People's sovereign right to alter their government'.[48] Over a century later the notion of a polity founded by a singular demos was again stated by the Supreme Court: 'the whole people of the United States asserted their political identity and unity of purpose when they created the federal system'.[49]

The creation of a national people in the birth of a federal constitution, and the creation of a direct institutional relationship between the federal government and the people of the whole country, are certainly not incompatible with the territorial pluralism that forms the foundations of the federal idea: the very concept of federalism comprises the balance between pluralism and union and this can manifest itself in different ways. But so homogenising did the American national vision become, that territorial pluralism within the American constitutional imaginary was consigned to the register of authority distribution. Even the states' rights debate, which dogged the early decades of the republic and led in part to Civil War, was not characterised by the promotion of strong and discrete state identities. A *regional* identity developed among the 'slave states', but the constitutional arguments that characterised the first half of the nineteenth century focused upon the meaning of the constitution and the founders' intentions in relation to the powers of *all* states.[50] These were not principally claims to asymmetrical entitlements of particular states on account of some form of demotic specificity. All states were perceived to be part of one demotic project and constitutional rights were viewed in this generalisable context as the entitlement of every state.

Overall then, from the early days of 'the Republic' a monistic republican vision of democracy supplanted a pluralised federal vision; and when viewed through the lens of either Lindahl's reflexivity or Loughlin's relational theory of sovereignty, this republican concept today does not differ greatly from the idea of a monistic demotic resource that underpins a unitary constitution.[51] Sovereign relations within American republican federalism are in effect singular, between one people and the constitution, albeit that the government of that one people is administered partly through a layer of territorial government.

[48] Amar, 'Of Sovereignty and Federalism', 1464, fn. 166. See also A.R. Amar, *America's Constitution* (New York: Random House, 2006), 14–16. Bruce Ackerman takes a similar view. The 14th amendment confirmed that 'the will of the nation was independent of, and superior to, the will of the states'. B. Ackerman, *We the People I: Foundations* (Cambridge MA: The Belknap Press of Harvard University Press, 1991), 81. See also B. Ackerman, *We the People II: Transformations* (Cambridge MA: The Belknap Press of Harvard University Press, 1998).

[49] *U.S. Term Limits, Inc. v. Thornton* [1995] 514 U.S. 779, 838 (Kennedy J. concurring).

[50] K.E. Whittington, 'The Political Constitution of Federalism in Antebellum America: The Nullification Debate as an Illustration of Informal Mechanisms of Constitutional Change' (1996) 26 *Publius* 1–24.

[51] To the extent that the very decision to federalise has recently been called a 'tragic' compromise. M. Feeley and E. Rubin, *On Federalism: Federalism as Tragic Choice* (Ann Arbor: University of Michigan Press, 2008).

(ii) Canada: the radical challenge of territorial constitutional authority

Canadian territorial subjecthood was personified through a succession of constitutional unions in the nineteenth century, the core purpose of which was the bringing together of the English- and French-speaking peoples of British North America. This process served to institutionalise the 'French fact' within the country, which over time coalesced largely around, although not exclusively in, the province of Quebec.[52] The bi-cultural reality of Canada, although always conditioned by the original conquest of aboriginal lands and, since the twentieth century, increasingly suffused by migrant multiculturalism, remains fundamental to the country's constitutional self-understanding. Canada over time took on a more overtly *bi-national* political and constitutional character as the cultural and linguistic specificity of Quebec as a province passed through its own nation-building process in the twentieth century.[53] And, despite efforts throughout Canadian history to build a singular conception of the people, it had become clear by the 1960s that Canadian federalism had not produced a process of demotic homogenisation comparable to the American historical journey. Instead, a deep popular dualism has played out with profound constitutional consequences for Canada since the late 1960s.

Canada made a self-conscious turn towards federalism in 1867 but the territorialisation of its constitutional arrangements long pre-date this. Even in the eighteenth century, the country's biculturalism was an important dimension in the developing constitutional story.[54] This can be traced back to the imperial competition between Great Britain and France in North America. New France was acquired by Britain in the Treaty of Paris (1763), which ended the Seven Years' War. New France became the Province of Quebec, a status it held from 1763 to 1791. The Constitutional Act of 1791 recognised the ongoing reality of French Canadian culture, as had the Quebec Act 1774. The 1791 Act also separated the province into Upper Canada, which was predominantly Anglophone, and Lower Canada, with its largely French-speaking population.

[52] New Brunswick and Ontario in particular also have significant francophone populations, but the fact that Quebec has always had an overwhelming French-speaking majority has made it, since 1867, the main institutional focus for Canada's francophone identity.

[53] Given the nature of Canada's constitutional structure, I will address this as an essentially bicultural constitutional discourse. Our account, which addresses the constitutional self-identity of Canada since the mid-nineteenth century, focuses upon English-French relations because it was in this story that the modern constitution was built and through this relationship that its contemporary problems came to a head. However, it is also increasingly the case that the role of Canada's aboriginal peoples has grown and that they too assert strong and distinct legal claims, founded upon deep territorial attachments and fundamental treaty rights, established with the British Crown. J. Borrows, *Freedom and Indigenous Constitutionalism* (Toronto: University of Toronto Press, 2016).

[54] S. Tierney, 'Misconceiving Federalism: Canada and the Federal Idea', in R. Albert (ed.), *Canada in the World* (Cambridge: Cambridge University Press, 2017), 34–58.

Canada began to take the constitutional form we recognise today through the Act of Union 1840,[55] which merged the legislatures of Lower Canada and Upper Canada into the United Province of Canada (Upper Canada now being known as Canada West and Lower Canada as Canada East).[56] The 'confederal' move, effected through the British North America (BNA) Act of 1867,[57] emerged from efforts to overcome the political difficulties and deadlocks within the United Province of Canada created by the Act of Union. It served to re-divide 'Canada' into the provinces of Ontario and Quebec, recognising Nova Scotia and New Brunswick also as provinces. The BNA Act 1867 therefore reframed the British colonies of North America: Canada, Nova Scotia, and New Brunswick were now federally joined in one Dominion of Canada on 1 July 1867.[58] In time, Canada would expand to include within its confederation ten provinces and three territories, but the structure of the constitutional state remains that created by the BNA Act.

By 1867, and in the shadow of the American Civil War, which for many within 'English Canada' highlighted the perils of territorial government, there was an inclination towards strong central government. As Hueglin comments: 'Although termed "Confederation", the union of 1867 was intended to be anything but.'[59] This centralising agenda however ran up against the bicultural dimension of Canada, as well as the territorial particularities of the other territories which came together in 1867, or which would later join confederation, as provinces. It was however French Canada whose influence in the move to a federal system was the most salient. The key aim of francophone representatives in the confederation debates was to overcome the homogenisation project of the first half of the nineteenth century.[60] For them, and in particular their leader Georges-Etienne Cartier, the purpose of a new federal arrangement would be to recognise the distinctiveness of French Canadian culture and offer it territorial protection.[61] The main political actors in English Canada, led by John A. Macdonald, although favouring a strong centralist regime,[62]

[55] Act of Union, 1840, 3 & 4 Vict., c. 35, renamed the British North American Act, 1840, by the Short Titles Act 1896, Sch. 1.

[56] See E. Brouillet, A.-G. Gagnon, and G. Laforest (eds), *The Constitutions that Shaped Us: A Historical Anthology of Pre-1867 Canadian Constitutions* (Kingston/Montreal: McGill-Queen's University Press, 2015).

[57] Renamed the Constitution Act 1867 by the Constitution Act 1982, part VII, s. 60.

[58] Constitution Act, 1867, 30 & 31 Vict., c. 3 (UK), RSC 1985, App. II, No. 11.

[59] Hueglin and Fenna, *Comparative Federalism*, 1st edn, 156.

[60] Captured infamously in the Durham Report: 'Lord Durham's Report on the Affairs of British North America' (1839). J.M. Bliss (ed.), *Canadian History in Documents, 1763–1996* (Toronto: Ryerson Press, 1996), 49–62; L.-G. Harvey, 'Confederation and Corruption: The Republican Critique of the Quebec Resolutions', in E. Brouillet, A.-G. Gagnon, and G. Laforest (eds), *The Quebec Conference of 1864: Understanding the Emergence of the Canadian Federation* (Kingston/Montreal: McGill-Queen's University Press, 2018), 220–232, 223–225.

[61] Hogg and Wright discuss how these two visions of confederation and its purpose have continued to dominate in the anglophone and francophone milieus respectively. P. Hogg and W. Wright, 'Canadian Federalism, the Privy Council and the Supreme Court: Reflections on the Debate About Canadian Federalism' (2005) 38 *University of British Columbia Law Review* 329–352, 330–331.

[62] R. Chignon, 'The Fathers of Confederation and the BNA Act: Constitution al Visions and Models', in E. Brouillet, A.-G. Gagnon, and G. Laforest (eds), *The Quebec Conference of 1864: Understanding the*

realised that a successful constitutional union would require compromise. Cartier, a leading voice for French Canada, agreed to such a compromise in the 1867 Act.[63]

The 1867 Act was indeed such a compromise. On the one hand there was recognition of the territorial prerogatives of all provinces created in 1867, which would also set the constitutional groundwork for admission of the new provinces that would later enter confederation. But on the other hand there was specific recognition of the French fact in Canada and its territorial concentration mainly in the province of Quebec.[64] In Canada's modern foundation there was therefore a dual dimension to the federal constitutional contract that emerged from the 1867 constitutional moment: what has been called a 'double compact'.[65] The constitution recognized the territorial constituent authority of its territories but it did so in different ways for different territories. The constitution accorded a general status of equality to the provinces and in time the proliferation of provinces would further serve the goal, which we saw in early American debates, of multiplying the centres of government across such a vast state for various pragmatic reasons. However, the constitution also recognised Quebec as a special province, accepting implicitly that it embodied one of Canada's two founding cultures.[66]

Quebec was essentially accorded asymmetrical recognition, with special autonomy in relation to language and religion built into the constitution. From the 1960s onwards Quebec would use these provisions to develop its own language policy, and it is also from this time that its cultural and political distinctiveness started fully to develop. Quebec's new assertiveness, illustrated by a referendum on 'sovereignty association' in 1980, created deep tensions at the time the constitution was formally repatriated from the UK in 1982, a process in which many Quebec nationalists felt the compact or contractual nature of the federation had not been respected.[67] Attempts to address this in elaborate proposals for constitutional change failed both in 1987 and 1992, culminating in a further 'sovereignty' referendum held by the province of Quebec in 1995. One of the most constitutionally

Emergence of the Canadian Federation (Kingston/Montreal: McGill-Queen's University Press, 2018), 29–48, 39.

[63] For which he was accused of betrayal by dissenting French Canadian voices. F. Rocher, 'Opponents of the 1864 Confederation Project: Criticism of the Future Regime', in E. Brouillet, A.-G. Gagnon, and G. Laforest, (eds), *The Quebec Conference of 1864: Understanding the Emergence of the Canadian Federation* (Kingston/Montreal: McGill-Queen's University Press, 2018), 179–219, 202–203.

[64] *Secession Reference*, para. 38.

[65] P. Romney, 'Provincial Equality, Special Status and the Compact Theory of Confederation' (1999) 32 *Canadian Journal of Political Science* 21–39; P. Romney, *Getting it Wrong: How Canadians Forgot Their Past and Imperilled Confederation* (Toronto: Toronto University Press, 1999).

[66] The pluralism of the Canadian provinces was aided by the Dominion status of Canada. The Canadian constitution in the nineteenth century remained subordinate to that of the UK and each province also enjoyed its own discrete relationship to the Crown through their own lieutenants governor, the vice regal representatives of the Monarch as head of state.

[67] K. McRoberts, *Misconceiving Canada: The Struggle for National Unity* (Toronto: Oxford University Press, 1997); G. Laforest, *Trudeau and the End of a Canadian Dream* (Montreal/Buffalo: McGill-Queen's University Press, 1995).

significant consequences of this was the *Secession Reference* brought to the Supreme Court of Canada by the Canadian federal government. In its wide-ranging Opinion the Court addressed the lawfulness of secession from the perspective of both international and Canadian constitutional law. In the course of doing so it also addressed the nature of Canada as a federal polity and the constitutional status of its constituent territories. This was the first time the Court had offered such a detailed reflection on the foundational legitimacy of the Canadian constitution, and its Opinion served to expose the tension between different understandings of the nature of the Canadian demos which had beset the country since confederation.

The Court addressed the complex history of Canada by noting that the constitution, while written, was also supported by four (unwritten) 'fundamental and organizing principles of the Constitution'. These are 'federalism; democracy; constitutionalism and the rule of law; and respect for minorities'.[68] The Court did not find there to be any hierarchy among these principles, but it is not insignificant that federalism is the first to which it refers. The Court also considered there to be an intimate relationship between federalism and democracy which led it to the demos question. Here we see the demotic tension play out as the Court moves from a conception of Canada that chimes with a monist account of modern state constitutionalism—'The Constitution Act 1867 was an act of nation-building'[69]—to a notion that the demotic composition of Canada is at the same time more complex than this. The Court qualifies its 'nation-building' analysis. 'The federal-provincial division of powers was a legal recognition of the diversity that existed among the initial members of Confederation, and manifested a concern to accommodate that diversity within a single nation by granting significant powers to provincial governments.'[70] The concept of a single nation is seemingly qualified by diversity, with the Court reaching towards a distinctive definition of what federal nationhood looks like. It is also worth noting that the Court is emphasising demotic difference in a way that is largely absent from the Federalist Papers' account of early American identity, and certainly from later analysis by the US Supreme Court of the nature of the American demos.

This reference to diversity is in itself of little constitutional significance, but elsewhere in its Opinion the Court elaborates on the demotic underpinnings of the Canadian confederation. In doing so it begins to articulate how the populations of the provinces constitute specific 'majorities' or 'collectivities'. 'The relationship between democracy and federalism means, for example, that in Canada there may be different and equally legitimate majorities in different provinces and territories and at the federal level.'[71] Indeed, the purpose of federalism is to recognise this

[68] *Reference Re Secession of Quebec* [1998] 2 SCR 217, para. 32.
[69] *Secession Reference*, para. 43.
[70] *Secession Reference*, para. 43.
[71] *Secession Reference*, para. 66.

demotic plurality: 'The function of federalism is to enable citizens to participate concurrently in different collectivities and to pursue goals at both a provincial and a federal level.'[72] There is of course nothing revolutionary in this statement. It is a non-controversial, indeed banal, truth within federal theory that federalism allows citizens to participate in different 'collectivities'—provinces and the nation-state. But what is more significant is the description of provinces and the federal government as containing different and *equally legitimate* majorities. In linking constitutional legitimacy in general, and constitutional federalism in particular, back to democracy, the Court is opening up the question of constituent power—who holds it and what its salience might be; and in describing the demoi of the provinces as equally legitimate popular collectives to that of the national people as a whole, the Court does seem to suggest that what is being recognised is the existence of *plural constituent authorities* within Canada, in other words constituent collectives who sustain a particular constitutional authority in reflexive relationship to the particularity of Canadian constitutional foundations. There are other nods in this direction. For example, the Court also uses the term 'peoples'. It does so in reference to the constitutional moment in 1867 itself. Although creating a unified state, the moment of confederation was one 'in which *different peoples* could resolve their disagreements and work together toward common goals and a common interest. Federalism was the political mechanism by which diversity could be reconciled with unity.'[73] This is a starkly different narration from the 'We, the People' motif that dominated the Philadelphia process.

We are left therefore with a certain ambiguity. 1867 was a nation-building moment. But it was one in which different peoples came together to form that nation which, once built, contained a number of equally legitimate majorities. It was, in short, a nation of peoples, the prospect of which, in the context of the nascent United States, so horrified Madison. In this way we see the Supreme Court of Canada reconcile Canada as a nation on the one hand, entirely consonant with the relationship between nation and state that has been a central feature of constitutional modernity, with the categorical significance of federal constitutionalism on the other hand. This does not deny the modern idea of a nation and its connection to the state but it does serve to complicate this idea. Canada is a nation but one which contains discrete territorial peoples within it; a concept fully compatible with the federal idea.[74]

The Court addresses the implications of constitutionally recognised territorial pluralism when it turns to the issue of Quebec secession itself. It declares that under

[72] *Secession Reference*, para. 66.

[73] *Secession Reference*, para. 43.

[74] In 1996 Samuel La Selva distinguished American and Canadian approaches to nationhood as follows: 'American federalist theory has focused on the kind of government the nation should have; Canadian federalist theory has concerned itself with whether there is a nation at all.' S.V. La Selva, *The Moral Foundations of Canadian Federalism* (London: McGill-Queen's University Press, 1996), 38.

the constitution of Canada there is no right of unilateral secession. A province seeking to secede must do so through a process of negotiations with its 'partners in confederation' and through the processes for constitutional change embedded within the constitution. However, the Court qualifies this general statement in a crucial way. It is:

> unable to accept the . . . proposition, that a clear expression of self-determination by the people of Quebec would impose no obligations upon the other provinces or the federal government. The continued existence and operation of the Canadian constitutional order cannot remain indifferent to the clear expression of a clear majority of Quebecers that they no longer wish to remain in Canada . . . The rights of other provinces and the federal government cannot deny the right of the government of Quebec to pursue secession, should a clear majority of the people of Quebec choose that goal, so long as in doing so, Quebec respects the rights of others.[75]

Under the constitution of Canada, and in light of the interaction of the four constitutional principles which the Court identified, the secession of Quebec, if it satisfies certain procedural and substantive requirements, cannot be constitutionally resisted.

This is astonishing recognition not only of provincial constitutional constituent authority but that this authority entitles provinces to ultimate self-determination, even to the point of leaving, not only the federal constitution, but the state itself. A fundamental article of faith within the modern state-nation nexus, consolidated after the Second World War by international law, has been the immutability of state borders. Nonetheless, the Supreme Court of Canada connects constitutional constituent authority back to foundational constituent power; parties to the federal contract can withdraw from that contract provided they do so in a constitutionally correct manner, respecting the procedural and substantive requirements set out by the Court. Robert Schertzer, in his subtle account of the Supreme Court of Canada's role as a facilitator of different narratives of federalism (to which we return in Chapter 10), argues that the *Secession Reference* stands out as the classic example of a 'recognizing decision'; namely, a decision that recognises different visions of federalism and their contested nature rather than imposing one vision upon the polity.[76] I began the chapter by arguing that federalism as a constitutional form should be reflexive, adapting itself institutionally to the particular popular composition of the polity and to the evolution of its demotic identities. The Supreme

[75] *Secession Reference*, para. 92

[76] R. Schertzer, *The Judicial Role in a Diverse Federation: Lessons from the Supreme Court of Canada* (Toronto: University of Toronto Press, 2016), 155.

Court of Canada in the *Secession Reference* helped facilitate a reorientation of the constitution's very self-perception.[77]

In Chapter 4 we discussed how, within the constitutional theory of the unitary state, constituent power is deemed either to have been exhausted in the moment of constitutional foundation or, if it survives, doing so as an abstraction, a totemic notion of the 'sovereignty of the people' that has in fact been subsumed by the constitution. Insofar as constituent power remains exercisable it only does so in an extra-constitutional way, by a people over-throwing an existing constitutional order and establishing a new constitution. The Supreme Court of Canada's Opinion in the *Secession Reference* offers a starkly different account. Provinces within Canada retain the authority to secede, to leave the constitutional order entirely. Crucially, this is not articulated as an intangible political right—as an extra-constitutional exercise that asserts a new constituent power *contra* the authority of the constitution. Rather it is a right that exists within the constitution, even though not recognised explicitly by the text of the constitution. It is not a new foundational constituent power to establish a new constitution: that would manifest itself once the province was independent and had embarked upon the task of establishing a new constitution. The act of secession takes place within the existing constitution as a manifestation of the ultimate logic of constitutional constituent authority.

The constitutional, and internally structured, character of this provincial constituent authority is clear from the way in which the Court sets out to explain the rules that condition its exercise. The process must include 'principled negotiation' with other holders of constitutional constituent authority within the federal constitution.[78] At the same time as it recognises the deep normative salience of the provinces' constituent constitutional authority, the Court also recognises that the Canadian constitutional founding in 1867 *was* normatively transformative. The provinces which were party to the foundation of the constitution or which became party to it later in time did not remain effectively independent states that could revert to an independent status as and when they wished. The constitution was a deep commitment to union. As such, it involved the pooling of authority under the constitution—the establishment of the constitution as a third order of rule, allocating authority to the central and provincial levels of government. But the provinces were and remained the fundamental subjects of the polity. Although their status was transformed by the constitution into constitutional subjects, they retained a connection back to the foundational moment by virtue of the identity they

[77] Schertzer also sees the *Secession Reference* opinion as a gear shift in federalism. By his analysis, from 1980 to 1998, 'approximately 64% of the Court's decisions on federalism '*imposed* a federal model' whereas after the *Secession Reference* decision until 2010 approximately 71% of its decisions were of a 'recognizing' nature. Schertzer, *The Judicial Role in a Diverse Federation*, 220.

[78] *Secession Reference*, paras 93–95, 97. See further discussion in paras 100–101, 103–104, 106, 149.

had then, and which they retained within the constitution.[79] Referring to the particular situation of Quebec within the constitution, the Court stated:

> The principle of federalism facilitates the pursuit of collective goals by cultural and linguistic minorities which form the majority within a particular province. This is the case in Quebec, where the majority of the population is French-speaking, and which possesses a distinct culture. This is not merely the result of chance. The social and demographic reality of Quebec explains the existence of the province of Quebec as a political unit and indeed, was one of the essential reasons for establishing a federal structure for the Canadian union in 1867. The experience of both Canada East and Canada West under the *Union Act, 1840* (U.K.), 3-4 Vict., c. 35, had not been satisfactory. The federal structure adopted at Confederation enabled French-speaking Canadians to form a numerical majority in the province of Quebec, and so exercise the considerable provincial powers conferred by the *Constitution Act, 1867* in such a way as to promote their language and culture. It also made provision for certain guaranteed representation within the federal Parliament itself.[80]

It is therefore the case that the constitutional constituent authority of the provinces connects in a deep and real way back to that foundational constituent power.[81] And it is in consequence of that connection that the Supreme Court recognised Quebec's *prima facie*, albeit not unilateral, right to secede in certain circumstances. In this we see the specificity of the federal constitution—as combining the twin dimensions inherent in the federal idea, union and plurality; the two operating in tension but also in a complementary way through constitutional authority that is transformative, but which does not enervate the constituent authority, of the constitution's territorial subjects.

This demonstrates an understanding of the foundational constituent power–constitutional constituent authority relationship that is particular to Canadian federalism. It is by no means a universalisable understanding that applies to all federal constitutions. Indeed, a civil war was fought in the United States on the very question of whether constitutional constituent authority allowed states to secede. After that war, which confirmed by force of arms that secession from the United States was not a political possibility, the Supreme Court also made clear that secession was not a constitutional right. In that case, involving Texas, the Court noted

[79] The Supreme Court of Canada reflects upon the constituent power of the territories in the period leading up to confederation in 1867. *Secession Reference*, paras 34–41.

[80] *Secession Reference*, para. 59.

[81] Indeed, societal particularity was not exclusive to Quebec: 'Federalism was also welcomed by Nova Scotia and New Brunswick, both of which also affirmed their will to protect their individual cultures and their autonomy over local matters. All new provinces joining the federation sought to achieve similar objectives, which are no less vigorously pursued by the provinces and territories as we approach the new millennium.' *Secession Reference*, para. 60.

that the constitution was promulgated, per its preamble, 'in Order to form a more perfect Union'. This, in the eyes of the Court, precluded any possibility of unilateral secession under the constitution. The 'constitution, in all its provisions, looks to an indestructible Union, composed of indestructible States'.[82]

> When ... Texas became one of the United States, she entered into an indissoluble relation ... All the obligations of perpetual union, and all the guaranties of republican government in the Union, attached at once to the State. The act which consummated her admission into the Union was something more than a compact; it was the incorporation of a new member into the political body. And it was final. The union between Texas and the other States was as complete, as perpetual, and as indissoluble as the union between the original States.[83]

A similar conclusion has been drawn in Australia. The preamble of the constitution is similar to that of the US. 'The people' of the colonies 'have agreed to unite in one indissoluble Federal Commonwealth'. It is generally taken to be the case that the constitution of Australia prohibits secession. This has been the case since an attempt by Western Australia to secede in the 1930s.[84] A joint select Committee of the UK Parliament, looking into the legality of the matter concluded:

> The [Commonwealth of Australia Constitution] Act gives no power to any State to secede. The Commonwealth itself has no power to amend the Constitution to the extent of enabling any State to secede. It is only by legislation in the Parliament of the United Kingdom, therefore, that the dissolution of the Commonwealth or the secession of any of its constituent parts can be effected.[85]

Even in the modern context where Australians of course do not recognise the UK Parliament as in any meaningful way the source of the legitimacy or authority of the Australian constitution, there is a widespread view that the constitution of Australia does not recognise a right to secede.[86]

Others have noted that Australian federalism was born from a situation of strong national identity, even stronger than the nascent national identity that marked the birth of American federalism. Kenneth Wheare observed that the Australian territories shared a 'sense of Australian nationality ...' long before the two major constitutional conventions in 1891 and 1897–1898 that led to federation in 1901. For

[82] *Texas v. White* [1868] 74 U.S. 700, 725.

[83] *Texas v. White*, 726.

[84] G. Craven, *Secession: The Ultimate States Right* (Melbourne: Melbourne University Press, 1986).

[85] Report by the Joint Committee of the House of Lords and the House of Commons appointed to consider the Petition of the State of Western Australia (UK Parliament House of Commons Parliamentary Papers, 1935).

[86] N. Aroney, 'Australia', in L. Moreno and C. Colino, *Diversity and Unity in Federal Countries* (Montreal: McGill-Queen's University Press, 2010), 30.

Wheare there were therefore 'Australians before there was an Australia'.[87] Aroney echoes this point in relation to Australia today, where there exists among the states only 'subtle variations in political culture'.[88] Other federal countries have also been founded in the name of a common peoplehood. For example, the constitution of Austria declares: 'Austria is a democratic republic. Its law emanates from the people.'[89] The Swiss Federal Constitution preamble, by contrast, recognises both the people of Switzerland and the Cantons.[90] In Germany the notion that the constitution might contain any right of secession was rejected in 2016.[91] The reasoning of the Court was founded expressly upon a monist conception of the demos. In addressing the question of a possible referendum on the secession of Bavaria, the Constitutional Court stated that the German federation was based upon the constituent power of the German people conceived in singular terms.[92] The secession of individual *Länder* was inconsistent with this and would be contrary to the constitution. Notably the Constitutional Court in Spain has sought to disavow the very idea of the Spanish constitution as a territorial pact. The Spanish Constitution of 1978 is not, according to the Spanish Constitutional Court, the result of any federal pact between prior existing entities, but a product of the will of the Spanish people as the exclusive holders of sovereignty.[93] This has been part of broader approach that considers secession inherently incompatible with the constitution's commitment to 'the indissoluble unity of the Spanish nation, the common and indivisible country of all Spaniards . . .'[94]

Federal constitutions can of course be founded upon the basis of indissolubility. In fact, there is a strong argument that a constitution containing a route to its own demise or allowing parties to leave makes no sense; that exit is always an unconstitutional or at least extra-constitutional act. Lincoln famously argued that 'perpetuity is implied, if not expressed, in the fundamental law of all national governments. It is safe to assert that no government proper ever had a provision in its organic law for its own termination.'[95] This asserts secession, without federal consent expressed through the amendment process, to be an inherently revolutionary act within a federal constitution. This was the view also taken by the US Supreme

[87] K.C. Wheare, 'Federalism and the Making of Nations', in A.W. Macmahon (ed.), *Federalism: Mature and Emergent* (New York: Columbia University Press, 1955), 28–43, 35.

[88] Aroney, 'Australia', 16–46, 19.

[89] Constitution of Austria, art. 1.

[90] Preamble to the Constitution of Switzerland, 'In the name of Almighty God! The Swiss People and the Cantons . . . adopt the following Constitution . . .'

[91] 2 BvR 349/16, BVerfG 16 December 2016.

[92] The Court was unequivocal that the *Länder* are not 'Masters of the Constitution' (*Herren des Grundgesetzes*). German Federal Constitutional Court, BVerfG, Beschluss, 16 December 2016, 2 BvR. 349/16.

[93] Constitutional Court of Spain, Judgments 76/1988, 247/2007, 31/2010, 42/2014. I am grateful to Pau Bossacoma i Busquets for discussion on this and related points.

[94] Constitution of Spain, art. 2.

[95] First Inaugural Address of Abraham Lincoln, 4 March 1861.

Court in *Texas v. White*. In stating that the union between Texas was indissoluble, the Court qualified this by noting there is 'no place for reconsideration or revocation, except through revolution or through consent of the States'.[96] The Court acknowledges that secession as a matter of fact can occur and that secession can even be facilitated by the Article V processes of constitutional amendment. What it rejects is that it is a unilateral constitutional right of any individual state, founded either upon territorial constituent power or constitutional constituent authority. In the end, the contrasting approaches taken by the Supreme Courts of the USA and Canada demonstrate that the federal idea leaves the question of secession to each constitution to manage, depending upon how it envisages the nature of constituent constitutional authority within its own polity.[97]

IV. Concluding remarks

Federal constitutionalism is founded through collective territorial subjecthood. Beyond this bare but crucial fact it leaves the demos question open for each federal constitution to navigate. This chapter has discussed two implications of this. The first is that constituent territories are fundamental constitutional subjects but their subjecthood has been neglected within a monist constitutionalist mindset that focuses almost exclusively upon individual citizenship. A second conclusion is that the federal constitution caters for differing forms of normative transformation in the nature and legal status of its territorial subjects than are possible in relation to individual citizens. It is possible for coherent sub-state demoi to be maintained within the constitution's demotic identity, and for these to remain constitutionally salient—relating to the polity through discrete relations of constitutional sovereignty: what I have termed constitutional constituent authority. This salience will depend upon the nature of the federal constitution and how it develops in reflection of plural identities over time, responding to the ongoing resilience or, alternatively, the dissipation of these identities. The contrasting approaches taken to the nature and significance of constituent territorial identities by constitutional courts illustrate this.

Ultimately, subjecthood in a federal system brings to the table the authority generative dimension of sovereignty, defining the subjects who warrant the constitution's ongoing legitimacy. In some federal constitutions, such as that of the United States, a republican vision sets the constitution on a trajectory whereby the very possibility of an original, pluralised conception of constituent power is

[96] *Texas v. White*, 726.

[97] For a thorough and sophisticated account of the theoretical issues at stake see P. Bossacoma Busquets, *Morality and Legality of Secession: A Theory of National Self-Determination* (London: Palgrave, 2019).

supplanted by a conception of individualised popular sovereignty, resulting in a conception of authority generation encapsulated in 'the people' that would become over time no different from the demotic backdrop of a unitary constitution. In other federal systems, where the salience of certain territorial identities remained strong, there is a much more complex story to be told about the validatory foundations of constitutional authority, involving not only individual citizens but the constituent constitutional authority of the territories themselves. We addressed Canada as an example. In an age of deep territorial cleavages, this example seems to offer a more realistic and indeed fruitful template for other countries developing federal constitutions in recognition of the plural sources of territorial constituent power that come together in these moments of constitution-making. In Chapters 8–10 we will explore how constitutional constituent authority remains a coherent political and legal resource across federal systems in the institutional life of most federal polities, albeit that it has in many cases been subordinated by a competing and overriding sense of a singular demotic self.

7
The Purpose and Principles of Federalism

I. Introduction

The function of any constitution is to transform political power into lawful authority. Each constitution does this in its own way and for its own purpose. It is also the case that certain constitutions perform this function in a sufficiently similar manner to warrant categorisation as particular families of constitutionalism. Federalism is such a genus of government: a federal constitution transforms political power into legal authority for a specific purpose; it is the aim of this chapter to explain this.

In Chapters 3, 4, and 5 we explored the nature of this transformation and its particular character in the history of modern constitutionalism. From these building blocks a definition of federalism can be offered that draws out the core, immanent, or 'meta' purpose that is, by definition, shared by all federal constitutions. Federalism is a specific genus of constitutional government for the modern state which, in the act of constitutional union, gives foundational recognition and accommodation to the state's constituent territorial pluralism. The purpose of the federal constitution is both to foster this foundational pluralism and to maintain the constitutional relationship between pluralism and union in the creation and reconciliation of different orders of government. From this definition flows a set of constitutional principles that underpin the purpose of federalism. The term 'principles' is used here not in the moral-normative sense of 'morally correct behaviour and attitudes', but rather in an ontological way: 'principles' as the logical implication or 'chain of reasoning'[1] that flows from the foundational character of federalism as a particular form of constitutional rule.[2] Principles, in this sense, do not attribute to federalism an externally derived narrative of 'the good'; rather they are the precepts that inhere to, and stem from, its constitutional purpose.

[1] Oxford English Dictionary.

[2] It is also the case that any constitution, whether federal or otherwise, is characterised by principles that flow as a matter of logic from the purpose of the constitution and implicitly from the text of the constitution. The Supreme Court of Canada observed this in its discussion of the principles which it identified as underpinning confederation: 'Although these underlying principles are not explicitly made part of the Constitution by any written provision, other than in some respects by the oblique reference in the preamble to the Constitution Act, 1867, it would be impossible to conceive of our constitutional structure without them. The principles dictate major elements of the architecture of the Constitution itself and are as such its lifeblood.' *Reference re Secession of Quebec* [1998] 2 SCR 217, para. 51.

The Federal Contract. Stephen Tierney, Oxford University Press. © Stephen Tierney 2022.
DOI: 10.1093/oso/9780198806745.003.0007

In this chapter I begin by distinguishing constitutional purpose from the political purposes that are often ascribed to federalism. I categorise these political purposes as instances either of 'strategic instrumentalism' or 'ideological instrumentalism', echoing the wrong turns taken in attempts to define federalism which we explored in Chapter 2. I argue, *contra* these approaches, that the purpose of federalism as a generic order of constitutional rule can only be properly understood by way of constitutional theory. Constitutional theory also leads us to the principles that flow logically from the meta-purpose of federalism. These, it is suggested, are recognition, autonomous government, associational government, and both vertical and horizontal reciprocity.

II. Attempts to elicit federalism's purpose: strategic and moral instrumentalism

In much of the political studies literature on federalism, 'purposes' takes on a categorically different character from an approach founded in constitutionalism. Constitutional theory seeks to explain how the generic foundational constitutional purpose and principles of federalism together set the federal polity upon a particular legal-normative path. By contrast, within politics scholarship there is a tendency to focus not upon the constitutional dimension of federalism as a particular type of polity, but rather upon the specific political intentions that are deemed to lie behind the creation of each federal system, emphasising the importance of the political motives of political actors, or deeper behavioural or structural undercurrents, influencing the moment of foundation; addressing why political actors chose a federal polity rather than explaining the detailed constitutional legal order in which this choice resulted. In fact, the significance of the very act of constitutionalisation is apt to be downplayed. The constitution is taken merely to be an instrumental vehicle through which political goals relating to, *inter alia*, human nature, economics, democratic stability, and state security are advanced.

While political motives are certainly significant in the formation of a federal constitution, as they are in the creation of any polity, my central claim is that these political imperatives, which are so diverse and at times mutually contradictory, cannot by themselves draw out the essence of the federal idea. This can only be derived from the foundationally fundamental fact of its constitutional instantiation and the legal-normative consequences this bears.

Across the vast literature on federalism all manner of political purposes have been ascribed to federal government. These can be categorised into two main groups: pragmatic purposes associated with building a strong state ('strategic instrumentalism') and ideological purposes which ascribe to the constitutional founding the advancement of a particular set of political values ('ideological instrumentalism'), the latter typically assessing whether federalism assists or inhibits the establishment and consolidation of a liberal polity. Within these two general groups, six further specific purposes can be identified: three relating to statehood and three to the maximisation of individual freedom, as this is understood by liberalism. I consider these six instrumental purposes in turn.

One historical trend in federal formation is the bringing together of territories into one state through a process of decolonisation. Examples include the United States of America, Canada, Australia, India, and Nigeria, each of which emerged through a gradual or an abrupt constitutional break with the United Kingdom. These territories were either already administered as one colony or dominion but in a territorially disaggregated way, or, notably in the case of the United States, Australia, and India, were composed of multiple territories independent of each other but subject ultimately to central colonial control. It followed that the post-colonial constitution of the newly independent, and unified, state gave recognition to the pre-existing reality of territorial pluralism, albeit in new and differing ways. In such a situation, recognition of territorial pluralism was not necessarily valued as a good in itself but as the only feasible way to forge both a new state and a new constitution. The consolidation of a large but diverse decolonising polity is therefore often presented as a strategic purpose behind federal constitutionalism.

A second political purpose which is frequently attached to the birth of federalism is the efficient administration of the state and the fostering of a national economy. This was a particular concern for states which cover large and, at the time of their creation, growing, territorial spaces, such as the USA, Canada, and Australia, as well as the nineteenth-century German Federation, and in the twentieth century the decolonising states of India, Nigeria, and Indonesia, which are also deeply pluralised. As with post-colonial unification, federalism is, upon this register, not envisioned primarily as a way to foster diversity; rather the pluralisation of government is a vehicle through which the state's central power can be channelled and made more manageable.[3]

A third purpose relating to state-building is the consolidation of state borders, security, and defence in the face of external threats.[4] One of the main defects identified in the Articles of Confederation system was the absence of strong central government, which left the American states vulnerable to foreign invasion.[5] As

[3] As John Stuart Mill put it in 1861: 'There is a limit to the extent of country which can advantageously be governed, or even whose government can be conveniently superintended from a single centre.' J.S. Mill, *Considerations on Representative Government* (London: Parker, Son and Bourn, 1861), Ch. XVII; J.S. Mill, *Utilitarianism, On Liberty and Considerations on Representative Government* H.B. Acton (ed.) (London: J.M. Dent & Sons, 1972).

[4] K.C. Wheare, *Federal Government*, 4th edn (London: Oxford University Press, 1963), 37. Riker famously argued that the construction of a strong system of common defence was *the* key motivation behind American federalism and, by extension, other federal systems: W. Riker, *Federalism: Origin, Operation, Significance* (Boston: Little, Brown and Company, 1964), 13; *The Development of American Federalism* (USA: Kluwer Academic Publisher, 1987), 11. This value was addressed in Chapter 4 in the context of nation-building.

[5] James Madison, Federalist No. 22 and see also Federalist 23–29, C. Rossiter (ed.), *The Federalist Papers* (New York: New American Library, 1961), 152–187.

Diamond argues, delegates measured the Articles 'by standards appropriate to nations because they wanted from the central body what only a national government could supply'.[6] In this respect, territorial pluralism and the multiplicity of governments which it implied, far from being taken to be a value, was seen as potentially dangerous to the welfare of the new polity. A variation of this argument is that a federal system, by fostering a common system of protection, also helps prevent small units from warring among themselves.[7] Federalism, if the only way to bring territories together, can therefore be considered to serve a useful purpose, but from this perspective it tends also to be seen as sub-optimal when compared to a unitary constitution: 'The great teaching of *The Federalist* is not how to be federal in a better way, but how to be better by being less federal.'[8] This strain within American constitutional thinking has been instrumental over time in setting the US on a centralising path, envisaging the quest for 'a more perfect union' to lie in a strong central government; a mindset that influenced constitution-making in other federal systems.

Together these three strategic instrumental approaches do not therefore focus upon territorially located societal pluralism as the core purpose of a federal constitution. Rather, they try to make a virtue of this reality by taking the (for many, unfortunate) fact of territorial pluralism and creating a constitution that will steer the polity in the direction of a strong, unified state with a primary focus upon unity and centralised government.[9]

[6] M. Diamond, 'What the Framers Meant by Federalism', in R.A. Goldwin (ed.), *A Nation of States: Essays on the American Federal System* (Chicago: Rand McNally, 1964), 24–41, 39. See also J. Jay, Federalist No. 4, Rossiter, *The Federalist Papers*, 45–50. This criticism extended to the lack of central authority over economic decision-making and the unsettled issue of supremacy, both strong features of the Federalist critique of the Articles of Confederation: A.R. Amar, 'Of Sovereignty and Federalism' (1987) 96 *Yale Law Journal* 1425–1520.

[7] Mill offers this view. He takes Switzerland as an example of a state held together by common defence even in the face of strong religious and other differences: 'The common interest arising from this cause has in Switzerland, for several centuries, been found adequate to maintain efficiently the federal bond, in spite not only of difference of religion when religion was the grand source of irreconcilable political enmity throughout Europe, but also in spite of the great weakness in the constitution of the federation itself.' J.S. Mill, 'Of Federative Representative Governments', in *Considerations of Representative Government*, Ch. XVII. A related advantage in creating a federal constitution, relevant in light of our discussion in the last chapter, is that it can help contain secessionism. This is the context in which federalism was addressed by Dicey: 'to reconcile the apparently inconsistent claims of national sovereignty and of state sovereignty . . .' A.V. Dicey, *Introduction to the Study of the Law of the Constitution*, 8th edn (London: Macmillan, 1915), 139. Dicey was of course preoccupied with the threat of Irish Home Rule. The danger of secession remains a key factor in debates concerning federalism in South Asia: M.G. Breen, 'The Origins of Holding-Together Federalism: Nepal, Myanmar, and Sri Lanka' (2018) 48 *Publius: The Journal of Federalism* 26–50.

[8] M. Diamond, 'The Federalist's View of Federalism', in G.C.S. Benson (ed.), *Essays in Federalism* (Claremont: Institute for Studies in Federalism, 1962), 21–64, 40.

[9] This tradition of assessing federalism through the lens of state-building instrumentalism remains core to federal scholarship today. Ronald Watts, in one of his final contributions to federal scholarship, cited approvingly various recent empirical studies which 'have indicated that federal political systems have, on balance, actually facilitated political integration . . . better than non-federal systems'. R.L. Watts, 'The Federal Idea and its Contemporary Relevance', in T.L. Courchene et al., *The Federal Idea: Essays in Honour of Ronald L. Watts* (Kingston-Montreal: McGill-Queen's, 2011), 13–27, 25–26. Notably, integration rather than pluralism was advanced by Watts as the benchmark of success.

A second group of political purposes ascribed to federalism derives from the presupposition that its primary goal is to serve certain ideological ends, largely derived from the methodological individualism of liberalism. The first of these is the notion that federalism is instrumentally useful in limiting public power by multiplying the sites of, and hence diffusing the threat to liberty posed by, government.[10] In this way federalism becomes just another weapon within a wider arsenal of separated powers and checks and balances in liberalism's battle to constrain political power.[11] Madison viewed public power as a threat to private liberty. Federalism was for him a form of government restraint which would adapt America's territorial pluralism towards the greater good of liberal republicanism.[12] In the emerging United States, federalism would bring the states together to build a unified nation. While a strong central government was greatly desirable to overcome the perceived weaknesses of the Articles of Confederation, a pluralisation of government would, despite the risk of weakening the national government, nonetheless help decrease the attendant danger of tyranny which Madison feared would accompany the centralisation of public authority.[13] In a number of the Federalist papers Hamilton and Madison express concern about the risk to private interests posed by over-weaning government, although they each, in different ways, argued against the strong presumption of the age that liberty could only survive in small polities.[14] Federalism

[10] J. Madison, Federalist No. 10, Rossiter, *The Federalist Papers*, 77–84, 77–78. See also J. Bryce, *The American Commonwealth*, 3 vols (London: Macmillan & Co. Ltd, 1919), vol. I, 350–353; S. Beer, *To Make a Nation: The Rediscovery of American Federalism* (Cambridge MA: Belknap, 1993), 38–88. Alan Taylor observes: '[T]he founders did not intend to create a national democracy. Instead, they designed a national republic to restrain state democracies, which they blamed for the union's woes.' A. Taylor, *American Revolutions: A Continental History, 1750–1804* (New York: W.W. Norton & Co., 2016), 373.

[11] In the US context Amar argues that there are 'powerful analogies between separation of powers and federalism, the two great structural principles of the Constitution.' Amar, 'Of Sovereignty and Federalism', 1493. He also observes: 'As with separation of powers, federalism enabled the American People to conquer government power by dividing it.' Amar, 'Of Sovereignty and Federalism', 1450.

[12] J. Madison, Federalist No. 51, Rossiter, *The Federalist Papers*, 320–325. In this paper he draws a clear connection between federalism and separation of powers. Bryce adapted this argument by suggesting that locating government at more local levels strengthens the capacity of citizens to oversee it. Bryce, *The American Commonwealth*, vol. I, 350–353.

[13] 'In a single republic, all the power surrendered by the people is submitted to the administration of a single government; and the usurpations are guarded against by a division of the government into distinct and separate departments. In the compound republic of America, the power surrendered by the people is first divided between two distinct governments, and then the portion allotted to each subdivided among distinct and separate departments. Hence a double security arises to the rights of the people. The different governments will control each other, at the same time that each will be controlled by itself.' J. Madison, Federalist No. 51, Rossiter, *The Federalist Papers*, 320–325, 323.

[14] This notion is famously associated with Montesquieu: 'It is, therefore, very probable that mankind would have been, at length, obliged to live constantly under the government of a single person, had they not contrived a kind of constitution that has all the internal advantages of a republican, together with the external force of a monarchical, government. I mean a confederate republic.... As this government is composed of petty republics, it enjoys the internal happiness of each; and with respect to its external situation, by means of the association, it possesses all the advantages of large monarchies.' C. de Secondat, Baron de Montesquieu, , ,*The Spirit of Laws* (London: Collingwood, 1823), vol. I, Book IX, Ch. I. Hamilton and Madison took issue with this argument for different reasons. Hamilton believed that careful institutional design would avert the risk of tyranny. A. Hamilton, Federalist No. 9, Rossiter, *The Federalist Papers*, 71–76. Madison went further, turning Montesquieu's argument on its head. A large population represented by a plurality of governments would lead to a complex matrix of

becomes in this way what we might call the 'Madisonian compromise': limiting government through its proliferation, and weakening it by creating more of it. Madison indeed spoke in favour of a 'compound republic' where there would be the 'double security' for liberty in both a vertical division of powers between two levels of government and a horizontal separation of powers within each level.[15] This focus upon federalism as an additional check on government also became a well-worn trope within American constitutional jurisprudence.[16]

A further motivation behind federalism flows from this, namely the pursuit of economic competition and accordingly, in terms of the liberal credo, enhanced economic efficiency. A common argument, again deriving initially from the American experience, is that the presence of a number of separately governed territories within a state creates competition among them; this encourages a number of innovations, for example regional policy experiments, which, if successful, can then be extrapolated elsewhere in the state.[17]

The economic efficiency argument can blend into a third liberal goal attributed to federalism: the maximisation of individual choice through competition. With a range of territorial jurisdictions within which the individual can choose to live or businesses to operate, competition will develop among these territories and their governments in the search for economic advantage, with subsequent benefits for

cross-cutting interests from state to state; and this would in turn be more likely than a small republic to avert the risk of factional domination: J. Madison, Federalist No. 10, Rossiter, *The Federalist Papers*, 77–84. See also Q. Taylor, '"A System Without a Precedent": The Federalism of the Federalist Papers', in A. Ward and L. Ward, *Ashgate Research Companion to Federalism* (Farnham: Ashgate, 2016) 175–192, 177–178; J. Madison, Federalist No. 45 and No. 46, Rossiter, *The Federalist Papers*, 288–294.

15 J. Madison, Federalist No. 51, Rossiter, *The Federalist Papers*, 320–325, 324. Crucially for Madison it was the constitutionalisation of power that was vital here. As Amar puts it in discussing Federalist 51: 'Madison's point here is crisper than the cliché that diffusion of political power will generally prevent tyranny. He implies that the Constitution's structure of government will help assure compliance with the specific legal rights established by that instrument.' Akhil Reed Amar, 'Of Sovereignty and Federalism', 1493. In this way, the creation of different sites of government was a more secure way of tightly constraining the exercise of government than mere 'parchment barriers against the encroaching spirit of power'. J. Madison, The Federalist No. 48, Rossiter, *The Federalist Papers*, 308–313, 308.

16 'Perhaps the principal benefit of the federalist system is a check on abuses of government power.' O'Connor J. in *Gregory v. Ashcroft* (90-50), 501 U.S. 452 (1991); *Garcia v. San Antonio Metropolitan Transit Authority*, 469 U.S. 528, 572 (1985) (Powell J., dissenting).

17 This approach found favour within 'rational choice' theorising, popular in the middle of the last century, e.g. in Tiebout's theory of 'sorting', which involved a form of market modelling of residential choice among jurisdictions made by citizens. Tiebout argued that people sort themselves into jurisdictional spaces that best suit their economic interests in relation to taxing and spending policy. C.M. Tiebout, 'A Pure Theory of Local Expenditures' (1956) 64 *Journal of Political Economy* 416–424. The argument also finds support in American jurisprudence. In *New State Ice Co. v. Liebmann* 285 U.S. 262, 310 (1932) (Brandeis J., dissenting), Justice Brandeis stated: 'one of the happy incidents of the federal system that a single courageous state may, if its citizens choose, serve as a laboratory; and try novel social and economic experiments without risk to the rest of the country . . .'. Another advantage associated with this purpose is that errors can be spotted locally and avoided elsewhere. M. Landau, 'Federalism, Redundancy and System Reliability' (1973) 3 *Publius* 173–196. For a sceptical view of the experimentation 'advantage' see Hueglin and Fenna who suggest that it can put pressure on governments to privilege business interests at the expense of national welfare standards. T.O. Hueglin and A. Fenna, *Comparative Federalism: A Systematic Inquiry*, 2nd edn (Toronto: University of Toronto Press, 2015), 45–46.

the citizen whose best interests are, according to a liberal world view, conceived largely in individualistic terms and premised upon a capitalist system of *laissez faire* economic liberty.[18] The third liberal purpose attributed to federalism can therefore combine with the first (limiting government by dividing it). In this way federalism is viewed as valuable for the way in which it can shield capitalism from strong, centralised democracy.[19]

In these six purposes, centred as they are in different manifestations of political instrumentalism, we get little sense that federalism is primarily a discrete constitutional category or that its fundamental purpose must be understood through the register of constitutionalism, except insofar as constitutionalism is conceived as a strong bulwark against over-reaching government power. Rather than being understood as a model of government that constitutionally recognises and accommodates societal pluralism across territories, it is in fact often envisaged as a mechanism with which to *overcome* territorial difference in pursuit of common goals for a societally unified polity. Madison took the view that institutional arrangements in a large republic would produce 'rational, deliberate majorities' that embody 'the permanent aggregate interests of the community'.[20] Furthermore, the territorial diversification of government is evaluated in essentially individualist terms, all within an essentially monist demotic register. Therefore, the six main political goals attributed to federalism coalesce around one common aim that characterises liberal nation-building more broadly: the fostering of a unitary demos within a strong state by way of a constitution that maximises individual freedom.[21]

[18] Each of the latter two arguments are put forward by Justice O'Connor in her Opinion in *Gregory v Ashcroft*: 'This federalist structure of joint sovereigns preserves to the people numerous advantages. It assures a decentralized government that will be more sensitive to the diverse needs of a heterogeneous society; it increases opportunity for citizen involvement in democratic processes; it allows for more innovation and experimentation in government; and it makes government more responsive by putting the States in competition for a mobile citizenry.' *Gregory v. Ashcroft*, 501 U.S. 452, 458 (1991) (O'Connor J.).

[19] Hamilton was unequivocal in the value he saw in pluralised government. 'There is one transcendent advantage belonging to the province of the State governments', namely, their role as 'the immediate and visible guardian of life and property'. A. Hamilton, Federalist No. 17, Rossiter, *The Federalist Papers*, 118–122, 120. Madison also associated property interests with the distribution of constitutional competences. 'The powers reserved to the several States will extend to all the objects which, in the ordinary course of affairs, concern the lives, liberties, and properties of the people ...'. J. Madison, Federalist No. 45, Rossiter, *The Federalist Papers*, 292–293. See also R.A. McGuire, *To Form a More Perfect Union: A New Economic Interpretation of the United States Constitution* (New York: Oxford University Press, 2003).

[20] J. Madison, Federalist No. 10, Rossiter, *The Federalist Papers*, 77–84.

[21] I have observed in earlier chapters that German federalism belongs to a different tradition. But those who focus upon the continental practice of federalism also tend to ascribe to it instrumental goals comparable to those attributed to American federalism, even if the normative instrumentalism takes on a more social democratic character. Hueglin and Fenna, *Comparative Federalism: A Systematic Inquiry*, 2nd edn, 114–115. The break-up of Prussia into a number of *Bundeslaender* in the birth of the federal constitution in 1949 is another example of the multiplication of territories being viewed as a defence against strong central rule. M. Umbach, *German Federalism: Past, Present and Future* (London: Palgrave, 2002), 207–208. See also C. Clark, *Iron Kingdom: The Rise and Downfall of Prussia, 1600–1947* (Cambridge MA: Harvard University Press, 2006).

Because the road to and from Philadelphia is one in which constitutional actors have attempted to mould federalism to meet a series of essentially political purposes—efforts which often distort the federal contract itself—subsequent commentators have found great difficulty in distilling the territorial pluralism that represents its essence as a constitutional idea and have instead attempted to articulate its constitutional purpose from these political strategies. In the end, we can identify three main distorting effects of this tradition of federal thinking and federal practice. The first is over-inclusiveness. Instrumentalist reasons presented for a federal constitution are in fact reasons for either state- and constitution-building in general or, more specifically, liberal state- or constitution-building in particular. For example, Riker's account of federal origins centres upon the claim that a material external or internal threat is central to the creation of any federal system.[22] Watts refutes this: 'while this factor has been important in a number of cases ... there are a number of other instances, such as Australia, where it was clearly not a major factor'.[23] However, Watts himself offers a long list of political reasons for federal formation which is so extensive that it can tell us very little about the constitutional specificity of the federal idea.[24] We see over-inclusiveness also within federal jurisprudence. I have noted the opinion of Justice O'Connor in *Gregory v. Ashcroft*, observing that it largely mirrors the main ideological instrumentalities advanced by liberal theory for a federal constitutional system. Despite a passing and somewhat vague reference to 'the diverse needs of a heterogeneous society' this opinion is so broad in the values it ascribes to federalism as to offer little if anything to explain or justify a constitutional foundation focused upon territorial pluralism.[25] A related point is that many of the purported merits of federalism could be achieved without it. To take the 'laboratory' argument, Jacob Levy argues:

> In its most technocratic understanding the metaphor is basically unrelated to federalism. A unitary state can order competing pilot projects to identify the best way to solve an agreed-on problem, and (as scholars of quasi-experiments in public policy know all too well) the policies that provinces just happen to adopt on their own are rarely well designed to allow precise and straightforward technical comparisons.[26]

[22] W. Riker, *Federalism: Origin, Operation, Significance* (Boston: Little, Brown and Company, 1964). 13.

[23] R.L. Watts, *Comparing Federal Systems*, 3rd edn (Montreal, QC, Canada: McGill-Queen's University Press, 2008), 63. Hueglin and Fenna also accuse Riker of 'over-simplifying', pointing out that German political union in the nineteenth century was principally inspired by economic integration and the desire for a customs union. Hueglin and Fenna, *Comparative Federalism: A Systematic Inquiry*. 2nd edn, 102.

[24] Watts, *Comparing Federal Systems*, 3rd edn, 66.

[25] This was discussed in Chapter 2. See also M. Feeley and E. Rubin, *On Federalism: Federalism as Tragic Choice* (University of Michigan Press, 2008), 22–24.

[26] J.T. Levy, 'Federalism, Liberalism, and the Separation of Loyalties' (2007) 101 *American Political Science Review* 459–477, 461.

Federal systems also do not necessarily provide optimally sized spaces for these types of policy experiment.

A second problem with instrumentalist approaches is that they can assume that the purpose of a constitutional enterprise is entirely deducible from practice. The risk in such a method, as we explored in Chapter 2, is that we alight upon a purported purpose and consequent principles of federalism that stem from the contingencies, and indeed accidents, of history. Several confusing effects flow from this assumption. One is that the search for purpose and principles becomes in effect an exercise in description, and as such of limited help is trying to define a genus of constitutionalism. We see this for example in the work of Rufus Davis, who describes the 'inescapable federal principle' as follows: 'that those matters of a "national", "general", or "common" interest should be vested in the central government, while matters of a "local" or "particular" interest should be left in the hands of the regional governments'.[27] Federal 'principle' is thus derived entirely from observing the most basic manifestation of federal practice. A further distraction is that the genus can come to be defined through one particularly influential instance of practice; I track throughout the book how the powerful influence of American constitutionalism has overwhelmed efforts to explain the purpose of federalism as an idea. A related difficulty is that the differing precedential influence of various federal systems can mean that instrumental purposes derived from one system can be extrapolated from the highly specific to the general. Certain purposes which may well have influenced dominant actors in the foundation of one polity but which were irrelevant to those in other states nonetheless come to be understood as part of federalism's generic purpose.[28]

This hints at a third major problem in instrumentalist approaches: that widely different and even conflicting purposes can emerge if we seek to define federalism by way of political ideology. Political actors who are instrumental in the foundation of one federal system may see it as a vehicle for maximising competition and hence individual freedom on a rational choice calculus; a possible consequence of this is deep disparities of wealth from one constituent territory to another. Alternatively, elites in another may see it as a way of pursuing social solidarity across a large space, intending federalism to bring with it equalisation corrections in tax yield and spending across the polity. The very meaning of federalism can thus become caught in an ideological trap, defined by its consequences and interpreted through widely differing prisms of political values. If one's primary goal is strong government, federalism's governmental pluralism can be seen as a pathological weakness;[29] if one overlays federalism with the prioritisation of a universalised

[27] S. Rufus Davis, *Theory and Reality: Federal Ideas in Australia, England and Europe* (Queensland: University of Queensland Press, 1995), 46.

[28] We see this e.g. in Riker's assessment of security concerns above.

[29] Dicey, a firm sceptic of any form of government that would adversely affect parliamentary supremacy, stated: 'Federal government means weak government.' Dicey, *Introduction to the Study of the Law of the Constitution*, 8th edn, 167.

conception of individual rights, federalism can come to be seen as a threat to this vision should particular territories within a federal polity adopt policies that are considered harmful to individual rights.[30] It is not my intention to argue for or against any particular ideological position on the merits or demerits of a federal system of government, but simply to observe that an approach based upon political instrumentalism, often overlain by moral constructivism, does not arrive at a generic constitutional purpose of federalism but instead tends to supplant definition with evaluation.

III. The constitutional purpose of federalism

My task, in contrast with those founded in political instrumentalism, is to elicit the particular *constitutional* purpose of federalism as a form of constitutional practice. It is of course the case that the federal constitution, like any constitution, is founded by political actors who seek in doing so to advance particular strategic or ideological political goals. But as we established in Chapter 3, the normative significance of a constitutional founding is a categorically different concern from the political motivations that bring a constitution into being. The very act of constitutionalising sets a polity on a particular legal path: it shapes the polity by husbanding political power within an authoritative institutional structure and it gives constitutional status to the constitution's constituent subjects, thereby helping to form their public identity. Our interest therefore is in the inherent rationale—which must by definition be shared by all systems bearing the name federal—for re-ordering political rule into lawful authority in a federal rather than a unitary way.

The purpose of a federal constitution is both to foster this foundational pluralism and to maintain the constitutional relationship between pluralism and union in the creation and reconciliation of different orders of government. The foundational constitutional pluralism of federalism therefore takes on a highly particular character, focused as it is upon territory. This must be clearly distinguished from other types of social diversity, in particular cultural pluralism, which is concerned with cultural particularity that is not principally tied to territory.[31] An error can easily flow from an over-generalisation of the link between diversity and federalism's inherent purpose. Feeley and Rubin argue correctly that diversity in

[30] Hueglin and Fenna, *Comparative Federalism: A Systematic Inquiry*, 2nd edn, 45. See also J. Vickers, 'The Gender-and-Federalism Research Field: Past, Present and Future', in John Kincaid (ed.), *A Research Agenda for Federalism Studies* (Cheltenham: Edward Elgar, 2019), 117–128; F.L. Neumann, 'Federalism and Freedom: A Critique', in D. Karmis and W. Norman (eds), *Theories of Federalism: A Reader* (Basingstoke: Palgrave Macmillan, 2005); Levy, 'Federalism, Liberalism, and the Separation of Loyalties', 475.

[31] W. Kymlicka, *Multicultural Citizenship: A Liberal Theory of Minority Rights* (Oxford: Oxford University Press, 1996); A. Sarat and T.R. Kearns (eds), *Cultural Pluralism, Identity Politics, and the Law* (Ann Arbor: University of Michigan Press, 2014).

the broadest sense—meaning cultural diversity—can be promoted without federalism, and indeed that some forms of diversity may not be well promoted by federalism: non-territorial bases of identity are by definition given a different and often weaker level of accommodation in a federal constitution than territorially located identities.[32] A federal constitution's purpose is overtly to prioritise territorially based attachments.[33] Although cultural specificity may well map onto segmented territorial identities within a federal state,[34] in legal-normative terms it is the territorial boundedness of the state's constituent territories with which the constitution is specifically concerned; with the legal consequences of giving foundational constitutional accommodation—through jurisdiction—to territorial units.[35] From this we can further refine the constitutional focus of federalism as 'jurisdictional territorial pluralism': the creation of individual systems of government for the constituent territories as well as a state-wide system of government for the polity as a whole; and it is the ultimate purpose of federalism that these different governments be reconciled with each other through institutions of rule across the polity: an implicit logic of any constitutional system is efficacy.

In Chapter 5 we discussed the deep scepticism that has attended federalism as a constitutional project. We noted how, for example, Carl Schmitt took the idea of the meaningful accommodation of territorial pluralism, implied by federalism, to be an impossibility for the modern state, given how his very conception of the sovereign state was tied up with presuppositions concerning a singular demos and

[32] Feeley and Rubin, *On Federalism: Federalism as Tragic Choice*, 52–54.

[33] There are situations where a federal system's creation of territorial government overlaps with other forms of accommodation of cultural distinctiveness. An example is Belgium in which the constitution recognises three constitutional territories (the Flemish region, Wallonia, and Brussels), but also three communities (Dutch, French, and German), the latter accommodating identity on a personal rather than geographical basis. Even in Belgium however these constitutional (cultural) identities largely map onto territory, so much so that the Flemish region and community have merged their institutions. Watts, *Comparing Federal Systems*, 3rd edn, 44. This type of territorial/cultural elision is by no means unusual in federal systems. Garth Stevenson argues that Canada in 1867 was founded upon a consociational principle. G. Stevenson, *Building Nations from Diversity: Canadian and American Experience Compared* (Kingston-Montreal: McGill-Queen's University Press, 2014), 25–27. See also M. Chevrier, 'The Making of a Dominion: The Completion of a Conquest', in E. Brouillet, A.-G. Gagnon, and G. Laforest (eds) *The Quebec Conference of 1864: Understanding the Emergence of the Canadian Federation* (Kingston/Montreal: McGill-Queen's University Press, 2018), 49–69, 59–64. The overwhelming demarcation of rights and duties in Canada is however territorially organised, a fact reflecting Watts' observation that: 'the constitutional distribution of power among *territorial* units is by far the most common pattern among federations.' Watts, *Comparing Federal Systems*, 3rd edn, 18.

[34] A particular feature of multinational or 'plurinational' federations: F. Requejo (ed.), *Democracy and National Pluralism* (London: Routledge, 2001; M. Keating, *Plurinational Democracy: Stateless Nations in a Post-Sovereignty Era* (Oxford: Oxford University Press, 2001); S. Tierney, *Constitutional Law and National Pluralism* (Oxford: Oxford University Press, 2004); W. Norman, *Negotiating Nationalism: Nation-Building, Federalism, and Secession in the Multinational State* (Oxford: Oxford University Press, 2006); A. Lecours, 'Federalism and Nationalism', in John Kincaid (ed.), *A Research Agenda for Federalism Studies* (Cheltenham: Edward Elgar, 2019), 140–150.

[35] For Tocqueville a virtue of federalism is that it facilitates a range of legal jurisdictions and in turn allows the law to vary in order to meet the needs of different societies within the states. A. de Tocqueville, *Democracy in America* (New York: Library of America, 2004), 182.

unitary constitution. It is no surprise that such a conceptual roadblock also affected 19th–early 20th-century accounts of federalism in the work of Madison, Mill, Bryce, and Dicey. Viewing federalism through the same nation-building prism with which unitary constitutions are viewed, each of these thinkers tended to see federalism as a short-term solution to manage territorial differences. Dicey's view, noted above, was characteristic of these approaches: 'Federalism, when successful, has generally been a stage towards unitary government.'[36] As Norman puts it: 'for Dicey there seems to be no principled basis for federalism. It is something you accept as a second best, and you should hope to grow out of it as soon as possible.'[37] A core aim of this book is to challenge the two-stage argument that underpins this scepticism: that the deep territorial pluralism which defines federalism is such a pathological threat to the existence of the state that it must be eschewed in favour of demotically monist unitary constitutionalism, and that where a constitution takes a federal form it must have the same demotic underpinnings and, therefore, source of sovereignty, as a unitary constitution.

Federalism is in fact a fruitful constitutional project because of, rather than despite, its deep and often complex territorial arrangements. The vitality of federalism lies precisely in the living constitutional tension between accommodating territorial difference while at the same time maintaining the viability of the modern state project through the reconciliation of different levels of government. Since the promise of federalism is, on the one hand, the accommodation of plurality (and hence difference), and, on the other, a common commitment to the federal constitution as a unifying project, these two goals, pluralism and union, must be ultimately reconcilable within federal idea's meta-purpose if federalism is to stand as a sustainable model of government, capable of generic applicability across very different states. Federalism, cast in this way, is a provocation to the dominant mentality of modern constitutionalism which suggests that only a narrowly construed singular demos producing an ultimately monistic order of constitutional rule can properly serve the modern state. The discrete constitutional purpose of federalism, which I now unpack, challenges this assumption in its contention that the dual goals of pluralism and union which both reflect the reality, and facilitate the aspirations, of societally complex societies, can and must be realisable and reconcilable through the federal idea of rule for the modern state.

[36] Dicey, *Introduction to the Study of the Law of the Constitution*, 8th edn , preface.

[37] Norman, *Negotiating Nationalism*, 89. I have also noted Madison's monist nationalism earlier in this chapter and in Chapter 6. The orientation of Mill's chapter in *Considerations on Representative Government*— 'Of Federal Representative Governments'—sees value in federal systems when conditions do not as yet exist for the establishment of a strong unitary constitution. As Porter puts it: '[h]is clear preference for a decentralized unitary government over a federal government is unmistakeable.' R.B. Porter, 'John Stuart Mill and Federalism' (1977) *Publius: The Journal of Federalism*, 101–124, 113. This mentality continued into the post-war period of federal constitution-building. Sir Ivor Jennings, although advising on new federations within the Commonwealth after the war, nevertheless wrote 'nobody would have a federal constitution if he could possibly avoid it'. W.I. Jennings, *Some Characteristics of the Indian Constitution* (Madras: Oxford University Press, 1953), 55.

IV. Purpose and principles of federalism: the matrix of territorial pluralism

It is necessary therefore to begin by confronting the tension between pluralism and union that lies at the heart of the purpose of federalism. Dicey argued that without a desire to unite, 'there is clearly no basis for federalism'. But he qualified this in what has become a famous aphorism: the inhabitants of territories coming together to form a federation 'must desire union, and must not desire unity'.[38] Although Dicey's own account of federalism was weighted heavily towards the overriding value of unity, this conceptual distinction is useful. The purpose of federalism is indeed to foster a union that promotes pluralism rather than a homogenising conception of unity.

Principles of federalism, immanent to this core purpose, flow as a matter of logic from it. They are not a search for an ideal system of government for the human condition. Federalism as a constitutional system is premised upon the very fact of a non-ideal or imperfect demotic situation as the lived reality of so many states. It is the very tension that stems from unsettled pluralism that usually leads constitution-builders to adopt federalism as a useful constitutional structure for a territorially segmented polity. That is not to say that federalism is a temporary sticking plaster, applied until territorially located identities can be overcome in the teleological pursuit of a 'more perfect' or 'ever closer' long-term unity, as writers from Madison to Dicey hoped and believed. It is instead a sociologically coherent response to the deep social reality of salient and lasting territorial specificities, the boundaries of which are no less real or meaningful for the fact that they are located within states. The principles of federalism flow from this reality; they are the constitutional precepts necessary to make federalism work as a coherent genus of constitutional rule for complex social settings.

In identifying the principles of federalism there is no rigid distinction between the twin pillars that characterise the federal contract: pluralism and union. The idea of federalism contains an inherent tension but it is not a pathology. Dicey, elaborating upon his vision of federal government, stated that the basis of federation is a 'combination of union and separation … the desire for national unity and the determination to maintain the independence of each man's separate State'.[39] This does to some extent capture the two elements of federal constitutionalism but, as do many writers, Dicey in the language of 'national unity' on the one hand and 'separation' on the other, seems to posit these as oppositional, and ultimately incommensurable, aims. My contention is that the federal idea promises not only a workable but also a fruitful relationship between pluralism and union. The founding act of a federal constitution creates different levels of government,

[38] Dicey, *Introduction to the Study of the Law of the Constitution*, 8th edn, 137.

[39] Dicey, *Introduction to the Study of the Law of the Constitution*, 8th edn, 138.

but federal pluralism is captured not only in the multiplicity of governments but also in their interaction and association:[40] territories have their own governments, but they also participate in the central level of government. The latter in turn has a state-wide jurisdiction giving it a direct relationship with citizens and bringing it into constant interaction with the governments of constituent territories. Therefore, the pluralism of federal government is better described, as is federal subjecthood, through the metaphor of matrix than that of levels. Federalism is not the creation of governmental silos but rather of avenues of interaction—and ultimately communion—of different levels, in order to foster an effective constitution and an effective state. In this way pluralism is not antithetical to union; the two dimensions of federalism, pluralism and union, should operate in a symbiotic relationship to the best advantage of each.

Flowing from the matrix of territorial pluralism are four principles which undergird, make effective, and thus advance the meta-purpose of federalism:

- the mosaic of recognition
- autonomous government
- associational government
- reciprocity

(i) The mosaic of recognition

In Chapters 3–6 we explored how a modern constitution is founded in the name of its subjects and is deemed to be legitimate on the basis both of the original consent (whether actual or symbolic) of these subjects, and the ongoing consent of each generation of constitutional subjects. Central to any constitution therefore is mutual recognition: the constitution acknowledges the significance of the constitution's subjects and in so doing ascribes legal status to them. In a reciprocal way the constitution's subjects recognise the authority of the constitution. It follows that this process also involves constitutionally conditioned transformation. In the act of constitutionalisation, and the recognition that comes with it, the founding (constituent) subjects become constitutional subjects and take on a new public identity in consequence of this. There is however a second dimension to the recognition owed to and required of a constitution's subjects. In the act of constitution-making the constitution's subjects must also acknowledge the constitutional status of their fellow subjects. A constitution for a state is not simply an agreement to co-exist: a resigned assent to perpetuate mutual solitudes within some over-arching legal order. The process involves appreciation that the transformative power of the

[40] J. Tully, *Strange Multiplicity: Constitutionalism in an Age of Diversity* (Cambridge: Cambridge University Press, 1995).

constitution creates new inter-subject relationships. The constitution has transformed the status of these subjects and as such each constitutional subject is called upon to recognise their own transfigured status, that of their fellow subjects, and the new collective constitutional subjecthood they share. We can call these two aspects of social reflexivity, respectively, vertical and horizontal recognition.

The vertical dimension of this mosaic is recognition of the authority of the constitution but it is more than this; it is also recognition of the legitimacy of that authority: an acceptance by the constitution's constituent subjects of the constitution's validity as a higher order system of rule that unites them in a constitutional union, not only subjecting them to its authority but also uniting their discrete identities in a common project whereby they forge a new collective identity around the constitution itself. In federal context this is the process of building a federal constitutional union. In this move the constitution recognises the *a priori* constitutional status of its territorial subjects; simultaneously, the territorial constitutional constituents acknowledge the validity of the constitution's authority. Vertical recognition both establishes the federal constitution as a normative order of rule for a modern state and also establishes the particularity of territorial subjecthood with all that this specificity—as explored in Chapters 5 and 6—implies.

In its horizontal dimension the process of mutual recognition in a federal constitution is also in the first instance fundamentally inter-territorial; a recognition that constituent territorial subjects are transformed by the constitution into constitutional territorial subjects, and that in this act of transformation each subject recognises the identity and prerogatives of every other as partners in this constitutional territorial union. Individual citizens are of course central to all of these processes, but the fundamental distinctiveness of a federal constitution is that individual subjecthood is mediated through the constitutionally foundational territorial pluralism that distinguishes a federal constitution from a unitary constitution.

This mosaic of recognition, combining the elements of pluralism and union, is common to all federal constitutions. However, the ways in which a federal constitution recognises, and in so doing accords status to, its constituent territories, and the ways in which they in turn offer recognition to the constitution of its authority and to their fellow constituents of their constitutional status, can vary considerably from one constitution to another. The diverse forms which constitutional recognition takes are explored further in Chapter 8 but it is useful to lay out in summary here the three different ways in which recognition can manifest itself.

The first of these is constitutional symbolism; an explicit statement of constitutional identity or status. The constitution, often in its preamble, can make such a declaration of its federal character, for example noting the foundational role of the federal polity's constituent territories or stating the shared commitment to union of those territories. Secondly, recognition can be tied up in the institutional design of the polity and the allocation of constitutional powers. On this institutional register recognition can be calibrated by comparing the relative governmental authority of constituent territories on the one hand and the central government on the other. Institutional design is concerned more with the principles of autonomous government and associational government than simply recognition, but as we will see when we turn to these principles below and in the remaining chapters of the book, institutional design and power allocation also bear heavily upon the matrix of recognition within a federal polity by framing the entire orientation of the federal constitution and demarcating, symbolically as well as institutionally, the balance within any federal constitution between pluralism and union. A third way in which recognition can manifest itself is in relation to those federal constitutions that offer differing or, as it were, asymmetrical recognition among the constituent territories themselves. Constitutionalism is reflexive, the authority it bears depends upon its legitimacy, and, in turn, that legitimacy derives from how the constitution encapsulates the demotic specificity of the polity in question. A federal constitution may recognise its constituent territories as constitutional equals, and they in turn may recognise each other also through the register of constitutional parity. Alternatively, a federal constitution may recognise its constituent territories as different *inter se*; ascribing particular constitutional status to certain territories and/or making differentiated provision through institutional design and the allocation of powers.[41] Such an asymmetrical approach is a particular feature of plurinational federations; those in which territorial particularity is most pronounced.[42]

The very idea of asymmetry within federal constitutionalism is a particular challenge to conceptions of federalism that have been built upon a monistic understanding of the demos: a vision of federalism that ties it clearly to the nation-building endeavour of default modern constitutionalism. At the vertical level, it requires an implicit understanding of the ongoing salience of territories within the constitution, and a recognition that these retain discrete and significant societal particularity despite the normatively transformative effect of the foundational constitutional act.[43] A genuine commitment to asymmetrical recognition within

[41] In the political studies literature asymmetry tends to be addressed very broadly, embracing what Watts describes as 'the cultural, economic, social, and political conditions affecting the relative power,' influence and relations of different regional units with each other and with the federal government'. Our concern is instead with constitutional asymmetry: 'the degree to which powers assigned to regional units by the constitution of the federation are not uniform'. Watts, *Comparing Federal Systems*, 3rd edn, 125.

[42] See n 34 above. Pelletier has commented: 'asymmetry is not merely compatible with the federal principle; it is intrinsic to federalism'. B. Pelletier, 'The Future of Quebec within the Canadian Federation', in A.-G. Gagnon (ed.), *Contemporary Canadian Federalism* (Toronto: University of Toronto Press, 2012), 469–482, 476. See also P. Popelier and M. Sahadzic (eds), *Constitutional Asymmetry in Multinational Federalism: Managing Multinationalism in Multi-tiered Systems* (United Kingdom: Palgrave-MacMillan, 2019).

[43] Asymmetry is of course not the only approach to recognising and accommodating territorial difference; the principle of equality can itself be a boon to weaker or smaller constituent territories. John Witherspoon in the mid-1770s noted that in the incorporating union of Scotland and England, the former was inevitably overwhelmed by the size of the latter. In light of this: 'Witherspoon's focus on the distribution of political power led him to the conviction that the states ought to be represented equally in the new confederation.' A.L. LaCroix, *The Ideological Origins of American Federalism* (Cambridge MA: Harvard University Press, 2011), 124.

a federal polity also depends significantly upon the horizontal plane, and the willingness of the territories themselves to recognise that one or more among them has such a level of societal distinctiveness as to merit both symbolic recognition of this fact and asymmetrical institutional design to accommodate this distinctiveness, very possibly at the expense of these other territories who by definition enjoy a less generous allocation of constitutional influence or authority.[44]

Across these three different sites of recognition, one generic fact remains: the success of any constitution in meeting the meta-purpose of federalism depends in part upon how it recognises the specific relationship between pluralism and union that characterises this particular constitution.

(ii) Autonomous government

The principle of autonomous government flows logically from federalism's commitment to territorial pluralism, as it does from the principle of recognition. Given that the point of constitutional recognition of a federal constitution's constituent territories is to affirm their status as the foundational constitutional subjects of the polity, it follows that the constitution must also create the institutional environment within which these territories can pursue their own societal objectives. Three implications flow from the salience of autonomy to the meta-purpose of federalism. First, it implies the need for real and not merely instrumental self-government; secondly, territorial autonomy is not characterised by only one institutional model but must be properly reflective of the specific demotic nature of each federal society; and thirdly, while it is certainly a central dimension of the federal idea, the principle of autonomy exists within, and must be conditioned by, the meta-purpose of federalism and the other principles that flow from it. I will address each of these in turn.

The federal identity of a constitution requires that the level of self-government accorded to constituent territories within a federal constitution must be meaningful, with sufficient decision-making independence and substantive powers to reflect each constituent territory's discrete societal specificity. This policy-making freedom can be said to inhere in the very idea of federalism in the same way that individual autonomy is immanent within the idea of a unitary constitution founded on liberal democratic terms.[45] If discrete territorial jurisdictions are so important

[44] Traditional federal theory, with its monist mindset, has considerable difficulties with the idea of asymmetry: C.D. Tarlton, 'Symmetry and Asymmetry as Elements of Federalism: A Theoretical Speculation' (1965) 27 *The Journal of Politics* 861–874. In a major recent research project Maja Sahadzic argues however that the assumption that federalism requires symmetry is not supported by evidence and is in fact a proxy for both integration and centralisation. M. Sahadzic, *Asymmetry, Multinationalism and Constitutional Law, Managing Legitimacy and Stability in Federalist States* (London: Routledge, 2021).

[45] Hueglin and Fenna, *Comparative Federalism: A Systematic Inquiry*, 2nd edn, 37. That is not to say of course that federalism is somehow inherently illiberal or in any way incompatible with liberalism, but simply that the purpose of a federal constitution is focused upon the constitutional accommodation of

that their specific accommodation is the defining register of the polity's constitutional character—flowing from their foundational constituent power, transformed by the constitution into constitutional constituent authority—then it follows that each territory should be allotted the institutional means to foster that specific jurisdiction in support of the particular identities, values, and policy preferences generated within that jurisdiction.

Here we see a fundamental point of demarcation between the constitutional purposes of federalism and the instrumental political purposes which have been ascribed to it. The latter often fail to recognise that meaningful autonomy for the state's constituent territories is of *inherent* significance to the very idea of federalism. Autonomy or self-government is of course universally recognised as a *feature* of federalism, but its status as a *principle* flowing logically from its generic constitutional purpose is often not recognised or is at least under-played. An approach that focuses upon the federal constitutional contract however is one that considers constituent constitutional authority to be the vital legitimising resource of the constitution's very authority, stemming as it does from the constitutional salience of the polity's foundational subjects. In this way autonomy is reconceived as a principle rather than a mere feature of federalism; an intrinsic rather than a contingent constitutional value which reflects the constitutionally embedded territorial pluralism at the heart of the federal idea. To have the capacity to give effect to the jurisdictional and societal specificities that underpin the salience of territorial constituent power, autonomous government within a federal constitution must therefore have strong and clear jurisdictional boundaries. Federal scholarship has identified 'cooperative federalism' as an increasingly significant feature of modern federalism. Cooperation is indeed vital among constituent territories and between them and the central government. But for autonomous government to be real, relationships must be voluntary and cannot be conditioned by a power imbalance which in reality compels 'cooperation'. For example, autonomy is not meaningful if regions are mere conduits for the implementation of national policy at the regional level or if their formal autonomy is in practice stripped away by the dominant political and economic power of the central government.[46]

Federal autonomous government is also categorically distinct from 'decentralisation', 'subsidiarity', or 'local government'; nor does it collapse into amorphous 'multi-level government'. Each of these alternative conceptualisations is in fact characterised by an essentially unitary rather than a pluralist conception of constitutional authority. This is most obvious in the case of local government which typically enjoys no constitutional status[47] but it is also clear in notions such as

territorial pluralism as part of a constitutional union and, beyond this, is not inherently reflective of any particular ideological approach to politics.

[46] This point is discussed as 'coercive federalism' in Chapter 9.

[47] Some constitutions do give constitutional recognition to local government but this is categorically different from federalism. Feeley and Rubin argue that federalism can be distinguished from local

subsidiarity and decentralisation, which each have one powerful central source of authority as their direct referent. A presupposition underpinning subsidiarity is that there exists one hierarchically superior level of government from which authority is dispersed; the lower level of government implements central decisions, albeit with some degree of discretion.[48] By contrast, federal constitutionalism means that the federal level of the polity and each of the constituent territories together constitute 'different and equally legitimate majorities'.[49] Federal autonomy implies the capacity of discrete self-determining units to make meaningful policy decisions within clear and protected jurisdictional limits. In this way the principle of autonomy, as a strong and distinct counterpoint to central government, goes against the grain of the default constitutional conception of modern statehood which extends a monistic conception of sovereignty to the authority distributive dimension of governmental rule.

This conclusion has implications for certain systems today which have a federal institutional structure but within which real autonomy for constituent territories is lacking. The term 'administrative federalism' is often used to characterise systems which are, in effect, models of decentralised central decision-making, such as the German constitution. Under the German system the central government is the general law-making authority and the *Länder* governments essentially implement, with some degree of discretion, centrally determined laws. Feeley and Rubin characterise administrative federalism as: 'a managerial strategy by which a centralized regime can achieve the results it desires in a more effective manner'.[50] In their view such a model lacks 'the most basic characteristic of federalism, where the subdivisions possess an area of independent decision making in which they can establish their own policies'.[51] This is however not the whole story. The influence of

government because of the scope for independent decision-making and formation of distinct policies within a federal system. M. Feeley and E. Rubin, *Federalism: Political Identity and Tragic Compromise* (University of Michigan Press, 2008), 30–31. In fact, the distinction is, in legal normative terms, more fundamental than this. The essence of federalism is the constituent nature of the constitution's territories and their foundational status as bearers of both foundational constituent power and constitutional constituent authority; the constitutional status of local government is not comparable to this.

[48] As Watts says of subsidiarity: 'it has a clearly hierarchical character, and it implies that ultimately it is for the "higher" body to decide at which level tasks should be performed'. Watts, *Comparing Federal Systems*, 3rd edn, 6. He is also critical of the lack of clarity as to where authority lies in relation to the exercise of the subsidiarity principle. Watts, *Comparing Federal Systems*, 92. For a deeper critique of the application of the subsidiarity principle to federalism see D. Golemboski, 'Federalism and the Catholic Principle of Subsidiarity' (2015) 45 *Publius* 526–551. He argues that much of the account of subsidiarity in recent federal discourse has been superficial and misplaced because it has 'tended to neglect or only superficially appreciate its foundations in Catholic social doctrine' which attributes to the term social and metaphysical as well as legal meaning.

[49] *Secession Reference*, para. 66 (discussed in Chapter 6). Levy goes so far as to argue that subsidiarity, with the suggestion of case-by-case assessments of where decisions can best be made, is inherently incompatible with federalism since federalism rests upon clear jurisdictional boundaries and clarity as to where *kompetenz-kompetenz* must rest. Levy, 'Federalism, Liberalism, and the Separation of Loyalties' (2007), 462.

[50] Feeley and Rubin, *On Federalism: Federalism as Tragic Choice*, 20.

[51] Feeley and Rubin, *On Federalism: Federalism as Tragic Choice*, 29.

the German *Länder* is felt in the making of national policy where they are heavily involved; 'integrated federalism' also bringing with it shared power.[52] It is certainly the case that constituent territories in such a system can use administrative powers to shape policy in different ways. One example is the spending power. Those who defend the idea that administrative federalism does involve meaningful autonomy argue that in such a system 'the constitutional expenditure responsibilities of the regional governments are significantly broader than would be indicated by the distribution of legislative powers taken alone'.[53] But within administrative federalism, even though central power is shared, it is not meaningfully divided; decision-making lies with the central institutions with no real policy-making autonomy for the constitution's constituent territories.[54] We need then to distinguish between formal or titular federalism and real manifestations of the federal contract. The federal principle is in the end made manifest not only through constitutional formalism—the very existence of constitutionally recognised territorial governments[55]—but in whether these give effect to the fundamental salience of constitutional constituent authority through meaningful autonomy.

A second feature of federal autonomy as a principle is that there is no set 'federal' way of designing either the different institutional forms of government within a federal constitution or the allocation of authority between the central government and the governments of constituent territories. The purpose of the principle is to deliver meaningful autonomy for the polity's constituent territories and this ultimately depends upon the nature of these territories and the specific terms of the federal contract. Therefore, federal autonomy can be manifested in a diverse array of institutional designs and competence allocations. Indeed, it is the case that in no two federal polities do constituent territories have exactly the same powers or institutional arrangements. It is also the case that a particular constitution may accord self-government to its constituent territories in asymmetrical ways, whereby one or more constituent territory is ascribed with different powers and/or different institutional arrangements than the other constituent territories. We will explore in

[52] 'In order to bring about a quasi-unitary system of public services and administration, legislative powers were concentrated at the centre. As a compensation for this loss of autonomous legislative powers, the Länder governments not only gained a right to co-determine national legislation through their membership in the second chamber of the national legislature, they were also assigned responsibility for implementing and administering most of those laws and policies.' Hueglin and Fenna, *Comparative Federalism: A Systematic Inquiry*, 2nd edn, 149.

[53] Watts, *Comparing Federal Systems*, 3rd edn, 100.

[54] This type of system has been called a 'joint decisions trap', a form of 'interlocked federalism' that requires 'a high degree of co-decision making'. R.L. Watts, 'The Federal Idea and its Contemporary Relevance', in T.L. Courchene et al., *The Federal Idea: Essays in Honour of Ronald L. Watts*, (Kingston-Montreal: McGill-Queen's, 2011), 13–27, 21. The term originates in F.W. Scharpf, 'The Joint-Decision Trap. Lessons From German Federalism and European Integration' (1988) 66 *Public Administration* 239–278.

[55] The German constitution does indeed entrench the legislative and administrative jurisdictions of the federal government and *Länder* respectively: Basic Law of the Federal Republic of Germany (1949).

Chapter 8 how institutional design within the federal idea is open to great diversity both across federal systems and within them.

A third point is that the principle of autonomy, while important, takes its place alongside the other principles inherent within federalism's meta-purpose. Hence it must also be reconciled with the deep relationship between pluralism and union that characterises this fundamental purpose and which conditions the nature and extent of autonomous government. The institutions and powers of self-government for any constituent territory must be designed and must operate in a way that accommodates also the autonomy of the other constituent territories and the role of the central institutions of government in making the constitutional system as a whole work in the interests of the common good. This is clear as we turn to the other principles of federalism in relation to which autonomy must be set in context.

(iii) Associational government

The accommodation of territorial pluralism within the federal contract is achieved not only by way of self-government, but also by the engagement of the constituent territories in the government of the central state: associational rule as the necessary complement to self-government.[56] The principle of democratic engagement is of course a broader principle that undergirds the very legitimacy of the modern constitution;[57] constitutional constituent authority being the logical extrapolation of foundational constituent power. The principle of associational government manifests itself within a unitary constitution in the capacity of citizens to choose representatives and call them to account. In a federal system the line of legitimacy from foundational consent to active engagement in the government of the state also applies, but it does so principally through the relationship between the constituent territories and the central institutions of the state; the collective nature of its constituents being the essential register of validity that distinguishes constituent power and constituent constitutional authority in a federal constitution from that of a unitary constitution. Associational rule flows within federal constitutionalism as a fundamental proposition inherent in the foundation of such a system, in the same way that individual engagement in the government of the state flows from the individualised premise that underpins unitary constitutionalism.

The idea of an active role for the state's constituent territories in the government of the state is taken for granted within federal scholarship, in the notion of 'shared rule'.[58] But, as we saw in relation to autonomous government, associational

[56] For some this, rather than autonomy, is the key benchmark of federalism: P. King, *Federalism and Federation* (London: Croom Helm, 1982), 19.

[57] John Stuart Mill was one of the first thinkers to draw a clear connection between the good of political participation for citizens within any democracy and federalism as one form of democratic government. Mill, *Considerations on Representative Government*, Ch. 17.

[58] D. Elazar, *Exploring Federalism* (Tuscaloosa: University of Alabama Press, 1987).

government is not simply a universal 'feature' of federal practice but rather a fundamental principle of federalism that flows inexorably from its foundational constitutional purpose. This is so for two reasons. The first rests in the very relationship between this principle and the principle of autonomy. Constituent territories require autonomy to pursue their specific jurisdictional interests. It follows that constituent territories must have a meaningful role also in the management of the central level of government, otherwise the autonomy of the constituent territories might be undone by powerful, contradictory forces. Central institutions have their own independent sphere of operation and demarcated powers. However, constituent territories retain an interest in how these institutions work and how these powers are exercised, just as the central government has an interest in how constituent territorial autonomy operates. Secondly, we have discussed how, within the meta-purpose of federalism, the idea of union functions as the essential complement to pluralism. To make the union dimension of the federal project meaningful, each constituent territory must commit and contribute to it by playing an active and constructive part in supporting, or at least not undermining, the constitutional authority of the central institutions (this point is returned to in the discussion of the principle of reciprocity below). Associational government therefore is not simply an instrumental device to bolster constituent territorial autonomy; by involving constituent territories in the government of the state as a whole the constitution can avoid the polity descending into silos where self-government becomes detached from the union dimension of the state, thereby undermining its very union nature.

Associational government is therefore not separable from autonomous government. Powers of the central level of government are powers in relation to the whole polity. While they may be set out in the constitution as resting exclusively in the central branch (we will see instances of this in Chapter 9), in practice they operate alongside and in overlapping ways with those of the constituent territorial governments. Given this close linkage, there has been a tendency to view autonomous government as antagonistic to central rule—a 'tragic compromise'. This is a conception that sees federalism as an unhappy outlier from the somehow 'natural' unitary order of modern constitutional rule.[59] It is not. Federalism is a discrete and self-conscious idea of constitutional rule for the modern state, and the relationship between autonomy and associational government is inherent in its very purpose.[60] It follows that autonomy and associational rule are not antonyms, they operate

[59] '[F]ederalism is more likely to be an option that people will resort to only when they feel a deep sense of alienation from the nation as a whole. In other words, it is a tragic situation.' Feeley and Rubin, *On Federalism: Federalism as Tragic Choice*, 60.

[60] As the Supreme Court of Canada put it, the purpose of the Constitution Act 1867 was: 'to establish a central government in which these Provinces should be represented, entrusted with exclusive authority only in affairs in which they had a common interest. Subject to this each Province was to retain its independence and autonomy and to be directly under the Crown as its head.' *Re the Initiative and Referendum Act* [1919] AC 935 (PC), 942.

over shared space; nor are they necessarily antagonistic to each other: federalism may be 'competitive', but it must also be sufficiently 'cooperative' for the overall federal project to prosper. Together, autonomy and associational rule constitute the complex matrix of territorial pluralism that characterises the federal contract; the federal polity's purpose is to foster a harmonious commitment to both principles.

A vision which sees this relationship in pathological terms—as irreconcilable silos—misses also the complex patterns of identity among citizens who feel allegiance to and identity with both their constituent territory and the state. Institutions exist at both territorial and central levels, and powers are accorded to each, in order to facilitate the diverse needs of citizens and respond to these dual or mixed identities. Government within a federal constitution should therefore not be seen as a division between levels but as a plural pattern within which different orders of rule interact in overlapping but complementary ways.[61] In this way associational government should not be conceived within the federal contract as a constraint on autonomy. Rather, by integrating the constituent territories into the central level of rule, associational government represents a form of co-ownership in the constitution and in the government of the state as a whole, and hence an extension of the very principle of autonomy. Such a conceptualisation in turn helps bolster the union dimension of the federal state by making the constitutional project more meaningful and relevant to its autonomous territories and, by making explicit their responsibility as players within the central institutions of the constitution, it can also foster the success of that constitutional project.

The same three implications flow from this principle as they do from autonomy. First, the principle of associational government must be meaningful. Associational government is an inherent commitment within the federal contract, not an instrumental device useful in pursuit of other goals. The role played by constituent territories at the central level of government is not satisfied by some loose conception of multi-level government but must be constitutionally recognised and guaranteed. Secondly, the particular form associational government will take within any constitution will depend upon the demotic nature of the polity. In Chapter 9 I will address how this principle has been institutionalised in radically different ways across federal constitutions, reflecting societal specificities. As with autonomous government, associational government can also accommodate asymmetry, for example giving particular territories certain special forms of representation in central institutions to reflect their particular demotic nature. Thirdly, in this section I have emphasised how the principle of associational government relates to that of autonomy and how the two are reconcilable and indeed complementary principles which together flow logically from the purpose of the federal contract. This reflects a broader point: the symbiotic relationship between pluralism and union

[61] A metaphor that has been used to describe modern federalism is 'marble cake': M. Grodzins, *The American System* D.J. Elazar (ed.) (Chicago: Rand McNally & Company, 1966).

that characterises the federal idea and which is reflected in each of its principles, a feature that becomes more apparent as we turn to reciprocity.

(iv) Reciprocity: a principle with two dimensions

'Territorial pluralism' is a vital component of the purpose of federalism but it must operate in a way that secures and strengthens federalism's constitutional commitment to union. We explored in Chapter 2 how the functional normativity of constitutional theory evaluates government as 'good' in the sense of it being efficacious: creating successful institutional forms in reflection of the constitution's core purpose. To this end federal government can only be good government if it situates territorial pluralism within a stable and successful polity. Constituent territories come together in a federal constitution with the purpose not only of guaranteeing their own prerogatives through autonomous and associative government, but also in a commitment to the vitality of the union constitution as a whole.

In this section of the chapter I argue that 'reciprocity' emerges as another inherent principle of federal constitutionalism which does much to capture the union dynamic essential to the federal contract. The principle of reciprocity encapsulates two discrete types of constitutional relationship. *Vertical reciprocity* concerns the relationship of cooperation required between the constitution's constituent territories on the one hand and the central government on the other, involving a commitment by both to the federal constitutional order itself: Kelsen's third order of rule within a federal system. *Horizontal reciprocity* reflects the further commitment by and within each of the constitution's constituent territories towards each other, encapsulated in the idea of inter-territorial solidarity. While vertical reciprocity captures the cooperation needed to make a polity with different levels of government operate effectively, the horizontal dimension is a deeper form of societal commitment to the common good.[62] While the first can be read as a logical necessity, the latter captures a demotic form of collaborative commitment, mutual reliance, and support among the constitution's subjects.

(a) Vertical reciprocity (comity)

The principle of vertical reciprocity stems from that of recognition. In Chapter 3 I drew out how the foundational moment of a federal constitution is characterised by the coming together of constituent territories to found the constitution. But this is not just a moment of normative mutual recognition, it is also a commitment to

[62] In recent times there has been an increased focus within the federalism literature on the issue of interdependence within federal systems: N. Bolleyer and L. Thorlakson, 'Beyond Decentralization—The Comparative Study of Interdependence in Federal Systems' (2012) 42 *Publius* 566–591; J. Schnabel, *Managing Interdependencies in Federal Systems: Intergovernmental Councils and the Making of Public Policy* (UK: Palgrave MacMillan, 2020).

the success of the constitution (and to its central level of rule) by constituent territories and by the constitution to the flourishing of the territories.

If the two levels of government are to cooperate constructively to make the polity work then institutional design is of course important, but just as vital is the *disposition* to do so and the fostering of a mentality of cooperation. As Watts puts it: 'Since federations involve accommodating and reconciling territorial diversity, a political culture emphasizing tolerance and compromise is an equally important prerequisite.'[63] Friedrich uses the terms *loyauté fédérale* and *bundestreue* or comity to express this value. He takes these to mean, as Burgess puts it, 'the fundamental commitment of the constituent units and their representatives to the overall needs of the larger federal system'.[64] Friedrich however, with his focus upon behaviour, sees comity in narrow terms, falling essentially upon officials at both levels of the state to engage in 'fair play': 'the presumption of a willingness to "give the other side a 'break', to be ready for compromise" wherever serious strains developed, to be, in other words, "pragmatic in the approach to problems" on which the federal and local authorities were divided or on which "their intrinsic interests clashed"'.[65]

The notions of *loyauté fédérale, bundestreue*, or comity are articulated in various ways within the federalism literature. Wheare identified what he called the 'federal principle',[66] while Elazar wrote of 'covenantal federalism' as a form of contract.[67] Riker focused more on the idea of federalism as a 'bargain' or process of 'bargaining' which is framed very much in terms of *realpolitik*, as founded upon a power balance; a tradition of political analysis stemming from game theory and rational choice theory. For Riker, federalism is essentially 'a bargain between prospective national leaders and officials of constituent governments for the purpose of aggregating territory, the better to lay taxes and raise armies'.[68] A federal system is only viable in Riker's view if neither the central government nor those of the constituent territories can overpower one another.[69] A more recent account of the underpinning federal commitment is encapsulated in Burgess' 'federal spirit'. This is an overtly normative account, discussed in Chapter 2, that sees federalism

[63] Watts, *Comparing Federal Systems*, 3rd edn, 68–69.

[64] M. Burgess, *In Search of the Federal Spirit: New Theoretical and Empirical Perspectives in Comparative Federalism* (Oxford: Oxford University Press, 2012), 14.

[65] Burgess, *In Search of the Federal Spirit*, 14.

[66] Wheare, *Federal Government*, 10–11.

[67] Although, as we have seen, Elazar's covenant was not in reality a contract among territories but rather an individualised conception of mutual cooperation largely indistinguishable from liberal social contract theory: 'the deliberate coming together of humans as equals to establish bodies politic in such a way that all reaffirm their fundamental equality and retain their basic rights'. Elazar, *Exploring Federalism*, 4–5. Larsen notes that 'a similar political-theological root can be found in the German term for a federation, *Bund*, which was originally used by Luther to describe the alliance between the people and God'. S.R. Larsen, *The Constitutional Theory of the Federation and the European Union* (Oxford: Oxford University Press, 2021), 94. This again emphasises an individualist strain within early federal theory, also evident in Althusius' idea of covenant: discussed in Chapter 2.

[68] Riker, *Federalism: Origin, Operation, Significance*, 11.

[69] Riker, *Federalism: Origin, Operation, Significance*. An approach that echoes that of Carl Schmitt.

as: 'a moral undertaking or enterprise in that it is based upon the faith and trust that is bound up in the commitment of a promise or a voluntary agreement, itself rooted in the recognition and equality of partnership. The moral basis of such an association or union arises from the presumed integrity and mutual respect of the participating entities.'[70] As Burgess acknowledges, the term 'federal spirit' was first used by Carl Friedrich. Friedrich's meaning differs however from Burgess', focused as it was on 'federal behaviour' and the types of political processes and outcomes that are needed to make a federal system work. In particular, a 'spirit of compromise and accommodation ... moulded by the knowledge that there are many rooms in a house that federalism builds'.[71] In this sense Friedrich's interest was similar to Riker's—an observational account of the durability, rather than the merits, of federal systems. Burgess goes further. For Burgess the notion of federal spirit is more than just a textual set of rules. It is manifest in a deeper constitutional and political culture of comity that *should* characterise the federal nature of the constitutional system as a whole. At its heart is the preparedness to act with integrity in relation to other parties, to compromise, and to be pragmatic in dealing with problems.[72]

Institutions can help foster this principle through associational government, requiring joint decision-making and hence giving all governments an incentive to make the constitution work. In Chapter 9 we will address various ways in which this can be done. But it is also the case that the constitutional and political culture of a federal system can vary on a scale between a more cooperative and a more competitive system. Although autonomy and association ought not to be antagonists, they can develop in this way. That said, a competitive relationship is not necessarily pathological for a federal system if it is accompanied by an overall commitment to the success of the system.

The three implications which we discussed in relation to autonomous and associational government again flow. Vertical reciprocity must be meaningful: there must be a real, and unforced, commitment to union by both the constituent territories and the central institutions. This can be reflected in the way the respective competences of constituent and central governments are constitutionally allocated and in the way institutional design is intended to foster cooperation. Reciprocity is about a valid exchange based upon a voluntary commitment. It is not forced acquiescence from a position of strength; the different governments must have real power and a successful federal constitution is one that holds these in balance in a productive relationship of interaction. As a relationship of genuine cooperation by equally legitimate political communities possessed of real constitutional authority it should not be a slippery slope to either centralisation or separation. Secondly,

[70] Burgess, *In Search of the Federal Spirit*, 7–8.

[71] C.J. Friedrich, *Trends of Federalism in Theory and Practice* (London: Frederick A. Praeger Publishers, 1968), 39.

[72] Burgess, *In Search of the Federal Spirit*, 13.

vertical reciprocity must be reflexive of the plural nature of federal society. The commitments that constituent territories give and what they expect of the central institutions is shaped by the constitution itself. If there is asymmetrical accommodation for certain territories then the reciprocal duties will vary accordingly. Finally, reciprocity must be understood, and find deep and real institutional expression, in relation to the other principles of federalism, recognition, autonomous and associational government. Therefore, although there are reciprocal rights and responsibilities which bind the constituent territories to pursue the health of the overall polity, this operates against the backdrop of clear and meaningful jurisdictional boundaries and legally demarcated fields of governmental interaction, rather than in relation to some nebulous and legally vague notion of multi-level government.

(b) Horizontal reciprocity (inter-territorial solidarity)

The principle of recognition also requires the mutual recognition among the federal state's constituent territories of each territory's existence, autonomy, partnership in associational government, and of the new relationships they form in a constitutional union; mutual recognition not only of the existence and constitutional salience of each, but of the fact that each has committed to a federal constitution and hence to the successful functioning of that constitution for the common good of every territory.

As a matter of logic, any constitution involves some sense of mutuality among its subjects. In seeking to thrive through a constitutional union, and in depending upon others to facilitate or at least not obstruct one's own good life, a subject must commit to the flourishing of others. What then is distinctive about horizontal reciprocity in a federal as opposed to unitary context? In a unitary constitution, subjecthood is understood as one community of individuals and any sense of common social solidarity operates upon the register of individual citizenship; modern social contract theory has largely been constructed upon trying to understand the reciprocal rights and responsibilities that flow from this constitutional construction.[73] The most fundamental point of departure for a federal constitutional contract is that constitutional obligations are established upon a territorial as well as an individual register, creating a territorially focused conception of social cohesion. Inevitably, different ideologies have been brought into play by commentators in an effort to explain what this means for a federal polity. Those who approach federalism from a social democratic perspective consider that reciprocity involves a commitment to a deep social solidarity; as Hueglin puts it, in a federal system 'social solidarity is extended not to individuals but to spatial collectivities'.[74] Those who approach federalism from a more libertarian perspective take a

[73] J. Rawls, *A Theory of Justice* (Cambridge MA: Harvard University Press, 1971).
[74] Hueglin and Fenna, *Comparative Federalism: A Systematic Inquiry*, 2nd edn, 40.

different view. A federal system is not primarily a site within which to foster social solidarity. Rather it is another forum for the playing out of the 'rational choices' of autonomous individuals. For libertarian liberals a federal constitution, just like a unitary constitution, should facilitate relatively deregulated competition among individuals and businesses. Federal systems are potentially attractive insofar as they add an additional, territorial site of competition and experimentation.[75]

Neither of these approaches, in bringing to the federal idea an externally generated instrumentalism, prioritises territorial distinctiveness as the fundamentally salient feature of federalism. Horizontal reciprocity should however be assessed by way of constitutional rather than political theory, primarily as a legal rather than an ideological commitment. As a principle, horizontal reciprocity stems logically from the decision to constitute a polity in the name of territorial pluralism. It is therefore a broad canvas and each federal constitutional system will choose to pursue this principle in its own way. At the moment of constitutional foundation or later, a federal system can of course be infused with a particular ideological approach on a register between social democracy and libertarian liberalism. The fundamental point however is that there are also inherent, constitutional, reciprocal duties which apply *ab initio* as a matter of legal commitment due to the foundational constitutional salience of territory to the polity.

It is possible to see the variety of possible approaches by citing a few brief examples. The German model has developed in a more social democratic way, with an approach to fiscal transfers that seeks to maintain equal social standards on an individual basis across the country. Canada does not go so far, but does seek to create a national floor of minimum individual standards. The approach in the USA is less systematic; in economic terms there is no national commitment to equal economic standards across territories but the federal spending power is huge and can be used directly within states as need is perceived to arise. There is also evidence that in federal systems with deep diversity the commitment to state-wide social solidarity can be weaker than in those which show greater cultural homogeneity across territory.[76]

While the federal principle of horizontal reciprocity does not dictate a particular ideological approach, it does encapsulate the inherent strain between pluralism and union within the federal idea. There are several pressure points that make the actualisation of horizontal reciprocity particularly difficult in certain types of federal polity. One is where considerable differences exist among constituent

[75] R.E. Wagner, 'Competitive Federalism in Institutional Perspective', in D.P. Racheter and R.E. Wagner (eds), *Federalist Government in Principle and Practice* (New York: Springer, 2001), 19–37.

[76] D. Miller, *On Nationality* (Oxford: Oxford University Press, 1995) As Weinstock puts it: 'citizens who are net contributors must feel strong solidarity with the beneficiaries . . . By creating new identities that are potentially rivals, federalism may thus impede the achievement of such desirable social objectives as the equitable distribution of material resources.' D. Weinstock, 'Towards a Normative Theory of Federalism' (2001) 53 *International Social Science Journal*, 75–83, 78. See also Y. Tamir, *Liberal Nationalism* (Princeton: Princeton University Press, 1995).

territories in terms of size, power, or wealth, resulting in protectionism by the bigger or wealthier territories on the one hand, and, on the other, resentment towards these territories by smaller or weaker territories.[77]

Federal constitutions can address disparities of size by, for example, according disproportionate (assessed by population size) institutional influence for smaller territories. One way is to give all territories equal representation in the second chamber of the federal legislature. The commitment to equal political representation in one chamber is explicable through the principle of associational government and has tended not to be particularly controversial. At the same time, disparities of wealth can be addressed by requiring redistribution through fiscal and spending policy, going so far as to seek some measure of economic equalisation or at least common standards across the state. This is not always readily accepted by wealthier territories who may assert for example the principle of autonomous government in defence of their own interests. The principle of reciprocity can therefore sit in tension with that of self-government, leading to hostility within territories which become net contributors to the general purse.

To take Canada's system of fiscal distribution as an example, this can be seen both as a commitment to a level of relative individual equality, based upon an individualised conception of social citizenship, and as vital in promoting national unity.[78] 'Equalisation payments' are made by way of federal government transfers to poorer provinces, for example by way of the Canada Social Transfer and the Canada Health Transfer, so that they can provide reasonably comparable public services to those available in wealthier provinces, without having to resort to significantly higher levels of taxation. This leads to debate about the meaning of 'reasonably comparable'. Furthermore, the system is resented by some voices within richer provinces, in particular Alberta, which has been a net contributor for over fifty years. In Germany, the principle of national redistribution is more readily accepted. There have been tensions, for example between the richer north and the poorer south, and at the time of reunification in 1990 with the impoverished east, but in general national equality is seen as part of a general social democratic commitment to minimum national standards, assessed individually.[79] A similar approach is also relatively uncontroversial in Australia. There, a sophisticated institutional apparatus is in place to ensure redistribution of tax revenue. The fact that this has until recently been administered by an independent body[80] boosts the system's legitimacy, but the broader point is that the Australian federal polity accepts the principle of distribution with an eye to equal national standards.

[77] *Comparing Federal Systems*, 3rd edn, 73–74.

[78] A. Lecours and D. Béland, 'Federalism and Fiscal Policy: The Politics of Equalization in Canada' (2010) 40 *Publius* 569–596, 570–571.

[79] See Hueglin and Fenna, *Comparative Federalism: A Systematic Inquiry*, 2nd edn, 190–191.

[80] Discussed in Chapter 9.

The tensions between relatively more and less affluent territories can be greater within federal systems characterised by deep diversity where constituent territories consider themselves to be discrete 'nations', especially where the bonds of union are more attenuated or accompanied by feelings of resentment or hostility. Andre Lecours has studied this issue in practice and has concluded that building bonds of social solidarity is much harder in multinational societies where there is resistance to redistribution beyond the sub-state 'national' group. He takes Belgium as a case study. Here the two major territorial groups, the Flemish and the Walloons, co-exist in a state of some tension. Originally poorer and less influential, since the 1960s Flanders has in economic terms overtaken Wallonia. With poor relations between the two territories, there is among some a strong disinclination to redistribute wealth from Flanders.[81] Similar tensions exist in Spain where Catalonia produces a disproportionate amount of Spain's GDP but where relations with the rest of the country have deteriorated over the past decade.[82] In the UK too there is the potential for considerable tension over finances stemming from the fact that England is so much the dominant actor in economic and political terms. This has however not led to separate government for England, while the devolved territorial governments in Scotland, Wales, and Northern Ireland receive a distribution of revenue in considerable excess of a per capita distribution.[83] This however has not stopped the rise of Scottish nationalism and a weakening of the bonds of social solidarity. If a federal system does indeed become little more than mutual co-existence of territories within a constitutional framework than a meaningful inter-territorial commitment to a common flourishing of the polity, the union itself can come under real strain.[84]

Further social factors can exacerbate or mitigate such tensions. Watts notes that if there is a large number of constituent territories within a polity it is harder for any one of these to dominate; whereas, in a smaller federal system, the existence of one powerful territory can lead to instability.[85] In Canada therefore, although there is resentment from Alberta over wealth redistribution, and further tensions emerging from Quebec nationalism, the existence of ten provinces, all with their own competing priorities, leads to different and shifting alliances within intergovernmental relations, with no one province exercising a dominant position, bearing out Madison's point that federalism may well work better in larger than smaller

[81] A. Lecours, 'Balancing Self-Rule and Shared-Rule: Sources of Tensions and Political Responses in Contemporary Political Systems' in A. López Basaguren and L.E. San Epifanio (eds), *The Ways of Federalism in Western Countries and the Horizons of Territorial Autonomy in Spain, vol. I* (Berlin: Springer, 2013), 103–113, 109.

[82] A. Castells, 'Catalonia and Spain: Political and Fiscal Conflict' (2014) 40 *Dans Pôle Sud*, 59–80 <https://www.cairn.info/revue-pole-sud-2014-1-page-59.htm>.

[83] S. Tierney, 'Brexit and the English Question' in F. Fabbrini (ed.), *The Law & Politics of Brexit* (Oxford: Oxford University Press, 2017), 95–114.

[84] House of Lords Constitution Committee, 'The Union and Devolution', HL Paper 149, 25 May 2016.

[85] Watts, *Comparing Federal Systems*, 3rd edn, 71–72.

polities. Spain is in some sense similar. There seventeen autonomous communities and two autonomous cities co-exist, several with strong cultural identities. Cross-cutting economic and other interests have tended, to some extent, to diffuse potentially separatist pressures stemming from Catalonia and the Basque Country on questions of cultural particularity and wealth distribution.[86]

What then does the principle imply? Although it certainly need not mean an ideological commitment to social equality any more than a unitary constitution implies such an obligation, the commitment of each territory to a common constitution for a common state implies a duty to make this work for all. Federalism is self-consciously social and collective in the very elevation of collectivities as the constitution's primary subjects. A federal constitution is founded upon the value of community—of a community of communities—and commits its constituent territories to mutual respect through the constitutional recognition of their respective governments as facilitators and guarantors of the collective interests of each. This implies that these territories must be able to flourish, if not all in exactly the same way, then at least in a comparable manner as part of the broader decision to found the constitution on plural territorial grounds.[87]

These factors certainly hint at the importance of social solidarity and provide a logical basis for redistribution. But we must also accept that the federal commitment can be thinner than this, marked by competitiveness among territories as well as between them and the central government; in other words, the principle of reciprocity implies some measure of 'territorial' solidarity which can certainly accommodate broader 'social' solidarity but it need not go so far as to imply, as a matter of constitutional necessity, equal social provision across the polity.[88] It follows that each federal constitution can accommodate asymmetry in its horizontal reciprocity. In seeking my territory to thrive, I must commit to others thriving. This comes with an obligation to allow each territory to thrive *as they are*, accepting that salient differences among territories can lead to different social policies which may incur a higher burden on the national purse; for example, to allow territories which

[86] Although Catalan–Madrid relations deteriorated sharply around the issue of a 'sovereignty' referendum in 2017.

[87] This principle operates even in situations of deep diversity. As one of the fathers of Canadian Confederation put it in 1865: '[W]e [are] of different races, not for the purpose of warring against each other, but in order to compete and emulate for the general welfare.' George-Étienne Cartier, Parliamentary Debates on Confederation (7 February 1865), 33. Documented by W.P.M. Kennedy (ed.), *Documents of the Canadian Constitution, 1759–1915* (Toronto: Oxford University Press, 1918), 618–629.

[88] A misunderstanding around this point led to a deep tension between federalism as an idea for government and the modern welfare state as it developed in the twentieth century. Laski, for example, was typical of a number of social democrats who came to view federalism as a hindrance to a social equality which they believed should be rigorously embedded within a national polity, regardless of territorial jurisdictions. H.J. Laski, 'The Obsolescence of Federalism' (1939) 98 *New Republic* 367. See also Pierre Elliott Trudeau, 'The Practice and Theory of Federalism', in P.E. Trudeau, *Federalism and the French Canadians* (Toronto: Macmillan of Canada, 1968) 124–150; S. Tierney, 'Pierre Elliott Trudeau and the Idea of Federalism' (2020) 99 *Supreme Court Law Review* 3–36.

represent cultural minorities to foster their specific linguistic or educational priorities. How the reciprocity principle plays out in practice is returned to in Chapter 9.

V. Concluding remarks

The distinct constitutional purpose of federalism is a radical challenge to modern democratic theory which is almost universally focused upon a monist demos and unitary institutional architecture. At the heart of the federal idea is territorial pluralism operational within a constitutional union. The federal contract is founded expressly in the tension between these realities. The purpose of federalism is not to resolve this tension but to find an equilibrium in the life of any federal system, appropriate to the social, political, and economic conditions of the polity in question. It is therefore vital to identify principles immanent to this purpose: the mosaic of recognition, autonomous government, associational government, and reciprocity in its vertical and horizontal dimensions. That is not to say that federalism is an easy subject for the management of the modern polity, particularly since it emerged as a model of government in parallel with the development of monist conceptions of peoplehood, nation, state, and sovereignty. It is also the case that the operation of the federal idea must be assessed in light of social change within any polity. On the one hand, processes of demotic homogenisation or a realignment of identities along non-territorial lines can leave a federal constitution redundant for a polity that no longer sees itself as defined by territorially demarcated differences. On the other hand, where that pluralism becomes so deep that one or more territories desire independent statehood, then the carefully crafted constitutional balance between pluralism and union may be fatally unsettled. Nonetheless, history has shown that federal constitutions are very malleable, both in original design and in evolving practice, and that they can stretch in ways that allow them to continue to serve polities even in the face of either declining or increasing demotic diversity. In the next two chapters we will explore the scope within the federal idea for institutional flexibility and how the principles inherent to federalism's purpose are highly adaptable to a wide range of federal constitutions.

8

Federal Constitutional Design I: Recognition and Autonomous Government

I. Introduction: constitutional theory and federal practice

In the last chapter we addressed the meta purpose of federalism and the principles that flow axiomatically from this purpose. In this chapter and the next we will see how these principles have taken life in the institutions of federal constitutions. My focus here is upon the principles of recognition and autonomy; in Chapter 9 I turn to the institutional manifestation of associational government and reciprocity. At this point in the book I move therefore from how authority is generated by the federal contract to how it is distributed—exploring the different ways in which the federal idea is given institutional life across federal systems.

Approaching the practice of federalism via the purpose and principles of federalism it is clear that the federal idea does not prescribe a definitive institutional prototype. Federalism, like any order of rule, must be dynamic and open to variation from place to place, depending upon the demotic and political conditions of each polity.[1] As Levinson puts it: 'To the extent that a given constitution "succeeds" or "fails", the reason is far more likely to involve its "degree of fit" with the demands presented by a given social order than its adherence to, or deviation from, abstract and universalistic notions of constitutional design.'[2] Federalism, just like unitary constitutionalism, leaves open a capacious range of institutional 'possibilities'.[3] Furthermore, within each federal system the centralisation-decentralisation relationship is always mutable, subject to shifts over time.[4] Accordingly, while there

[1] A. Benz and J. Broschek, 'Federal Dynamics: Introduction', in Benz and Broschek (eds), *Federal Dynamics: Continuity, Change, and the Varieties of Federalism* (Oxford: Oxford University Press, 2013), 1–23, 2.

[2] S. Levinson, 'Reflections on What Constitutes a "Constitution": The Importance of "Constitutions of Settlement" and the Potential Irrelevance of Herculean Lawyering', in D. Dyzenhaus and M. Thorburn (eds), *Philosophical Foundations of Constitutional Law* (Oxford: Oxford University Press, 2016), 75–94, 76.

[3] J. Tully, 'On Local and Global Citizenship: An Apprenticeship Manual', in *Public Philosophy in a New Key: Volume II, Imperialism and Civic Citizenship* (Cambridge: Cambridge University Press, 2008), 246.

[4] P. Dardanelli et al., 'Conceptualizing, Measuring, and Theorizing Dynamic De/Centralization in Federations' (2019) 49 *Publius: The Journal of Federalism* 1–29.

The Federal Contract. Stephen Tierney, Oxford University Press. © Stephen Tierney 2022.
DOI: 10.1093/oso/9780198806745.003.0008

is a core genus of rule that can be called 'federal', there is no generic institutional template of federalism.[5]

Although the federal contract is institutionally commodious, at its heart is the need to balance the dynamic tension between pluralism and union that characterises the federal idea. This relationship has been core to the analysis of most federal scholars and has often proved vexing. Daniel Elazar tells us that 'all federal systems have in common institutional arrangements that connect constituent units horizontally and vertically with the federal level through institutional mechanisms allowing both shared rule and self-rule'.[6] This pithy account has been so influential as to have taken on the character of an aphorism—'the epigram of federalism'[7]—widely deployed as capturing the federal idea itself. Despite its attractive simplicity—'being sufficiently generic that no one can disagree'[8]—this definition does not in fact focus upon the constitutional distinctiveness of federalism which I sought to elicit in my account of federal constitutional principles. Ronald Watts does however attempt to orientate the same balance from a constitutional perspective: 'federations represent one distinct species in which neither the federal nor the constituent units of government are constitutionally subordinate to each other'.[9] In this approach Watts seems to reflect Kelsen's three orders of federal rule: 'each has sovereign powers derived from the constitution rather than from another level of government, each is empowered to deal directly with its citizens in the exercise of its legislative, executive and taxing powers, and each is directly elected by its citizens'.[10] This account, while defining federalism in constitutional terms, is however still characterised by a narrow positivism which presents the institutional instantiation of federalism as a proxy for the federal idea itself. Nonetheless, Watts does highlight that the relationship between pluralism and union is tied inexorably to the relationship between politics and law; the task that follows is to extract how the founding purpose and principles of federalism are made manifest in institutional design. My concern in this book is also squarely with the constitutional nature of federalism's practical instantiation, but it is precisely the fact that constitutionalism from place to place is built from so much 'bricolage'[11] that brings such deep

[5] Even Ronald Watts, who brought to federal studies a dedicated attempt to identify institutional commonalities across federal systems, recognised that 'the application of the federal idea has taken a great variety of forms'. R.L. Watts, *Comparing Federal Systems*, 3rd edn (Montreal, QC, Canada: McGill-Queen's University Press, 2008), 7.

[6] D. Elazar, *Exploring Federalism* (Tuscaloosa: University of Alabama Press,, 1987), 28.

[7] Watts, *Comparing Federal Systems* 1.

[8] F. Palermo and K. Kössler, *Comparative Federalism: Constitutional Arrangements and Case Law* (Oxford: Hart Publishing, 2017), 4.

[9] R.L. Watts, 'The Federal Idea and its Contemporary Relevance', in T.L. Courchene et al., *The Federal Idea: Essays in Honour of Ronald L. Watts* (Kingston-Montreal: McGill-Queen's, 2011), 13–27, 15.

[10] Watts, 'The Federal Idea and its Contemporary Relevance', 15. The reader will observe that this legal-institutionalist approach strongly echoes Wheare's 'jurisdictional' account of federalism—K. Wheare, *Federal Government*, 4th edn (Oxford: Oxford University Press, 1963), which as we will see in this and later chapters has deeper roots in early American federal jurisprudence.

[11] M. Tushnet, 'The Possibilities of Comparative Constitutional Law' (1999) 108 *Yale Law Journal* 1225–1309, 1229.

institutional diversity to the functional life of the federal idea. As Rufus Davis once put it, the essence of federalism lies in 'the creation of a specific kind of jural relationship between law-making authorities, not in the material quality of the functions vested in the general and regional governments'.[12]

It is my contention that the special jural relationship that characterises the federal idea is the fundamental constitutional bond between pluralism and union. It follows that recognition, autonomy, associational rule, and reciprocity, which together create this bond, do not exist in silos or indeed as counterpoints, but rather as essentially complementary principles. As we now explore, in institutional terms this means that within any federal system a territorially based level of government must operate in relation to a viable and effective central order of government. Although the federal idea does not bring with it a particular institutional template, a constitutional theory of federalism recognises that institutions are central to constitutionalism; without institutional realisation, a foundational constitutional purpose can never be more than an idea. It is only in the careful and societally reflexive design of institutions, and in the allocation of powers, that the complex and delicate relationship between pluralism and union can find a balance in the lived reality of any federal contract. It follows that the federal idea is adaptable to new and diverse political conditions, allowing federal institutions to be shaped in innovative ways. It also follows that certain constitutional systems, not necessarily treated as 'federal' within the canon of institutionalist federal studies, will fit the definition of federalism if they are premised upon, and seek to pursue, the core purpose and principles of federalism as a discrete idea for government.

II. Institutionalising federalism: pluralism and union

The essential complementarity of the different principles of federalism is reflected within institutional design across three registers: symbolism/identity, institutional architecture, and governmental competences. Each of these leaves open the space for significantly different design among federal systems and for asymmetry within them. A particular principle may map more obviously onto one or more of these registers than do others. For example, the principle of recognition is reflected particularly in the symbolism of, or totemic declarations made by, the constitution, and in the deep but at times amorphous constitutional identity that flows from these; autonomous government is guaranteed principally in the allocation of governmental competences; while the principle of associational rule is largely captured through institutional architecture. The principle of reciprocity, in both its

[12] R. Davis, 'The "Federal Principle" Reconsidered' (2008) 1 *Australian Journal of Politics & History* 223, 225.

dimensions, tends, like recognition, to assume more inchoate institutional manifestation and can be identified across all three registers.

(i) The principle of recognition

In Chapter 7 I explained the principle of recognition through the metaphor of a mosaic that combines, in complex ways, vertical and horizontal dimensions. The constitution recognises and identifies the constituent territories as its foundational subjects, while they in turn recognise the constitution's authority and the constitutional status of one another as joint partners in the federal constitutional project. Recognition also plays a transformational role: in these acts of recognition the constituent territories take on a new common identity as collective constitutional subjects, shaping a new joint enterprise.

The mosaic of recognition manifests itself in a federal constitution primarily through symbolism or self-declaration—the constitution expressly assuming a federal identity in its very title or preamble.[13] Such explicit language is however missing from the first federal constitution, that of the United States. This reflects both the nebulous meaning of the very term 'federal' in 1787 and also the deeply ambiguous American constitutional commitment to territorial pluralism both at the time of constitutional founding and ever since.

In the nineteenth century the term federal, with or without the prefix 'con', found more explicit articulation. We see this first in the Swiss 'Federal Constitution of the Swiss Confederation' of 1848, which provides in the preamble: 'The Swiss Confederation, with a view to strengthen the Union of the Confederates, to maintain and promote the unity, power and honour of the Swiss nation, has adopted the following Federal Constitution.'[14] It is notable that by the mid-1800s the term 'federal' was still conceptually embryonic, evident in its interchangeability with 'confederal'. The establishment of the modern Canadian constitution two decades later[15] was also deemed by the founders to be an exercise in 'confederation'.[16] However, terminological fluidity was a feature of this process, reflected in a

[13] 'Most federal constitutions refer to the constitutive authority by which the federation was legally constituted.' N. Aroney and J. Kincaid, 'Comparative Observations and Conclusions', in N. Aroney and J. Kincaid (eds), *Courts in Federal Countries: Federalists or Unitarists?* (Toronto: University of Toronto Press, 2017), 482–540, 490.

[14] Federal Constitution of the Swiss Confederation 1848, preamble. The 1999 constitution's preamble removes references to the (con)federal relationship, but states that the Swiss people and the cantons are 'resolved to renew their alliance so as to strengthen liberty, democracy, independence and peace in a spirit of solidarity and openness towards the world'. The title remains: Federal Constitution of the Swiss Confederation 1999.

[15] The British North America Act 1867, 30 & 31 Vict. (UK), c. 3.

[16] E. Brouillet, A.-G. Gagnon, and G. Laforest (eds), *The Quebec Conference of 1864: Understanding the Emergence of the Canadian Federation* (Kingston/Montreal: McGill-Queen's University Press, 2018).

reference to federal unity in the preamble to the British North America (BNA) Act 1867.[17]

The Commonwealth of Australia Constitution Act of 1901, like the BNA Act, does not contain the word 'federal' in its title but it does so in the preamble, which makes its constitutional purpose clear: 'Whereas the people of New South Wales, Victoria, South Australia, Queensland, and Tasmania, humbly relying on the blessing of Almighty God, have agreed to unite in one indissoluble Federal Commonwealth under the Crown of the United Kingdom of Great Britain and Ireland . . .'.[18] Unlike the BNA Act, this explicit badge of federal identity also appears in the body of the Act, for example in the name of the central legislature.[19]

The Australian constitution emerged after a period of intense academic interest in federalism. Work by J.S. Mill, James Bryce, Edward Freeman, and A.V. Dicey, as we have seen throughout the book, drew upon the word 'federal' to describe the USA, Canada, and various multi-territorial polities in Europe. By the turn of the twentieth century therefore, and despite the highly varied practice within constitutional texts themselves, the word federal was becoming the default description for those constitutions which chose to give foundational recognition to territorial pluralism as the primary badge of constitutional identity. In the course of the ensuing century, other constitutions with a similar foundational commitment also tended to adopt the term. The title of the post-war German constitution, *Bundesrepublik Deutschland*, is uniformly translated into English as the *Federal* Republic of Germany. While its title hearkens back to the German Confederation of 1815 and the German Empire's federal constitution of 1871 (which was in practice heavily dominated by Prussia), it has generally been categorised as part of the family of federal constitutions emanating from Philadelphia.[20]

In the process of post-war decolonisation, a number of constitutions adopted the term 'federal' in either titles or preambles: the Federation of Nigeria (1960), United States of Indonesia (1949, defunct), Federation of Malaya (1948, independent 1957,

[17] 'Whereas the Provinces of Canada, Nova Scotia, and New Brunswick have expressed their Desire to be federally united into One Dominion under the Crown of the United Kingdom of Great Britain and Ireland, with a Constitution similar in Principle to that of the United Kingdom . . .'. This act of federalisation was however also described as a 'union' in the long title of the 1867 Act: 'An Act for the Union of Canada, Nova Scotia, and New Brunswick, and the Government thereof; and for Purposes connected therewith'; and neither the terms 'federal' nor 'confederal' appear in the body of the 1867 Act. The German Confederation created by the Congress of Vienna in 1815 was not a federal constitution since it was essentially a league of formally independent states until constitutional unification came about in the birth of the German Empire in 1871. Nonetheless, the fluid use of the term 'confederation' after 1815 is notable, given that the same term came to characterise Switzerland and Canada which were, in contrast to the looser union of the German lands, clearly constitutional systems for a state as we understand the concept today.

[18] Commonwealth of Australia Constitution Act 1901.

[19] 'The legislative power of the Commonwealth shall be vested in a Federal Parliament . . .'. Commonwealth of Australia Constitution Act 1901, s. 1.

[20] H. Steinberger, 'Historic Influences of American Constitutionalism upon German Constitutional Development: Federalism and Judicial Review' (1998) 36 *Columbia Journal of Transnational Law* 189–208, 202, 207–208.

defunct), Federation of Ethiopia and Eritrea (1952, defunct), Pakistan (1956), the Federation of Saint Kitts and Nevis (1983), the constitution of the United Arab Emirates (1971), the Federal Republic of Cameroon (1961, defunct), the United Kingdom of Libya (1951, defunct), and the Mali Federation (1959, independent 1960, defunct). The Indian constitution is somewhat opaque. The constitution is authored, per the preamble, by 'We, the people of India' and the constitution makes no reference to federalism at all.[21] On the other hand, Article 1 declares: 'India, that is Bharat, shall be a Union of States.'[22]

One ought not to read too much into a preamble, particularly given its limited normative authority, but it can be significant in helping to shape constitutional culture. Recognition can however also manifest itself in the allocation of constitutional powers between the constituent territories and the central government and in the institutional design of the polity. In both of these dimensions it is possible to compare the respective political strength and prominence that different constitutions intend to give to the constituent territories' governments on the one hand and central government on the other, and from this institutional architecture deduce the broader constitutional status which the constitution accords to the constituent territories. Furthermore, on both symbolic and institutional registers recognition can also play a role in articulating different levels of constitutional accommodation among the constituent territories themselves. A federal constitution may recognise its constituent territories, and they in turn recognise each other, through the register of constitutional equality. Alternatively, a federal constitution may in fact recognise its constituent territories as different *inter se* and ascribe to them differentiated constitutional status and/or make variegated provision through institutional design and the allocation of powers.

The very idea of asymmetrical subjecthood is a challenge in light of the monist default of modern constitutionalism which envisages subjecthood *qua* citizenship in exclusively individual terms, as we explored in Chapters 6 and 7. Because liberal individualism has become the ideologically dominant backdrop to federal as well as unitary constitutionalism, the idea of recognising different legal rights among constitutional subjects, even when viewed through a territorial prism, often meets with confusion or indeed hostility.[23] Nonetheless, such an asymmetrical approach is today a particular feature of 'multinational' federations:[24] federal states which

[21] '*We, the People of India*, having solemnly resolved to constitute India into a *Sovereign Socialist Secular Democratic Republic* and to secure to all its citizens: . . . and to promote among them all *Fraternity* assuring the dignity of the individual and the unity and integrity of the Nation; . .. ' Constitution of India, preamble.

[22] The reference to a union of states was itself a compromise. Proposals to insert 'federal' in the first clause of the preamble were rejected at the drafting stage: <https://www.constitutionofindia.net/constitution_of_india/the_union_and_its_territory/articles/Article%201>.

[23] B. Barry, *Culture and Equality: An Egalitarian Critique of Multiculturalism* (Cambridge MA: Harvard University Press, 2001).

[24] S. Tierney, *Constitutional Law and National Pluralism* (Oxford: Oxford University Press, 2005); W. Norman, *Negotiating Nationalism: Nation-Building, Federalism, and Secession in the Multinational State* (Oxford: Oxford University Press, 2006).

include constituent territories within which a distinct national identity exists. One example is Canada. The BNA Act 1867 recognised the founding provinces by way of institutional symmetry as we explore later in the chapter, but at the same time it did offer some specific accommodation to Quebec's distinctiveness in language, religion, and civil law.[25] In these instances of institutional asymmetry there was not however an accompanying symbolic acknowledgement of difference. A strong trope within Canadian constitutional identity has been 'provincial equality'.[26] Despite the rise of Quebec nationalism, the constitution has not been amended to offer any explicit recognition of Quebec's particularity, even by the Constitution Act 1982 through which the Canadian constitution was finally patriated from the UK Parliament.[27] An attempt to recognise Quebec as a 'distinct society' failed in 1987,[28] as did a further process of reform in 1992.[29] However, since then the Canadian body politic has taken a symbolic stride—recognising Quebec as a nation,[30] even though this has occurred only through a parliamentary motion rather than by way of formal constitutional change or even a statute.

Other constitutions have adopted asymmetrical recognition of their constituent territories, at least at the level of constitutional practice. These include the constitutions of Belgium, India, Malaysia, Russia, and Spain. An example of a constitution that moved from a position of largely formalistic territorial equality to a more nuanced recognition of difference is India. The constitution in 1947 was characterised by the symbolic and actual constitutional equality of the territories. However, this changed over time. Between 1954 and 1966 the states came increasingly to be defined territorially on ethno-linguistic grounds. For example, six new states were created from Assam while Punjab's particular religious characteristics were also recognised.[31] The new approach to asymmetrical recognition is particularly notable in relation to Jammu and Kashmir which was given special status in 1949.[32] But, on the other hand, this also reflects the central parliament's extraordinary power to amalgamate states or to create new states by dividing existing territories.[33]

The Indian example highlights that the success of any constitution in meeting the constitutional purpose of federalism depends upon how accurately it reflects the territorial particularity of the polity and how well this particularity is recognised

[25] Constitution Act 1867 (UK), 30 & 31 Vict., c. 3, Part VI, s. 92(13) (Property and Civil Rights) and s. 93A (religion and schools); also Part IX, s. 133 (Language).

[26] P. Romney, 'Provincial Equality, Special Status and the Compact Theory of Canadian Confederation' (1999) 32 Canadian Journal of Political Science 21–39.

[27] Constitution Act 1982, being Sch. B to the Canada Act 1982 (UK), c. 11.

[28] Meech Lake Accord (1987).

[29] Charlottetown Accord (1992).

[30] House of Commons Debates, 39–1, No. 087 (27 November 2006), 1000–1005.

[31] The changes were very wide-ranging—for full details of the territorial reorganisation of India see the States Reorganisation Act of 1956.

[32] Constitution of India, art. 370.

[33] Constitution of India, art. 3 and part VIII. Today India has twenty-eight states and eight union territories.

inter se by the constitution's territorial subjects. Canadian scholars for decades have focused upon how the failure of the Canadian constitution to recognise fully Quebec's societal particularity was mirrored by a deeper misunderstanding among Canadian citizens of how the deep diversity between English and French Canada had prompted the decision to found a federal constitution in 1867.[34] Charles Taylor has argued that the flourishing of Quebec as a society was not only important to Quebec itself but was central to the self-definition of Canada as a territorially pluralised 'political society'.[35] If the constitution does not in form or practice recognise territorial pluralism as its underpinning constitutional purpose then the question arises whether federalism is still a useful constitutional model for the state. And if a particular constituent territory comes to believe that the constitution does not adequately recognise its own particularity it may no longer consider the state a legitimate vehicle for its own society. It is clear nonetheless that a pronouncement in the title or preamble of a constitution is not in itself sufficient to give real federal identity to a constitution, nor does its absence necessarily indicate that a constitution is not federal. The federal nature of each system has to be assessed principally by the benchmarks of constitutional competence and the architecture of the constitution's institutions. To take forward this analysis we turn first to autonomous government.

(ii) The principle of autonomous government

The autonomy of the federal state's constituent territories is an inherent principle that flows logically from the constitutional purpose of federalism. Like the principle of recognition, it must be given meaningful legal force by a federal constitution. The ways in which authority is apportioned between the constituent territories and the central government of the state can vary greatly from one federal polity to another, but what is of primary importance to the constitutional theory of federalism is that the division is a matter of constitutional law; this rather than the substantive content of the division of powers demarcates federalism from a unitary order of government.

Autonomy therefore requires to be situated in the context of sovereignty and the relationship between the authority generative and the authority distributive dimensions of constitutional law. Although the autonomy of constituent territories within a federal constitution is primarily a matter of authority distribution, the legitimacy of constitutional authority always operates in relationship with its source.

[34] K. McRoberts, *Misconceiving Canada: The Struggle for National Unity* (Oxford: Oxford University Press, 1997); P. Romney, *Getting it Wrong: How Canadians Forgot Their Past and Imperilled Confederation* (Toronto: University of Toronto Press, 1999).

[35] C. Taylor, 'Shared and Divergent Values', in R.L. Watts and D.M. Brown (eds), *Opinions for a New Canada* (Toronto: Toronto University Press, 1991), 53–76, 64–65. See also M. Burgess, *Comparative Federalism: Theory and Practice* (Abingdon: Routledge, 2006), 114.

I have argued that a federal constitution, compared to a unitary constitution, is characterised by an active relationship between generated and allocated authority; in a federal constitution the constituent territories, as authors of the constitution and the generators of its authority, become institutionalised as both fundamental and active players in the state's governance. This vital relationship between territorial constituent power and territorial constitutional authority remains fundamental to any analysis of the specific institutions and powers through which constituent territories exercise self-government.

Authority allocation is addressed across two vectors. The first is the schema of authority distribution: the institutional method by which the constitution demarcates powers between constituent territories and the central government. The second is the content of this distribution: which powers go, respectively, to which order of government. It is possible to draw out general trends in authority allocation between constituent territories and the central government. Throughout this analysis we will note how the constitutional purpose of federalism directs us to assess authority delineation across the registers of meaningfulness, reflexivity, and complementarity, the benchmarks I used in explaining the principles of federalism in Chapter 7.

(a) The architecture of authority distribution

One approach to allocating constitutional competences within federal constitutions is to enumerate the powers allocated to the centre, with all unenumerated or residual powers falling within the jurisdiction of the constituent territories. In a sense this is the high point of constituent territorial autonomy, specifically limiting the authority of the central government while leaving the powers of the territories relatively open-ended. James Madison took this model to be a feature of a 'federal' system of effectively independent entities: a form of decentralisation which today would typically be characterised as a 'confederal' system.[36] This was indeed the model contained in the Articles of Confederation,[37] and although many involved in the Philadelphia process sought a more centralising model than the Articles, this system of authority distribution was adopted by way of the 10th amendment to the new constitution.[38] As Madison himself put it in his reflections on the draft document, powers accorded to Congress 'are few and defined. Those which are to remain in the State governments are numerous and indefinite'.[39]

[36] J. Madison, Federalist No. 45, C. Rossiter (ed.), *The Federalist Papers* (New York: New American Library, 1961), 288–294, 290–291.

[37] Articles of Confederation (1777), art. 2.

[38] US Constitution, amend. 10.

[39] J. Madison, Federalist No. 45, Rossiter, *The Federalist Papers*, 288–294, 292. Madison was in fact opposed to the amendment altogether and instrumental in changing the draft text of the 10th amendment to reduce its impact. K.L. Lash, 'James Madison's Celebrated Report of 1800: The Transformation of the Tenth Amendment' (2006) 74 *The George Washington Law Review* 165–200, 171–172.

The Swiss federal constitution of 1848 took a similar approach, allocating residual powers to the cantons.[40] A key point of difference is that whereas the American constitution is, beyond the 10th amendment, silent as to the authority of the states, the Swiss constitution is more detailed, allocating powers on an article-by-article basis, articulating the respective limits of cantonal and national parliamentary authority.[41] The 1848 model was a prototype for those later federal constitutions which have enumerated the allocation of competences in a more granular way; it stands out however as exceptional for the degree of autonomy it guarantees the constitution's constituent territories. This is manifest in other ways, such as the role of the cantons in administering federal law.[42] Nonetheless, as I will discuss below, the Swiss constitution changed over time; indeed it was the deep entanglement of the cantons in federal administration that helped facilitate the diminution of cantonal autonomy in favour of powers exercised concurrently with the federal government.

The Australian constitution also allocates residual powers to the states but differs from the American model—and pre-empts later Swiss developments—in setting out a detailed list of concurrent powers to supplement the short list of exclusive federal powers which it contains.[43] Another example in this vein is, to an extent, Germany. The constitution of 1949 allocates residual powers to the *Länder*.[44] The German federal model is however principally characterised by the deep integration of the *Länder* governments and the central government. This alerts us to the fact that formal architecture of authority distribution, including the location of residual powers, is far from the whole story of central/constituent territorial relations.

An alternative to the American approach is to detail the exclusive powers of each branch while adding a list of concurrent powers.[45] The Swiss constitution of 1999 marks a gear shift in this direction, coupling its more detailed approach to listing the competences of the cantons and the federal government with shared competences.[46] The Indian constitution similarly contains three lists. It has been argued that the very fact of enumerating state powers in the Indian constitution was 'intended to limit the scope of the national government'.[47] That may be so, but this model is complemented not only by enumerated federal powers and a list of

[40] Federal Constitution of the Swiss Confederation 1848, art. 3: 'The Cantons are sovereign except to the extent that their sovereignty is limited by the Federal Constitution. They exercise all rights that are not vested in the Confederation.'

[41] Federal Constitution of the Swiss Confederation 1848, arts 73–74.

[42] P. Mahon, 'Judicial Federalism and Constitutional Review in the Swiss Judiciary', in A. Ladner et al., *Swiss Public Administration: Making the State Work Successfully* (Lausanne: Palgrave MacMillan, 2018), 137–155, 144.

[43] Commonwealth of Australia Constitution Act 1900, s. 107.

[44] Artis 30 and 70 (*contra* art. 73 which enumerates federal powers).

[45] N. Steytler (ed.), *Concurrent Powers in Federal Systems: Meaning, Making, and Managing* (Leiden: Brill and Nijhoff, 2017).

[46] Constitution of Switzerland, Title Three, Ch. 2.

[47] Palermo and Kössler, *Comparative Federalism*, 140.

concurrent powers but also by the vesting of residual powers in the central government.[48] The Indian approach was to delineate power allocation in more detail, going further than the Canadian and Australian approaches by generating a more comprehensive list of all powers.[49] Article 248 has been interpreted by the courts as a mop-up clause, allocating to the federal government those matters not contained in the lists.[50]

When comparing India to the first federal constitutions it is clear that differing approaches emerged from very particular historical circumstances, highlighting the societal reflexivity of federal constitutionalism. Those federations in which the constituent territories were pre-existing polities tended to allocate residual powers to the territorial governments. By contrast, in states where the governments of constituent territories were first created at the moment of federal constitutional foundation, the reverse is the case, as we see explicitly in the Indian constitution and more implicitly in relation to Canada.[51] The BNA Act 1867 adopted a two-lists approach,[52] in part to avoid the American precedent which was seen as vesting excessive powers in the states. Section 91 sets out areas of exclusive jurisdiction of the federal Parliament, while section 92 lists those areas within the sole purview of the provinces.[53] While the Canadian constitution does not attempt to articulate a comprehensive list of concurrent powers, it does specifically provide for the sharing of authority in a limited number of areas, notably agriculture and immigration.[54] Importantly, section 91 is a comprehensive allocation of authority. Like the Indian constitution nearly a century later, section 91 vests the residual power in the federal government through a broad, sweeping-up provision, authorising the federal

[48] Constitution of India, art. 248. The Malaysian constitution also has the three-list format (with special supplementary lists for the states of Sabah and Sarawak). However, residual legislative power goes to the state legislature. Constitution of Malaysia, art. 77.

[49] V. Niranjan, 'Legislative Competence: the Union and the States', in S. Choudhry, M. Khosla, and P. Bhanu Mehta (eds), *The Oxford Handbook of the Indian Constitution* (Oxford: Oxford University Press, 2016), Part 5, Ch. 26, 467.

[50] *Union of India v. H S Dhillon AIR* (1972) Indian SC 1061.

[51] The Canadian foundational story is complex because it was elongated over time through the Quebec Act 1774, (UK) 14 Geo. III, c. 83 and the British North America Act 1840 (UK) 3 & 4 Vict., c. 35. In some sense the 1867 Act marked the union of existing territories; although given new names by the BNA Act, Ontario and Quebec had distinct governmental arrangements that preceded 1867. At the same time however the colonies of Nova Scotia and New Brunswick were united with the newly characterised 'provinces' of Ontario and Quebec within the Dominion of Canada.

[52] BNA Act, 1867 (UK), 30 & 31 Vict., c. 3, Part VI, ss 91 and 92.

[53] The historical circumstances are complex. A clear intention of the founders was, in contrast to the US constitution, to accord residual powers to the national government. In that regard the enumerated list of federal government powers was intended to be illustrative only and not comprehensive. E. Bedard, 'The Centralizing Federalism of Cauchon', in E. Brouillet, A.-G. Gagnon, and G. Laforest (eds), *The Quebec Conference of 1864: Understanding the Emergence of the Canadian Federation* (Kingston/Montreal: McGill-Queen's University Press, 2018), 103–116, 112–113. See also T.O. Hueglin and A. Fenna, *Comparative Federalism: A Systematic Enquiry*, 2nd edn (Toronto: University of Toronto Press, 2015), 159.

[54] Constitution Act 1867 (UK), 30 & 31 Vict., c. 3, Part VI, s. 95. Another example is s. 94A. The federal legislature may make laws for pensions, however this is not a supreme power; its exercise does not affect the operation of provincial laws on the matter.

Parliament to legislate in areas not allotted to the provinces in order to guarantee 'peace, order and good government'.[55]

With the promulgation of increasingly detailed constitutions, and with further provision for concurrent powers, the issue of residue has become less important in most modern federal constitutions. It remains of some conceptual significance however because it offers a constitutional guide as to hierarchy. Constitutional draftsmen, and in time those vested with the task of constitutional interpretation, still had to decide where the last word lay in relation to any shared or unenumerated powers.[56] The American constitution is not explicit about this, but the 'supremacy' clause in Article VI makes clear that the constitution itself operates above the authority of laws made by the states,[57] a provision which has in practice, and through judicial interpretation,[58] served to strengthen the federal branch.[59] The federal judiciary has also reinforced this dominance through the doctrine of 'pre-emption', whereby state legislation is deemed to be forestalled by existing federal legislation,[60] with the federal courts taking a generous view of the range of competences to which federal arrogation applies.[61]

In a similar way the Indian constitution, by supplementing its three lists with the principle of federal paramountcy, has also done much to centralise the federal system,[62] at times with the active assistance of the Supreme Court.[63] The

[55] H.A. Smith, 'The Residue of Power in Canada' (1926) 4 *Canadian Bar Review* 432–439. The centralising intention is clear. See N. Aroney, 'Formation, Representation and Amendment in Federal Constitutions' (2006) 54 *American Journal of Comparative Law* 277–336, 291–292.

[56] S. Mogi, *The Problem of Federalism; A Study in the History of Political Theory* (New York: The Macmillan Company, 1931).

[57] 'This Constitution, and the Laws of the United States which shall be made in Pursuance thereof; and all Treaties made, or which shall be made, under the Authority of the United States, shall be the supreme Law of the Land ... any ... Laws of any State to the Contrary notwithstanding.' US Constitution, art. VI.

[58] *Ware v. Hylton*, 3 US (3 Dall.) 199 (1796); *McCulloch v. Maryland*, 17 US (4 Wheat.) 316 (1819); *Pennsylvania v. Nelson*, 350 US 497 (1956).

[59] There is evidence that James Madison would have preferred the federal government to have been given a veto power. D.B. Robertson, *The Original Compromise: What the Framers Were Really Thinking* (New York: Oxford University Press, 2013), 168. But in the end the supremacy clause has served successfully to consolidate its dominant constitutional position.

[60] *Gibbons v. Ogden*, 22 US (9 Wheat.) 1 (1824); *Brown v. Maryland*, 25 US (12 Wheat.) 419 (1827); *Pacific Gas & Electric Co v. State Energy Resources Conservation & Development Commission*, 461 US 190 (1983). See also R. Epstein and M. Greve (eds), *Federal Preemption: States' Powers, National Interests* (Washington DC: Aei Press, 2007).

[61] *Missouri v. Holland*, 252 US 416 (1920); *Pennsylvania v. Nelson* 350 US 497 (1956). See also J.F. Zimmerman, *Federal Preemption: The Silent Revolution* (Ames: Iowa State University Press, 1991). Although it has also been pointed out recently that states could make better use of the regulatory power conferred by the federal government to resist federal policy. J. Bulman-Pozen and H.K. Gerken, 'Uncooperative Federalism' (2009) 118 *Yale Law Journal* 1256–1310. In light of the overwhelming power of the US federal government discussed later in this chapter and the next, it is not clear how realistic this option of obstructionism would be in practice, even if the political will to pursue it should exist.

[62] Constitution of India, art. 254 and Sch. 7, List III. The constitution also contains a federal override power—Constitution of India, art. 249(1). The exercise of this power requires a supermajority in parliament. An equivalent executive power is contained in art. 257(1). Art. 251 also provides that law made by the federal Parliament will prevail over inconsistent law made by a legislature of a state.

[63] Discussed in Chapter 10.

Malaysian constitution also provides for federal supremacy in the event of a conflict between federal and state law.[64] The German constitution similarly provides for the supremacy of federal law over *Länder* law[65] and the pre-emptive validity of national law in areas of concurrency.[66] Again, the courts have been instrumental, interpreting federal supremacy in broad terms.[67] A further, albeit indirect, consolidation of federal power in the German constitution results from conditions imposed upon the *Länder* to comply with the constitution's fundamental principles, including republicanism and democracy.[68] This 'homogeneity clause' imposes a set of conditions upon *Länder* powers that 'significantly limits subnational constitutional autonomy'.[69] It has served to give the federal government a further role, supported by the courts, as guarantors of the ideological structure of the entire polity.[70]

A major trend in the development of federal constitutions has indeed been the centralisation of decision-making power. In some cases this was the clear intention of the founders, manifest in the allocation of the residual power to the centre and in pre-emption clauses. In India, the Constituent Assembly that drafted the 1950 constitution decided that the best model for India was 'a federation with a strong Centre'.[71] But it is also the case that the trajectory of centralisation and decentralisation within federal constitutional systems has often gone against the grain of foundational institutional design. The US constitution contained a strong steer towards state autonomy in the 10th amendment, but over time the US constitution took on a strong centralising drive. Several factors over time served to weaken the effect of the 10th amendment. One is the other provisions of the Bill of Rights which guarantee individualised liberties across the country. The nationalising impetus of these amendments was consolidated through the 14th amendment, and the broad interpretation given to it, which served to extend the coverage of first nine amendments to state as well as Congressional law-making and executive administration. It is also the case that the US constitution, although enumerating

64 Constitution of Malaysia, art. 75. The trajectory of the Malaysian constitution has been in many ways centralising: F. Hutchinson, 'Malaysia's Federal System: Overt and Covert Centralisation' (2014) 44 *Journal of Contemporary Asia* 422–442.

65 Constitution of the Federal Republic of Germany, art. 31.

66 The *Länder* can only legislate 'so long as and to the extent that the Federation has not exercised its legislative power by enacting a law'. Constitution of the Federal Republic of Germany, art. 72(1).

67 Chapter 10.

68 Art. 28(1) states *inter alia* that: 'The constitutional order in the Länder must conform to the principles of a republican, democratic and social state governed by the rule of law, within the meaning of this Basic Law . . .'

69 Palermo and Kössler, *Comparative Federalism*, 135.

70 83 BVerfGE 37 (Foreign Voters I) —see Palermo and Kössler, *Comparative Federalism*, 415. The Swiss constitution, in moving towards ever greater concurrency, also includes pre-emption powers which bolster the authority of the federal government (Federal Constitution of the Swiss Confederation 1999, art. 49—see also arts 62, 63, 74, and 123). The Australian constitution has also conferred a determinative voice upon federal legislation in important ways—Commonwealth of Australia Constitution Act 1900, ss 51 and 109.

71 M.P. Jain, 'Nehru and the Indian Federalism' (1977) 19 *Journal of the Indian Law Institute* 392–418, 401–402.

very few powers, tends to allocate those which it does provide for to the federal government. Article I, sections 7, 8, and 9 assign specific powers by reference exclusively to the federal order of government, remaining silent as to the powers of the states. These provisions have been deployed by the central government greatly to expand its sphere of authority. In particular, the 'necessary and proper' clause,[72] the 'general welfare' clause,[73] and the 'commerce' clause,[74] together with the supremacy clause in Article VI, have been instrumental in the gear shift of constitutional power over the past two centuries. The reasons behind this development are far more complex than simply the text of the constitution, but the vagueness and laconic nature of the written word created a zone of ambiguity which allowed the federal government, supported by the judiciary, to expand the meaning of constitutionally allotted federal power.

Interpretation has therefore been vital to federal centralisation. In the USA the federal courts have animated the brief list of federal powers in a way that has played 'havoc with the original design'.[75] This is a common trend in other countries also, with federal courts fostering the accrual of more and more central control. In relation to the Australian constitution, context is also important. The constitution came with a seemingly high level of state autonomy, leaving residual power to the states. However its trajectory, like that of the USA, has been centralising. Although the founders intended to limit strictly the jurisdiction of the central government, over time the constitution has 'manifestly failed to do so'.[76] Although the 'single list' approach to articulating the powers of the federal government is more detailed in the Australian constitution than the US, Cheryl Saunders draws the general conclusion that a single list of central powers 'offers little effective limit' to the scope of the federal power 'in the absence of competing powers expressly assigned to the states'.[77]

Centralisation has also been a feature of administrative federalism in Germany, Austria, and to some extent Switzerland. While the German *Länder* have a potentially strong role in helping to make central policy, they have little territorially

[72] 'To make all Laws which shall be necessary and proper for carrying into Execution the foregoing Powers, and all other Powers vested by this Constitution in the Government of the United States, or in any Department or Officer thereof.' US Constitution, art. I, s. 8, 18. See G. Lawson et al., *The Origins of the Necessary and Proper Clause* (Cambridge: Cambridge University Press, 2010); James Madison, Federalist No. 44, Rossiter, *The Federalist Papers*, 280–288, 285.

[73] 'The Congress shall have Power To ... provide for the ... general Welfare of the United States.' US Constitution, art. I, s. 8, 1.

[74] US Constitution, art. I, s. 8, 3.

[75] Hueglin and Fenna, *Comparative Federalism*, 2nd edn, 144.

[76] Hueglin and Fenna, *Comparative Federalism*, 2nd edn, 165. And see A. Fenna, 'The Centralization of Australian Federalism 1901–2010: Measurement and Interpretation' (2019) 49 *Publius: The Journal of Federalism* 30–56.

[77] C. Saunders, 'The Constitutional Arrangements of Federal Systems: A Sceptical View from the Outside', in J.J. Hesse and V. Wright (eds), *Federalizing Europe? The Costs, Benefits, and Preconditions of Federal Political Systems* (Oxford: Oxford University Press, 1996), 49–69, 54.

specific autonomy beyond the implementation of national policy.[78] The complex system of administrative federalism is set out in Part VII of the Basic Law. On matters within the exclusive legislative power of the Federation, the *Länder* have power to legislate only when and to the extent that they are expressly authorised to do so by a federal law.[79] There is also provision setting out in detail matters falling under exclusive federal jurisdiction and matters subject to concurrent legislative powers.[80] Essentially the role of the *Länder* is one of implementation: to 'execute federal laws in their own right',[81] but this is subject to federal oversight.[82]

Austria has a similar system, providing exclusive powers of federal implementation of national law[83] but also setting out areas of federal legislative business which the *Länder* must implement.[84] Switzerland too has moved in this direction. Despite strong cantonal powers set out in the 1848 constitution, we have noted that in practice a number of powers have come to be exercised concurrently by the centre and the cantons. The 1999 constitution both reflected this historical trend and was instrumental in taking it further. Although the 1999 constitution provides that the federal government 'shall allow the Cantons all possible discretion to organise their own affairs and shall take account of cantonal particularities',[85] it defines many powers as jointly held.[86] Power sharing is now 'the norm',[87] which has in effect been a way of enhancing national power. Although the structure of powers is now based upon three lists—federal, national, and shared power—the *modus operandi* of Swiss government is administrative federalism similar to Germany,[88] whereby cantons in effect largely implement national framework legislation.[89] That said, it would be a mistake to assume that Switzerland is as centralised as Germany or Austria; Swiss federal culture is still distinctive. As Dietmar Braun puts it, 'though both countries follow the logic of "administrative federalism" … Germany follows a "unitary" rationale with centralizing tendencies in the distribution of legislative

[78] A. Kaiser and S. Vogel, 'Dynamic De/Centralization in Germany, 1949–2010' (2019) 49 *Publius* 84–111.

[79] Basic Law for the Federal Republic of Germany 1949, art. 71.

[80] Basic Law for the Federal Republic of Germany 1949, arts 72–74.

[81] Basic Law for the Federal Republic of Germany 1949, art. 83. The Basic Law also reserves certain matters to central administration: art. 87.

[82] Basic Law for the Federal Republic of Germany 1949, art. 84. The *Länder* in certain circumstances also execute federal laws on federal commission—art. 85.

[83] The Federal Constitutional Law of Austria 1920, art. 10.

[84] The Federal Constitutional Law of Austria 1920, art. 11. See further related provisions in arts 12–14. Matters of *Länder* jurisdiction are set out in arts 15–16. Notably art.15a provides that: 'The Federation and the Land can conclude agreements between themselves concerning matters of their current scope of competence.'

[85] Federal Constitution of the Swiss Confederation 1999, art. 46(3).

[86] For example, art. 45 concerning canton participation in federal decision-making; art. 55 relating to consultation in foreign policy decisions.

[87] Hueglin and Fenna, *Comparative Federalism*, 2nd edn, 163.

[88] A. Ladner, N. Soguel, Y. Emery, S. Weerts, and S. Nahrath (eds), *Swiss Public Administration: Making the State Work Successfully* (Berlin: Springer, 2020).

[89] The Federal Constitution of the Swiss Confederation, art. 46.

authority while Switzerland follows a "non-centralized" organization ... which values the self-determination of member states highly.'[90] The formal allocation of powers to the cantons therefore retains some significance, if only in reminding the federal government that it is dependent upon the cantons for effective administration of national policy.[91]

Formal jurisdictional autonomy can therefore be undermined by concurrent powers, even where a lengthy and detailed list of powers is allocated to constituent territories. Another factor that has facilitated centralisation is the allocation of general or residual revenue and spending power to central governments. The power of the purse has been significant in implementing federal government policies and it has also had indirect constitutional significance in allowing federal governments to stretch fairly terse constitutional powers by claiming to be spending money on issues of 'general welfare', 'commerce', 'good government', and the like. Central governments have also been able to tie constituent territories to central policy through central financial grants which can come with conditions of policy uniformity.[92]

There are also deeper structural factors in play in either fostering or constraining centralising tendencies. Perhaps the most significant is the growth of government in general over the past two centuries. Early federal systems anticipated a relatively clear division of competences, what Kenneth Wheare called 'coordinate federalism',[93] through which constituent territorial governments and the central government would have relative independence to formulate and implement policy. Since the mid-nineteenth century however, governments at both federal and territorial levels have taken on responsibility for more and more areas of public health, welfare, education, the environment, etc. A consequence of this is that the clear-cut allocation of powers into central and territorial silos has for long not been feasible, replaced by an expansion in the range and complexity of inter-jurisdictional interaction. Whether concurrent powers are expressly provided for or not, they exist in all federal constitutions and, as the state has grown, have proliferated to the point where the principle of autonomy can only be understood in the context of shared powers. It is also the case that new areas of responsibility have increasingly taken

[90] D. Braun, 'Multilevel Governance in Germany and Switzerland', in H. Enderlein et al. (eds), *Hand-book on Multi-level Governance* (Cheltenham: Edward Elgar, 2010), 168–183, 169–170. South Africa is another constitutional system that has adopted a 'German administrative federalism' model in a more centralising way than Switzerland. D. Braun, 'Federalism in South Africa—Can it work?' (2009) *Université de Lausanne Travaux de Science Politique/Political Science Working Paper Series*, No. 41. <https://serval.unil.ch/resource/serval:BIB_7E73EA722BCD.P001/REF.pdf>.

[91] Watts, *Comparing Federal Systems*, 3rd edn, 31. It is also the case that in Switzerland the central government does not have the same power to give directions to the territories in implementing its policies as does the German federal government. The recognition in art. 3 that the cantons are both sovereign 'except to the extent that their sovereignty is limited by the Federal Constitution' and hold the residual power, is also of general significance to the relative centralisation/decentralisation of the system.

[92] R.M. Bird, 'The Spending Power in Federal Countries' (2009) SSRN paper, <https://papers.ssrn.com/sol3/papers.cfm?abstract_id=1529322>

[93] Wheare, *Federal Government*, 4th edn, , 10.

on a 'national' character as federal states have sought to achieve common standards across the polity. Here the role of the central government in setting common policy, administering its delivery, and paying for its provision become crucial factors. In a number of federal states a strong uni-national mentality has developed which is now of far greater salience as a focus of identity for citizens than territorial attachments, leaving little reason to oppose the accrual of central power in the name of territorial autonomy.[94] In light of these factors, it is clear that the institutional allocation of powers is not the whole story, and that the centralising tendency of many federal constitutions is a consequence of political practice, the interpretation of the constitution in a centralising way, and deeper cultural plate changes below the institutional surface of the polity.

While the inexorable growth of central power is a common trend, it is by no means a universal truth. We see a contrasting story to that of the USA, Australia, Germany, and Switzerland when we turn to Canada. It was thought by the drafters the BNA Act in 1867 that a two-list system would provide for a stronger central government, and more tightly circumscribe territorial competence, than had the limited number of federal powers set out in the US constitution.[95] Despite this purpose and design, the story of Canadian federalism has been complex and fluctuating. The two-list approach may have opened the door institutionally to greater centralisation than did the constitutions of the USA or even Australia. It is also the case that dynamics of coordination and uniformity advanced by the Canadian federal government, similar to those in other federal states, 'have generally been backed by the political process and upheld by the courts'.[96] However, Canada, in comparison to these other systems, developed in a far less centralising way.

There are undoubtedly additional institutional factors that have contributed to this, such as the lack of a supremacy clause in the BNA Act 1867.[97] The Canadian constitution also lacks an express residual powers provision. These two design features have certainly drawn the courts into numerous disputes over where respective powers lie and who has the final word in relation to particular competencies.[98]

[94] This is set against the backdrop of, and has been consolidated by, the ideology of liberal universalism: 'The original idea that federalism would allow different jurisdictions to practise different values has run up squarely against the modern world's commitment to universal human rights, whether that be in respect of racial issues, sexual choice, gender equality or a range of other subjects.' Hueglin and Fenna, *Comparative Federalism*, 2nd edn, 140.

[95] P. Hogg and W. Wright, 'Canadian Federalism, the Privy Council and the Supreme Court: Reflections on the Debate About Canadian Federalism' (2005) 38 *University of British Columbia Law Review* 329–352, 333.

[96] Palermo and Kössler, *Comparative Federalism: Constitutional Arrangements and Case Law*, 140.

[97] Although as Hodge points out, 'Dominion leadership could employ the executive machinery of disallowance to shortstop provincial ambition.' W.C. Hodge, 'Patriation of the Canadian Constitution: Comparative Federalism in a New Context' (1985) 60 *Washington Law Review* 585–632, 604, fn. 59.

[98] Detailed in Hogg and Wright, 'Canadian Federalism, The Privy Council and the Supreme Court: Reflections on the Debate about Canadian Federalism'.

As we will see in Chapter 10 however, the approach of the Canadian courts has, over time, been considerably less centralising than that of the US Supreme Court. Overall therefore, it is clear that constitutional design is only part of the story of centralisation. A more plausible explanation than the division of competences in the constitution is that different social and demotic factors have been instrumental in shaping the different trajectories of American and Australian federalism on the one hand and Canadian federalism on the other. A unified national demos grew within both the USA and Australia and the federal government in each system assumed to itself the role of representing this demos through a direct relationship with the state's citizens as a national body. Accordingly, each country, without strong territorial differences, found less need for territorial autonomy. Individual equality rather than territorial difference became the crucial ideological benchmark against which constitutional culture developed. As Saunders notes in relation to Australia: 'A national preoccupation with equity or equality . . . tends to be reflected in the assignment of power to the federal government or in other mechanisms designed to achieve the same result.'[99] In Canada, by contrast, the country's bicultural identity was the central reality that underpinned the 1867 process and this has continued to overshadow the development of the central-provincial power relationship, with Quebec particularly active in demanding respect for provincial autonomy. As Hueglin and Fenna argue: 'Given the country's bicultural nature, the intention of making Canada a strongly centralized federal system was probably doomed under any scheme of dividing powers.'[100] And Canada is not alone in such a reality. Other constitutional systems with similarly deep, territorially situated, cultural differences such as Belgium, Spain, and the United Kingdom have seen autonomy grow over time, reflecting the strong desire for self-government by one or more of their constituent territories.[101]

It follows from the deep pluralism of these states that institutional design since the 1970s has been expressly shaped to recognise territorial difference; a notable feature is that territorial autonomy has been tailored to the particularities of each state and, in asymmetrical ways, to reflect also their internal complexity. Spain emerged from Franco's rule in the late 1970s with a new, complex constitution that combined a strong centre with detailed and asymmetrical accommodation of the country's 'historical nationalities': Catalonia, the Basque provinces, and Galicia. The constitution provided for an exclusive area of central jurisdiction, but also for separate Statutes of Autonomy. One example of asymmetry is that, after promulgation of the 1978 constitution, five of the seventeen Autonomous Communities were assigned what was tantamount to residual authority, while the federal government

[99] C. Saunders, 'Constitutional Arrangements of Federal Systems' (1995) 25 *Publius* 61–79, 70.

[100] Hueglin and Fenna, *Comparative Federalism*, 2nd edn, 148. See also S. Tierney, 'Pierre Elliott Trudeau and the Idea of Federalism' (2020) 99 *Supreme Court Law Review* 3–36.

[101] S. Tierney, *Constitutional Law and National Pluralism* (Oxford: Oxford University Press, 2004).

retained residual power in relation to the rest.[102] More significantly, the constitution allowed the territories to assume self-government in their own ways and at their own pace. While many have taken on the powers on offer, it has been the 'historical nationalities' that have been most keen to maximise their autonomy. They were entitled to take a 'fast track' in drawing down initial autonomy[103] and have used this to consolidate distinct and significant self-governing authority.

The Belgian constitution of 1831 had a centralising aim and initially left residual powers with the central government. But with the rise of sub-state nationalism, particularly in Flanders, constitutional reform followed by way of a series of developments from 1970 onwards. In the most significant constitutional reform, in 1993, which declared Belgium to be federal, residual powers were reallocated to the constituent territories and most powers now exist as exclusive competences. Constituent territories exist in a complex relationship with cultural communities established in the First State Reform of 1970. There is also much asymmetry between the powers of the regions and those of the communities. Within all of this complexity, the overall trend in the past half century has been towards more and more decentralisation, a centrifugal dynamic encouraged by the lack of any supremacy clause in the Belgian constitution.

In the UK the devolved administrations in Scotland and Wales, created between 1998 and 1999, have also seen their devolved powers increase considerably.[104] Although these powers are not codified within a system that lacks a written constitution, devolution is itself a matter of the highest constitutional significance and has seen statutory recognition of a constitutional convention that protects territorial autonomy,[105] as well as a statutory commitment to the permanence of devolved institutions.[106]

To conclude, it is clear that the story of federalism in most states is one of increasing central authority and diminishing territorial authority, a process involving the complex mixture of institutional design, interpretive disposition, and structural changes in the role of the state. Even seventy-five years ago Wheare observed: 'There is one general tendency in all federal governments … The general governments have grown stronger.'[107] In seeking to explain this phenomenon, some look to institutional features such as a two-list system, the location of residual authority, a power of pre-emption, and the degree of detail in competence allocation as important factors. Each of these can of course play a role but there are deeper factors of constitutional and political culture that either foster or constrain

102 For the division of competences see Constitution of Spain, arts 148–149.

103 The Constitution of Spain, arts 149 and 151 set out this process.

104 Scotland Acts 2012 and 2016 and Government of Wales Act 2006; Wales Acts 2014 and 2017.

105 Scotland Act 1998, s. 28(8); Government of Wales Act 2006, s. 107(6).

106 Scotland Act 1998 s. 63A; Wales Act 2017, s. 1

107 Wheare, *Federal Government*, 4th edn, 236. To take the example of the American system, Robert Nagel has also talked of the 'implosion' of American federalism. Robert F. Nagel, *The Implosion of American Federalism* (New York: Oxford University Press, 2001).

centralising tendencies. At the same time, in a number of federal or federalising states, territorial autonomy has remained strong or has indeed grown in significance. It is apparent that the demotic nature of the polity is therefore of considerable significance to the fostering of relative centralising or decentralising dynamics; the existence or absence of strong territorial identities and the desire within the polity to give these institutional expression through constitutional autonomy play a vital part in the trajectory of federal constitutionalism. In those states where constituent territories retain a strong identity, there is a deeper sense that the power distribution dimension of the constitution is tied to, and legitimised by, the power generational act of constitutional foundation. In this context constituent territories uphold the fundamentality of the federal contract in actively resisting centralisation. It is therefore particularly in these federal systems that we see deep tensions emerge in relation to those areas of government in the modern state where shared powers, and through them the accrual of central power, are a growing reality. We see clearer evidence of these stresses as we turn to the substantive allocation of competences in federal systems.

(b) Substantive division of competences

The tension between pluralism and union at the heart of the federal contract, the focus of federal debates both at and since the Philadelphia convention, in many ways comes to a head in the substantive division of competences. Federalists, in their critique of the dysfunctionality of the Articles of Confederation, argued that the central government required meaningful areas of exclusive responsibility to make the nascent United States viable as an international power.[108] Despite this, the constitution's enumeration of federal powers was very modest when viewed from today's perspective. This is unsurprising in an age where the reach of public authority in general was fairly limited. As a consequence, the emphasis of the framers was much more upon institutional design and the issue of representation than it was upon competence distribution.

The tension between pluralism and union has played out differently in every federal system inaugurated since then, with each polity taking its own approach to the allocation of powers. Nor is it the case that particular architectures of division—for example, whether or not a system adopts a two-list approach or the way in which residual powers are allocated—offer a definitive guide as to which powers go to which level.[109] Nonetheless, certain powers are in general allocated by federal constitutions to the central branch. Today national governments within federal polities tend to have been allotted, or at least have accrued, responsibility for the major tasks of managing the modern state: macro-economic policy, regulation

[108] See e.g. A. Hamilton, Federalist No. 11, Rossiter, *The Federalist Papers*, 84–91; J. Madison, Federalist No. 20, Rossiter, *The Federalist Papers*, 134–138.

[109] N. Aroney, 'Formation, Representation and Amendment in Federal Constitutions' 280.

of the currency, fiscal policy including revenue collection and spending, trade and commerce (both internal and external), foreign affairs, defence policy, and security. As we have seen, this accretion of competence has often occurred within older constitutions through expansive interpretation of terse constitutional provisions, while more modern constitutions tend to set these powers out in far greater detail.

Despite most central governments now having responsibility for a similar range of matters, it is not always easy to find within the literature in-depth theoretical explanations of what should be allocated to sub-state constituent territories and why. Analysis can consequently be tautological, assuming that 'national' matters and 'local' matters are respectively self-evident.[110] The federal idea does in fact provide a principled basis for the allocation. The inherent constitutional commitment to union implies that the central institutions need sufficient powers to fulfil a key role—sustaining the constitution as an effective legal order, thus enabling the state to function both domestically and as a viable international actor. The principle of autonomy on the other hand requires that the constitution allocate to sub-state constituent territories those powers necessary to make their self-government meaningful. Every federal system must find its own alignment between these competing goals.

As we address the division of powers within federal systems we find however that the same two structural features that encouraged a centralising architecture of power allocation have also affected the allocation of specific powers themselves: namely the emergence of new areas of competence within the modern state as the sphere of public law has expanded, and the developing matrix of shared powers that flows from these. The most obvious area in which both dynamics have been in play, resulting in the accumulation of powers by the centre and its dominant role even in areas where competences overlap, is the economy. The national government generally has competence for economic policy, currency, and revenue collection and redistribution. Therefore, as the state's role in social policy has expanded, so too has the significance of the taxing and spending powers to reflect the growing scale and cost of social provision. At the same time however the role of constituent territories in social affairs has also grown, given the extensive overlap that has developed between economic policy and social provision in areas that are often territorial competences such as health, education, language, and culture.[111] Kenneth Wheare considered the scope for independent economic activity to be crucial to territorial autonomy. For the federal principle to operate meaningfully, it followed for Wheare that central and regional governments must each have under

[110] D. McGregor, *The Government of Canada* (Toronto: University of Toronto Press, 1949), 96; S. Rufus Davis, *Theory and Reality: Federal Ideas in Australia, England and Europe* (Queensland: University of Queensland Press, 1995), 46.

[111] M. Keating, 'Beyond the Nation-State: Territory, Solidarity and Welfare in a Multiscalar Europe' (2021) 9 *Territory, Politics, Governance* 331–345.

its own independent control financial resources sufficient to perform its exclusive functions. Each must be 'financially co-ordinate with the other'.[112] As I have discussed however, the very idea of 'exclusive functions' within federal systems has largely been overtaken by the growth of the public sphere at both national and territorial levels and the inevitable overlap that emerges between making social provision and paying for it. Furthermore, given that overlap now extends beyond classic areas such as health and education into so many ancillary fields of social policy, it can be hard to identify meaningful areas of complete autonomy within any modern federal constitutional system. At the same time, as the central government has expanded its role in social policy however, territories have also sought to use their powers to make policy in various new areas. These endeavours can hinge upon the constitutional capacity to raise taxes, or at least to decide how to spend tax revenue collected at the centre. If these powers do exist, constituent territories can follow different ideological directions from those taken by the centre or by other territories: for example, a constituent territory can establish itself as a relatively high or low tax zone, spending less or more respectively on public services. Such divergence in approach can of course rub up against demands for equal treatment across the polity which I address when we turn to the principle of reciprocity in the next chapter. A related issue is that the spending power of territories can be asymmetrical. This can be an accident of fortune—territories with more natural resources or with wealthier residents or resident companies can raise more revenue, giving them in practice more scope to develop discrete policy. But it can also be a result of deliberate constitutional recognition. In Spain for example, the Basque Country and Navarre have traditional 'foral' rights to raise taxes that other autonomous communities do not. In Belgium, the regions have some tax-raising powers, while the communities rely upon transfers from the federal government. And in the UK Scotland has very different tax-raising powers from Wales and Northern Ireland, while most of England is taxed entirely by Westminster.

Some federal systems have established such strong patterns of overlap and shared competence between central and territorial levels, particularly in relation to the spending power, that the very meaningfulness of territorial autonomy is brought into question. We have noted how, in systems of administrative federalism, competences are so interconnected that in the end one central policy tends to be set; the role of the territories is principally to give effect to this. While discretion at the level of policy implementation may be built into the system, such is the level of integration across the federal polity in terms of fiscal and social policy that constituent territories do not enjoy any real policy autonomy. Institutionally, systems such as Germany and Austria were modelled in this way, but the broader trend across federal constitutions towards increasingly shared powers has served

[112] Wheare, *Federal Government*, 4th edn, 97.

to consolidate an institutional architecture that in any case already favoured integrated policy-making. Competences over taxing and spending have allowed the central government in most federal systems to appropriate areas of concurrent jurisdiction such as social and welfare policy, and even venture into areas that are often an exclusive power of the constituent territories, such as education. For Watts, the spending power 'has frequently proved to be a Trojan horse for federal dominance'.[113]

I have noted that the principle of autonomy requires that constituent territories have the powers necessary to develop discrete and meaningful self-government; in other words the requisite powers to flourish as distinct societies.[114] Therefore, it is often the case that constituent territories are allocated powers in relation to culture, education, and language policy. As Watts observes: 'Generally the more the degree of homogeneity within a society the greater the powers that have been allocated to the federal government, and the more the degree of diversity the greater the powers that have been assigned to the constituent units of government.'[115] This is only partly true. Culture was a particular preoccupation of early federal systems which were founded upon the basis of deep cultural diversity. A major reason why the Swiss constitution in 1848 was so different from its American predecessor was the extent to which it required to manage linguistic as well as religious divisions, both of which were largely territorially concentrated. The demarcation of competences, designed to give the cantons powers over cultural policy, survives into the 1999 constitution. The cantons have authority over church–state relations, education, and the determination of official languages in each canton,[116] the last of which we return to shortly. The BNA Act 1867 was also shaped in part by the essentially bicultural nature of the polity, but in this we find a variable approach which oscillated between a centralising agenda, formed around a strong central government, and the ascription of competence over language and education to the provinces. Insofar as Canada is less centralising today than other federations has, therefore, more to do with its development over time than its original design.

[113] Watts, *Comparing Federal Systems*, 3rd edn, 92. To take one example, Fenna observes how significant the spending power has been to the centralising trajectory of the Australian constitution: 'A constitution drafted in the 1890s left the majority of domestic governance responsibilities to the States. Within two decades, though, a process, continuing to this day, was underway whereby the financial power and the policy reach of the Commonwealth expanded in an apparently inexorable and irreversible fashion.' A. Fenna, 'The Centralization of Australian Federalism 1901–2010: Measurement and Interpretation' (2019) 49 *Publius* 30–56, 30.

[114] In fact, it is not easy to identify which powers constituent territories tend—or need—to have. Cheryl Saunders, having offered a familiar account of those powers that should go to the centre within a federal constitutional system, finds it more difficult to identify a similar level of generality in relation to sub-state powers: Saunders, '*Constitutional Arrangements of Federal Systems*', 70.

[115] Watts, *Comparing Federal Systems*, 3rd edn, 84.

[116] Federal Constitution of the Swiss Confederation 1999, arts 62 (Education), 70 (Languages), and 72 (Church and State).

In all of these issues the question of competence over culture relates to the tax and spending powers. The Canadian demarcation of economic policy to the centre and culture to the provinces has been complicated by two opposing dynamics. One is that federal spending has been required to support the ever-growing area of social provision within provinces. The other is the view taken by Quebec nationalists that the pursuit of societal particularity required the development of a distinct economic and welfare policy if the francophone society of Quebec is to remain salient within North America;[117] in consequence, other provinces also seek economic powers to promote their own policy agendas. And so we see that in federal systems with the greatest territorial diversity, and hence the strongest demarcation of competences in the field of culture, there can also arise the greatest pressure for competence over fiscal policy.

I began the chapter by highlighting that autonomy must not only be meaningful, it must also be reflexive in relation to the other principles of federalism. This point is crucial when it comes to the allocation of powers surrounding culture in a federal constitution: in particular, the goal of pluralism sits in tension with that of union. Just as constituent territories seek autonomy to promote and protect their cultural specificity, the central government seeks control of cultural policy, for example over language and education, in order to help build a national identity. The issue of language can be particularly controversial. The fostering, and often the imposition, of a 'national' language has been key to nation-building within federal as well as unitary states. In federal polities where cultural differences are not principally territorially demarcated, such as the USA, Australia, or Germany, there is little need for territorialised powers over language policy. However, in those federal states where territorial national minorities, with their own minority language, are a key feature of the state's identity, there can be deep contestation over language policy.[118]

A number of federal systems make specific provision for different official languages; it is also the case that constituent territories can have significant autonomy in relation to language accommodation and protection. The constitution of Switzerland of 1848 established German, French, and Italian as national languages,[119] and gave the cantons authority in this area. Despite its otherwise centralising tendencies, the 1999 constitution restates this[120] and adds Romansh as an official language, giving the cantons the power to regulate this.[121] Notably however,

[117] D. Beland and A. Lecours, 'Sub-State Nationalism and the Welfare State: Quebec and Canadian Federalism', (2006) 12 *Nations and Nationalism* 77–96.

[118] S.K. Mitra, 'Language and Federalism: The Multi-Ethnic Challenge' (2001) 53 *International Social Science Journal* 51–60.

[119] The Federal Constitution of the Swiss Confederation 1848, art. 109.

[120] The Federal Constitution of the Swiss Confederation 1999, art. 70(1).

[121] The Federal Constitution of the Swiss Confederation 1999, art. 70(2).

this provision recognises that language is also a national issue and one in which the cantons owe each other reciprocal duties.[122]

Another example is Canada where both French and English are protected as official languages under the Constitution Act 1982,[123] but where any legislature can take measures to 'advance the equality of status or use of English and French'.[124] In Belgium, the constitution acknowledges that the country is divided into four 'linguistic regions', and that 'the boundaries of the four linguistic regions can only be changed or corrected by a law passed by a majority of the votes cast in each linguistic group in each House, on condition that a majority of the members of each group is present and provided that the total number of votes in favour that are cast in the two linguistic groups is equal to at least two thirds of the votes cast'.[125] Article 129 further provides that: 'The Parliaments of the Flemish and French Communities, to the exclusion of the federal legislator, regulate by federate law, each one as far as it is concerned, the use of languages' for administrative, education, and employer-employee relations purposes. In Spain, the constitution states that Castilian is the official language of Spain,[126] while also providing that the 'other Spanish languages shall also be official in the respective Self-governing Communities in accordance with their Statutes'.[127]

Another issue I have noted as a central feature of the federal idea is asymmetry. We see this in the allocation of powers, most markedly in relation to the issue of culture. In many federal constitutions, particularly those with no strong territorially demarcated cultural differences, all constituent territories are allocated the same powers by the constitution. This is the case in the US constitution. In Australia, powers are also allotted symmetrically, as they are in Austria and Germany; in both of the latter constitutions there is only one legal category of constituent unit—*Länder*—to which equal constitutional authority is issued. But in federal polities with deeper territorial diversity there can be considerable divergence of competence across territories. To this end, territories with a strong identity may seek competence not only over culture and language but at a deeper level over citizenship, seeking to pluralise this very concept in pursuit of a claim that the territory constitutes a distinct public space, in some cases contending that the sub-state territory is a 'national' space. Immigration is traditionally allocated as an exclusive competence of the central branch but in a number of federal systems certain territories seek competence both to attract migrants to the territory and also to

[122] The constitution is also alive to the presence of minorities within cantons. Accordingly, it also limits cantonal authority in this area: '[i]n order to preserve harmony between linguistic communities, the Cantons shall respect the traditional territorial distribution of languages and take account of indigenous linguistic minorities'. Art. 70(1).

[123] Constitution Act 1982, Part I, (G)(16)(1).

[124] Constitution Act 1982, Part I (G)(16)(3).

[125] Constitution of Belgium, art. 4.

[126] Constitution of Spain, s. 3(1)

[127] Constitution of Spain, s. 3(2).

manage the integration of new citizens,[128] in this way communicating the discrete values of the constituent territory and in so doing exercising a form of sub-state nation-building themselves.[129]

Another area in which constituent territories have made recent moves to extend competence is international relations. Like migration and citizenship this is traditionally an exclusive central power within federal constitutions. The American constitution, as we have seen, is terse in its allocation of competences and began life in a period where the notion of the state as international actor was still in its infancy. However, even here, the federal government was given exclusive jurisdiction to regulate international and inter-state commerce and to declare war,[130] while the states were explicitly prevented from such actions (either completely or without the consent of Congress).[131] This competence has also been consolidated by the courts as it has in Australia.[132] However, in federal constitutions, particularly those with deep diversity, territories have sought greater international presence and freedom to pursue their own international relations.[133] This can manifest itself in different ways. If the central government is amenable, it can involve attendance with the central government at international treaty-making processes, in international organisations, or at conferences or other venues where the country is represented. Through this 'paradiplomacy' constituent territories seek to have a role in 'the definition of the state's international position on matters where they are domestically competent'.[134] But it can go further, involving the territories in representing themselves and asserting their own discrete identity internationally, in some cases opening consulates or directorates general abroad. In certain situations constituent territories have a role even in negotiating international agreements in areas within their own competence.[135] Belgium goes further than other federal constitutions

[128] P. Skerry, 'Many Borders to Cross: Is Immigration the Exclusive Responsibility of Federal Government?' (1995) 25 *Publius* 71–85.

[129] I. Dam, 'Immigration and Sub-State Nations. Theorizing the Nexus', in K. Detterbeck and E. Hepburn (eds), *Handbook on Territorial Politics* (Cheltenham: Edgar Elgar Publishing, 2018), chapter 18.

[130] US Constitution, art. 1(8).

[131] US Constitution, art. 1(10).

[132] *United States v. Curtiss-Wright Export Corporation*, 299 US 304 (1936) and *Youngstown Sheet & Tube Company v. Sawyer*, 343 U.S. 579 (1952); in *Australia: Commonwealth v. New South Wales* (1923) 32 CLR 200 at 210; *Koowarta v. Bjelke-Petersen* (1982) 153 CLR 168 at 215 (Stephen J.); *Commonwealth v. Tasmania* (1983) 158 CLR 1, 298–299 (Dawson J.).

[133] H.J. Michelmann and P. Soldatos (eds), *Federalism and International Relations: The Role of Subnational Units* (Oxford: Clarendon Press, 1990); F. Aldecoa and M. Keating (eds), *Paradiplomacy in Action: The Foreign Relations of Subnational Governments* (London: Frank Cass, 1999); A.S. Kuznetsov, *Theory and Practice of Paradiplomacy: subnational governments in international affairs* (New York: Routledge, 2014); J.A. Schiavon, *Comparative Paradiplomacy* (Nueva York: Routledge, 2019).

[134] A. Lecours, 'Balancing Self-Rule and Shared-Rule: Sources of Tensions and Political Responses in Contemporary Political Systems', in A. López Basaguren and L.E. San Epifanio (eds), *The Ways of Federalism in Western Countries and the Horizons of Territorial Autonomy in Spain*, vol. I (Berlin: Springer, 2013), 103–113, 103.

[135] Quebec has signed many treaties and has representatives in other states in directorates general of the Quebec government: C. Kirkey, S. Paquin, and S. Roussel, 'Charting Quebec's Engagement with the International Community' (2016) 46 *American Review of Canadian Studies* 135–148. There

in permitting the conclusion of international treaties by constituent territories in their areas of competence.[136]

The example of foreign affairs again illustrates the ever-increasing range and depth of overlapping powers within federal constitutions. For example, even when the central state has general competence to negotiate international agreements, the constituent territories may well have a role in the ratification of agreements.[137] Furthermore, the central government may be dependent upon the cooperation of the constituent territories for the effective implementation of any international obligations it enters into, if the subject matter of the treaty falls within territorial competence. A number of constitutions—Canada, Germany, Australia—give constituent territories a significant role in implementing international agreements.[138] This can put pressure on the state to ensure that the territories are kept informed of, and even have a significant say in the conclusion of, treaties themselves. A dramatic example arose in 2016 when Belgium declared that it was unable to sign the Canada–Europe Trade Agreement (CETA), a free-trade deal between Canada and the European Union. The reason was that Wallonia and the French Community were unwilling to endorse it, as required by the Belgian constitution. In the end disagreement was resolved and the agreement was finally concluded, but the affair demonstrates how a formerly exclusive central government competence is an increasingly shared power in certain federal systems.

Overlap arises also in the complex patterns of identity in modern federal states. A significant issue is the status of minorities not only within the state as a whole but within constituent territories themselves. I have noted how the Swiss constitution delimits the authority of the cantons in relation to language.[139] In a similar way, the BNA Act 1867 gives the Canadian federal government a responsibility in relation to minority education,[140] which for example caters for the protection of

are considerable tensions between the federal government and Quebec in relation to these initiatives: Lecours, 'Balancing Self-Rule and Shared-Rule: Sources of Tensions and Political Responses in Contemporary Political Systems', 109.

[136] Constitution of Belgium, art. 167(3). The constitutional lassitude towards territorial international engagement extends beyond deeply diverse federal systems. The German constitution, which otherwise grants an exclusive power over international relations to the federal government, has been changed to give the *Länder* a role in participating in the EU—Basic Law, arts 23(2), 23(6), 50. Lecours discusses the German approach: Lecours, 'Balancing Self-Rule and Shared-Rule: Sources of Tensions and Political Responses in Contemporary Political Systems', 110–111; and the powerful position of Belgium's constituent units, concluding, 'the decentralization of foreign relations has worked well' in Belgium: Lecours, 111.

[137] For example, in relation to Belgium's ratification of EU treaties—Constitution of Belgium, art. 168.

[138] Basic Law for the Federal Republic of Germany 1949, art. 32; Commonwealth of Australia Constitution Act 1900, art. 16; see also Federal Constitution of the Swiss Confederation 1999, art. 55.

[139] The constitution declares (art. 4) that the national languages are German, French, Italian, and Romansh. These are also designated as 'official languages' by art. 70. However, the constitution further provides that 'The Cantons shall designate their official languages. In order to preserve harmony between linguistic communities, they shall respect the traditional territorial distribution of languages, and take into account the indigenous linguistic minorities.' Art. 70(2).

[140] The Constitution Act 1867, 30 & 31 Vict., c. 3, s. 93(4).

French speakers within majority English-speaking provinces. It also has responsibility for 'Indians and Lands reserved for the Indians'.[141] In India, the federal government has even more extensive responsibilities and can direct state governments to comply with the laws of Parliament,[142] which could cover matters relating to minority languages, education, etc.

Another feature of deep diversity is that it has led to interesting experiments in the division and sharing of competences. Belgium combines a territorial and cultural approach, with some powers allocated to regions and some to communities. We have also noted the Spanish 'draw down' model. This in many ways captures the fluidity of the federal idea:

> At least implicitly, it acknowledges that time and circumstance will change what at any given moment may appear as the most reasonable and effective distribution of powers. And, by avoiding the enumerated finality of the classical list approach, it suggests that the role of constitutions in federal systems of divided governance is to provide not so much juridical finality as political guidance in search of mutually acceptable solutions.[143]

Saunders observes that, beyond the standard set of powers that typically go to the central government, 'the allocation of powers reflects the history and values of the polity and the purposes of the federation'.[144] There is in fact no hard and fast model of federal power allocation. Rather these reflect the society in question. They also change over time as the nature of the constitutional polity changes.

Overall we see in the history of federalism a considerable tension in play. The growth of the modern state has led to centralisation since many of the powers that have become so significant to the modern state—economic policy, taxation, and international relations—are typically the preserve of the central government. There is however a marked distinction between federal systems where the territories reflect a national demotic homogeneity and those where at least one territory is a site of deep cultural distinctiveness. It is this issue more than any other that has led to constituent territories seeking out greater powers, for example in the area of culture, and then seeking further powers over language, citizenship, taxation policy, public spending, and even international relations, in order to protect and promote their societal distinctiveness.[145] But the ongoing salience of territorial pluralism to

141 The Constitution Act 1867, 30 & 31 Vict., c. 3, s. 91(24).

142 Constitution of India, art. 256.

143 Hueglin and Fenna, *Comparative Federalism*, 2nd edn, 165.

144 Saunders, 'Constitutional Arrangements of Federal Systems', 70.

145 As André Lecours observes in relation to Canada: 'it is the territorial diversity of the country, primarily but not exclusively nationalism in Québec, along with the original centralized nature of the Canadian federation, that fundamentally accounts for why Canada has not centralized like so many other federations.' A. Lecours, 'Dynamic De/Centralization in Canada, 1867–2010' (2019) 49 *Publius* 57–83, 57.

the federal idea extends well beyond the issue of deep cultural difference. Pressure for the recognition and pursuit of particular interests can grow as constituent territories use their constitutional power to generate distinct policies in pursuit of economic self-interest. In Canada, the post-war growth of major cities such as Toronto, Vancouver, and Calgary encouraged decentralisation as powerful forces within and beyond these cities sought to harness the constitutional autonomy of the provinces to promote economic development, migration, and the exploitation of natural resources.[146] In federal systems local elites will seize upon the powers they have and use these strategically even in the absence of strong territorial identities.[147] In this way territorial pluralism can take on new trajectories and the principle of autonomy can be used to develop this pluralism in new and unexpected ways, at all times emphasising and indeed weaponising the 'specific kind of jural relationship' that is the essence of federalism. Within federal systems therefore, the principle of autonomy remains a vital dynamic. In order to reflect the founding commitment of the federal contract it must in all cases be meaningful; it must be reflective of the specific societies, economies, values, and policy priorities of the territories within a federal polity; and it must be open to asymmetry if the distinctiveness of the sub-state territories *inter se* requires such a heterogeneous approach.

III. Concluding remarks

The principles of recognition and autonomy are manifestations of the authority distributive dimension of federal constitutional sovereignty. But each, in particular recognition, also articulates the categorically distinctive nature of authority generation within a federal constitution—the fundamental salience of its constituent territories to both the identity and the lived political reality of a federal constitution. The vitality of federalism as a discrete order of rule hinges upon the meaningful application of these principles within a federal constitutional setting. Recognition can be an ephemeral principle, articulated by way of constitutional symbolism and identifiable too in the various institutional structures through which the significance of its constituent territories is embedded in any federal constitution. Autonomy is a more active, and arguably a more significant, marker of

[146] It is also the case that while recent decades have seen decentralisation in areas such as agriculture, citizenship, immigration, and natural resources, there has been centralisation in the area of language (in light of Canada's commitment to bilingualism) and social welfare, reflecting the principle of reciprocity which we address in the next chapter. Lecours, 'Dynamic De/Centralization in Canada, 1867–2010', 76.

[147] John Nugent argues that in the US, despite a nationalisation of the demos, states have 'increased their capacity for democratic, professional, and effective self-governance'. J.D. Nugent, *Safeguarding Federalism: How States Protect Their Interests in National Policymaking* (Norman: University of Oklahoma Press, 2009), 225. As Zackin puts it 'whether or not states persist as meaningful normative communities, we must take them seriously as institutions with the capacity to preserve themselves and to shape national policy'. E. Zackin, 'What's Happened to American Federalism?' (2011) 43 *Polity* 388–403.

the relevance of the federal idea today. It has also been a key battleground where rival visions of the constitution—territorial self-determination v. authority centralisation—play out. Within this arena, perhaps the most notable story is in fact the changing nature of public power itself within the modern state. The nature of autonomy has developed, regardless of respective centripetal or centrifugal ideologies, due to the changing functions of the state which have produced overlapping constitutional competences and encouraged a tendency towards policy homogenisation. At the end of the Second World War Kenneth Wheare argued that: 'The ideal distribution of powers between governments in a federation is the one in which each government is able to act independently within its own watertight sphere of responsibility.'[148] Sixty years later Ronald Watts, in many ways a great admirer of Wheare, flatly contradicted this: 'overlaps of jurisdiction are unavoidable because it is virtually impossible to define absolutely, watertight compartments of exclusive jurisdiction'.[149] This new reality serves to complicate the application of the principle of autonomy by altering the context within which it operates, but it does not diminish the constitutional significance of autonomy itself. We have seen how constituent territories have also used the expansion of 'the public' sphere to develop their own sites of political self-government. The expansion of public power and the complex web of overlapping competences which it has produced serves to emphasise the inter-relationship between autonomy and the other dimension inherent in federal constitutionalism's immanent tension, that of union. It is to the latter that we turn in the next chapter.

[148] Wheare, *Federal Government*, 4th edn, 14.
[149] Watts, *Comparing Federal Systems*, 3rd edn, 87.

9

Federal Constitutional Design II: Associational Government and Reciprocity

I. Introduction

Any federal constitution must arrive at a workable equilibrium between the key dimensions of federalism's meta-purpose: pluralism and union. Having addressed in the last chapter the principles which best reflect the federal goal of pluralism we now turn to the principles of associational rule and reciprocity which provide balance to a federal constitution, emphasising its character as a constitutional and political union. It is also the case however, as we have explored in relation to overlapping competences, that pluralism and union, far from being antonyms, are essential halves of one whole; and that all four principles therefore interact symbiotically in support of the overall purpose of a federal constitution: the foundational recognition and accommodation of the state's constituent territorial pluralism; the federal constitution acts both to foster this foundational pluralism and to maintain the constitutional relationship between pluralism and union in the creation and reconciliation of different orders of government. In this chapter we will explore further how the four principles of federalism combine in complex and inextricable ways in the institutional instantiation of any federal system.

II. The principle of associational government

The creation of a central branch of government is an essential feature of any federal constitutional system. Its principal task is to consolidate the polity as an effective union but to do so in a way that also reflects the inherent pluralism that underpins its constitutional meta-purpose. This two-dimensional goal is captured by the principle of associational government. Although, as we explored in the last chapter, the allocation of substantive powers is an important aspect of this principle, it is more clearly reflected in the design of the central institutions of the state. The principle can be institutionalised across all three sites of governmental authority—executive, legislative, and judicial; or its manifestation can be more restricted, limited for example to the central legislature. Despite the scope for significant institutional

The Federal Contract. Stephen Tierney, Oxford University Press. © Stephen Tierney 2022.
DOI: 10.1093/oso/9780198806745.003.0009

variation, what is vital to the viability of any federal system is the meaningful involvement of the constituent territories, in some way, in the central branch of governmental authority.

Associational rule brings with it a relationship not just between the central organs of the state and the constituent territorial governments but between the central government and the people of the whole state, the latter helping to forge demotic as well as institutional bonds of union. It is often argued that one of most crucial legal-normative moves made through the inauguration of the United States constitution was the creation of such a direct relationship.[1] A natural corollary of a constitution founded in the name of 'We, the People of the United States', the purpose of which was 'to form a more perfect Union …', was that the citizens of the constituent territories also became citizens of the new polity in that moment of constitutional founding. It is in this original federal union, combining these two sets of relationships, that the federal contract comes to be characterised not by silos of divided authority but by an interconnected plural matrix of rule; and it is in the arguments which shaped the US constitution that we see how the federal idea is open to a wide spectrum of institutional instantiation, ranging from stronger to weaker roles for constituent territories in patterns of associational government.

(i) Legislature

The institutional and demotic features of associational government come together most vitally in the architecture of the central legislature. This must provide a balance between accommodating territorial pluralism on the one hand and functioning as an effective central law-maker for the whole polity on the other. There are three dimensions to the realisation of this dual-purpose: the *level of representation* accorded to the constituent territories in the central legislature; the *design* of the second ('federal') chamber—in particular, whether the constituent territories are represented therein directly or indirectly; and the *authority* of that chamber in relation to the 'national' chamber of the central parliament.

(a) Level of representation

Bicameralism tends to play a key role in facilitating the dual role of associational government in fostering both pluralism and union within a federal system. The typical division involves one chamber designed to cultivate the direct relationship between the central government and all citizens of the polity, and another that reflects the status of the constituent territories as the foundational subjects of the

[1] A point made by Madison himself: J. Madison, Federalist No. 39, C. Rossiter (ed.), *The Federalist Papers* (New York: New American Library, 1961), 240–246, 241–242.

constitution. This has been called 'dual representation'[2] and while it may be an exaggeration to say that 'all fully federal systems have a bicameral legislature',[3] bicameralism has become a key characteristic of most federal systems.[4]

Despite the consistency of bicameralism among federal legislatures, the level of constituent territorial representation within federal legislatures varies greatly.[5] Among the many debates that surrounded the United States' constitutional founding, the issue of institutional design was more prominent in the discussions of the Philadelphia Constitutional Convention than the allocation of authority between the central Congress and the states.[6] A vital question was whether the central legislature should better reflect either one national majority or a constitutional commitment to equal state power. The result, emerging as part of the 'Connecticut compromise', was a Senate characterised by the same level of representation for each state regardless of size which would act as a territorial counter-weight to the 'national' House of Representatives, in which states are represented in proportion to their aggregate share of the national population.[7]

The US Senate is indeed the clearest manifestation within the US constitution of the foundational constituent power of the states, a point recognised by Madison himself as evidence of a 'federal' (i.e. confederal) dimension of the constitution.[8] The American upper house is also a high point of constituent territorial representation within modern federal systems, becoming a model for other early federal systems such as Switzerland and Australia, which both adopted a similar form of second chamber representation,[9] and occasionally for later systems such as

[2] T.O. Hueglin and A. Fenna, *Comparative Federalism: A Systematic Inquiry*, 2nd edn (Toronto: University of Toronto Press, 2015), 205.

[3] U.M. Amoretti, 'Introduction: Federalism and Territorial Cleavages', in U.M. Amoretti and N. Bermeo (eds), *Federalism and Territorial Cleavages* (Baltimore: The Johns Hopkins University Press, 2004), 9.

[4] W. Swenden, *Federalism and Second Chambers* (Bern: Peter Lang Publishing, 2004), 25; N. Aroney, 'Formation, Representation and Amendment in Federal Constitutions' (2006) 54 *American Journal of Comparative Law* 277–336, 287.

[5] R.L. Watts, *Comparing Federal Systems*, 3rd edn (Montreal, QC, Canada: McGill-Queen's University Press, 2008), 147.

[6] S.M. Milkis and M. Nelson, *The American Presidency: Origins and Development, 1776–2018*, 8th edn (Thousand Oaks: Sage, 2020), 17–20.

[7] The Connecticut Compromise was essentially an agreement between the largest state Virginia, which wanted the central legislature to be entirely weighted according to population, and the smallest New Jersey, which favoured a Congress based wholly upon state equality. A.L. LaCroix, *The Ideological Origins of American Federalism* (Cambridge MA: Harvard University Press, 2010), 147–158; T. Anderson, *Creating the Constitution: The Convention of 1787 and the First Congress* (Pennsylvania: Penn State University Press, 1993), 63–72. For discussion of the role intended for the House of Representatives, see J. Madison, Federalist Nos 56 and 58, Rossiter, *The Federalist Papers*, 346–350, 356–361.

[8] J. Madison, Federalist No. 62, Rossiter, *The Federalist Papers*, 376–382.

[9] Commonwealth of Australia Constitution Act of 1901, s. 7(3) allocated six senators for each original state 'until Parliament otherwise provides'. Today this also takes account of the federal territories. The Senate currently comprises seventy-six members: twelve from each state, two from the Australian Capital Territory, and two from the Northern Territory: Representation Act 1983, s. 3. In Switzerland, the federal legislature is bicameral, composed of the National Council (Nationalrat) and the Council of States (Standerat). Twenty cantons have two representatives in the Standerat, and a further six cantons have only one representative. Constitution of Switzerland 1999, art. 150.

Brazil.[10] In general, lower houses in federal bicameral parliaments are elected, like the US House of Representatives, to reflect the distribution among the territories of the national population, although in some countries territorial weighting also applies in this chamber. We see this for example in Brazil.[11] The composition of the Canadian House of Commons also reflects a territorial element.[12] Such cases are however rare, and even within these systems the additional weighting for constituent territories is minimal compared to territorial representation in the federal upper house.

Among more modern federal systems the equal representation of constituent territories even in the territorial chamber is rare. The German Bundesrat has a complex system of seat allocation. There are in fact four population categories of *Länder* which are allocated respectively three, four, five, or six block votes in the chamber from least to most populous *Länder* respectively.[13] Austria has a similar model of weighted representation to Germany but one that is closer to a proportional system. The largest *Land* can have up to twelve members of the second chamber and the smallest must be allotted at least three.[14]

Federal systems adapt the second chamber to suit their specific societal circumstances. In general, Indian states are represented in the Council of State (Rajya Sabha) largely based upon share of the country's population.[15] But in 1956 India created six new states in the northeast of the country.[16] On account of their relatively small size, these were not given the level of representation accorded to existing states. As one commentator observes: 'If India had followed the U.S. model, these new states, containing barely one percent of India's population, would have to be given 25 percent of all the votes in the upper chamber.'[17]

Canada's Senate is organised uniquely on the basis of regional rather than specifically provincial representation.[18] The British North America Act 1867 grouped

[10] Brazil's Senate is composed of three members from each of the twenty-six states, as well as three from the federal district. Constitution of Brazil 1988, art. 46.

[11] In Brazil, the Chamber of Deputies is elected on the basis of proportionality but this is qualified in that states are guaranteed a minimum of eight members and a maximum of seventy members—Constitution of Brazil, art. 45.

[12] Seats are in general allotted on a proportional basis but there is also constitutional provision to ensure that each province has at least as many MPs as senators and to guarantee that each province has, at any time, at least as many Members of Parliament as it had in 1985 (the date of the coming into force of the Constitution Act 1985, Representation). Constitution Act 1982, s. 51(1) and (2).

[13] Basic Law for the Federal Republic of Germany 1949, art. 51(2).

[14] Constitution of Austria, art. 34(2).

[15] Constitution of India, art. 80(4). Rajya Sabha is the upper house, elected by members of state legislatures, though the president may also nominate members to this house. For the number of state representatives in the House of the People (Lok Sabha) see art. 81(2). Lok Sabha is the lower house, consisting of 543 members directly elected by citizens representing parliamentary constituencies. Bills may originate in either house but must be approved by both and receive assent by the president to become acts of Parliament.

[16] State Reorganisation Act 1956, ss 5–11.

[17] A. Stepan, 'Federalism and Democracy: Beyond the U.S. Model', in D. Karmis and W. Norman (eds), *Theories of Federalism: A Reader* (London: Palgrave Macmillan, 2005), 255–268, 260.

[18] D.E. Smith, *The Canadian Senate in Bicameral Perspective* (Toronto: University of Toronto Press 2003).

the provinces into regions and then allocated an equal number of seats to these regions.[19] At the time of the pre-confederation debates, Canada consisted of three 'regions': Canada West, formerly Upper Canada (which became Ontario), Canada East, formerly Lower Canada (which became Quebec), and the Maritime region. The Maritime provinces, Nova Scotia and New Brunswick, fearing that they could be swamped by Ontario and Quebec, voted as a block in the constitutional deliberations of 1867. At the same time Quebec, also fearful of the growing strength of the predominantly Anglophone Ontario, was insistent that it should have representation equal to Ontario and the Maritime region in order to protect French Canadian interests.[20] Today the regional principle still applies despite the addition of further provinces and territories over time. In 1915 the Western Provinces (Alberta, British Columbia, Manitoba, and Saskatchewan) were allotted block representation in the Senate.[21] The current division of Senate seats applies as follows: Ontario, Quebec (which are both also single provinces), the Maritime provinces (Nova Scotia, New Brunswick, and Prince Edward Island[22]), and the Western provinces (Saskatchewan, Manitoba, Alberta, and British Columbia) each get twenty-four seats, while the province of Newfoundland and the territory of Labrador get six and the other three territories three each.[23]

The fact that the Western provinces have grown in both population and economic power has served only to foster resentment and calls for the Senate either to be reformed or abolished.[24] The Canadian Senate is certainly an odd creature, not least for its mode of appointment, to which we will return, but it does serve to demonstrate, as does the Indian upper house, how federal systems will shape their second legislative chambers to fit the specificities of their own demotic composition and territorial complexity.

It is notable that India and Canada are also characterised by deep territorial diversity. So too is Belgium. However, despite its deep and polarising territorial and cultural pluralism, the Belgian second chamber was for a long time unusual among federal systems in being characterised by strict national majoritarianism. This changed however with constitutional reforms in 2014 which removed the system of direct election of the country's senators and introduced a new and complicated system of indirect election through appointment by the territorial parliaments, as well as the representative assemblies of its linguistic 'Communities', discussed below.

19 Constitution Act 1982, s. 22.

20 F. Rocher, 'Opponents of the 1864 Confederation Project', in E. Brouillet, A.-G. Gagnon, and G. Laforest (eds), *The Quebec Conference of 1864* (Kingston/Montreal: McGill-Queen's University Press, 2018), 179–219, 209; L.-G. Harvey, 'Confederation and Corruption', in E. Brouillet, A.-G. Gagnon, and G. Laforest (eds), *The Quebec Conference of 1864* (Kingston/Montreal: McGill-Queen's University Press, 2018), 227–228.

21 The Constitution Act 1915, s. 1.

22 Which joined Confederation in 1873.

23 The Constitution Act 1982, s. 22.

24 An attempt to reform the Senate in 1992 was unsuccessful: Draft Charlottetown Accord 1992, cl. 4.

The tendency towards territorial weighting makes second chambers of central importance to the principle of associational government. The American Senate serves as an influential and yet distorting precedent. Debates about representation at Philadelphia focused little upon territorial diversity among the states, or even upon disparities of size between large and smaller states, but rather upon the role of the Senate (often with an eye to the influence of slave-owning states[25]) in distributing power and weakening the federal government.[26] For many delegates the key goal was to produce an upper house that was, in Edmund Randolph's words 'less than the House of Commons ... to restrain, if possible, the fury of democracy'.[27]

In countries which, like the USA, are in relative terms territorially homogeneous, such as Australia, Germany, and Austria, the design of the second chamber has been relatively uncomplicated.[28] In other systems such as Canada, India, and Belgium the design of the second chamber has been a more complex issue. In Canada, Quebec saw the national legislature as key to protecting its own specific society, which, as we have seen, prompted others to seek some level of equality with Quebec.[29] Reform of the second chamber in India in the 1950s attempted to strike a balance between accommodating territorial diversity and the coherence of the constitutional system as a whole, while in Belgium the increasingly centrifugal pulls upon the state led to a complete reorganization of the Senate in recognition of Belgium's deep and complex diversity. The particular tensions that affect associational government within culturally heterogeneous federal societies also play out in other ways in the design on federal legislatures.

(b) Design of the second chamber

The design of federal second chambers varies from polity to polity. One key distinction is between directly elected and indirectly appointed second chambers. While the

[25] Taylor records that almost half of the fifty-five men who took part in the proceedings of the Constitutional Convention were slave-owners. A. Taylor, *American Revolutions: A Continental History 1750–1804* (New York: Norton, 2016), 25. Delegates from 'slave states' were anxious to avoid a diminution of their influence within the central branch of government. Anderson, *Creating the Constitution*, 91–94.

[26] S.M. Milkis and M. Nelson, *The American Presidency: Origins and Development, 1776–2018*, 8th edn (Thousand Oaks: Sage, 2020), 20–21.

[27] Cited in M. Farrand, *Records of the Federal Convention* I (New Haven: Yale University Press, 1911), 58. See also J. McHenry, 'Papers of Dr. James McHenry on the Federal Convention of 1787' (1906) 11 *The American Historical Review* 595–624, 598. Quoted by Anderson, Creating the Constitution, 117.

[28] Although we have noted that federal legislation extended representation in the Australian Senate to Australia's territories. This seemed to contradict s. 7 of the constitution which provides that the second chamber is to be 'composed of senators for each state'. The law was upheld by the High Court on the basis largely of s. 122 which gives the federal Parliament authority to 'allow the representation of... [a] ... territory in either House of the Parliament to the extent and on the terms which it thinks fit'. *Western Australia v. Commonwealth* (1975) 134 CLR 201 (First Territory Senators' case); *Queensland v. Commonwealth* (1977) 139 CLR 585 (Second Territory Senators' case).

[29] M. Chevrier, 'The Making of a Dominion', in E. Brouillet, A.-G. Gagnon, and G. Laforest (eds), *The Quebec Conference of 1864* (Kingston/Montreal: McGill-Queen's University Press, 2018) 49–69, 64.

norm for the lower house (or national chamber) is direct election across the country, members of upper 'territorial' chambers may either be elected by the citizens of the territories or take their seats through designation by territorial governments. The general tendency is towards direct election, but the German Bundesrat stands out for the highly particular way in which it is constituted. Members of this chamber are delegates of, and hold office in the name of, their respective *Land* governments.[30] Austria operates in a similar way. Members of the Federal Council or Bundesrat are elected by the legislatures of the *Länder* on a proportional representation basis.[31] In both countries this leads to the direct control of the second chamber by the *Länder*. For example, in the German Bundesrat representatives in the second chamber hold office *ex officio* as members of the *Land* executive and vote as a 'quasi-diplomatic'[32] block under the instruction of their respective *Land* administration.[33]

The German and Austrian systems represent a particularly high degree of indirect representation. In other federal countries, direct election is now the norm. The American Senate, although originally appointed by the state legislatures,[34] has been directly elected since the coming into force of the 17th amendment.[35] The Australian Senate in a similar way is elected directly by the people of each state.[36] Switzerland does not have a second chamber in the council style of the Bundesrat. Although the constitution leaves to the cantons how representatives to the Council of States should be elected,[37] each canton now provides for direct election to the upper house.

In other federal constitutions, particularly those characterised by deep pluralism, the composition of the second chamber does not follow any fixed pattern. The Canadian Senate is an outlier not only due to its 'regional' representation but also in the way senators are appointed: by the governor general on advice of the federal prime minister, holding office until their retirement at seventy-five. This system of appointment is in some ways more similar to that of judges than legislators. Executive appointment is clearly questionable as a matter of democratic principle[38] but it also diminishes the authority of the Senate to stand up to the House of Commons, even if its members wish to do so, which they often do not. Although

[30] Basic Law for the Federal Republic of Germany 1948, art. 51(1). By contrast, members of the Bundestag are 'representatives of the whole people, not bound by orders or instructions and responsible only to their conscience' —art. 38(1).

[31] Constitution of Austria, art. 34.

[32] D.C. Smiley and R.L. Watts, *Intrastate Federalism in Canada* (Toronto: University of Toronto Press, 1985), 56.

[33] Basic Law for the Federal Republic of Germany 1948, art. 51(3).

[34] Constitution of the United States, art. 1, s. 3.

[35] Constitution of the United States, 17th Amendment (ratified 8 April 1913).

[36] Commonwealth of Australia Constitution Act, s. 7.

[37] Constitution of Switzerland, art. 150(3).

[38] A. Benz and J. Broschek, 'Introduction', in A. Benz and J. Broschek (eds), *Federal Dynamics: Continuity, Change, and the Varieties of Federalism* (Oxford: Oxford University Press 2013), 10.

senators are intended to represent regional groups of provinces, it has been noted that 'as a result of the method of appointment, [they tend] ... to display little accountability to regional interests, and to vote instead generally on party lines'.[39]

Belgium and Spain have mixed models of appointment. I have noted the radical change to the Belgian constitution undergone in 2014. This led to a model of indirect election. Of the sixty senators, fifty are appointed from the parliaments of the territories and communities: twenty-nine senators are appointed by the Flemish Parliament, ten by the Parliament of the French community, eight by the Parliament of Wallonia, two by the French-language group of the Parliament of the Brussels-Capital Region, and one by the Parliament of the German-speaking community. Ten further senators are 'co-opted', meaning that six are elected by the Dutch-language group of the Senate and four by the French-language group.[40] Spain also has a distinctive hybrid model of second chamber composition. Under the constitution the Senate is the 'House of territorial representation'.[41] It is however constituted largely through 'provinces' rather than the autonomous communities which are the principal constituent territories of the Spanish constitution. Four senators are directly elected from each province. This is supplemented by the appointment of one senator by each autonomous community legislature. These legislatures have the opportunity to appoint one further senator for every one million inhabitants of each autonomous region.[42] It is therefore largely a proportional model, meaning that larger autonomous communities, such as Andalusia and Catalonia have a significant number of senators, currently nine and eight respectively, out of fifty-seven.

The radically different ways of constituting second chambers prompts the question as to which approach, in particular the contrasting models of direct election versus the German 'council' model, best reflects the purpose of federalism. The move to a directly elected US Senate is widely seen as part of a 'nationalising' project that weakened the influence that the states could bring to bear in the Congress.[43] In purely institutional terms however there is no reason for this. Although directly elected, senators are chosen within states ostensibly to represent these states. The American Senate could have developed and maintained a strong territorial persona, despite direct election, if the political culture of the US had been inclined in this direction. The nationalisation of the Senate bears out the argument that the accrual of constitutional authority and political power by the central branch of government is often an issue of constitutional and societal culture more than institutional form.

[39] Watts, *Comparing Federal Systems*, 3rd edn, 151.
[40] Constitution of Belgium 1831, art. 67(1).
[41] Constitution of Spain 1978, art. 69(1).
[42] Constitution of Spain 1978, art. 69(4).
[43] J.S. Bybee, 'Ulysses at the Mast: Democracy, Federalism, and the Sirens' Song of the Seventeenth Amendment' (1997) 91 *Northwestern University Law Review* 500–572, 547–567.

We see this also when we turn to Germany. The German model of second chamber composition starkly contrasts with that of the US Senate, promising an even stronger role for the constituent territories in the central legislature. Indeed the Bundesrat, through its direct selection by, and answerability to, the governments of the *Länder*, seems ideally suited to protect and promote territorial pluralism. It has even been called 'the only truly federal chamber'.[44] Nonetheless, it has in its political practice not acted as a bulwark of *Länder* autonomy. Far from it. The Parliament as a whole has evolved in its practice into one of the most centralised of any federal system, the Bundesrat working in a highly integrated way with the Bundestag to develop common national standards across most areas of policy. The Bundestag, like the US Senate, again supports the conclusion that demotic homogeneity is a more significant determinant than chamber design of whether or not a second chamber will play a strongly integrationist role in associational government and national policy-formation within a federal constitutional system.

(c) Authority and functions of the second chamber

The authority and functions of second chambers can be assessed by way of three variables: the legislative capacity of the territorial chamber; its non-legislative powers, in particular the role of the second chamber in making or confirming executive appointments or in ratifying international agreements; and the second chamber's function as a deliberative forum, helping to frame national political debates or call the executive to account, and in this way exercising political as well as legal influence.

In its distribution of legislative authority, the American constitution gave the Senate an equal role to that of the House of Representatives. This applies at both the initiation and in the passage of law: bills can be introduced in the Senate and no law can pass without its consent.[45] Such co-equal law-making authority characterises a number of other second chambers including those in Switzerland,[46] Canada,[47] Australia,[48] India,[49] Argentina,[50] Brazil,[51] and Mexico.[52] The US Senate takes on particular importance however due to its composition (state equality), the prestige of its members, and its oversight powers in

[44] Hueglin and Fenna, *Comparative Federalism*, 2nd edn, 36.

[45] There is one minor exception to equal power of introduction in that all bills for raising revenue must originate in the House of Representatives. Constitution of the United States 1789, art. I, s. 7(1). Even in this regard however, the Senate still has a determining role in that it 'may propose or concur with Amendments as on other Bills'.

[46] Federal Constitution of the Swiss Confederation 1999, arts 148(2) and 156(2).

[47] Canadian Constitution Act 1982, s. 17.

[48] Constitution of the Commonwealth of Australia 1900, s. 53(5).

[49] Constitution of India 1950, s. 107(2).

[50] Constitution of Argentina 1853, arts 44 and 75.

[51] Constitution of the Federative Republic of Brazil 1988, arts 61 and 65.

[52] Constitution of Mexico 1917, arts 50 and 72(a).

relation to central executive competence to which we will return. In other systems the lower house has the authority to override objections by the upper chamber.[53]

The US Senate's law-making power is bolstered by the separation of the legislature from the executive. In parliamentary systems, where the executive sits in the legislature and has greater scope to influence the legislative agenda, the lower house tends to be more powerful.[54] The upper house in parliamentary systems also tends to have less power in relation to finance and the passage of money bills.[55] That said, there are examples of powerful second chambers within parliamentary systems. The Australian Senate is one, which has authority to reject any bill including money bills, which can lead to dissolution of Parliament itself.[56]

The German constitution can be categorised as a parliamentary system and indeed the Bundesrat is considerably less powerful than the Bundestag. At the same time it plays a key role in a highly integrated national law-making body, a role bolstered by the direct participation of the *Länder* governments in its composition. The Bundesrat does have an absolute veto over a limited range of matters concerning state legislative responsibilities,[57] giving it, in Watts' view, 'strong political leverage'.[58] But in general the Bundesrat only has a suspensive veto over federal legislation; its opposition can be overridden by the Bundestag.[59] Furthermore, since many of its responsibilities concern the implementation of national laws rather than the pursuit of territorial autonomy, its authority is in practice strictly circumscribed. Therefore, the strong political leverage of which Watts talks is felt more in the Bundesrat's integrated role in the formation of national policy. The Bundesrat can be said to take on more of a co-governance role in the interests of union than an assertive veto role in the name of pluralism. Or as Hueglin puts it, the central legislative process 'contains the kind of cooperative and coordinated compromises that intergovernmental relations elsewhere have to achieve afterwards'.[60] To this end a Mediation Committee, composed of sixteen representatives from the Bundestag and sixteen from the Bundesrat representing each *Land*, plays an important role in arriving at agreement on legislative proposals, greatly reducing the prospect

[53] Constitution of Spain, art. 90; Constitution of Belgium, art. 78(2); Constitution of Austria, art. 42(4).

[54] Watts, *Comparing Federal Systems*, 3rd edn, 153.

[55] A.A. Preece, 'Financial Powers of Upper Houses', (2002) 4 *University of Notre Dame Australia Law Review* 115–143

[56] Constitution of the Commonwealth of Australia, s. 57.

[57] Basic Law for the Federal Republic of Germany 1948, arts 76–78. This includes a veto power in relation to federal legislation affecting the *Länder*. Art. 77(2a) requires the Bundesrat to vote on a bill within a reasonable time if its consent is required.

[58] Watts, *Comparing Federal Systems*, 3rd edn, 154. Notably, however, the 2006 reform of the federal constitution reduced the range of competences over which Bundesrat approval is necessary.

[59] One area where Bundesrat consent is required is if a bill regulates matters without any scope for the *Länder* to deviate from its provisions. Art. 84(1).

[60] Hueglin and Fenna, *Comparative Federalism*, 2nd edn, 51.

of conflict during the law-making process itself.[61] Kössler and Palermo point to the political weight of this body: 'even if a simple majority would be sufficient in theory, much broader support is necessary in practice, as majorities in both the Parliament and the Federal Council have to confirm the compromise decision of the mediation committee afterwards'.[62] In this sense, the German second chamber is a strange hybrid. The institutional design of the Bundesrat is indeed truly federal as Hueglin and Fenna suggest, but this is not borne out by the authority it has. Rather than a chamber designed to promote and protect regional differences its focus is very much upon integration rather than policy diversity.

In India the lower house—the House of the People (Lok Sabha)—is clearly dominant. Although the Council of States (Rajya Sabha) generally has equal jurisdiction,[63] the House of the People is far larger.[64] In the event of disagreement, the size of the lower house allows it to override the views of the Council of States very easily. The constitution does provide for a process whereby the two chambers can be brought together in a joint sitting in the event of deadlock over legislation.[65] This provision has been very sparingly used in the history of the Indian constitution (for three bills—in 1961, 1978, and 2002) and the House of the People, given its size and status, is able to control these discussions.

Second chambers can exert their influence also through non-legislative powers, for example in relation to executive appointments or international relations. The American Senate's status is greatly enhanced by its jurisdiction in both of these areas. It possesses a veto over key executive appointments, including appointments to the federal judiciary,[66] and it has special powers in relation to the ratification of treaties.[67] Another highly significant power relates to the impeachment of the president, where the Senate acts as the court of adjudication.[68] The German Bundesrat also enjoys significant roles beyond law-making, particularly in relation to federal appointments. The constitution provides that the upper and lower houses each elect half the members of the Federal Constitutional Court.[69] The president

[61] C. Koggel, 'The Mediation Committee of the Bundestag and Bundesrat: A Special Institution of German Constitutional Law' (2016) 44 *International Journal of Legal Information* 35–42.

[62] P. Francesco and K. Kössler, *Comparative Federalism: Constitutional Arrangements and Case Law* (Oxford: Hart Publishing, 2017), 192–193.

[63] An exception is that finance and taxation bills must originate in the House of the People. Constitution of India 1947, art. 109.

[64] The Lok Sabha has a potential 550 members compared to a maximum 250 representatives in the Council of States. The Constitution of India 1950, arts 81(1) and 80(1).

[65] Constitution of India 1950, art. 108.

[66] Constitution of the United States 1789, art. II, s. 2, cl. 2.

[67] Constitution of the United States 1789, art. II, s. 2, cl. 2: the president has the 'power, by and with the advice and consent of the Senate, to make treaties, provided two thirds of the Senators present concur'.

[68] The House of Representatives has the power to impeach the president (Constitution of the United States 1789, art. I, s. 2, cl. 5 and art. II, s. 4, cl. 1. The Senate acts in a judicial capacity (art. I, s. 3, cls 6–7 and art. II, s. 4). In such proceedings, the chief justice of the Supreme Court presides in the Senate (art. I, s. 3, cl. 6).

[69] Basic Law for the Federal Republic of Germany 1948, art. 94(1).

of the Federal Republic is elected by the national Parliament 'Federal Assembly', comprised of equal numbers of the Bundestag and Bundesrat.[70] The constitution of India contains a very similar model of election of the federal president.[71]

Second chambers can also exercise softer power, particularly as deliberative *fora* through which the political concerns of the constituent territories can be aired and by which both legislative and executive policy of the central government can be scrutinised. In many ways this is an issue of political culture. We have seen for example that in Germany the dominant political mindset has been to build national consensus rather than to foster territorial particularity. This has greatly depleted the autonomy dimension of federalism but it has also given the *Länder* significant indirect influence in national policy through the Bundesrat. By contrast, the Canadian Senate is in fact relatively strong (technically equal[72]) in terms of its formal role in the law-making process[73] and yet its actual influence on both law-making and national executive policy is very weak.[74] As we have discussed, the political weakness of the Senate was in many ways a conscious intention in 1867.[75] In the nineteenth century the House of Lords was a powerful branch of the Westminster legislature and the framers in Canada were keen to avoid the level of gridlock that could at times beset the British legislative process. For the same reason, the American precedent of a Senate that would offer a check on a strong, centralised lower house was not attractive. The Canadian drafters in fact favoured a powerful central government focused in the House of Commons, particularly when they looked to the constitutional malaise that had beset the USA since the 1850s. The fact that the Senate is to all intents and purposes appointed by the prime minister has also diminished its moral authority. The Canadian legislature is therefore imbalanced, one might say *de facto* unicameral, with the Senate failing to provide the level of territorial influence that is so crucial to effective associational rule.[76]

Second chambers vary across federal systems both in terms of their legislative and other competences but also for the ways in which they have used the constitutional authority they do possess. Constitutional culture has been a strong factor in the development of constitutional practice. Notably, the significance of second chambers is often described, even by federal theorists, in terms of the role they

[70] Basic Law for the Federal Republic of Germany 1948, art. 54(1) and (3).

[71] Constitution of India 1950, arts 54 and 55.

[72] Constitution Act 1867, s. 17.

[73] Although, as in the Constitution of India, money bills must begin in the lower house, the House of Commons—Constitution Act 1867, s. 53.

[74] Earning it opprobrium: 'the most criticised institution of government in Canada': C.E.S. Franks, *The Parliament of Canada* (Toronto: University of Toronto Press, 1987), 186.

[75] P. Buckner, 'Canadian Constitution-Making in the British World', in E. Brouillet, A.-G. Gagnon, and G. Laforest (eds), *The Quebec Conference of 1864* (McGill-Queen's University Press, 2018), 70–101, 88, 91–92.

[76] Watts, *Comparing Federal Systems*, 3rd edn, 153.

play in dividing and hence weakening the authority of the central government, rather than in allowing constituent territories an active role in the central branch.[77] Ronald Watts famously analysed second chambers in terms of their character 'as "veto-players" constraining democratic majorities'.[78] The very orientation of this schema is notable. The notion of 'veto-players' immediately supposes that the lower house in a federal legislature should have the primary role in legislating upon 'national' policy. The territorial chamber, whatever the constitution may say, is seemingly not envisaged as a co-equal policy-maker but merely as a check on the more powerful (or at least more legitimate) house, perhaps revising or scrutinising the legislation and, *in extremis*, rejecting it. The term 'democratic majority' is also telling. The lower house is seen as representing a singular demos, which is conceived monistically. The territorial chamber by contrast is not described as representing other, equally legitimate democratic majorities. This monist demotic mindset has in fact led to robust criticisms of those second chambers which are composed on the basis of territorial equality, as 'undemocratic'.[79] As Macedo puts it, in relation to the US Senate: 'unequal representation in the Senate is often regarded as the greatest democratic flaw' in the American constitutional system.[80] That the House of Representatives which is deemed to speak for the 'whole population' is weaker than the chamber of states simply does not compute with an approach to the demos which in effect mirrors that of a unitary constitution.

This debate posits 'democracy' and 'federalism' as contrasting justifications for legitimate rule.[81] If one accepts that these two principles are in fact separable then it is very difficult to justify a second chamber that strongly represents territorial interests. Watts, in his counter to the demos-constraining argument, says that federations are potentially 'demos-enabling' and 'might be described as "democracy-plus"'. The reason for this is that federalism can maximise 'the opportunity for citizens' preferences to be achieved, because they establish alternative arenas for citizen participation and because they provide for governments that are smaller and closer to the people'.[82] This mirrors the ideologically infused approaches to federalism which we discussed in Chapter 7. But in the end subsidiarity-related

[77] We have discussed how weakening the central government of the nascent United States was a recurring goal for Hamilton and Madison. It was also how the Australian Senate was envisaged. Alfred Deakin, a key figure in the federation movement in Australia, commented that a sober upper house might restrain the 'spectacle of a democracy carried hither and thither by violent impulses to opposite points of the compass within short periods of time'. Cited by S. Marchant, 'The Historical Traditions of the Australian Senate: the Upper House we had to have', PhD thesis, Australian National University, 2009, 14 <https://openresearch-repository.anu.edu.au/bitstream/1885/49337/2/02whole.pdf>.

[78] Watts, *Comparing Federal Systems*, 3rd edn, 155.

[79] S. Levinson, *Our Undemocratic Constitution. Where the Constitution Goes Wrong (And How We the People Can Correct It)* (New York: Oxford University Press, 2005), 6–7. See also M.J. Klarman, *The Framers' Coup: The Making of the United States Constitution* (New York: Oxford University Press), 2016.

[80] S. Macedo, 'Toward a More Democratic Congress? Our Imperfect Democratic Constitution: The Critics Examined' (2009) 89 *Boston University Law Review* 609–628, 610.

[81] Palermo and Kössler, *Comparative Federalism: Constitutional Arrangements and Case Law*, 175.

[82] Watts, *Comparing Federal Systems*, 3rd edn, 155.

arguments offer no real justification for the massively disproportionate influence a small constituent territory has in a second chamber such as the US Senate, for example Rhode Island having the same number of seats as California. The underlying purpose of the federal contract and its essential commitment to territorial pluralism is the only way to justify this, based upon the fundamentality of associational government, organised upon a territorial register, to the very idea of federalism as a genus of constitutional government. The inherent constituent authority of the constituent territories, stemming from their foundational constituent power, underpins the specificity of a federal constitution and in doing so establishes federal constitutionalism as an order of rule composed of multiple, legitimate democratic majorities. This is not undemocratic; it is, rather, a fundamentally different model of democratic justification from that premised upon a singular conception of the constitutional people. National policy-making in a federal constitution should be conceived as an exercise in plural territorial deliberation as well as in national deliberation; a federal central legislature should be seen as the coming together of different and overlapping self-determining polities within one collective decision-making arena. It is this which justifies the strong powers and functions of federal second chambers as co-decision-makers and not merely as veto players. It is also the case however that this foundational justification for federal second chambers as a voice for territorial constituent authority has largely been lost within a federalist discourse shaped by a monistic demotic mentality; and in turn this has served to alter the practice of federal bicameralism in the direction of homogenised national policy at the expense of pluralism.

(ii) The federal executive

Associational rule can be more difficult to accommodate, both in theory and practice, at the executive level, given the largely singular conception of government that dominates modern constitutionalism. This is clearly the case in presidential systems. The American constitution, a pioneer in so many ways for the modern constitutional state, created a separate Executive branch in Article II of the Constitution, 'vested in a President of the United States of America.'[83] The president was set to become a dominant authority, institutionally independent of both the federal Congress and the states. This singularity and detachment were consolidated through the direct accountability of the president to the people (subject to the indirect election method through the electoral college, discussed below). Over time a strong central executive has come to symbolise the intimate relationship between federalism and the modern state. However, powerful central authority also

[83] Constitution of the United States 1789, art. II, s. 1, cl. 1.

exists in deep tension with a territorially pluralist commitment to associational rule which, as we have seen, is better captured through a national legislature with the room it provides for various approaches to pluralised rule, even if the federal legislature does not always play such a role. As Ackerman observes in the US context: 'the very existence of such a presidency endangers the very federalist values motivating the creation of the senate in the first place'.[84]

Although the US constitution offers the clearest model of a strong, independent national executive, a singular conception of executive government has also developed within parliamentary systems. The British notion of the Crown was transformed in the age of democracy, through its connection to the legislature, into a Leviathan of central authority, the Crown in Parliament.[85] Much of the executive authority of the monarch was transferred to the prime minister and other Crown ministers through their exercise of prerogative powers. This system was inherited from the United Kingdom by federal Australia and Canada among others. The preamble to the British North America Act 1867 declares that the new constitution is 'similar in Principle to that of the United Kingdom', while the Commonwealth of Australia Constitution Act 1901 notes that the states agree to unite 'under the Crown of the United Kingdom of Great Britain and Ireland'. In a parliamentary system not only does the executive sit within, and remain answerable to, parliament but the prime minister and cabinet tend to be conceived as possessed of a single legal personality.[86]

In European federal systems strong central governments are also the norm. Although these tend to be republics rather than monarchies (Belgium and Spain being exceptions), consolidated cabinet government is a common characteristic, often built upon cross-party coalitions. We have also observed how Germany, Austria, and Switzerland are parliamentary systems without a clear demarcation between executive and legislative roles. This extends executive influence to the law-making process in important ways.

It is clear therefore that whether a federal system is presidential or parliamentary, whether republican or monarchical, strong central executives are a dominant feature of the modern federal constitution. We will now address both how the executive is appointed and how executive rule operates within federal systems, exploring what, if any, scope exists for direct territorial involvement in the machinery of central executive authority.

[84] B. Ackerman, 'The New Separation of Powers' (2000) *Harvard Law Review* 633–729, 673.

[85] G.C. Moodie, 'The Crown and Parliament' (1956) 10 *Parliamentary Affairs* 256–264.

[86] There is criticism, echoing Ackerman's point about the US presidential system, that inter-executive federalism which has developed within parliamentary systems, whereby the central and territorial executives come together to make important federal decisions, 'often leaves the federal second chamber out in the cold'. E. Delaney, 'The Federal Case for Judicial Review', unpublished paper. See also W. Swenden, *Federalism and Second Chambers* (Bern: Peter Lang Publishing, 2004), 349.

Although the American president is a singular, institutionally independent office, the states, through the electoral college system, do retain a strong role in the method by which the president is elected. This is largely a proportional system but it gives some extra weight to smaller states.[87] States also have control over their own part in the process. They are designated 'districts' for the purpose of nominating electors and they can choose their own electoral system for this purpose. However, once elected, the president acts with considerable operational independence. Although dependent upon Congress for the making of law which the president might propose, the president has substantial independent executive powers under Article II, powers which have grown over time.[88] Crucially, the president is operationally independent not only of Congress but also of the states.

A number of federal constitutions operate with a presidential system, for example, Argentina, Brazil, and Nigeria, while Russia has a semi-presidential system which also includes a prime minister. Canada and Australia are very different, each are constitutional monarchies and the executive power is headed by the prime minister, appointed by the monarch's representative as the leader of the party holding, or most likely to hold, the confidence of the House of Commons or House of Representatives, respectively. In Germany, we have noted that the president, who is formally head of state, is elected by an electoral college comprising the Bundestag and an equal number of members elected by the legislatures of the *Länder*.[89] However, the real executive power rests with the chancellor and cabinet. The chancellor is formally elected by the Bundestag after proposal by the federal president.[90] It follows that the chancellor and cabinet are responsible to the Bundestag only. However, given the very particular form of bicameralism in Germany, the national executive must govern through parliament as a whole where the *Länder* are, at least in institutional terms, strongly represented in the Bundesrat. In theory, therefore, the Bundesrat can exert considerable influence upon the central executive as it can over the Bundestag.

In Austria, the president is head of the executive and is popularly elected.[91] 'The Federal Chancellor and, on his recommendation, the other members of the Federal Government are appointed by the Federal President.'[92] The appointment of the federal chancellor or the whole federal government is 'countersigned by the newly appointed Federal Chancellor', however their dismissal does not require a countersignature.[93] Switzerland is a unique system that does not operate on the basis of an

[87] 'Each State shall appoint, in such manner as the legislature thereof may direct, a number of electors, equal to the whole number of Senators and Representatives to which the state may be entitled in the Congress.' Constitution of the United States 1789), art. II, s.1, cl. 2.

[88] M. Crenson and B. Ginsberg, *Presidential Power: Unchecked and Unbalanced* (New York: Norton, 2007).

[89] Basic Law for the Federal Republic of Germany 1949, art. 54(1) and (3).

[90] Basic Law, art. 63.

[91] Austria, The Federal Constitutional Law of 1920, art. 60.

[92] Austria, The Federal Constitutional Law of 1920, art. 70(1).

[93] Austria, The Federal Constitutional Law of 1920, art. 70(1).

individual executive head. Instead the Federal Council, comprised of seven members, acts as a collective federal executive. This body elects from among its number the president of the Confederation on a yearly basis. Both the Federal Council and, ultimately, the president of the Confederation, are elected by the Federal Assembly which is the joint sitting of both chambers of the national Parliament.[94] The clear intention of the constitution is to ensure that the Federal Council reflects the country's territorial pluralism. The constitution is in fact explicit in providing that the Council should represent the country's regions.[95] Until 1999 no canton could have more than one representative on the Federal Council.

Through what we might call 'the German model', the executive body in Switzerland is immersed in, and answerable to, Parliament. This pattern, which is also largely replicated in Austria, does offer a strong institutional opportunity for the constituent territories to influence the national executive in the formation of national standards. There are different ways to view the outcome of such a process. It can be seen as an ideal example of associational government in practice—central policy formed by territorial interests—or it can be viewed as the effective capture of the constituent territories by the central government; in effect, the executive dominates the formation of national policy which can then be implemented with no risk that competing policies will be developed within the territories. But if the latter outcome is, in practice, a more accurate description of these systems, this is surely more an issue of political culture than institutional design. A model which, in institutional terms, gives the constituent territories such a strong role in policy formation holds considerable promise for associational rule by bringing the executive level of government firmly within constituent territorial influence.

The alternative to a highly integrated national executive is intergovernmentalism. That this would emerge as the main way in which territorial governments would influence central executive decision-making was largely unforeseen by the founders of early federal constitutions. Intergovernmental relations (IGR) have therefore developed mainly through political practice as a consequence of the growth in concurrent areas of jurisdiction within modern federal systems.[96] The purpose of intergovernmental relations is the successful management of joint or shared competence and the mitigation of potentially harmful knock-on consequences resulting from the exercise of discrete powers. It also functions to prevent conflict

[94] Federal Constitution of the Swiss Confederation 1999, arts 168(1) and 176(2). An even more radical model exists in Belgium where the constitution requires that the federal government be comprised of an equal number of French-speaking and Dutch-speaking ministers, with the exception of the prime minister. Constitution of Belgium (1831, art. 99.

[95] The Federal Constitution of the Swiss Confederation 1999, art. 175(4) seeks to ensure that the seven members of the Federal Council reflect diversity as to language and regional identities that the constitution promotes in relation to the National Council and Council of States (arts 149 and 150).

[96] For a detailed study of the evolution of intergovernmental relations across twelve federal constitutions see J. Poirier, C. Saunders, and J. Kincaid (eds), *Intergovernmental Relations in Federal Systems: Comparative Structures and Dynamics* (Oxford: Oxford University Press, 2015).

or to help resolve it without recourse to legal remedies. Canada is an example of a country where inter-executive relations have become very significant.[97] A prominent forum is the intergovernmental conferences of first ministers which have been used particularly in pursuit of major constitutional change. These were most significant in a period from the 1970s to the1990s, covering the period leading up to patriation of the constitution and the constitutional turmoil that resulted from this. Since then, Canadian IGR has tended to operate in more prosaic ways, but they remain vital to the functioning of the system.[98] IGR is therefore another example of how it is not possible to track constituent territorial influence upon associational rule simply by reference to constitutional provisions. In the Canadian context these patterns of central-territorial interaction have 'grown organically' from a constitution that makes no mention of them,[99] to become a crucial dynamic within Canadian federalism, with a strong bilateral as well as multilateral character.[100] They have been formalised over time through dedicated executive structures at federal and provincial levels.[101] Switzerland has one of the few constitutions that expressly provides for IGR[102] and this has been instrumental in both establishing and formalising the system.[103] India too has an elaborate system that operates generally on a multilateral basis, with a very strong voice for the federal government.[104] Australia also has a very elaborate system of intergovernmental relations. Australia formalised its meetings of first ministers through the creation of the Council of Australian Governments (COAG) in 1992. This operated until 2020 although it has, at least for now, been replaced by a 'National Cabinet'.[105]

In countries where the second legislative chamber operates strongly in the formation of national policy, such as Germany, this type of inter-executive

[97] N. Karazivan, 'Cooperative Federalism v Parliamentary Sovereignty: Revisiting the Roles of the Executive, the Legislative and the Judicial Branches', in A.-G. Gagnon and J. Poirier (eds), *Canadian Federalism and its Future: Actors and Institutions* (Montreal/Kingston: McGill-Queen's University Press, 2019), 291–335.

[98] R. Simeon and A. Nugent, 'Parliamentary Canada and Intergovernmental Canada: Exploring the Tensions', in H. Bakvis and G. Skogstad (eds), *Canadian Federalism: Performance, Effectiveness and Legitimacy*, 3rd edn (Don Mills: Oxford University Press, 2012), 59–78.

[99] G.J. Inwood, *Understanding Canadian Federalism: An Introduction to Theory and Practice* (Toronto: Pearson, 2013), 113.

[100] Inwood calculated in 2013 that there were more than 1,500 intergovernmental agreements in Canada and that, of these, 85 per cent were bilateral. Inwood, *Understanding Canadian Federalism*, 113.

[101] C.M. Johns, P.L. O'Reilly, and G.J. Inwood, 'Formal and Informal Dimensions of Intergovernmental Administrative Relations in Canada' (2007) 50 *Canadian Public Administration* 21-–41.

[102] Federal Constitution of the Swiss Confederation 1999, art. 48(1): the cantons may 'establish common organisations and institutions'.

[103] Largely operable through Conferences of Cantonal Directors. For a detailed account see N. Bolleyer, *Intergovernmental Cooperation: Rational Choices in Federal Systems and Beyond* (Oxford: Oxford University Press, 2009), 93–110.

[104] R. Saxena, 'The Working of Cooperative and Collaborative Federalism in India: Understanding Intergovernmental Relations', (2021) 67 *Indian Journal of Public Administration* 153–164.

[105] G. Hitch, 'Scott Morrison Says National Cabinet Here to Stay, Will Replace COAG Meetings in Wake of Coronavirus', ABC News, 29 May 2020 <https://www.abc.net.au/news/2020-05-29/coag-scrapped-national-cabinet-here-to-say-coronavirus-update/12300636>.

engagement is less prominent, largely because the executives interact, albeit indirectly, within the legislature itself. By contrast, in Austria where the second chamber is less influential, the Conference of the *Länder* Governors takes on greater significance.[106] In Switzerland too, despite Article 48, IGR is also characterised by executive/legislative cross-over. In these three states, policy tends to be agreed in the national Parliament, leaving the role of the cantons to implement this, for which they are given funds.[107] The policy discretion of the canton executives is, concomitantly, strictly circumscribed and so the role of executive intergovernmentalism becomes less significant.

The United States, with its clear separation of both legislative and executive powers and federal and state competences, stands out as a constitutional system without any formal or semi-formal institutions of IGR. Instead, channels of IGR are more dispersed. Complex patterns of cooperation take place, but these are often bilateral between particular state executives and the federal government. They also involve a complex interplay with Congress, often through Congressional committees.[108] Unsurprisingly, the Senate with its high level of state representation is particularly central to these processes and the system involves a sophisticated system of Congressional lobbying both by state representatives and by private actors, including corporations. The complex mix of multilateral, bilateral, public, and private activity which together constitute or influence IGR in the US has famously been described as 'marble cake' federalism.[109]

There is, in short, no standard way of managing inter-executive relationships. What matters is that each federal system finds a way of doing so that makes a reality of associational rule—giving the constituent territories a meaningful say in the formation of central government policy-making that affects the territories and in the implementation of that policy within their territories. It is also crucial that associational government works in a way that cushions the influence of the centre upon the autonomy of the territories. IGR has however often had limited influence in reining in the growth of central executive power, in particular the spending power. This is the main power of the centre that impacts upon the constituent territories; the political power of the purse diluting in practice the constitutional autonomy of the territories. One way in which this occurs is through direct central spending in the territories. Of course, the centre often has a general spending power for the

[106] P. Bussjager, 'Austria's Cooperative Federalism', in G. Bischof and F. Karlhofer, *Austrian Federalism in Comparative Perspective* (Innsbruck: Innsbruck University Press, 2015), 11–33, 16.

[107] A. Gamper, 'Legislative Functions of Second Chambers in Federal Systems' (2018) 10 *Perspectives on Federalism* 117–133.

[108] F. Palermo, 'Beyond Second Chambers: Alternative Representation of Territorial Interests and Their Reasons' (2018) 10 *Perspectives on Federalism* 50–68, 56–57. See also J. Kincaid, 'Intergovernmental Relations in the United States of America', in J. Poirier and C. Saunders (eds), *Intergovernmental Relations in Federal Systems* (Montreal-Kingston: McGill-Queen's University Press, 2002), 33–44.

[109] M. Grodzins, *The American System*, D.J. Elazar (ed.) (Chicago: Rand McNally & Company, 1966).

whole country, but it can target this, spending specifically within certain territories over the heads of the territorial governments, either by financing infrastructure projects directly or by funding bodies or entities other than the territorial governments, for example by the use of grants to cities. Where the central government chooses to give grants or disbursements to the constituent territories it can exercise influence by attaching conditions for how this is to be spent, for example ring-fencing this money for use in pursuit of a national policy. A further device is to tie federal spending grants to agreements on common policy approaches. This type of fiscal transfer is therefore entirely dependent upon arrival at the level of detailed policy alignment advanced by the central government. It may be open to the territorial government to resist such pressure but the attraction of the funding and the political fall-out from refusing to accept it can leverage territorial acquiescence in central policy initiatives. As in so many areas, the expansive exercise of the federal spending power has often been supported by the federal courts.[110]

IGR can operate bilaterally as well as multilaterally. Specific agreements between a particular constituent territory and the central government allow for policies to be tailored to the needs of that territory. This is also a way in which asymmetries within the constitution can be respected; for example, in relation to specific powers held only by certain constituent territories, or in relation to policy such as language or education that particularly impacts upon certain territories. One risk however is that the central government will have an even more dominant relationship with one territory than it has in multilateral negotiations with all of the constituent territories. A different risk is to the reciprocal relationships within the system as whole. Bilateral relationships can suit particularly large, rich, or powerful territories which, in bypassing other territories through the formation of discrete relationships with the central government, can secure particular advantages for themselves. We return to this in addressing the principle of reciprocity below.

IGR can also assume an important horizontal dimension, with agreements among the constituent territories rather than with the centre. Such inter-territorial cooperation is a particular feature of the American and Swiss systems—'federalism without Bern' or 'federalism without Washington'[111]—and is generally seen to be a

[110] For example, in *Canada: Reference re Canada Assistance Plan (BC)* [1991] 2 SCR 525 where the Court decided that the federal government was not constrained from introducing a bill to Parliament determining the distribution of welfare benefits to the provinces, despite the fact that the bill would amend the Canada Assistance Plan previously agreed with the provinces. British Columbia had no reasonable expectation that its consent to this alteration was required. In the United States, the Supreme Court has allowed the withholding of federal funds to states that do not comply with certain conditions. See *South Dakota v. Dole* 483 U.S. 203 (1987). However, the Court has more recently found that provisions of the Affordable Care Act, which withheld federal funds from states failing to extend Medicaid coverage in specified ways, went beyond the limits of the Spending Clause in art. 1, s. 8 of the US Constitution. *National Federation of Independent Business v. Sebelius* 567 U.S. 519 (2012). See E. Patterson, 'The Spending Power after NFIB: New Direction, or Medicaid Exception?' (2015) 68 *SMU Law Review* 385–425.

[111] D.J. Elazar, *American Federalism: A View from the States* (New York: Thomas Y. Crowell Company, 1972), 174.

growing feature of IGR.[112] For example, the Council of the Federation established in Canada in 2003 comprises the premiers of the Canada's provinces and territories, meeting twice each year;[113] the Council for the Australian Federation (CAF) in 2006 which, in a similar way to its Canadian equivalent, is comprised of the premiers and chief ministers of Australia's states and territories.[114] Each of these bodies seeks to promote interests common to the constituent territories which they feel are neglected by the federal government. Such relationships are perfectly consistent with the federal idea. Territories can use their autonomy in this way and such relationships can help bolster the union dimension of a federal system by strengthening the bonds of recognition and interdependence among constituent territories.

In the end, the principle of associational rule is capacious. Institutional design in the management of executive government can vary greatly. But ultimately vertical and horizontal processes of IGR, whatever forms they take, must be orientated towards consolidating the federal union while also respecting the other principles central to the federal contract. This requires a particular mindset; an approach to government that is cooperative and deliberative, in recognition of the complex matrix of relationships in any federal system, and of the fact that the powers of each locus of government are limited. In the end successful associational government always relies upon political cooperation and a shared constitutional commitment to union; the constitution can foster and induce harmonious intergovernmentalism but it cannot force it; to attempt to do so is to bely the territorial constituent authority upon which its legitimacy and validity rest.

(iii) The judiciary

The judiciary today plays an increasingly significant role in shaping the dynamics of federalism.[115] There is of course, within the principle of associational government, a need to reach agreement as to the meaning of the constitution and a consistent approach to its interpretation. Whether the system has different legal orders, and whether the appointment and management of the judicial system is pluralised, a common feature of federal systems is the tendency to vest responsibility

[112] N. Behnke and S. Mueller. 'The Purpose of Intergovernmental Councils: A Framework for Analysis and Comparison' (2017) 27 *Regional & Federal Studies* 507–527.

[113] It was intended to 'institute a new era of intergovernmental collaboration by promoting a constructive dialogue between the partners of the federation'. Preamble, Council of the Federation — Founding Agreement (2003).

[114] The primary CAF objective is to address issues not currently being addressed by the Commonwealth government, while facilitating common understanding. A. Tiernan, 'The Council for the Australian Federation: A New Structure of Australian Federalism' (2008) 67 *Australian Journal of Public Administration* 122–134.

[115] N. Aroney and J. Kincaid (eds), *Courts in Federal Countries: Federalists or Unitarists?* (Toronto: University of Toronto Press, 2017).

for ensuring consistent interpretation in an apex court. Such courts have assumed great salience in determining the path of the constitution itself. Therefore, over time, the direction of the constitution as one that continues to emphasise the central constitutional importance of the federal idea or one that moves in an increasingly centralising trajectory, has depended to a large extent upon the federal judiciary; an issue we address in detail in the next chapter.

How judges are appointed and how they fit into the system of associational government is therefore of the highest importance. The autonomy of constituent territories within a federal system creates different jurisdictions: discrete regimes of legal competence within the overall jurisdiction of the constitutional polity. This however need not translate into different legal *systems*. Certainly in some federal constitutions territorial legal systems and judicial systems exist alongside the central legal system and court structure. Common law federal constitutions are more likely to have plural legal systems. An example is the United States where the states have their own court structures, distinct from the federal legal system, but united by the constitution and the supervisory competence of the Supreme Court. The constitution expressly provides for a federal judicial branch with general jurisdiction.[116] Decisions of state courts, including state supreme courts, are appealable to the Supreme Court if the matter touches upon the interpretation of the federal constitution, federal law, or international relations. As we will see in the next chapter, the US Supreme Court has taken a very expansive approach to its own jurisdiction, and in particular has interpreted the 14th amendment to extend widely its jurisdictional oversight of state law.

The same structure applies in Canada and Australia where discrete territorial jurisdictions come together in the highest federal court, and is also a feature of Switzerland despite its civilian system. In Canada, the Supreme Court is the final court of appeal in both federal and provincial matters.[117] In these countries, distinctive legal systems can in part be a legacy of aggregation, in some cases territories which came together to form the federal constitution already had court systems in place as part of their discrete systems of government within pre-existing constitutional arrangements. Where federal constitutions emerge within already existing states, multiple court systems are less common. In this latter category, authority over the entire legal system may lie at the central level of government, as it does in Belgium, or it can be a shared power, as it is in Germany, where the court system is unified but administration of it is divided between the central and territorial levels. In Germany, *Länder* courts deal with lower level cases but, since the Basic Law establishes a unified court system,[118] federal courts operate as courts of

[116] 'The judicial power of the United States shall be vested in one Supreme Court, and in such inferior courts as the Congress may from time to time ordain and establish.' Constitution of the United States 1789, art. III, s. 1.

[117] The Supreme Court Act (RSC, 1985, c. S-26). Under s. 35 of this act, the 'Court shall have and exercise an appellate, civil and criminal jurisdiction within and throughout Canada.'

[118] Basic Law for the Federal Republic of Germany 1948, art. 92.

appeal with full judicial power and final exclusive jurisdiction vested in the Federal Constitutional Court.[119]

Another feature of judicial federalism is that national control of the courts can grow. Palermo and Kössler cite this as a trend, noting Switzerland as an example of a dual system 'where the judicial powers of the national level are constantly expanding'.[120] It is the case therefore that, whether a federal constitution has a specialist constitutional court or a supreme court of general jurisdiction, federal matters are dealt with by courts with jurisdiction wider than just federal matters. Belgium is in fact the only system within which a constitutional court was created to deal specifically with federal disputes,[121] and even here its jurisdiction has considerably expanded from this original purpose.[122]

One key issue I address in the next chapter is the role of the courts in bolstering central authority within a number of federal systems. One question that arises is the extent to which systems of judicial appointment are responsible for this. Patricia Popelier has undertaken detailed empirical work on this issue. She addressed eleven federal systems and concluded: 'If subnational authorities are not involved in the selection of judges and courts do not represent the federal structure, courts seem more likely to take a centralist stance.'[123] Others are sceptical that judges appointed by the federal level from constituent territories on a quota basis, or even by the governments of constituent territories themselves, act as representatives of that territory or understand their role in that way.[124] Robert Schertzer discusses this as a broader point about territorial representation at the centre:

> the assumption that including ethno-national minorities in central government institutions will result in the protection and promotion of their home group in decision-making is questionable. This is because there are, in any diverse polity, multiple competing ideas about the ethno-national nature of the state and the related distribution of powers and resources via systems such as federalism.[125]

[119] Basic Law for the Federal Republic of Germany 1948, arts 92 and 93. For an account of different models see G. Appleby and E.F. Delaney, 'Federalism, Judicial Systems', *Max Planck Encyclopaedia of Comparative Constitutional Law* (Oxford: Oxford University Press, 2017).

[120] Palermo and Kössler, *Comparative Federalism: Constitutional Arrangements and Case Law*, 162.

[121] P. Popelier and K. Lemmens, *The Constitution of Belgium: A Contextual Analysis* (Oxford: Hart Publishing, 2015), 196–197.

[122] In 2017 it was observed that competence disputes, which in the mid-1980s constituted 100 per cent of the docket, now 'account for only 12 percent of its cases'. P. Popelier, 'Federalism Disputes and the Behavior of Courts: Explaining Variation in Federal Courts' Support for Centralization' (2017) 47 *Publius: The Journal of Federalism* 27–48, 30.

[123] Popelier, 'Federalism Disputes and the Behavior of Courts, 29.

[124] This is in any case very rare. Erin Delaney notes: 'In the world's actually existing major democratic federations, only the Supreme Court of Canada has explicit subnational representation mandated by law. Supreme Court Act (R.S.C. 1985, c. S-26) (requiring 3 of the 9 Supreme Court justices to be members of the Quebec bar).'

[125] R.S. Schertzer, *The Judicial Role in a Diverse Federation: Lessons from the Supreme Court of Canada* (Toronto: University of Toronto Press, 2016).

A strong role for constituent territorial governments in central judicial appointments does not therefore necessarily lead to any self-perception on the part of federal judges that they have a territorially representative role. We have noted that federal judicial appointment in the United States is a power vested in the president, 'with the advice and consent of the Senate'.[126] This offers states a potentially significant role to bargain for territorial representation or for conventions to have developed as to territorial balance.[127] In fact, in deciding whether or not to ratify judicial appointments, the Senate in recent times has been far more concerned with issues of jurisprudential (or openly political) ideology than geography. By contrast, the Canadian constitution highlights how a system in which the constituent territories have less apparent influence in central judicial appointments can develop in a 'territorially representative' direction. In Canada all judges, both provincial and federal, and including the nine justices of the Supreme Court, are appointed by the federal government.[128] The Supreme Court of Canada was established in 1875[129] but the method of appointment remains unchanged.[130] This serves in practice to vest considerable power in the prime minister. Despite federal judicial appointment being a unilateral power of the central executive, conventions developed that sought to ensure that judicial appointments reflect Canada's territorial diversity. A principal constitutional practice which emerged was that at least three Supreme Court judges should be appointed from Quebec; the 1985 Act put this convention into law.[131] Other conventions include that three judges should come from Ontario, two from the Atlantic provinces, and one from the Western provinces.[132] The way in which territorial background has become such an issue in Canadian judicial appointments, despite a deeply unpropitious appointment model in which the provinces have no meaningful voice, can only be explained by the societal and

[126] Constitution of the United States 1789, art. II, s. 2, cl. 2.

[127] 'The early United States also had an unofficial convention of regional balance.' Erin Delaney, 'The Federal Case for Judicial Review', unpublished paper. See also J. Rakove, *Original Meanings: Politics and Ideas in the Making of the Constitution* (New York: Vintage, 1996).

[128] Nominally in the name of the governor general but in reality by the prime minister. Constitution Act 1867, s. 96 vests in the governor general power to appoint all judges in each province (except probate courts in Nova Scotia and New Brunswick). Ss 97 and 98 set out that provincial judges should be appointed from the bars of the province in question. Typically, independent judicial advisory committees assess the qualifications of lawyers who apply for these positions. A recommendation is then sent to the minister of justice. See 'Preserving Independence in the Judicial Appointment System: Report of the Standing Committee on Justice and Human Rights', House of Commons, 39th Parliament, 1st Session, 2007.

[129] However, final appeal lay to the Judicial Committee of the Privy Council until 1949 when power was transferred via the Supreme Court Act Amendment of 1949 (Can. 2nd sees.), c. 37.

[130] Supreme Court Act (RSC, 1985, c. S-26), s. 4(2).

[131] Supreme Court Act (RSC, 1985, c. S-26), s. 6.

[132] This was conventional from 1949 to 1978, but the pattern was broken when a second Atlantic judge was appointed. The pattern returned and currently exists on today's Court, but is not formal law. There are also arguments that Supreme Court appointments should reflect other aspects of Canada's territorial diversity, e.g. in the appointment of a Supreme Court judge with aboriginal origins.

jurisdictional particularity of Quebec which in turn has led to a broader territorial approach to judicial appointments.

Although Germany has an integrated legal system, the *Länder* have a significant role in judicial appointments. As noted above, the Basic Law provides that the Bundestag and Bundesrat each elect eight of the Federal Constitutional Court's sixteen members. Each election requires a two-thirds majority.[133] This requires cross-party support. In practice, negotiations in the Bundesrat are generally focused upon legal merit and to some extent the ideological disposition or adjudicatory approach of the judge; geography or the notion of somehow representing particular *Länder* or geographical areas do not register in any meaningful way. In Australia, judicial appointments are also a responsibility of the federal government.[134] There is a legal duty to consult with state attorneys general[135] but final determination is with the federal government.

(iv) Conclusions on associational government

It is clear that the federal idea has often become lost in the development of associational government within modern, complex federal constitutions. Monistic conceptions of the demos have tended to produce a notion of union—detached from autonomy—as a discrete value vested in a free-standing central level of government which, in a number of systems, operates without meaningful territorial involvement let alone control.

A consequence has been a tendency to overlook or indeed negate the foundational constitutional purpose of federalism. This requires that union should play out in close relationship to pluralism. The monist mindset that has been brought to the development of central government in a federal system has seen equal representation in the central legislature caricatured as 'demos-constraining' rather than as an entirely appropriate way in which to reflect the complex reality of the federal demos—a demos of different foundational demoi—manifest in the ongoing sovereign relationship between foundational constituent power and constitutional constituent authority. A strong role for constituent territories in the central branch of government is in fact a logical consequence of territorial constitutional subjecthood and of the constitutional aspiration to foster the polity's territorial pluralism. That is not to say that a powerful role for constituent territories necessarily involves the assertion of strong territorial identities or an antagonistic approach to the making of national policy. In many federal states, as we have seen,

133 Basic Law for the Federal Republic of Germany 1948, art. 94.

134 Technically the governor general: Constitution of Australia 1901, s. 72(i): 'The justices of the High Court and of the other courts created by parliament . . . shall be appointed by the Governor-General in counsel.'

135 High Court of Australia Act 1979, s. 6.

associational government happily operates in pursuit of common national policy. Each federal polity needs to respond to its own multi-societal realities in balancing territorial representation with a broader national project. However, it is also the case that the overwhelming trajectory within most federal systems over time has been the accretion of more and more authority by the central institutions, or the use of existing authority to strengthen these institutions at the expense of territorial autonomy or a share in associational rule. This is increasingly given effect through soft power exercised for example through the revenue raising and spending capacity of the federal government which can supplant the formal influence which the constitution seems to guarantee to the constitution's constituent subjects.

Into this mix, at the executive level, has come IGR. These operate in diverse ways but they often depend upon the political strength of the territories as much as institutional structure, as territories seek to protect their autonomy from central encroachment. Even where there is a formal IGR structure this can fall prey to political power. The Council of Australian Government is one example. It lost much of its importance and was largely dominated by the federal executive. As Anderson observes: 'the greater resources of the Commonwealth and its dominant role in setting the agenda for COAG meetings has inevitably meant that the bureaucracy supporting COAG would take its lead from the centre. This suggests that the form of executive federalism that COAG has fostered is one which has supported greater centralisation within the federation.'[136] It is also clear that the nature of institutions within the constitution cannot be separated rigidly from any account of the division of powers; associational government therefore becomes a complex story of the interplay among institutional design, authority distribution, constitutional culture, and political power. In many ways therefore the principle of associational rule is a litmus test of the very endurance of the federal idea. In some federal systems the union dynamic of federalism has proven to be so strong that the very salience of federalism as the fundamental constitutional principle of the polity is brought into question. It is largely in those countries where territorial cultural diversity remains salient that constituent territories continue to assert strongly the constitutional prerogatives of associational government as an essential bulwark of the other principles of federalism.

III. Reciprocity

(i) Vertical reciprocity (comity)

The principle of reciprocity is core to the constitutional purpose of federalism, flowing from the idea of union as the necessary complement to pluralism. This has

[136] G. Anderson, 'The Council of Australian Governments: A New Institution of Governance for Australia's Conditional Federalism' (2008) 31 *University of New South Wales Law Journal* 493–508, 506.

two dimensions: vertical and horizontal. 'Vertical reciprocity' involves a commitment by the constituent territories to the constitutional contract itself. It therefore implies a duty on the part of constituent territories to cooperate with the national level of government in working for the overall success of the federal project. Federal constitutions can make express provision for vertical reciprocity. The Swiss constitution provides that the federal government—'the Confederation'—and the cantons 'shall support each other in the fulfilment of their duties and shall generally cooperate with each other'.[137] Furthermore, they 'owe each other a duty of consideration and support ... [and] shall provide each other with administrative assistance and mutual judicial assistance'.[138] Similarly, under the Belgian constitution, all governments must '[i]n the exercise of their respective responsibilities ... act with respect for federal loyalty, in order to prevent conflicts of interest'.[139] The constitution of South Africa sets out principles of cooperative government and IGR, imposing duties upon the different levels of government, including a duty to be 'loyal to the Constitution, the Republic and its people'.[140] It also anticipates an act to 'establish or provide for structures and institutions to promote and facilitate intergovernmental relations'.[141] Most federal constitutions however contain no such explicit requirement and instead the principle manifests itself more opaquely in three main ways: demotic allegiance, institutional architecture, and the distribution of competences.

(a) Demotic allegiance

The commitment by constituent territories to the constitution requires, most crucially, the allegiance of each territory's citizens, characterised by the constitutional creation of a national citizenship. A federal constitution is a distinctive order of rule but it is also a genus of constitutionalism for the modern state. As such, it requires to put in place the foundations for viable statehood as well as effective constitutionalism. A vital way of doing this is to give the constitution, and indeed the central level of government, a direct relationship with, and jurisdiction over, citizens across the entire state. The construction of a strong state was a key concern for the federalists at Philadelphia, and it is no coincidence that a national citizenship emerged as a central feature of Madison's constitutional vision.[142] Mill, in his mid-nineteenth-century reflections on federalism, recognised this as a vital dimension of the American constitution and, more broadly, essential to the success of any federal system.[143]

137 Federal Constitution of the Swiss Confederation 1999, art. 44(1).
138 Federal Constitution of the Swiss Confederation 1999, art. 44(2).
139 Constitution of Belgium 1831, art. 143(1). This provision was introduced in 1993.
140 Constitution of South Africa, art. 41(1)(d).
141 Art. 41(2)(a).
142 J. Madison, Federalist No. 39, Rossiter, *The Federalist Papers*, 240–246, 240–241.
143 J.S. Mill, *Utilitarianism, On Liberty and Considerations on Representative Government*, H.B. Acton (ed.) (London: J.M. Dent & Sons, 1972), 367.

National citizenship exists in tandem with the relationship between citizens and the constituent territory to which they belong, and federal polities have sought to manage these overlapping demotic relationships in different ways. Germany does so through both governmental practice and jurisprudential articulation of the principle of *Bundestreue* or federal loyalty.[144] There is however a delicate balance to be struck. Such loyalty cannot be imposed by a top-down approach—central institutions telling the citizens of constituent territories what their duty is. Such a commitment among citizens to the success of the polity can only develop organically. In general, federal systems have been highly successful in this role, with commitment to the constitution growing in strength and with the central government coming clearly to be seen as more than just a siphon for the constituent territories. Citizen allegiance to the federal constitution therefore co-exists with different levels of affinity to constituent territories, establishing a complex matrix of citizenship as discussed in Chapter 6, but a matrix which varies across, and even within, federal polities as each constitutional system finds its own way to manage and balance citizen aspirations for pluralism and union.

(b) Institutional architecture

We have seen how a federal system tends to take on a hybrid institutional structure, reflecting the dual commitment to pluralism and union that underpins the idea of federalism. An example is the central legislature where one house is designed to represent the undifferentiated people of the whole state, and a second chamber plays the role more as a house of the territories. This mix of different levels of government is what Madison called 'partly federal and partly national', or a 'compound republic'.[145] The danger to the principle of reciprocity can emerge if institutional imbalance is built into the system or emerges over time. For example, if the central legislature coupled with a strong central executive becomes too powerful then federalism's foundational purpose is itself in jeopardy. This is as much a behavioural as an institutional design issue. Both levels of government must work towards the success of the system, showing loyalty to the system through mutual respect for the competence and institutional prerogatives of the other.

[144] It was cited in an early case by the German Constitutional Court—BVerfGE 1, 299 (315), 1952. In this case the Court made comity a legal standard and asserted that the Basic Law required both the federal government and the *Länder* to conduct their business in a manner 'friendly to the idea of federation' (*bundesfreundliches Verhalten*). See G. Kisker, 'The West German Federal Constitutional Court as Guardian of the Federal System' (1989) 19 *Publius* 35–52, 50.

[145] '[I]n the sources from which the ordinary powers of the government are drawn, [The Constitution] is partly federal and partly national.' James Madison, Federalist No. 39, Rossiter, *The Federalist Papers*, 240–246, 240; and 'In the compound republic of America, the power surrendered by the people is first divided between two distinct governments.' J. Madison, Federalist No. 51, Rossiter, *The Federalist Papers*, 320–325, 323.

(c) Competences

The principle of vertical reciprocity is also manifest in the allocation of constitutional authority among the governments of the federal constitution, in particular through shared or concurrent powers. Shared powers are those that can only be exercised by both levels of government working cooperatively; concurrency on the other hand emerges in relation to competences accorded separately to each order of government but which overlap. The latter is a potentially messy arrangement, leaving it possible for a particular government to plant its flag first and exercise authority within its own jurisdiction. This can make it difficult, at least politically or practically, for the other level to legislate in a different way. The central level is often assisted in areas of overlap by an express or implied paramountcy rule within the constitution, whereby the federal courts will accept that its voice on a concurrent matter should take precedence.

In addition to such clauses, the central order of government, as we have discussed, is greatly consolidated by the authority to raise and spend money. It is through this power that it performs its role of consolidating the state—providing for its defence, its welfare, and its internal and external commerce. Watts notes that in nearly all federations 'the majority of major revenue sources have been assigned to the federal governments'.[146] This has been a growing trend and it is in fact the case that central authorities can use these powers to further the principle of reciprocity itself, by helping to promote efficient policies, avoiding unnecessary duplication, pre-empting tax wars, and enabling the equitable distribution of resources.[147] In this way a strong federal spending power can be exercised to promote the federal union, assisting weaker or poorer constituent territories, through for example fiscal transfers. This can be vital in giving constituent territories the resources they need to make their autonomy meaningful; another consequence can be the consolidation of their commitment to the federal project.

Significant imbalances in wealth can arise across the polity due to various socio-demographic differences: natural resources, size and dispersion of population, age and social mix of the population, relative urbanization, etc. Therefore, simply giving constituent territories their own revenue-raising power is not in itself a solution to imbalances. In fact, complete autonomy over tax-raising powers can result in very different levels of social services across the federal state: horizontal imbalances. Natural resources have become a focal point within federal systems because of the imbalances that can result when certain territories enjoy great natural wealth. In Canada this is a significant issue. Western provinces such as Alberta benefit greatly from forestry and carbon reserves. Accordingly, national competence in relation to tax and spending policies is important to ensure national standards which make the federal system work for all provinces. Similar tensions exist

[146] Watts, *Comparing Federal Systems*, 3rd edn, 96.
[147] Watts, *Comparing Federal Systems*, 3rd edn, 95–96.

in relation to relatively wealthy states in India such as Andhra Pradesh, Gujarat, Maharashtra, and Tamil Nadu and prosperous *Länder* in Germany, for example, Bavaria and Baden-Württemberg. It is a particular tension in pluri-national federal systems if sub-state nations whose ties to federal loyalty can be weak are further diminished by a sense that they subsidise the rest of the country, a frequent complaint from Flanders in Belgium and Catalonia in Spain.

Strong central spending powers can however be used in less benign ways or in ways that, perhaps inadvertently, have negative consequences for territorial autonomy. Certain constitutions do limit the purposes for which the central spending power can be used. In Switzerland and Germany it is restricted,[148] while Belgium has a very high level of fiscal decentralisation.[149] However, some constitutions explicitly empower the central government to spend or to provide grants to territorial governments even in areas beyond central government jurisdiction.[150] It is also the case that legal rules can be something of a grey area. Constitutions may not explicitly allow central governments to spend in areas of constituent territorial jurisdiction but nor do they tend expressly to forbid it. Much then rests upon constitutional interpretation and in many federal systems such as the USA[151] and Canada[152] the courts tend not to strike down central spending in areas of exclusive territorial jurisdiction.

As well as spending money the central government can also exert influence by issuing grants. The grant-giving power is an example of soft power; the federal government extending its reach in more subtle ways than actively spending in territorial areas: issuing monies with conditions attached, requiring that they be used for specific purposes. The central government can therefore use its power to promote its own policies; constituent territories may resent the control but they will also be reluctant to reject financial support. Ronald Watts conducted a detailed study of the federal spending power in federal constitutions. He found that in the USA grants to the states are always conditional, while at the other end of the

[148] In Switzerland, the Federal Assembly determines the expenditure of the Confederation, adopts a budget, and approves federal accounts. Federal Constitution of the Swiss Confederation 1999, art. 167. However, it may only give grants or subventions when empowered by federal statute. In Germany, the budget is set out in law at the start the fiscal year.

[149] Constitution of Belgium, Title V.

[150] Watts notes that the constitutions of Australia, India, and Malaysia explicitly recognise 'the authority of their federal governments to provide grants to state governments for *any* purpose, whether that purpose is under federal government jurisdiction or not'. Watts, *Comparing Federal Systems*, 3rd edn, 101.

[151] *South Dakota v. Dole* and *National Federal of Independent Business v. Sebelius* discussed above.

[152] B.H. Kellock and S. LeRoy, 'Questioning the Legality of the Federal "Spending Power"' (2007) 89 *Public Policy Sources* 1–26. The Supreme Court of Canada has recently upheld the authority of the federal Parliament to impose a tax on carbon emissions. *References re Greenhouse Gas Pollution Pricing Act 2021* SCC 11. The Court noted that global warming causes harm beyond provincial boundaries and therefore took the view that it such a matter of national concern under the 'peace, order and good government' clause of the constitution as to justify federal taxation.

spectrum, grants in Belgium came with conditions in only 6 per cent of cases.[153] It is also the case that in the USA and in Australia, the conditions attaching to central government grants tend to be highly specific; in other countries, such as Canada, they are less so.[154] It is notable that in countries with deep territorial cultural pluralism such as Belgium and Canada, the constituent territories tend to be left with more freedom in determining what to do with distributed funds. However, even in Canada, belying older practice, grants can come with the condition 'to implement federal priorities'.[155]

For the federal polity to work on the basis of reciprocity, the commitment of the central branch to pluralism is just as important as that of the constituent territories to union. The overwhelming story however is of the taxing and spending powers being used to consolidate central power. These powers are so influential that, even where they do not expressly invade territorial competences, in practice they can circumscribe tightly the environment within which territorial powers are exercised. Wheare noted that the 'financial autonomy' of regional governments 'is always conditional upon their working within the framework of currency and credit determined in the last resort by the general government—so far as such matters are determined by governments at all'.[156] The classic example of how, instead of promoting vertical reciprocity, the central branch has accrued more and more influence to itself is the USA. The constitution left open the balance of competences and gave the states a strong role in associational rule through the Senate. But the financial power of Congress has served to diminish both the autonomy of the states and meaningful associational government. Congress, through the spending power, has effectively forced the states into a system of 'co-operative federalism', which is in reality dependence upon Washington. So powerful is the central role that it is better described as 'regulatory federalism' or even 'coercive federalism'.[157] This process of centralisation has happened over a long period of time. It is consolidated particularly at times of economic or other national crisis, when national problems seem to call for national solutions.[158] Power shifts that occur during times of economic depression or the exigencies of war often remain in place when the crisis is

[153] See also Watts, *Comparing Federal Systems*, 3rd edn, 106.

[154] Referring to the British North America Act of 1867 Kenneth Hanssen wrote over fifty years ago: 'The only explicit provisions of the constitution that confer upon the federal government power to transfer money to the provinces are the sections providing for what are known as the statutory subsidies which were unconditional grants to the provinces.' K. Hanssen, 'The Constitutionality of Conditional Grant Legislation' (1966) 2 *Manitoba Law Journal* 191–199, 195.

[155] Watts, *Comparing Federal Systems*, 3rd edn, 100.

[156] K.C. Wheare, *Federal Government* (New York: Oxford University Press, 1946), 99.

[157] Whereby the states in the latter half of the twentieth century were essentially forced to accept uniform policy imposed by Congress: J. Kincaid, 'From Cooperative to Coercive Federalism' (1990) 509 *Annals of the American Academy of Political and Social Science* 139–152.

[158] G.C.S. Benson, *The New Centralization* (New York: Farrar and Rinehart, 1941).

over; the long-term legacy being the undermining of the very balance at the heart of the principle of vertical reciprocity.[159]

There are other areas where shared or concurrent powers require cooperation among governments or at least a disposition not to frustrate the authority of the other level. One example is international relations. As we discussed earlier in the chapter, typically the central branch has exclusive competence to conclude international agreements. However, the ratification and/or successful implementation of such agreements may depend upon the constituent territories, particularly where the subject matter of the agreement covers areas of constituent territorial competence. This illustrates how imperative it is that the central government works towards a cooperative relationship even in relation to areas within its own jurisdiction, given the interconnectedness of competences in a modern federal constitution.

Federal constitutional systems are now more complex than ever before and powers are increasingly shared between levels. The issue of balance between pluralism and union can become a complex story of relative economic and political power played out in the context of constitutional competence. Constituent territories are also adept at using courts to assert their constitutional prerogatives even in systems of inter-territorial societal homogeneity[160] It is certainly not a one-sided game and the growth in importance of IGR bears this out. The principle of vertical reciprocity is promoted if the constitution embeds a commitment by each order of government to the flourishing of the other. However, this principle depends more upon a federal political culture underpinning constitutional practice; if structural power dynamics shift to the point where one order dominates the other, the federal principle itself is jeopardised.

(ii) Horizontal reciprocity (social solidarity)

In addressing the principle of recognition in the last chapter I noted that the federal idea manifests itself also in the mutual recognition of the constituent territories; the acknowledgement that each is an elemental subject of the federal constitution. This foundational salience gives rise to reciprocal rights and duties; in effect, the

[159] In fact such a subtle move towards centralisation was anticipated by a number of the founders. Yarborough argues that Madison and Hamilton expected that support for the strongly federal aspects of the constitution would wane as the people came to 'experience the advantages of the national government'. She also believes they were correct to do so: 'To a considerable extent, The Federalist's expectations have been borne out. The Constitution has been amended to limit the participation of the states in the national government, and the people have turned increasingly to the national government, rather than the states, for solutions to their economic and social problems.' J. Yarbrough, 'Rethinking "*The Federalist*'s View of Federalism"' (1985) 15 *Publius* 31–53, 36.

[160] J.A. Gardner, 'The Theory and Practice of Contestatory Federalism' (2018) 60 *William and Mary Law Review* 507–588.

substantive obligations that flow from the horizontal dimension of recognition. The principle of horizontal reciprocity manifests itself in more inchoate or indirect ways than the other principles of federalism and is most obviously identifiable in the playing out of these other commitments. The principles of autonomy and associational rule within a plural territorial environment imply that each territory will recognise that others too are entitled to self-government and a representational role at the centre commensurable with their own entitlement. This begs the question however as to the nature of these mutual duties and how they should be fulfilled institutionally.

We noted in relation to vertical reciprocity how the central government can use its fiscal and spending powers to correct disparities of wealth across the state. This can clearly be seen from one perspective as a threat to constituent territorial autonomy. But from another it is an essential element of federal constitutionalism, recognising the salience of each constituent territory to the federal project and the need for some level of material parity across territories for each to feel properly part of the federal project. The fact that richer or stronger territories accept such a reality makes this a form of horizontal as well as vertical recognition: acknowledgement that one's partners in the foundational federal commitment must be able to take part in the federal constitutional project as viable and effective governments and societies.

Wealth distribution is therefore also core to the principle of horizontal reciprocity but this dimension of reciprocity raises questions about how duties implicit within the federal contract are understood and articulated by the constituent territories themselves. There are two issues in play. First, how wealth redistribution is rationalised within a federal constitution: whether it is viewed through a territorial lens or on the basis of individual justice; and secondly, the differing ways in which the principle of horizontal reciprocity is given effect within federal systems: through either grants or direct central spending.

We have seen in earlier chapters how liberal ideology has come to over-power the federal idea, raising objections to the idea of asymmetrical representation at a political level, for example in the central legislature. This extends also to the principle of horizontal reciprocity which has been respectively bolstered and undermined by two different versions of liberalism. On the one hand the principle has come to be understood by social democratic liberals as a commitment to an individualised conception of social solidarity. The purpose of distribution by this conception is not principally to facilitate the functioning of effective societies within a federal system but to achieve, as closely as possible, individual equality in social provision across the state in matters such as health, education, and social welfare. On the other hand, arguments against wealth distribution tend to be based upon libertarianism and a general antipathy towards high taxation and wealth redistribution by the state, whether for federal or non-federal purposes. This latter position clearly informs the economic liberalism of the Federalist Papers, where a federal system was presented as a vital guarantee against 'the equal division of property'.[161] Since, for classical liberals, the pluralisation of government is not seen as a value in itself but as a vehicle for individual autonomy and the protection of individual interests, federalism's worth is assessed instrumentally through the lens of *laissez faire* approaches to economic management.

Each of these approaches misses the fundamental point that the purpose of federalism, as a discrete constitutional idea, is to be found not within alternative ideological accounts but in an inherent constitutional commitment to territorial pluralism within a state political project. The goal of horizontal reciprocity, when alleviated of ideological baggage, is therefore to balance territorial union and pluralism and reflect their essential complementarity within any properly functioning federal constitution. Horizontal reciprocity is crucial to foster union but it should not be elided with individual equality across the entire polity; if it is, it can serve to undermine the principle of autonomy for constituent territories; real autonomy is hard to maintain if there is a blanket requirement for equal individual standards across the country in areas that are wholly or partly within territorial jurisdiction. Constituent territories in coming together to form a federal constitution as opposed to a unitary one commit legally to do so, *inter alia*, in order to give ongoing constitutional recognition and efficacy to inter-societal difference. The federal idea does not therefore automatically imply a commitment to individual material equality across the polity; respect for the autonomy of constituent territories and to recognising their societal particularities may in fact preclude such an outcome. It might also be observed that liberal societies tolerate vast disparities of wealth and power that are not territorially located. A liberal argument for equalisation of resources across territories does not translate into an argument for equalisation of wealth *within territories*; in reality it is an argument that the fruits of economic inequality manifest themselves in the same way across the polity. This may be a liberal commitment, it is not a federal one.

This leads to the conclusion that while horizontal reciprocity argues for some degree of inter-territorial wealth distribution to make the union of territories viable, each federal system can interpret this principle in its own way upon a spectrum of greater or lesser territorial autonomy, allowing scope for constituent territories to pursue their own social policies based upon varying ideological positions or societal priorities. This is entirely consistent with the federal principle insofar as it does not undermine the coherent functioning of the constitution or of the state as a whole.

This final qualification does not disguise the tension inherent within the federal idea. Federal constitutional systems can legitimately decide that excessive imbalances across territories are both unfair in relation to the commitment to union and

[161] For Madison, an 'improper or wicked project'. J. Madison, Federalist No. 10, Rossiter, *The Federalist Papers*, 77–84, 77.

potentially destabilising; and therefore that significant differences in economic or tax policy across the state would undermine the solidarity essential to the federal contract: for example, if a territory uses its autonomy to lower corporation taxes to such an extent that businesses are attracted from one part of the federation to another, or in a way that makes the territory significantly wealthier than others. Some disparities can arise accidentally, for example where certain territories benefit from favourable natural resources such as oil, minerals, or timber. Again a federal system can legitimately allow these territories to benefit disproportionately from this or can decide upon more or less even distribution of revenues from the exploitation of such resources.

Given that the principle is open to different manifestations, how have federal systems approached the principle of horizontal reciprocity in practice? One common position within federalism is indeed towards 'equalisation'. In some systems this is provided for by the constitution itself. The Canadian constitution states that: 'Parliament and the government of Canada are committed to the principle of making equalization payments to ensure that provincial governments have sufficient revenues to provide reasonably comparable levels of public services at reasonably comparable levels of taxation.'[162] Notably this is not a commitment to individual equality. A guarantee of 'reasonably comparable levels' of public services offers scope for a calibrated and potentially shifting balance between respecting provincial autonomy on the one hand and making the federal project attractive and viable to less wealthy provinces.

The approach taken by the German constitution contains a subtle but important difference. In relation to concurrent powers, the federal Parliament has the right to legislate 'if and to the extent that the establishment of equal living conditions throughout the federal territory or the maintenance of legal or economic unity renders federal regulation necessary in the national interest'.[163] The authority to establish and maintain 'equal living conditions' is a more precise commitment than 'reasonably comparable levels' of service in Canada, and indeed this has been generally interpreted to warrant equal conditions for individuals across the whole polity.

The Indian constitution offers yet another difference in approach. It provides for the constitution of a Finance Commission every five years to make recommendations as to 'the distribution between the Union and the States of the net proceeds of taxes' and 'the principles which should govern the grants-in-aid of the revenues of the States out of the Consolidated Fund of India'.[164] This has operated alongside a Planning Commission which was established by the government of India in the

[162] Canadian Constitution Act 1982, s. 36(2). A similar provision is found in the Federal Constitution of the Swiss Confederation 1999, art. 135: Equalisation of financial resources and burdens.
[163] Basic Law for the Federal Republic of Germany 1948, art. 72(2).
[164] Constitution of India, art. 280(3).

early 1950s and operated until 2014. This had various responsibilities, including notably, a duty to 'formulate a plan for the most effective and balanced utilisation of the country's resources'. These two commissions have in practice encouraged a strongly equalising initiative across the federation. The constitution however also balances Article 280 with the autonomy principle: 'The Union or a State may make any grants for any public purpose, notwithstanding that the purpose is not one with respect to which Parliament or the Legislature of the State, as the case may be, may make laws.'[165]

The absence of specific constitutional provision has not prevented the establishment of such a system. Australia introduced a comprehensive scheme of equalization in 1933 despite no explicit constitutional commitment to equalisation. This is based upon Goods and Services Tax redistribution, managed by the federal government on the advice of the Commonwealth Grants Commission.[166] The aim is for 'Horizontal Fiscal Equalisation', but the grants to the states are issued without conditions, leaving them to adopt their own services which can create variation across states.

These examples illustrate that equalisation is typically achieved through a combination of taxation, whereby wealthier territories pay more, and by grant distribution, through which poorer territories receive more. As to the method of calculating the sums involved, in some countries there is an agreed formula, in others there is an independent body or commission to determine it—Australia and India are examples of the latter, as to some extent is Belgium where a National Solidarity Intervention allows for unconditional transfers from the federal government to federated entities where income tax income is below the national average. In a number of systems the constituent territories are themselves actively involved in determining how the equalisation process works. In Germany, Austria, and Switzerland equalisation measures/redistributive grants are determined by the federal legislature. Since territorial representatives have a significant voice in parliament they tend to exert a strong influence over decisions involving fiscal transfers and spending policy.

Most federal systems now see some form of equalisation as essential to constitutional and societal cohesion. The USA and Mexico are unusual in having no such arrangements. The trajectory within federal constitutions has tended to be towards more detailed models and processes of equalisation. Australia brought in a VAT system in 1999 and the federal government distribute this sales tax in an equalized way on the recommendation of the Commonwealth Grants Commission (CGC). This model and the role of the CGC more broadly is something of a high water mark in the formalisation of financial and equalization arrangements in federal systems. Grewal argues that Australia has 'adopted arguably the most elaborate and

[165] Constitution of India, art. 282.
[166] Commonwealth Grants Commission Act 1973.

comprehensive approach' to fiscal equalisation of any federation.[167] In a similar way Switzerland introduced a complex and detailed commitment to equalisation by way of a referendum in 2004.[168] This still permits cantons some level of tax and spend autonomy but the overwhelming commitment is to levelling out wealth among cantons.[169]

Canada, as we have noted, is to some extent a point of contrast, providing a floor of equality rather than a ceiling, promoting 'equal opportunities' rather than equal services.[170] In this way it differs from Germany and Australia which are more radically equalising on an individual basis.[171] It does however seek to arrive at integrated social services and an equalising approach to fiscal distribution.[172] At the same time, the Canadian model of reciprocity takes account of demotic differences, in particular Quebec's distinctiveness. One way in which this takes institutional form is through 'opt outs'. When a national policy is arrived at in a number of areas it is open to provinces to decide to pursue their own policy.[173] A province that does so then receives a share of the money to further its own approach. Numerous provinces take advantage of this but it has primarily been drawn upon by Quebec to promote distinct policies. In this way a balance is arrived at; transfers and a search for equalisation reflect the principle of horizontal reciprocity, but opt-outs allow this to be tempered by the principle of autonomy. The Canadian approach demonstrates how the principle of reciprocity is not a synonym for equality. It also shows how equality itself is a complex idea that must take account of the particular needs of different territories.

Horizontal reciprocity very much represents the central tension within the federal idea—a commitment that is fundamental to the union dimension of federalism but which can, depending upon how it is implemented, pose a significant challenge to the principle of autonomy. However, the range of options and the differences in approach that apply across federal systems emphasises that this principle, like the other principles implicit within the federal constitutional idea, is a malleable one, adaptable to the societal particularities of any federal constitution.

[167] B.S. Grewal 'Federalism and Fiscal Equalization: Should India Follow the Australian Path?', in I. Copland and J. Rickard (eds), *Federalism: Comparative Perspectives from India and Australia* (New Delhi: Manohar, 1999). See also E.M. Gramlich, '"A Fair Go": Fiscal Federalism Arrangements', in R.E. Caves and L.B. Krause (eds), *The Australian Economy: A View from the North* (Sydney: Allen & Unwin, 1984), 231–274.

[168] R.L. Frey and G. Wettstein, 'Reform of the Swiss Fiscal Equalisation System', CESifo DICE Report 1/2008 <https://citeseerx.ist.psu.edu/viewdoc/download?doi=10.1.1.862.4854&rep=rep1&type=pdf>.

[169] S. Mueller and S. Keil, 'The Territoriality of Fiscal Solidarity: Comparing Swiss Equalisation with European Union Structural Funding' (2013) 5 *Perspectives on Federalism* 122–148.

[170] Constitution Act of 1982, s. 36(1).

[171] Hueglin and Fenna, *Comparative Federalism*, 2nd edn, 173.

[172] A. Lecours and D. Béland, 'Federalism and Fiscal Policy: The Politics of Equalization in Canada' (2010) 4 *Publius* 569–596.

[173] Opt-outs can also be taken in certain circumstances from constitutional amendments, discussed in Chapter 10.

IV. Concluding comments

This chapter has addressed the principles that bolster the dynamic of union within the federal idea. At the same time these principles also emphasise that territorial pluralism is inherent within the federal idea as much as do the principles of reciprocity and autonomy. Since a federal constitution is a constitutional project for the modern state, it requires for its efficacy a viable and effective central government. But this is only part of the authority distributive dimension of federal constitutional sovereignty, operable alongside the authority of territorial governments. Crucially, the combination of both is not a synonym for constitutional sovereignty; this is generated by the constitution's territorial constituent subjects in their interaction with the constitution itself. The central branch of government must therefore be designed to reflect the pluralism inherent to the federal contract. To this end it is best described through the conception of associational government.

Without a commitment to associational rule that fully involves the territories in the government of the state the state project itself can be undermined. As Watts pointed out: 'Where particular regional groups have had inadequate representation and influence in the federal institutions, the resulting alienation has directed itself into separatist movements.'[174] He cites a number of failed federations in Asia and the West Indies.[175] It is no coincidence that among a number of modern constitutional systems which are currently under strain, including Spain and the UK, a lack of influence at the centre for the state's constituent territories is often alluded to as a key constitutional weakness[176] and improved intergovernmentalism a key remedy,[177] helping to bolster the union by making it more relevant within territories.

It is however the case that, in a number of federal systems, so monist is the demotic base of the state that associational rule has become highly integrated in practice, or is exercised not in order to promote territorial pluralism but in reflection of state-wide ideological divisions. In this way, central institutions which were designed to give constituent territories significant influence over central government come in time not to be used by these territories to promote territorial pluralism but are merely sites within which national party politics play out.[178] On the other

174 Watts, *Comparing Federal Systems*, 3rd edn, 181.

175 Watts, *Comparing Federal Systems*, 3rd edn, 181–182.

176 House of Lords Constitution Committee, 'The Union and Devolution', HL Paper 149, sess. 2015–16, 25 May 2016. On Spain, Requejo states bluntly: 'There are no clear procedural rules of "shared government" in the Spanish constitutional framework.' Ferran Requejo, Is Spain a Federal Country? <http://50shadesoffederalism.com/case-studies/spain-federal-country/>.

177 House of Lords Constitution Committee, 'Intergovernmental Relations in the United Kingdom', HL Paper 146, sess. 2014–15, 27 March 2015; V. Cuesta-López, 'Intergovernmental Relations in Spain and the United Kingdom: The Institutionalization of Multilateral Cooperation in Asymmetric Polities' (2014) 6 *Perspectives on Federalism* 299–318.

178 A recent analysis of party behaviour in the US Congress found that 'both parties routinely abrogate state authority in order to advance other valuable policy ends'. M.E. SoRelle and A.N. Walker,

hand, in other federal systems where territorial identities remain highly salient, territories seek to use associational rule to assert the pluralism of the polity and the central institutions can become sites of intense power struggle but also vital arenas for the making of consensual decisions.

The same differences in political culture affect how the related principles of vertical and horizontal reciprocity play out. Each of these principles is essentially about constitutional commitment, the commitment of the different levels of government to the constitution itself and its undertakings, and the commitment of each constituent territory to the prospering of every other. Addressing federalism by way of its purposes rather than from the perspective of an ideal institutional form raises a broader existential question. The constitutional design of a federal state may be a poor fit for the demotic or political make-up of the federal polity in question. This may be so from the very foundation of the constitution or it may develop over time, whereby the societal nature of the polity changes to the point where the underlying societal conditions are no longer suited to a federal constitution, or at least to a federal constitution in the form institutionalised by the constitution. Federalism is, like all constitutional systems, a functional tool, designed to husband political power in particular ways for that specific society. It must therefore be open to change to meet the evolution of the society itself. And if a society no longer values federalism then it should feel able to transform the constitution in a direction better suited to it. Change is therefore a vital element of federal constitutionalism and it is to this subject that we turn in the next chapter.

'Partisan Preemption: The Strategic Use of Federal Preemption Legislation' (2016) 46 *Publius* 486–509, 486–487. Cited by E. Delaney, 'The Federal Case for Judicial Review', unpublished paper.

10

Dynamics: Changing Federal Constitutions

I. Introduction

All constitutional systems change over time. And while change may take place through formal processes of amendment it can also occur more incrementally by way of shifts in constitutional culture and practice, often reflected in, or conditioned by, important decisions of constitutional courts. In this chapter I address the dynamics of constitutional change in federal systems across each of these dimensions. My key enquiry is how the constitutional purpose of federalism, and the principles which flow from it, shape the dynamics of federal constitutionalism in theory and in practice. In defining the purpose and principles of federalism in earlier chapters I discussed how a federal constitution is a complex matrix of authority that must constantly manage the tension between pluralism and unity. To this end the mechanics of constitutional change should offer an appropriate safety valve, relieving pressure in the system and adjusting the direction of the constitution, possibly towards greater territorial pluralism or stronger union as the interplay between the polity's underlying political conditions and the temper of its internal societies shifts.

This raises the question of entrenchment and its suitability to a federal constitution. Is the balance between pluralism and union better maintained through constitutional provisions that embed foundational institutional arrangements, or by a more fluid constitutional arrangement that facilitates political openness, allowing stresses within the system to be eased through flexible pathways to change? I begin the chapter by considering a general trend in modern constitutionalism towards rigid constitutions, assessing arguments both for and against deep entrenchment in federal systems. At the heart of this enquiry is the highly particular nature of federal constituent power which we discussed in Chapters 3 and 5. In Section II I address the theory of constitutional amendment within federal systems and from there, in Section III, turn from theory to institutional arrangements, cataloguing the different ways in which federal constitutions in practice manage formal constitutional change and addressing both the institutional architecture of constitutional amendment and the ways in which different entrenchment rules can apply to different constitutional provisions within federal systems. In light of this discussion of federal theory and practice I argue that different areas of political life lend themselves, respectively, to stronger or weaker constitutional insulation within a federal constitution. This can be contrasted with entrenchment design for unitary

The Federal Contract. Stephen Tierney, Oxford University Press. © Stephen Tierney 2022.
DOI: 10.1093/oso/9780198806745.003.0010

constitutions which reflects a monist conception of the demos. Throughout the chapter I consider how processes of change can serve either to consolidate the federal purpose of a constitution, helping the federal contract to flourish, or to undermine it by moving the constitution in a more unitary direction. In this context I address, in Section IV, how change is managed or developed by the courts. Judicial interpretation within federal systems, as within unitary constitutions, has proven to be crucial to the evolution of constitutional meaning, in some cases serving to transform fundamentally the very character and identity of the federal contract.

II. Constitutional change and the federal contract: between entrenchment and deliberation

Constitutions are more than mere rule books. They serve to manage political power by transforming it into lawful authority, but the process of encapsulating the dramatic original moment in one foundational written settlement also carries with it deep inter-temporal salience, meaning that the constitution takes on symbolic as well as institutional potency. We see this in the origins and subsequent political and social reification of the American constitution, made in the name of We, the People of the United States; a statement that creates and defines the demotic self as much as it constitutes the order of rule through which the people is set to shape its collective public life. The result is two-fold. At the institutional level constitutions entrench rules beyond ordinary law-making; while on the demotic register, they also assume a totemic significance as receptacles for, and generators of, political identity and ideological values.[1]

Increasingly we see the deepening of, and greater interconnection between, these two roles.[2] Constitutions are today framed with ever tighter rigidity. This trend has various strands. One is that new constitutions tend to be longer and more detailed.[3] Another is that constitutional change becomes harder to achieve due to deeper entrenchment including eternity clauses[4] and the notion of unamendable constitutional provisions leading to the judicially developed concept of 'unconstitutional amendments'.[5] As a matter of mentality, institutional inflexibility leads

[1] G.J. Jacobsohn, *Constitutional Identity* (Cambridge MA: Harvard University Press, 2010).

[2] For a recent, seminal account of the process of constitutional amendment in comparative relief see R. Albert, *Constitutional Amendments: Making, Breaking, and Changing Constitutions* (Oxford: Oxford University Press, 2019).

[3] For example, the US constitution of 1789 was comprised of 7 articles, while that of India, promulgated in 1950, has 395 articles in 22 parts and the Constitution of Iraq, 2005 144 articles.

[4] S. Suteu, *Eternity Clauses in Democratic Constitutionalism* (Oxford: Oxford University Press, 2021).

[5] Y. Roznai, *Unconstitutional Constitutional Amendments: The Limits of Amendment Powers* (Oxford: Oxford University Press, 2017). This notion that there are limits to the constitutional amendment process is a particular feature of Indian constitutional jurisprudence: *Kesavananda Bharati v. State of Kerala*, 1973 AIR 1461; *Indira Nehru Gandhi v. Raj Narain*, 1975 AIR 2299. It does however highlight, as Roznai demonstrates, a general trend towards more assertive judicial decision-making through

inexorably to ideological instrumentalism. With constitutions increasingly envisioned not just as road maps for lawful political decision-making but as statements of collective political identity, political values come to be elevated above, and insulated from, the realm of political disagreement. This process of constitutional consolidation, indeed crystallisation, is often aided, or driven, by the judiciary which, in its interpretive function, can articulate and further embed moral-normative values,[6] generally those of liberalism.[7] Given liberal theory's assumptions about the inherent, universal, and overriding value of methodological individualism, this has produced a form of ideological constitutionalism made to travel and we see the trend towards constitutional rigidity spread throughout the contemporary world in processes of constitution-making as well as at the more prosaic level of interpretation.[8]

The question then arises: how consistent is strong constitutional entrenchment with the federal idea? I have argued that the federal idea is in essence a *constitutional* idea and that overlaying this idea with political ideology has served to obscure its essential purpose. In this chapter a key argument I present is that the mode of entrenchment of any federal constitution should be focused upon federal constitutionalism's essential purpose and that, beyond this, a flexible approach to constitutional change is better suited to manage the tension at its heart. As Hueglin and Fenna put it: 'Permanent deliberation among multiple participants is not just a practical consequence of the federal division of powers, it is a basic federal principle in its own right.'[9] The Supreme Court of Canada offered a similar view in its seminal reflections upon Canadian constitutional history: 'The federal structure of our country ... facilitates democratic participation by distributing power to the government thought to be most suited to achieving the particular societal objective having regard to this diversity.'[10]

In fact, one of the contradictions within the federalism literature is between approaches which emphasise the importance of written constitutions to the federal project (I discuss this tradition in the next section of the chapter) and another strain which stresses the need for political openness to allow the federal idea to flourish. Friedrich was one scholar who identified the need for political openness in his idea of 'federal behaviour',[11] a pragmatic approach that emphasises the

'strong-form' judicial review. See also M. Tushnet, *Weak Courts, Strong Rights* (Princeton: Princeton University Press, 2008).

[6] R. Hirschl, *Towards Juristocracy: The Origins and Consequences of the New Constitutionalism* (Harvard: Harvard University Press, 2007).

[7] J. Goldsworthy, 'Questioning the Migration of Constitutional Ideas: Rights, Constitutionalism and the Limits of Convergence', in S. Choudhry (ed.), *The Migration of Constitutional Ideas* (Cambridge: Cambridge University Press, 2009), 115–141.

[8] S. Choudhry, 'Migration as a New Metaphor in Comparative Constitutional Law', in S. Choudhry (ed.), *The Migration of Constitutional Ideas* (Cambridge: Cambridge University Press, 2009), 1–36.

[9] T.O. Hueglin and A. Fenna, *Comparative Federalism: A Systematic Inquiry*, 2nd edn (Toronto: University of Toronto Press, 2015), 48.

[10] *Reference re Secession of Quebec* [1998] 2 SCR 217, para. 58.

[11] Discussed in Chapter 7.

ultimate salience of deliberative method (compromise and the accommodation of other viewpoints) over specific institutional design within any federal project. Friedrich describes the 'federal spirit' of 'federal behaviour' as 'a highly pragmatic kind of political conduct, which avoids all insistence upon "agreement on fundamentals" and similar forms of doctrinaire rigidity. Such behaviour proceeds in the spirit of compromise and accommodation. It is moulded by the knowledge that there are many rooms in a house that federalism builds.'[12] This notion has earlier origins in Althusius' idea of consociation, 'the art of living together'.[13] Although Althusius was describing the pre-modern world and not the system of modern federal constitutions with which we are concerned in this book, his focus upon the need for cooperation when a multiplicity of societies come together to form one polity[14] resonates into the modern federal era.

A common thread across this literature suggests the need for political openness to manage the tension at the heart of federalism between pluralism and union. In doing so it demonstrates that this tension is not a pathology of federalism but rather its key characteristic, one that requires federalism to remain dynamic in order to accommodate the complex political interactions it produces. As Hueglin and Fenna argue, the question of who does what in a federal system 'cannot be decided once and for all by a final allocation of powers ... it requires a permanent political process of negotiation and compromise according to changing times and circumstances.'[15] In this context, a federal constitution should not be viewed as a 'settlement'. The constitutional contract is one designed to manage tensions, and as such a key part of this should be its openness to revision.

Despite the seemingly compelling reasons to leave federal constitutionalism open to the political process, federal practice has itself tended towards, and indeed led the way in promoting, constitutional entrenchment, beginning with the deeply embedded US constitution. Federal scholars, often basing their analysis upon the American precedent, have long taken the view that federalism is characterised by deep entrenchment. Dicey argued that '(f)ederalism ... means legalism',[16] while

[12] C.J. Friedrich, *Trends of Federalism in Theory and Practice* (London: Frederick A. Praeger Publishers, 1968), 39. For a similar view see J. Broschek, Conceptualizing and Theorizing Constitutional Change in Federal Systems: Insights from Historical Institutionalism' (2011) 21 *Regional and Federal Studies* 539–559, 548; and A.A. Ninet and J.A. Gardner, 'Distinctive Identity Claims in federal Systems: Judicial Policing of Subnational Variance' (2016) 14 *International Journal of Constitutional Law* 378–410, 380: 'Federalism ... is a structure of governance that is likely to be in nearly constant motion. Federalism expressly contemplates, and indeed invites, intergovernmental contestation not only within the established constitutional framework, but over the dimensions of the constitutional framework itself. The regular and predictable outbreak of these kinds of conflicts thus reflects not a design flaw but the existence of a healthy, well-functioning, and indeed organically alive federal system.'

[13] J. Althusius, *Politica Methodice Digesta, Atque Exemplis Sacris et Profanis Illustrata*, [1603], F.S. Carney (ed. and trans.) (Indianapolis: Liberty Fund, 1995), I.5.

[14] Discussed by T.O. Hueglin, *Early Modern Concepts for a Late Modern World: Althusius on Community and Federalism* (Waterloo: WLU Press, 1999), 63.

[15] Hueglin and Fenna, Comparative Federalism: A Systematic Inquiry, 1st edn, 96.

[16] A.V. Dicey, *Introduction to the Study of the Law of the Constitution*, 8th edn (London: Macmillan and Co., 1915), 175.

Bryce categorised federal constitutions as 'rigid'.[17] Since these accounts have derived the idea from practice, it is harder to explain the appropriate balance between fixed and open constitutionalism. Accounts of where the line should be drawn tend to be vague. For Watts, what is needed in federal constitutions 'is a balance between rigidity and flexibility'.[18] Hueglin and Fenna offer a similar prescription: 'Somewhere between that rigidity at one extreme, and the flexibility of plain majority rule at the other, lies the typical level of agreement required in federal systems.'[19]

The notion of entrenchment is now so universally accepted as to be the subject of little reflection, the justification for it being caught up within a wider story of liberal republicanism and the entrenchment of individual rights. Among early writers however it is notable that entrenchment was seen to serve a very specific purpose: to ensure the efficacy of the institutional design and authority distribution inherent in the original federal structure.[20] In the mid-twentieth century Kenneth Wheare, in emphasising the salience of constitutional embeddedness to federal constitutionalism, also focused upon this institutional dimension.[21]

To some extent this can be seen as a simple extension of the fact that federal constitutionalism is a contract: '[a]t the bargaining table, the original participants want ... assurances about their irrevocable powers and rights written into constitutional stone.'[22] It is therefore necessary to narrow down the specific purpose of entrenchment within federal systems in order to overcome the apparent paradox that federalism as a genus of constitutionalism often manifests rigidity in its processes of constitutional change while also bearing a core purpose that seems to require political flexibility. The key to resolving this conundrum is to be found in the purpose of federal constitutionalism itself. Federalism involves a fundamental commitment to the constitutional salience of its constituent territories. It is, as a consequence, important to protect this commitment beyond the reach of simple 'national' majoritarianism. But at the same time, federalism is born from a particular manifestation of constituent power which, as we explored in earlier chapters, leads to an active and unsettled form of constitutional constituent authority through which the constitution's constituent territories play an active part in the management of the distributive dimension of sovereignty. We have explored in Chapters 8 and 9 how this plays out in the day-to-day relations of authority between and among the different levels of government: in interactions between legislatures

[17] J. Bryce, 'Flexible and Rigid Constitutions', in J. Bryce, *Studies in History and Jurisprudence* (Oxford: Oxford University Press, 1901), 200.

[18] R.L. Watts, *Comparing Federal Systems*, 3rd edn (Montreal, QC, Canada: McGill-Queen's University Press, 2008), 162.

[19] Hueglin and Fenna, *Comparative Federalism: A Systematic Inquiry*, 2nd edn, 275.

[20] For Dicey, the key purpose of federal entrenchment was that the foundational allocation of functions and powers within the constitution could not be altered unilaterally by either branch of government. A.V. Dicey, *Introduction to the Study of the Law of the Constitution*, 3rd edn (London: Macmillan and Co., 1889), 134–135; see also 8th edn, 139–140.

[21] K. Wheare, *Federal Government*, 4th edn (Oxford: Oxford University Press, 1963), 55–57.

[22] Hueglin and Fenna, *Comparative Federalism: A Systematic Inquiry*, 2nd edn, 277.

and by way of intergovernmentalism at the executive level. An approach to constitutional entrenchment that inhibits this latter role would be counter-productive to federalism's constitutional purpose.

The situation then is in fact not paradoxical. Entrenchment is required in federal constitutionalism but unless the extent to which this inhibits the playing out of political disagreement is limited it can do damage to the federal contract. A federal constitution should protect the core foundational commitment to territorial pluralism, guaranteeing the autonomy and participation in associational government of the constituent territories (doing so in a way that reflects the particularities of pluralism within each federal society). At the same time however federal constitutionalism requires to be cautious in extending its reach beyond the institutional framework of the polity. If, for example, it strays too far into the realm of identity formation or the circumscription of political values, it risks both constricting the discretion of constituent territories to foster their own societal identities and values, and constraining the freedom they require to engage fully in shaping the development of the federal polity in all its plurality over time. For this reason the moral normativism that has come to overlay modern constitutionalism with detailed political ideology seems particularly ill-suited to the federal contract and its need to remain open to political responsiveness.

III. Formal processes of change in federal constitutions

In turning to the practice of federal constitutional entrenchment there are two dimensions to consider, one of process and the other of substance: the different ways in which federal constitutions provide for their own amendment, and whether levels of entrenchment vary within a constitution according to subject matter. In relation to the former, process issue, the vital question is the respective roles played by the different actors involved across two stages of the process: proposal and ratification. In relation to the latter issue the question we will address is whether matters crucial to the federal nature of the polity enjoy heightened levels of protection.

(i) How are federal constitutions changed?

The fundamental salience of the constitution's foundational constituent territories to the federal contract demands that these territories should have a central role in its amendment. As we will now explore, although each federal constitution has its own model of constitutional amendment[23]—giving effect to constitutional

[23] For a survey of the mechanics of change in federal systems see A. Benz and F. Knüpling (eds), *Changing Federal Constitutions: Lessons from International Comparison* (Toronto: Barbara Budrich Publishers, 2012).

constituent authority in its own way—certain trends are discernible across federal constitutions which allow us to talk about a distinctly 'federal' approach to constitutional amendment. One notable theme is a dominant role for the central government in the proposal of amendments but a stronger role for the constituent territories in deciding whether or not to accept these changes.

(a) Proposing amendments

While in certain federal constitutions, including that of the United States, the constituent territories can play a formal role in proposing constitutional amendments, in general this role rests with the central government, with constitutional authority typically vested in the legislative branch. The degree to which constituent territories enjoy any indirect impact upon proposal decisions rests therefore upon their influence, through associational rule, upon the central branch.

Article V of the United States constitution provides that two-thirds of both Houses of Congress can propose amendments. A second route also exists, whereby two-thirds of the state legislatures can call a convention for proposing amendments, a process that has never occurred. Germany and India do not adopt this latter route but otherwise their constitutions replicate the 'proposal' element in the American system, providing that amendments emerge exclusively within the national legislature, and that a two-thirds majority is required in each chamber to validate such a proposal.[24] These processes involve respectively the US Senate, the Bundesrat, and the Rajya Sabha, each of which is a territorially weighted chamber, giving constituent territories indirect influence in amendment proposals. In Australia, constitutional amendments must also be proposed by the Commonwealth Parliament in the form of a bill. Proposals do not however require a weighted majority but can be proposed by a simple majority. This therefore also requires the support of the territorially weighted Senate.[25] The Swiss constitution is unusual in providing that amendment proposals come from the Federal Assembly or directly from the citizens. If a popular initiative proposing a constitutional amendment is signed by 100,000 people over a period no longer than eighteen months, then a referendum must be held on the issue.[26]

Several important matters can be drawn from these variations. The proposal process can be addressed on a scale of relative ease to relative difficulty. In the United States the super-majority requirement has, in practice, made it difficult

[24] Constitution of India, art. 368(2); Constitution of Germany, art. 79(2).

[25] Commonwealth of Australia Constitution Act 1900 (Imp) 63 & 64 Vict., c. 12, s.128. If one house rejects the proposal but the other house votes for it twice it can go forward.

[26] Art. 194(1) provides that: 'A partial revision of the Federal Constitution may be requested by the People or decreed by the Federal Assembly'; a total revision 'may be proposed by the People or by either of the two Councils or be decreed by the Federal Assembly' (art. 193(1)). It may also be noted that any federal legislation that is challenged by 50,000 citizens or 8 cantons must go to a referendum. This gives citizens in the cantons an important power over not just constitutional change but the very law-making process at the centre.

even to initiate the process of constitutional change, part of a wider account of the US constitution's inflexibility. A second point is that the power of constituent territories to propose can vary. In those situations where territorial governments can propose change this can be a general power to propose change in any area. This is the case in Canada[27] and the United States through the convention route and in other systems where constituent territories have such a role.[28] A final and significant point is that the approach taken by most federal systems, of vesting the proposal power in the central branch of government, has meant in practice that proposals for change, where they touch upon the federal nature of the constitution, has produced a tendency to expand central power, a matter to which we return.

(b) Ratification of amendments

The ratification process tends to offer a stronger role for constituent territories. In most systems this involvement remains indirect, through territorial representation in the federal legislature. However, since ratification within parliament often involves super-majorities within one legislative chamber or multiple majorities across both chambers this can give the constituent territorial representatives a potential veto role. A number of federal constitutions operate this way, vesting ratification in the hands of the federal parliament by way of super-majority. The constitutions of India,[29] Malaysia,[30] Argentina,[31] Mexico,[32] Ethiopia (in a joint sitting),[33] Nigeria,[34] Pakistan,[35] Russia,[36] and Germany[37] all require that amendments be ratified by a super-majority in both houses of the federal parliament. In other federal systems (Australia and Switzerland) ratification of constitutional

[27] Constitution Act 1982, s. 46(1): 'The procedures for amendment under sections 38, 41, 42 and 43 may be initiated either by the Senate or the House of Commons or by the legislative assembly of a province.'

[28] The constitution of Brazil also offers a role in the proposal process to the constituent territories. Amendments may be proposed by one-third of the members of the Chamber of Deputies or the Federal Senate or by the president of the Republic, or more than one-half of the Legislative Assemblies of units of the Federation, each manifesting its decision by a simple majority of its members (art. 60). In Spain, s. 166 provides that the procedures around proposing constitutional amendments are governed by s. 87(1) and (2). Those provisions state that 'Legislative initiative belongs to the Government, the Congress and the Senate, in accordance with the Constitution and the Standing Orders of the Houses.' However it is also open to the 'Assemblies of Self-governing Communities' to request the Government 'to adopt a bill or … refer a non-governmental bill to the Bureau of Congress and delegate a maximum of three Assembly members to defend it'.

[29] Art. 368(2).

[30] Art. 159(3).

[31] Art. 30 which requires a supermajority of the Congress.

[32] Art. 135.

[33] Art. 105(2)(a).

[34] Art. 9(2).

[35] Art. 239(1) and (2).

[36] Arts 136 and 108(2): 'federal constitutional law shall be considered to have been adopted if it is approved by a majority of not less than three quarters of the total number of members of the Council of Federation and not less than two-thirds of the total number of deputies of the State Duma'.

[37] By art. 79(2) amendments 'shall be carried by two thirds of the Members of the Bundestag and two thirds of the votes of the Bundesrat'.

amendments can involve the direct engagement of the constituent territorial governments or their citizens through referendums.

We may observe several systems in more detail for illustrative purposes. In India an amendment's ratification can be given effect in the same way as its proposal, by a two-thirds majority in the two houses of Parliament. However, it is also the case that certain matters of particular constitutional importance also require the approval of 50 per cent of the state legislatures.[38] Other constitutions explicitly require a super-majority of constituent territory legislatures for ratification.[39] The United States constitution is unusual in vesting the ratification power exclusively in the hands of the states. For an amendment to be passed, it must have the support of either three-quarters of the state legislatures or conventions in three-quarters of the states. The latter process has only been used once, to approve the 21st amendment, repealing 'Prohibition', and remains a method beset by uncertainty. In either of its variants, the ratification formula gives the states considerable power, allowing a minority of states, even those with very small populations, to block proposals for change.

The significance of constitutional amendment to a federal system is evident in the process by which Canada ended any meaningful constitutional connection to the United Kingdom in the formal 'patriation' of the constitution in 1982. The main purpose of this process was to arrive at a new and indigenous amendment formula for the Canadian constitution. Ironically, the controversy which it provoked, involving Quebec's relationship to Canada, revolved around the amendment process by which this new formula was promulgated.

Until the passage of the Constitution Act 1982 the method of amending the Canadian constitution—contained in the British North American (BNA) Act 1867—involved the Canadian Parliament presenting a proposal to the UK Parliament which, by convention, and in light of the Statute of Westminster 1931, always gave formal effect to such a proposal. There was general acceptance that the federal government was required, by convention, to seek provincial consent before asking the UK Parliament to amend the constitution. However, disagreement emerged as to whether it was bound by the advice it received and whether the convention required unanimous provincial consent.

The initial request to patriate the constitution and create a new amendment formula through a revised Constitution Act was submitted to the UK Parliament in 1981[40] without provincial consent. This was challenged by the provinces. The Supreme Court of Canada took the view that, while not legally enforceable, a convention of 'substantial provincial consent' existed.[41] Quebec then brought a second challenge, arguing that its own consent was specifically required in the amendment

[38] Indian Constitution 1950), art. 368(2).
[39] Canada is an example discussed below.
[40] Hansard vol. 15 col. 87, 22 December 1981.
[41] *Re Resolution to amend the Constitution* [1981] 1 SCR 753.

ratification process. The Court rejected both this contention and the related implication that the convention would only be satisfied by unanimous provincial consent.[42] In the end the formula adopted in 1982 is a complex one, offering a range of different ratification models. These are addressed in detail below, but what is notable is that of the five different ways in which a Canadian constitutional amendment can be ratified, four involve a direct role for the provincial legislatures. By building in a multi-stage process and super-majority requirements, and by introducing different veto points throughout the process, the Canadian constitution, like those of the United States and Australia, is in practice now very difficult to amend.[43]

Other constitutions, notably Switzerland and Australia, give a direct role to the constituent territories but do so by involving citizens directly in the ratification process. The Swiss constitution marks a high point of popular participation in constitutional change, guaranteeing the peoples of the cantons a say in both partial and total revision of the constitution.[44] This gives a considerable veto power to small cantons. As Palermo and Kössler observe: 'with optimal dispersion in the smallest cantons, only 10 per cent of the Swiss electorate could theoretically block a constitutional amendment'.[45] Despite this potential for blockage, specific amendments are passed regularly, more than 100 having been adopted since the late nineteenth century.[46] The Swiss constitution also allows for total revision of the constitution through amendment,[47] and indeed the constitution was re-ordered in 1999.

The Australian model adopted on 1 January 1901 follows that of Switzerland. As we have seen, in Australia amendments are proposed exclusively by an absolute majority in the national Parliament. They must however then be approved in a referendum by both a majority of the national vote and a majority of voters in a majority of the states.[48] This ratification process demonstrates, in Aroney's view, that the principle by which 'the federation consists of both one "people" and a plurality of "peoples" is entrenched within the Constitution'.[49] And notably, in contrast to

[42] *Reference: Objection by Quebec to a Resolution to amend the Constitution* [1982] 2 SCR 793. See also S. Tierney, 'Le formalisme constitutionnel strict: la toxine britannique, l'antidote canadien?', in F. Rocher and B. Pelletier (eds), *Le nouvel ordre constitutionnel canadien: du rapatriement de 1982 à nos jours Sous la direction* (Québec: Presses de l'Université du Québec (PUQ), 2013), 291–313.

[43] See D.S. Lutz, 'Toward a Theory of Constitutional Amendment', in S. Levinson (ed.), *Responding to Imperfection: The Theory and Practice of Constitutional Amendment* (Princeton: Princeton University Press, 1995), 237–274, 261.

[44] Art. 140(1)(a) —amendment to the constitution must be put to 'the People and the Cantons'. Proposals are 'accepted if a majority of those who vote and a majority of the Cantons approve them'. Art. 142(2) and (3).

[45] F. Palermo and K. Kössler, *Comparative Federalism: Constitutional Arrangements and Case Law* (Oxford: Hart Publishing, 2017), 182–183.

[46] Watts, *Comparing Federal Systems*, 3rd edn, 163.

[47] Arts 192 and 193.

[48] Australian Constitution, s.128.

[49] N. Aroney, 'Formation, Representation and Amendment in Federal Constitutions' (2006) 54 *The American Journal of Comparative Law* 277–336, 302.

the Swiss process, most amendment proposals put to referendum in Australia fail to pass.[50]

Constitutional amendment in Australia, as it was in Canada, was for a long time complicated by Australia's relationship to the United Kingdom, detaching as it did through a gradual process of decolonisation to Dominion and then Commonwealth status. The debate over ultimate authority was more an issue of abstract constitutional theory than real constitutional salience; for example, whether sections 1 to 9 of the Commonwealth of Australia Act 1900 could be altered only by the Imperial Parliament.[51] As Quick and Garran put it, 'the amending power can amend the Constitution, but the Constitution Act is above its reach'.[52] This has been, at least since the passage of the Statute of Westminster, an issue of no real political significance; the Australian constitution and its alteration being entirely a matter of indigenous concern as it has been in Canada since 1982.

The prominent role for constituent territories, whether directly or indirectly, in the ratification of constitutional amendments does highlight the ongoing salience of constitutional constituent authority in many federal systems. However, in order to capture more fully the role that constituent territories enjoy in the amendment process it is necessary to turn to the interaction between process and substance in federal constitutional amendment.

(ii) How, what, and why should federal constitutions entrench?

A number of federal constitutions have the same amendment formula for all matters, others provide varied levels of constitutional embeddedness for different matters. Those which do not differentiate include the constitutions of the USA and Australia, although each of these as we will see has its own significant exception to this general rule. In reviewing those constitutions which do contain varied amendment processes, the starting point of our enquiry is the federal nature of the polity itself. It is in fact common for federal systems to include either specific, super-majority amendment rules that seek to preserve the federal nature of the polity, or veto powers for constituent territories in relation to matters that are particularly vital to their own constitutional status and authority. Such veto powers are typically

[50] By 2020, of nineteen national referendums in Australia, proposing forty-four constitutional amendments in total, only eight have been carried. Parliamentary Education website <https://peo.gov.au/understand-our-parliament/having-your-say/elections-and-voting/referendums-and-plebiscites/>.

[51] P.C. Oliver, 'Parliamentary Sovereignty, Federalism and the Commonwealth', in R. Schütze and S. Tierney (eds), *The United Kingdom and the Federal Idea* (Oxford: Hart Publishing, 2018), 49–72, 66.

[52] R. Quick and R. Garran, The Annotated Constitution of the Australian Commonwealth [1901] (Sydney: Sydney Legal Books, 1976), 989, cited by Oliver, 'Parliamentary Sovereignty, Federalism and the Commonwealth'.

exercised either by the state's legislature or through a referendum within the constituent territory.

The German constitution is a well-known example that protects the federal nature of the state from alteration through an eternity clause.[53] The Brazilian constitution has a similar provision.[54] See also Austria,[55] Malaysia,[56] and South Africa,[57] where the constitutions also only require super-majority assent in the federal legislature for constitutional amendments concerning the federal character of the polity. The Swiss constitution specifically protects the existence and territory of the cantons.[58] Any change in the number of cantons or in the territory between cantons requires the consent of the citizens and the cantons concerned.[59]

No such specific guarantee is enumerated in the Indian constitution, but the Supreme Court has read the permanence of the federal nature of the polity into the constitution in its articulation of the 'basic structure' doctrine.[60] In Australia meanwhile the constitutionality of any amendment that purports to abolish the federal system is a matter of debate.[61] The very description in the preamble of the Australian constitution as 'federal' lends force to the contention that this aspect of the constitution is so foundational as to be beyond the remit of constitutional amendment.[62]

In addition to the federal nature of the constitution, federal constitutions can also protect the specific constitutional powers and institutional role of constituent territories. The South African constitution guarantees that if a draft amendment concerns the powers of particular provinces then it must, for its ratification, be approved by the legislature of the province in question.[63] The Indian constitution provides that any amendment affecting the representation of states in the national legislature requires a specific threshold—approval by the national Parliament and ratification by the legislatures of not less than one-half of the states.[64] Another example is the United Kingdom constitution which can be changed simply by act of Parliament. Recently Parliament has sought to inhibit its own power in a federal direction. The Scotland Act 1998 as amended provides that the Scottish Parliament

[53] As it does other core commitments including the Basic Law itself and the guarantee of human dignity within it (art. 1(1)). The Basic Law also provides that amendments 'affecting the division of the Federation into Länder [and] their participation on principle in the legislative process' shall be inadmissible: art. 79(3) of the Basic Law.

[54] Constitution of Brazil, art. 60(4).

[55] Constitution of Austria, art. 44(1).

[56] Constitution of Malaysia, art. 159(3).

[57] Constitution of the Republic of South Africa, art. 74(3).

[58] Constitution of Switzerland, art. 53(1).

[59] Art. 53(2) and (3).

[60] *Kesavananda Bharati v. State of Kerala.*

[61] Watts, *Comparing Federal Systems*, 3rd edn, 164.

[62] G. Craven, 'Would the Abolition of the States be an Alteration of the Constitution under Section 128?' (1989) 18 *Federal Law Review* 85–121.

[63] Constitution of the Republic of South Africa, s. 74(8).

[64] Constitution of India 1996, art. 368(2)(d).

and government are 'a permanent part of the United Kingdom's constitutional arrangements' and 'are not to be abolished except on the basis of a decision of the people of Scotland voting in a referendum'.[65] By the doctrine of parliamentary supremacy, Parliament could repeal these provisions but their constitutional significance in recognition of constituent territorial authority is nonetheless considerable, given that, in political terms, their unilateral revocation is unthinkable.[66]

We have noted how the Canadian Constitution Act 1982 created a backlash among the provinces. The new amendment formula it brought with it was also controversial, particularly in Quebec. The Canadian constitution's approach to amendment is complex, creating five different forms of amendment: those that can be effected exclusively by the federal branch;[67] those requiring a resolution of both chambers of the federal Parliament and ratification of at least two-thirds of the provincial legislatures (seven out of ten), representing at least 50 per cent of the population of Canada;[68] those requiring provincial unanimity,[69] reflecting the centrality of federalism to the constitution itself; those allowing the legislature of each province to amend the constitution of that province;[70] and other matters targeted at specific provinces which require a resolution of the federal Parliament and the consent of the legislature of each province to which the amendment applies.[71] Although provincial unanimity only applies to the amendment of a limited number of provisions within the constitution (section 41), the amendment model as a whole, with a strong and direct provincial role required for the majority of salient constitutional amendments, emphasises how the 1982 Act, despite the opposition which its mode of promulgation provoked, in substance is very respectful of Canada's federal nature, and as a whole reaffirmed the territorial foundations of federal constitutional authority first declared in 1867.

The strong voice guaranteed to the provinces across the amendment process is undoubtedly a consequence of the deep territorial diversity of Canada, a feature emphasised in the constitutional machinations of the ensuing fifteen years. Attempts in the 1980s and early 1990s to increase Quebec's influence over the amendment process failed, but in 1996 the federal Parliament passed the Act

[65] Scotland Act 1998, s. 6363A An identical provision is contained in the Wales Act 2017, s.1(1) in relation to Welsh devolved institutions.

[66] M. Loughlin and S. Tierney, 'The Shibboleth of Sovereignty' (2018) 81 *Modern Law Review* 989–1016.

[67] Constitution Act 1982, being Sch. B to the Canada Act 1982 (UK) 1982, c. 11, s. 44.

[68] Constitution Act 1982, s. 38(1). There is also a rider to this/ s. 38(2) and (3) allowing provinces effectively to opt out of 'any proposed amendment that derogates from the legislative powers, proprietary rights or other rights or privileges of the legislature or government of a province'.

[69] Constitution Act 1982, s. 41. The matters requiring the support of the Senate, the House of Commons, and the legislative assembly of every province are the right of a province to a number of members in the House of Commons not less than the number of Senators by which the province is entitled to be represented at the time; the use of the English or the French language; and the composition of the Supreme Court of Canada.

[70] Constitution Act 1982, s. 45.

[71] Constitution Act 1982, s. 43.

Respecting Constitutional Amendments which provides that no minister shall present to Parliament a resolution to authorise an amendment to the constitution of Canada unless the amendment has first been consented to by a majority of provinces, including Ontario, Quebec, British Columbia, two or more of the Atlantic provinces, and two or more of the 'Prairie provinces'.[72] This gives Quebec, and indeed other regions, a legal veto over constitutional change, although not one that itself enjoys embedded constitutional status.

Canada also provides an example of how courts can be instrumental in bolstering the amendment role played by constituent territories. The Supreme Court of Canada (SCC) has ruled that any amendment to change term limits for senators cannot be effected only by the federal Parliament but would require in addition the consent of seven provinces representing more than 50 per cent of the population per sections 38 and 42(1)(b) of the 1982 Constitution Act. Furthermore, the SCC took the opportunity in the same reference case to observe that the Senate could not be abolished without the consent of all ten provinces under section 41(e).[73] This decision reinforces the principle of associational government as a central plank of the Canadian federal contract.

The American constitution contains two avenues of constitutional change but these are alternative models that can each be applied in relation to any constitutional amendment. This offers the states a very powerful role since no constitutional amendment can pass without the support of three-fourths of the state legislatures. There is one addition to this general rule, providing specific protection to the federal nature of the constitution in relation to the Senate representation for individual states. Article V provides that 'no state, without its consent, shall be deprived of its equal suffrage in the Senate'.[74] The Australian constitution, whose authors drew heavily upon the American model, also tends towards a generic mode of amendment, regardless of subject matter. It does, however, contain an exception to this in relation to the associational rule in the national legislature. Each state is guaranteed a particular level of representation in both houses of the federal Parliament and this cannot be changed without the support in a referendum by the electorate in the state concerned.[75]

To conclude this section, although federal constitutions differ greatly we can draw several conclusions concerning the issue of entrenchment. The first is that federal constitutions tend to give constituent territories a significant say particularly in ratification processes. In substantive terms, the amendment process is often

[72] An Act Respecting Constitutional Amendments, SC 1996, c. 1. Notably this provision does not apply to amendments where the expression of dissent procedures already apply under s. 38(3) of the Constitution Act 1982 or to amendments that carry a veto power under ss 41 and 43.

[73] *Reference Re Senate Reform* [2014] 1 SCR 704. See also An Act Respecting Constitutional Amendments, SC 1996, c. 1.

[74] US Constitution, art. V.

[75] Australian Constitution, s. 128.

shaped to protect, in particular, the federal nature of the polity and/or the governmental status of the constituent territories. Indeed, the institutional architecture is invariably better protected than the distribution of powers within a federal system. As we noted in the last chapter, the distribution of powers can be very vulnerable to central encroachment in a way that institutional architecture tends not to be.

The question arises therefore as to how well federal constitutional entrenchment models fit with the purpose underpinning the federal contract. The German mode of entrenching the federal nature of the polity by way of an eternity clause is inflexible but it is in fact entirely congruous with the purpose and principles which underpin the federal contract. The federal nature of a federal constitution is its core identity; it is not part of the contract which should be open to revision: rather it constitutes the essence of the contract itself. If the German people decide that the state should no longer be organised on a federal basis, this would serve to overturn this founding identity and founding contract; it is appropriate therefore that this would require a new foundational moment and a new source of constituent power, one founded in a national demos rather than plural territorial subjects.

IV. Constitutional interpretation in federal systems

Judicial oversight of a constitution, including judicial review of the constitutionality of legislation and government acts, is now a default assumption in almost all modern constitutional systems, federal or unitary.[76] In federal systems, where the judiciary has taken on the vital role of defining the lawful competence of the central and territorial branches of government, courts have in some cases transformed the meaning of the constitution through this process; as Saunders observes: '[c]onstitutional interpretation is almost as important as the constitution itself in examining the intersection between constitutionalism and federalism.'[77] In this section of the chapter we will consider how the role of the courts has grown within federal systems and what this means for federal constitutionalism and the continuing salience of the federal idea.

[76] Ethiopia is one exception where the second chamber of the national legislature, rather than a court, has the power to interpret the constitution—art. 62. This does however co-exist with art. 80(1): 'The Federal Supreme Court shall have the highest and final judicial power over Federal matters.' See also A. Fiseha, 'Constitutional Adjudication through Second Chamber in Ethiopia' (2017) 16 *Ethnopolitics* 295–313; G.T. Hessebon and A.K. Idris, 'The Supreme Court of Ethiopia: Federalism's Bystander', in N. Aroney and J. Kincaid (eds), *Courts in Federal Countries: Federalists or Unitarists?* (Toronto: University of Toronto Press, 2017), 165–192. The United Kingdom is partly exceptional. Here the Supreme Court does not have the authority to nullify acts of Parliament although it can declare incompetent legislation from the devolved legislatures which exceeds devolved authority.

[77] C. Saunders, 'Federalism and Constitutionalism: Challenges Presented by Dominant Conceptions of the Unitary State', in J. Kincaid (ed.), *A Research Agenda for Federalism Studies* (Cheltenham: Edward Elgar Publishing, 2019), 39–49,. . . See also A. Sagar, 'Constitutional Interpretation in Federations and its Impact on the Federal Balance' (2011) 3 *Perspectives on Federalism* E1–E22.

One important structural difference across federal systems stems from differing legal traditions and types of system. In continental federal systems such as Germany, Austria, Belgium, and Spain the court system tends to be unified, with judges subject to one national system of appointment and operating within one national jurisdiction. Another feature of continental systems is a dedicated constitutional court with exclusive jurisdiction in the area of constitutional interpretation, separate from an appellate function in relation to ordinary law. Common law federal systems often differ across both of these registers. They characteristically have a Supreme Court which combines a general appellate jurisdiction with the authority to interpret the constitution; the US constitution established a model for this system[78] and it has largely been followed in the common law world by Australia, Canada, India, Malaysia, and the United Kingdom.[79] Common law systems can also have a plurality of different court systems operating at central and territorial levels: examples include the United States, Canada, Australia, and the UK. As we saw in Chapter 8, in constitutions with multiple legal systems, judges at the territorial level tend to be appointed at that level. This is however not always the case; for example, in Canada, provincial judges are appointed by the federal government, formally by the governor general.[80]

These differences have fostered distinct families of legal culture across federal systems. In common law federal systems the highest court has tended to assume a very active role in interpreting and hence shaping the meaning and direction of the constitution, a role that can be attributed in part to the breadth of its jurisdiction. Given the combination of appellate and constitutional functions, various processes can give rise to adjudication on federal matters: intergovernmental disputes; challenges to governmental competence (of either level of government) brought by private individuals or arising tangentially in the course of wider litigation; and, in some cases, a 'reference' procedure, allowing governments or other actors to question constitutionality even in the absence of an active legal dispute. Canada is a prime example of the last of these, where prominent reference cases have, for example, tested the legality of secession[81] and the constitutional procedure required to give effect to Senate reform.[82]

By contrast, in continental federal systems such as Germany, partly because federal disputes must be raised as a matter of special constitutional procedure, it is often considered wise by the different governments involved to reach intergovernmental

[78] Art. III of the constitution provides that 'the judicial Power of the United States shall be vested in one supreme Court', and that this judicial power 'shall extend to all Cases, in Law and Equity, arising under the Constitution'.

[79] The United Kingdom Supreme Court was created in 2010 but it largely assumed the existing roles of the Appellate Committee of the House of Lords and the domestic jurisdiction of the Judicial Committee of the Privy Council.

[80] Constitution Act 1982, s. 96.

[81] *Reference Re Secession of Quebec* [1998] 2 SCR 217.

[82] *Reference Re Senate Reform* [2014] SCC 32.

agreement and thus avoid the legalisation of political disputes. It is however difficult to assess the extent to which a more restricted judicial role is attributable to institutional design. I have noted the integrated nature of decision-making within German federal constitutional culture. Switzerland is another example where political actors tend to avoid recourse to the courts over federal disagreements. The Swiss Federal Supreme Court (FSC) is a curious hybrid of continental and common law models. The Swiss Court is not limited to constitutional adjudication. Its jurisdictions are federal law; international law; inter-cantonal law; cantonal constitutional rights; the autonomy of the communes and other cantonal guarantees in favour of public law corporations; and federal and cantonal provisions on political rights.[83] The constitution does not give the FSC the power to strike down federal legislation,[84] and while it does have this power in relation to the cantons, it is reluctant to use it.[85] This is also part of a broader constitutional culture, encouraged by the text of the constitution itself: 'The Confederation and the Cantons shall support each other in the fulfilment of their duties and shall generally cooperate with each other.'[86] From this it follows that: 'Disputes between Cantons or between Cantons and the Confederation shall wherever possible be resolved by negotiation or mediation.'[87] The appointment model reflects this search for consensus: judges of the FSC are elected by the Federal Assembly.[88] The South African constitution adopts a similar adjudicatory approach: a party to a dispute 'must exhaust all other remedies before it approaches a court to resolve the dispute.'[89]

What does tend to unite both common law and continental systems (even those where judicial review is resorted to only sparingly) is a commitment to one final site of adjudicatory decision-making. Although the existence of distinct legal systems within common law federal systems is significant from the perspective of territorial autonomy, this is superseded by judicially enforced constitutional supremacy, very similar to that in continental systems. One feature of those federal constitutions where the courts are active constitutional players is that this role has

[83] Federal Constitution of the Swiss Confederation 1999, art. 189.

[84] Federal Constitution of the Swiss Confederation 1999, art. 190.

[85] Lienhard et al. comment: 'the Court will declare cantonal norms to be unconstitutional only if it appears impossible to apply them in conformity with the Federal Constitution.' A. Lienhard et al., 'The Federal Supreme Court of Switzerland: Judicial balancing of Federalism without Judicial Review', in N. Aroney and J. Kincaid (eds), *Courts in Federal Countries: Federalists or Unitarists?* (Toronto: University of Toronto Press, 2017), 404–439, 417.

[86] The Federal Constitution of the Swiss Confederation 1999, art. 44(1). The Swiss constitution also provides an alternative to judicial review in that federal legislation may be subject to a ratifying referendum: art. 141(1). As Watts observes: 'This has in practice reinforced the consensus character of federal politics in Switzerland since the threat of a referendum has induced a practice of seeking maximum support (not just a bare majority) in the Parliament for federal legislation. The usual passage there of legislation by much more than a narrow majority reduces the potential vulnerability of legislation to a subsequent referendum challenge.' R. Watts, 'Federation as a Method of Ethnic Conflict Resolution', in M. Burgess and J. Pinder (eds), *Multinational Federations* (London: Routledge, 2007), 225–247, 237.

[87] Art. 44(3).

[88] Art. 168.

[89] Art. 41(3).

increased in recent times. This is of course a wider phenomenon within modern constitutionalism,[90] but in the federal context this has been encouraged by the growth of government in the modern polity, spreading into areas of overlapping or at least unclear competence division.

The US Supreme Court acted early to assert its role as ultimate constitutional arbiter,[91] and significant early cases involved the nature of the federal system itself,[92] a move that was firmly consolidated after the Civil War.[93] And we can say that, despite periods where it has been more restrained in relation to state competences, the overwhelming trajectory of more than 200 years of judicial supremacy has been a centralising one.[94] Particularly in the twentieth century, the Supreme Court facilitated a massive accrual of power to the centre through a very generous interpretation of the 'general welfare' clause[95] and the 'commerce clause'.[96] A further development in the 1980s (despite arguments that the Court was in this period less amenable to the expansion of the federal power) was a decision that Congress had the power to extend the Fair Labor Standards Act, and the requirement of a minimum wage, to the states.[97] Watts takes this case as indicating 'the apparent abdication ... by the Supreme Court of its role as an umpire within the federal system'.[98]

The Court's facilitation not only of federal government power but also of the homogenisation of national standards, particularly through the filter of individual rights, was facilitated by the post-Civil War amendments, in particular the 14th, which in the twentieth century was interpreted in a way that extended the constitutional bill of rights to the states and in so doing served significantly to curtail

[90] Hirschl, *Towards Juristocracy.*

[91] *Marbury v. Madison*, 5 US 137.

[92] *Chisholm v. Georgia*, 2 US (2 Dall.) 419 (1793); *McCulloch v. Maryland*, 17 US (4 Wheat.) 316 (1819).

[93] *Texas v. White*, 74 US (7 Wall.) 700 (1869).

[94] I. Somin, 'The Supreme Court of the United States: Promoting Centralization More Than State Autonomy', in N. Aroney and J. Kincaid (eds), *Courts in Federal Countries: Federalists or Unitarists?* (Toronto: University of Toronto Press, 2017), 440–481.

[95] *Massachusetts v. Mellon* and *Frothingham v. Mellon*, 262 US 447 (1923); *Helvering v. Davis*, 301 US 619 (1937); *United States v. Butler*, 297 US 1 (1936). This was especially a feature during the period of 'economic nationalism' and large welfare state intervention of the New Deal era. Further centralisation in the latter part of the twentieth century was facilitated by *South Dakota v. Dole*, 483 US 203 (1987).

[96] *Gibbons v. Ogden*, 22 US (9 Wheat.) 1 (1824); *United States v. Jones & Laughlin Steel*, 301 US 1 (1937) and *United States v. Darby*, 312 US 100 (1941); *Wickard v. Filburn*, 317 US 111 (1942); *Southern Pacific Co v. Arizona*, 325 US 761 (1945). 'Between 1937 and 1995, the Supreme Court did not invalidate a single federal law as beyond Congress's Commerce Clause authority.' Somin, 'The Supreme Court of the United States: Promoting Centralization More Than State Autonomy', 456. The first in which it did so was *United States v. Lopez*, 514 US 549 (1995). There is a sense that from the 1980s the Supreme Court began to show a new deference to the states. Somin concludes however that the impact on the scope of federal power of the so-called 'federalism revolution' begun under Chief Justice Rehnquist 'has so far been limited'. Somin, 460; and that this was 'seriously undermined' by *Gonzales v. Raich* 545 US 1 (2005). Less clear at this stage is the potential impact of *NFIB v. Sebelius*, 132 US 2566 (2012), the Court's ruling on constitutional challenges to the Affordable Care Act.

[97] *Garcia v. San Antonio Metropolitan Transit Authority*, 469 US 528 (1985).

[98] R.L. Watts, 'The Federal Idea and its Contemporary Relevance', in T.L. Courchene et al., *The Federal Idea: Essays in Honour of Ronald L. Watts* (Kingston-Montreal: McGill-Queen's, 2011), 13–27, 21.

their autonomy. The result is that, despite a constitutional guarantee that residual powers rest with the states and the accreditation of so few enumerated powers to the centre, the pattern of judicial interpretation has been one in which the states' powerful constitutional status has been greatly eroded over time.[99] As Hueglin and Fenna put it: 'judicial interpretation [has] played havoc with the original design'[100] of the constitution.

In other systems the judiciary has also interpreted the constitution in a centralising direction, often in the face of constitutional text that seems to intend a very different approach. As we saw in Chapter 8, the Australian constitutional framers sought, in a way similar to the US founders, to guarantee strong state powers precisely to avoid overweening central authority. However, the High Court in Australia has acted as a motor for stronger federal power in a way similar to the US Supreme Court, interpreting the constitution 'in a manner widely at variance with the intentions and expectations of its founders'.[101]

A number of federal courts have followed the American model in using ambiguity in the text of the constitution and the existence of concurrent powers to tip the balance towards the centre. Saunders observes that in India and Malaysia, conflict over concurrent powers 'is usually resolved in favour of the federation'.[102] In each of these cases much turns on the institutional self-perception of the court that it is a branch of the central government, and of a conceptual elision of the central branch of government and the federation as a whole; Saunders' use of the term in relation to Malaysia bearing this out. Kelsen's idea of three levels of government (discussed in Chapter 5) has largely been lost in such a construction. The approach taken by all of these courts is premised essentially upon a monistic conception of the demos like that which was so much a driver of American federal jurisprudence and became the dominant conceptual backdrop to Australian federal adjudication. A similar approach is evident in Australian case law where the High Court has spoken of the 'comparative superiority of the position of the Commonwealth in the federal structure'.[103]

[99] R. Sandler and D. Schoenbrun, *Government by Decree: What Happens When Courts Run Government* (New Haven: Yale University Press, 2003); B. Friedman, *The Will of the People: How Public Opinion Has Influenced the Supreme Court and Shaped the Meaning of the Constitution* (New York: Farrar, Straus & Giroux, 2009).

[100] Hueglin and Fenna, *Comparative Federalism*, 2nd edn, 156.

[101] N. Aroney and J. Allan, 'An Uncommon Court: How the High Court of Australia Has Undermined Australian Federalism' (2008) 30 *Sydney Law Review* 245–294, 246. They also argue: 'Nothing in the language of the Australian Constitution, or its structure, or the process that was used to adopt it, or the basis upon which its approval by the voters was promoted, or the likely original understandings of most of those voters, or anything else at the time would have suggested that the States would become the enfeebled, emasculated creatures they have become. Put slightly differently, no one, or almost no one, would have guessed or predicted that virtually all of the important division of powers cases would eventually go the Commonwealth's way.' Aroney and Allan, 247. See also B. Selway and J.M. Williams, 'The High Court and Australian Federalism' (2005) 35 *Publius* 467–488.

[102] Saunders in J. Kincaid (ed.), *A Research Agenda for Federalism Studies* (Cheltenham: Edward Elgar, 2019), 128.

[103] *Pape v. Commissioner of Taxation* [2009] HCA 23, 80.

Some consider that judicial centralisation is attributable largely to institutional design. Cheryl Saunders suggests that a single list of 'federal' powers without an equivalent list of territorial powers fosters a centralising process by failing to offer specific textual restrictions on the former.[104] In the US constitution the commerce and general welfare clauses can be said to invite judicial largesse in the absence of enumerated and balancing state competences. The cases certainly bear this out. In *Darby* the US Supreme Court stated that in relation to the commerce clause, and the regulation of interstate commerce, the authority of Congress 'is complete in itself, may be exercised to its utmost extent, and acknowledges no limitations other than are prescribed in the Constitution'. This is a power that 'can neither be enlarged nor diminished by the exercise or non-exercise of state power'.[105] A very similar approach has been taken in Australia despite residual power resting with the states.[106] The Australian federal Parliament's competences in relation to trade and commerce, taxation, and external affairs[107] have each been interpreted expansively by the High Court.[108] The Court has also failed to assert the very specific constituent role of the states within the constitution, an example being Senate reform. Federal legislation in 1973 extended Senate representation to the country's two territories, the Australian Capital Territory and the Northern Territory of Australia.[109] This was challenged by Western Australia and Queensland as contradicting section 71(1) of the Constitution Act which clearly states that the Senate is to be 'composed of senators for each state'. The High Court however upheld the legislation.[110]

In Chapter 8 I addressed how the spending power has assisted the central branch in expanding its institutional reach. Courts have aided this development either through active or passive acquiescence. In Canada the federal government has been notoriously aggressive in deploying its financial power within areas of partial or even exclusive provincial jurisdiction. Although politically controversial, it has not led to notable defeats for the federal government before the courts, with

[104] C. Saunders, 'Constitutional Arrangements of Federal Systems' (1995) 25 *Publius* 61–79, 69–70. Watts supports this view: 'Paradoxically, in such federations as Canada, India and Malaysia, where the centralist founders enumerated what were intended to be limited specific provincial powers, there has been a tendency for the courts to read those powers broadly, thus tempering the expansion of federal authority.' Watts, *Comparing Federal Systems*, 3rd edn, 90.

[105] *United States v. Darby*, 312 US 100, 114 (1941). An early case took a similar approach, confirming that the states are unable to limit federal power or give it different application: *Gibbons v. Ogden*, 22 US (9 Wheat.) 1 (1824), 196.

[106] *New South Wales v. Commonwealth* (2006) 229 CLR 1. An early seminal case is *Amalgamated Society of Engineers v. Adelaide Steamship Co. Ltd* (1920) 28 CLR 129, HCA 54.

[107] Constitution of the Commonwealth of Australia, s. 51.

[108] Nicholas Aroney has argued that 'the scope of federal legislative powers ... are interpreted as widely as the language used can sustain'. N. Aroney and J. Kincaid, 'Comparative Observations and Conclusions', in Aroney and Kincaid, *Courts in Federal Countries*, 482–539, 506.

[109] Senate (Representation of Territories) Act 1973. Authority for Parliament to make laws for the government of any territory is set out in s. 122.

[110] *Western Australia v. Commonwealth* (1975) 134 CLR 201 (First Territories Representation case); *Queensland v. Commonwealth* (1977) 139 CLR 585 (Second Territories Representation case).

Brouillet noting: 'Although the Supreme Court of Canada has not yet been asked to rule directly on the constitutionality of conditional spending by the federal government in areas of exclusive provincial jurisdiction, several *obiter dicta* suggest that it does not consider the spending as a normative act requiring an assessment of constitutionality.'[111] The Trojan Horse of central spending is also evident in the historical development of American and Australian federalism, again without strong judicial resistance.[112] The courts in India and Malaysia have also allowed the federal government to use tax and spending powers to expand beyond their enumerated areas of jurisdiction.[113]

Another institutionally based analysis is offered by Aroney who argues that whether a federal system is conceived in aggregative or devolutionary terms 'can have a decisive influence on the way in which its constitution is interpreted'.[114] The case Aroney makes is persuasive but he is also aware that we need to look beyond this for an explanation as to why the courts have tended to strengthen the powers of the federal government at the expense of the constituent territories, across aggregative systems (such as the US and Australia) as well as devolutionary systems such as India, with such enthusiasm. There is in fact nothing inevitable about this given the federal structure of any of these constitutions and the existence of constitutional provisions that would have provided equal or stronger justifications for a restraining hand upon central expansion. The residual powers model in both the US and Australian constitutions were seemingly a mandate for strong autonomy for the constituent territories. These could have been read to protect or even expand territorial powers, rather than the reverse. As Watts says: 'in practice there has been a tendency in these federations [i.e. those where residual powers were left to the constituent territories] for the courts to read the maximum "implied powers" into the specified federal authority at the expense of the scope of the undefined residual state powers'.[115] To do so they have often moved well beyond the ordinary meaning of the text.

Perhaps the most significant factor in this process is that institutional centralisation has been underpinned by a judicial understanding both of the judiciary's own

[111] E. Brouillet, 'The Supreme Court of Canada: The Concept of Cooperative Federalism and its Effect on the Balance of Power', in Aroney and Kincaid, *Courts in Federal Countries*, 135–164, 143.

[112] *Massachusetts v. Mellon* and *Frothingham v. Mellon*; *Helvering v. Davis*; *Butler*; *South Dakota v. Dole*. In Australia the breadth of the taxation power was demonstrated by *Pape*—above.

[113] Watts, *Comparing Federal Systems*, 3rd edn, 101.

[114] N. Aroney, 'The Federal Condition: Towards a Normative Theory' (2016) 61(1) *The American Journal of Jurisprudence* 13–31, 30.

[115] Watts, *Comparing Federal Systems*, 3rd edn, 89–90. This interpretation is supported by recent studies of the role of federal courts in the US and Australia respectively: Somin, 'The Supreme Court of the United States: Promoting Centralization More Than State Autonomy'; N. Aroney, 'The High Court of Australia: Textual Unitarism vs Structural Federalism', in Aroney and Kincaid, *Courts in Federal Countries*. This is also the pattern in a number of other federal countries: N. Aroney and J. Kincaid, 'Comparative Observations and Conclusions', in Aroney and Kincaid, *Courts in Federal Countries*, 482–539, 483–484.

institutional position and of the demos itself. In the constitutions I have addressed there is a growing institutional self-perception among top courts that the judiciary is a branch of the central government; beyond this is a deeper conceptual elision of the central branch of government and the federation as a whole. The US constitution of course provided that the federal courts were located conceptually within the federal or central branch of government, but this also is a wider assumption within other systems in which notions of the federal government and the federal system as a whole come to be elided, at least implicitly.

This approach is in turn premised upon a monistic conception of the demos like that which was so much a driver of American federal jurisprudence and became the dominant conceptual backdrop to Australian federal adjudication. In the latter system the *Engineers'* case marked a watershed. Aroney and Kincaid observe that in its early decisions the High Court took the view that the constitution embodied a compact between independent states 'interpreting federal power narrowly and constructing a strong doctrine of intergovernmental immunities on that basis'. In the *Engineers'* case this changed, with a new vision of a national Australian people emerging, and the federal government taken to represent the will of this monistically constructed people. Since this case Aroney and Kincaid argue, the Court 'has interpreted federal power very widely and limited the intergovernmental immunity doctrine to preserving state government "autonomy"'.[116] This is evident in *Pape v. Commissioner of Taxation* where the High Court reinforced a national view of the constitution, according to which Australia is no 'mere aggregation of the federating colonies'. And a clearer articulation of the idea of nation-building that lies behind this jurisprudence can be found in *Davis v. The Commonwealth*:

> The Constitution summoned the Australian nation into existence, thereby conferring a new identity on the people who agreed to unite 'in one indissoluble Federal Commonwealth', melding their history, embracing their cultures, synthesizing their aspirations and their destinies. The reality of the Australian nation is manifest, though the manifestations of its existence cannot be limited by definition. The end and purpose of the Constitution is to sustain the nation. If the executive power of the Commonwealth extends to the protection of the nation against forces which would weaken it, it extends to the advancement of the nation whereby its strength is fostered.[117]

Notably the High Court, like the US Supreme Court, is seen as a creature of the central branch of government: 'The judicial power of the Commonwealth shall be vested in a Federal Supreme Court, to be called the High Court of Australia, and in

[116] Aroney and Kincaid, 'Comparative Observations and Conclusions', 492–493.
[117] (1988) 166 CLR 79, 110.

such other federal courts as the Parliament creates, and in such other courts as it invests with federal jurisdiction.'[118] Appointment of judges also rests with the central branch, through the governor general in council.[119]

Australia and the USA are of course characterised by a high level of territorial homogeneity. But are there courts where the demos is similarly homogeneous but where the judicial approach is less centralising? It is often argued that the German Constitutional Court is more balanced in its outlook,[120] where the *Länder*'s powers are better respected. However, such analysis must be set in the context of a system in which there is a nation-wide commitment to centralising common standards and where this is achieved through the agreement on national policy within the national parliament. The Court need not act as the driver of centralisation in a system where the constituent territories do not often assert strong autonomy but are in fact happy to act as agents who administer agreed national standards.

In India, which is certainly not culturally homogeneous across territories, the overwhelming story has been one of centralisation of power fostered by the Supreme Court. It has been argued that in recent times the Court has been more accommodating of territorial autonomy,[121] but this scarcely impacts upon the way in which the Court has fostered a 'unitarist'[122] approach since the 1950s.

The fact that institutionalism can only go so far in explaining judicial centralism is borne out also by the fact that courts can moderate the impact of a more centralist institutional design by promoting greater respect for territorial pluralism. A key example of the latter role is to be found in Canadian constitutional history. The BNA Act 1867 was promulgated with a more centralising intention than was the US constitution. As we have noted in earlier chapters, by the mid-1860s, the strong constitutional authority accorded to the American states in 1787 was perceived by Canadian constitutional designers to be a cause of America's constitutional malaise.[123] However, over time, Canada's constitution developed in a more decentralising direction than that of the US or indeed that of Australia, and key to

[118] Constitution of the Commonwealth of Australia, s. 71.

[119] S.72.

[120] A. Benz, 'The Federal Constitutional Court of Germany: Guardian of Unitarism and Federalism', in Aroney and Kincaid, *Courts in Federal Countries*, 213.

[121] R. Saxena and W. Swenden, 'The Indian Supreme Court and Federalism' (2017) 17 *Fédéralisme Régionalisme* 1–12.

[122] M. Tewari and R. Saxena, 'The Supreme Court of India: The Rise of Judicial Power and the Protection of Federalism', in Aroney and Kincaid, *Courts in Federal Countries*, 223–255.

[123] E. Brouillet, A.-G. Gagnon, and G. Laforest, '1864: A Pivotal Year in the Advent of the Canadian Confederation', in E. Brouillet, A.-G. Gagnon, and G. Laforest (eds), *The Constitutions that Shaped Us: A Historical Anthology of Pre-1867 Canadian Constitutions* (Kingston/Montreal: McGill-Queen's University Press, 2015), 3–25, 11. Peter Russell observes that to the Canadian founders at the 1864 Quebec Conference 'the only federal system they knew, the American, seemed thoroughly flawed. Their earlier decision to give residual power to the central rather than the local legislatures aimed at reversing what many regarded as the most dangerously decentralizing feature of the American constitution.' P. Russell, *Constitutional Odyssey: Can Canadians Become a Sovereign People?*, 2nd edn (Toronto: Toronto University Press, 1993), 23.

this has been the different ways in which it has been interpreted. As Kössler and Palermo put it, contrasting the different but equally significant influence of judges to the development of Canada and other early federal systems: 'Jurisprudence in Canada has likewise turned the federal Constitution on its head, but in the opposite direction.'[124]

The constitutional history of Canada is complex due to its slow disentanglement from the United Kingdom. The fact that this was not finally achieved until 1982 meant that London exerted an influence on Canadian constitutional development not only through the Westminster Parliament but also in the interpretation of the 1867 Act, latterly through the Statute of Westminster of 1931. Until the middle of the twentieth century, final determination of the meaning of the BNA Act lay in the hands of the Judicial Committee of the Privy Council (JCPC). Although the Supreme Court of Canada (SCC) was founded in 1875, it did not become the ultimate arbiter of the constitution until 1949. The JCPC and the SCC, albeit to varying degrees over time, together have taken a very different approach to the balance between central and territorial powers than other common law federal courts.[125] This can be attributed principally to a very particular constitutional culture that has had to evolve to manage deep territorial diversity, rather than to a different approach to constitutional drafting than that adopted in the US and Australia.

The story is not entirely binary. The growth of government within the modern state has encouraged centralisation in Canada as it does in other federal systems, and at times the judicial branch has helped facilitate this, the Supreme Court of Canada in particular. Indeed, the JCPC's role until the late 1940s is often viewed as a high point in the judicial protection of provincial prerogatives.[126] One reason for this is that it developed the doctrine of 'watertight compartments', seeking to insulate the competences, respectively, of the provinces and the federal government from interference by the other branch through exclusive jurisdiction.[127] The SCC took on its constitutional role at a time when the notion of watertight jurisdiction became increasingly unrealistic as federal systems during and after the economic depression of the 1930s and the Second World War required to adjust to massive increases in public power and new areas of public law competence. The SCC therefore had to take account of new areas of government activity not clearly provided for in the text of the BNA Act 1867. The notion of exclusive jurisdiction came to be superseded to a large extent by other doctrines which envisage the constitution as

[124] Palermo and Kössler, *Comparative Federalism: Constitutional Arrangements and Case Law*, 268.

[125] Brouillet, 'The Supreme Court of Canada: The Concept of Cooperative Federalism and its Effect on the Balance of Power', 149.

[126] 'There is no doubt that the Privy Council favoured the provinces in federalism cases.' P. Hogg and W. Wright, 'Canadian Federalism, the Privy Council and the Supreme Court: Reflections on the Debate About Canadian Federalism' (2005) 38 *University of British Columbia Law Review* 329–352, 339.

[127] *Canada (AG) v. Ontario (AG)* [1937] AC 326, 354 (JCPC).

a 'living tree' which grows and changes over time and the 'double aspect' doctrine whereby one aspect of a competence may fall within the purview of the provinces, while another aspect is a matter of the federal government's jurisdiction. This new approach, which focuses upon overlapping responsibilities, has to some extent encouraged a centralising mentality. Key to this has been the Court's tendency to prioritise federal paramountcy. In recognising federal law as taking precedence over provincial law, the Court has facilitated moves by the federal government to legislate and act in areas that were previously considered to be matters of exclusive provincial competence.[128]

It is certainly true that the SCC has been generous in its interpretation of the powers of the federal government when compared with the approach taken by the JCPC, and that it is has been over time at least modestly, and at time significantly, centralising.[129] However, it is still markedly less so than the US Supreme Court. The fact that the Canadian constitution enumerates provincial as well as central powers gives the Court a concrete counterpoint to federal powers which the US Supreme Court lacks. However, it is also the case that the list system in Canada was intended to *circumscribe tightly*, rather than expressly guarantee, provincial jurisdiction. Furthermore, the BNA Act contains general federal powers which could have been interpreted as expansively as equivalent provisions have been in the US and Australia. An example here is the 'peace, order and good government' clause, a general power vested in the federal government, contained in section 91 of the BNA Act. This general power is comparable to the Necessary and Proper clause in the US constitution but has been interpreted more strictly.[130] The JCPC set a different tone in its understanding of the federal idea from that set by other federal common law courts, and while the SCC has rolled back from this somewhat, it is still markedly more protective of constituent territorial powers than the US Supreme Court has been. The role of the Indian Supreme Court is a complex one. It has generally supported the centralisation of power but at the same time it has been argued that 'the Supreme Court *has become* an effective guardian of federalism through its jurisprudence on President's Rule and the constitutional entrenchment of federalism as part of the basic structure'. At the same time 'it has upheld a restrictive reading of the powers of the states in treaty-making powers, state reorganization and ... in matters of national security'.[131]

[128] Hogg and Wright, 'Canadian Federalism, the Privy Council and the Supreme Court: Reflections on the Debate About Canadian Federalism', 347–350.

[129] Hogg and Wright, 'Canadian Federalism, the Privy Council and the Supreme Court: Reflections on the Debate About Canadian Federalism'; Brouillet, 'The Supreme Court of Canada: The Concept of Cooperative Federalism and its Effect on the Balance of Power'.

[130] *R v. Crown Zellerbach Canada Ltd* [1988] 1 SCR 401. See also Brouillet, 'The Supreme Court of Canada: The Concept of Cooperative Federalism and its Effect on the Balance of Power', 155. The SCC has certainly been more willing to accept the federal government's use of this power than the JCPC was, but it is still a much more restrictive power than the necessary and proper clause has proven to be. P.W. Hogg, *Constitutional Law of Canada* (Toronto: Carswell, 1997), ch. 17.

[131] Saxena and Swenden, 'The Indian Supreme Court and Federalism', 9.

Robert Schertzer's book on the SCC offers us a theoretically informed empirical account that helps explain the very different approach taken by the SCC from the US Supreme Court, demonstrating how constitutional adjudication in Canada has in large measure been shaped to reflect, and respond to, the country's territorial diversity and the conflict it can produce. Schertzer analyses Canadian federalism and the approach taken to it by the SCC in dialogic terms as both a deliberative conversation and an ongoing process of negotiation around constitutional meaning. Schertzer takes the meaning of Canadian federalism to be unsettled, suggesting that it is viewed by political actors, including the courts, through three different prisms: pan-Canadian, provincial-equality, and multinational. He takes the view that the appropriate role for the Court is not to impose one of these visions but to recognise them and let them play out.[132] The Court gives the federal system enhanced legitimacy by recognising this complex and contested reality within the country's political life. As Schertzer puts it: 'In practice this means promoting the use of a host of intergovernmental relations mechanisms (such as bilateral and multilateral forums or intergovernmental agreements) to encourage mutually agreeable outcomes to conflicts over the division of powers and responsibilities. It also means recognizing and reinforcing that there is significant cross-over between each order of government's areas of responsibility—even if they are presented as "exclusive" to a particular order in the constitution'.[133] Successful decisions of the SCC should, in Schertzer's view, be 'recognising' decisions, not 'imposing' decisions.

In other countries marked by deep diversity the courts are called upon to play a similar role, arriving at what Peeters and Mosselmann describe as an 'equilibrium' approach in Belgium.[134] But within the fraught divisions of Belgian political life the Court can come to be seen as an agent of the federal government, as relations between certain territories and the central government deteriorate. A similar role has been demanded of the Constitutional Tribunal in Spain.[135]

It is of course possible for a federal court to take a 'recognising' approach, in Schertzer's term. In Chapter 6 we explored how the SCC in the *Secession Reference* Opinion offered a reading of the constitution that strove to understand Canadian federalism in the context of history and the very particular territorial pluralism through which it was founded and which it was intended to serve. In doing so, it moved away from a narrowly positivist approach which it adopted in the early

132 R. Schertzer, *The Judicial Role in a Diverse Federation: Lessons from the Supreme Court of Canada* (Toronto: University of Toronto Press, 2016), 88.

133 Erin Crandall review.

134 P. Peeters and J. Mosselmans, 'The Constitutional Court of Belgium: Safeguard of the Autonomy of the Communities and Regions', in Aroney and Kincaid, *Courts in Federal Countries*, 69–102, 102.

135 E.C. Adam, 'The Constitutional Court of Spain: From System Balancer to Polarizing Centralist', in Aroney and Kincaid, *Courts in Federal Countries*, who argues that the Court has in recent times adopted a centralising approach which has further polarised relations between Catalonia and the rest of the country.

1980s during the 'patriation' of the constitution from the United Kingdom. At that time the Canadian federal government requested patriation of the constitution from the UK Parliament without first securing the consent of the provinces. The Statute of Westminster 1931 provided that the UK Parliament would not legislate for Canada without its consent.[136] A convention developed to the effect that Parliament would not exercise this power without the request and consent of the federal Parliament and of the provincial legislatures. Therefore the decision to seek patriation without formal provincial consent was challenged by the provinces in court. In the *Patriation Reference* the SCC found that since the process of requesting the transfer of ultimate constitutional authority from the Westminster Parliament was largely a matter of constitutional convention, it was not the Court's place to give legal effect to conventions. It did however seek to articulate the content of the convention of provincial consent to constitutional change that in its view had developed over time. The Court concluded that, by convention, a request to London for constitutional change required 'a substantial degree of provincial consent'.[137] This stayed the hand of the federal government which then negotiated with the provinces and arrived at a package of change agreed to by all but the government of the province of Quebec. In a subsequent legal challenge by Quebec the Court found that this convention of consent did not specifically include Quebec. In the end the federal government proceeded with the request for patriation and the creation of a new domesticated amendment formula without Quebec's consent.

The Court was widely criticised for an approach that paid insufficient attention to the real nature of Canadian federalism, in particularly the salience of the French fact, or binational or pluri-national nature, of the country; in other words, for not recognising that Quebec's embodiment of so much of the French Canadian presence in the country entitled it, by convention, to a veto over such change. The Court clearly could not enforce any convention but having gone down the line of articulating the content of conventions it was open to criticism for doing so politically and incorrectly. Political relations between Quebec and the rest of Canada were exacerbated by two failed attempts at comprehensive constitutional revision in 1987 and 1992 and by the failed Quebec sovereignty referendum in 1995. It is in this context that the *Secession Reference* Opinion was so significant, playing a role in helping to restore healthier federal relations.

Overall however the role of courts in such a context within deeply pluralised federal systems is rare. Aroney and Kincaid conclude in their edited book on federal courts that 'despite the importance of managing multinational conflict in territorially heterogeneous Belgium, Canada, Ethiopia, India, Nigeria, Spain, and Switzerland, we do not find high courts being major direct players in managing

[136] S. 4.

[137] *Reference re: Amendment of the Constitution of Canada (Patriation Reference)* [1981] 1 SCR 753, 904–905.

such conflict; conflict is managed (or mismanaged) mainly through political processes'.[138] There are good reasons for this. The judiciary is not an appropriate branch to develop the constitution. It lacks the political legitimacy to do so. Also judges are by training and methodology ill-suited to this task. Interpretation of legal text, as done by judges as technicians, cannot be expected to engage fully with the federal idea as the larger canvas upon which the text is written, and in any case they should be very wary of doing so. Australian jurisprudence offers a typical example of how federal courts bring a narrow positivism to the balancing of important constitutional principles. As Saunders observes: 'Until recently, the successive phases of its interpretation (Section 92) revolved almost exclusively around the words of the section and the previous case-law, rather than the role the section was fulfilling in the constitutional system. There is nothing surprising about this from the standpoint of the courts: these are the usual tools of statutory interpretation under the common law.'[139] From this it is clear that legal technique is not necessarily a good tool nor courts an appropriate forum through which to understand federal purpose and the complexities of the relations of authority within it. It is notable therefore that in civil law systems the role for the court in adjudicating upon federal principles has been more strictly circumscribed.[140] Palermo and Kössler observe that despite the 'transformative' role played by the courts within a number of common law countries this is not a general pattern.

> For various reasons, the impact of judicial decisions on federal systems has been much less significant in other countries. Among these reasons are the quantity and standing of constitutional jurisprudence, the probability of constitutional court judgments being prevented or overturned by mechanisms involving the two political branches of government, the degree of scepticism towards judicial power and resulting limitations of its scope and, finally, the approach to constitutional interpretation.[141]

Such an approach is more constitutionally appropriate. In the first section of this chapter, in relation to constitutional entrenchment, I argued that a federal constitution should appropriately protect the institutional parameters of the system, rather than a wider set of political values or policies. The latter is best left to the plural political processes that operate within a federal system. The constitution should regulate the rules of the political game, it should preempt the game itself by predetermining its outcome. This same principle applies to constitutional interpretation and hence to the appropriate role for judges in a federal system. A federal

138 Aroney and Kincaid, 'Comparative Observations and Conclusions', 501.

139 Saunders in John Kincaid (ed.), *A Research Agenda for Federalism Studies* (Cheltenham: Edward Elgar, 2019), 128, 131.

140 Watts, *Comparing Federal Systems*, 3rd edn, 85.

141 Palermo and Kössler, *Comparative Federalism: Constitutional Arrangements and Case Law*, 268.

system does of course need to change incrementally through constitutional practice as well as through formal amendment, but this should be done through political actors. A forum for this is the central parliament through associational rule, another is intergovernmental relations. These are the vital sites within a federal system that help avoid disputes reaching courts. The fact that Canada also has a strong tradition of intergovernmentalism may help explain why its jurisprudence has tended to be more balanced.

The role for a federal court is best preserved for those situations where political agreement is simply not possible and where unavoidable disagreement over the interpretation of the constitution remains. Notably the South African constitution requires the exhaustion of intergovernmental negotiations before a matter can be referred to the court. It also allows courts to refer disputes back to governments if efforts to resolve matters politically are deemed to be inadequate.[142] Notably, the SCC in the *Secession Reference* Opinion was restrained in its approach. Finding that there could be a situation where Quebec had the right to seek to secede, the Court refused to discuss what the appropriate process should be, stating that this was for political actors to determine.[143] In this approach the Court showed an appropriate measure of restraint: a federal court should help to frame the debate and to facilitate political interplay among different federal visions but leave the political institutions to determine how these should both operate and be re-shaped through practice and convention.

V. Concluding remarks

Federal constitutions must be open to change. Indeed the tension that sits at the heart of the federal idea between unity and pluralism demands the space to adjust to the societal particularities of each federal system and to social, political, and economic changes over time. Today, however, we live in an age of ever more detailed and deeply entrenched constitutions. Furthermore, a principal impetus behind this move is the subjection of constitutions to a more elaborate ideological substructure, elevating more and more values and policy preferences beyond the reach of day-to-day political decision-making. This is not new. The Bill of Rights, added to the US constitution, was an early indication of how constitutions would be used to establish political morality. But this phenomenon is now more pronounced and widespread than ever.

The move to ideologically thicker constitutions sits in a state of considerable tension with the federal contract. The federal idea that underpins this contract recognises the salience of territorial differences and that these may well produce

[142] Constitution of the Republic, s. 41(4)).

[143] *Secession Reference*, para. 153.

different political positions and values across the federal polity. The constitution should therefore allow these differences to be reflected in policy divergence, all within the parameters of maintaining a coherent state project. It is in this context that I argue that the federal idea requires agreement and constitutional protection for the institutional design and allocation of competences but that it should leave other matters to the political system and to pluralism.

It is in this context that a centralising approach taken by the judiciary also belies the constitutional idea of federalism. Watts came to the conclusion that federation as a form of government may be said ultimately to result 'in rule by judges rather than by elected representatives'.[144] The assertiveness of judges within many federal systems has tended to unsettle, and in some cases completely supplant, the original design of institutions and competences. This runs counter to the pluralistic promise inherent in the federal contract. Courts in federal systems should understand their constitutional position through the prism of Kelsen's three orders of rule, situating themselves apart from, and hence as a neutral arbiter between, federal and constituent governments. Even this role should be approached modestly, helping to protect the design of federal institutions and interpreting competences in ways that promote the principles that underpin the federal contract; and most crucially helping to preserve the space within which political deliberation can take place among the constituent territories and between them and the central government.

[144] Watts, *Comparing Federal Systems*, 3rd edn, 161.

11
Federalism: A Constitutional Idea for our Time

I. Introduction: the anatomy of the federal contract

Federalism is a specific genus of constitutional government. It took its first institutional form at the Philadelphia Constitutional Convention in 1787 but its broader significance over time has been in the management of the territorial variety and complexity of many modern states. The United States in the 1780s was establishing itself as a continental power and required a system of government that would allow it to do so while also recognising the distinct polities that together constituted this new country. These two aims were not easily reconcilable, and certainly could not be synthesised by deducing an idealised model of territorial government from first principles. It was therefore inevitable that the first modern federal constitution came to be drafted through contestation, pragmatism, and compromise; a jerry-built structure that amalgamated the self-interest of the drafters, moments of philosophical principle, and selective, and invariably self-serving, comparative borrowing. This is not to disparage the idiosyncrasies of American constitutional foundations. This process of 'bricolage',[1] far from delegitimising the system that emerged, captures perfectly the essence of constitutionalism as a discrete area of human endeavour. Constitutional theory, in distinction to political theory, is characterised by such an iterative interplay between idealised conceptions of government, the reality of political power, institution-building, and the conditioning legal rules that together give life to constitutionalism as the praxis of government; constitutions emerge from the interface between concept and practice as path-determining legal-normative instruments, regulating political activity in different ways within each polity for the purposes laid down in law by their framers and thereafter developed by their subjects and institutional actors.

In this book I have considered how modern constitutionalism in general and federal constitutionalism in particular have each been heavily influenced by the American experience. It is clear that all modern constitutional systems share similarities, and that many of these points of resemblance stem from the 1789 prototype. This paradigmatic precedent has in many ways been intellectually enriching

[1] M. Tushnet, 'The Possibilities of Comparative Constitutional Law' (1999) 108 *Yale Law Journal* 1225–1309, 1229.

The Federal Contract. Stephen Tierney, Oxford University Press. © Stephen Tierney 2022.
DOI: 10.1093/oso/9780198806745.003.0011

to the materialisation of the federal idea, but over time, as the American template came to be seen not only as the progenitor of federalism as a constitutional concept, but as the detailed blueprint for its institutional instantiation, this influence has tended to distort federal constitutionalism as both an idea and a practical form of government capable of wider and more flexible applicability.

My task in this book has been to retrieve the nature of federal constitutionalism as a discrete but broad species of constitutional government, one that has developed through the dialectic of theory and practice, but one which has done so by way of many and varied institutional manifestations. From the perspective of constitutional theory, it is ultimately misconceived to search for a definitive institutional model of federal government. The constitutional idea of federalism must instead be pieced together from its various instantiations over time and from place to place. It is a discrete idea for government that flows immanently from the core legal-normative purpose that unifies all polities within the federal family of modern constitutionalism; a unifying purpose that I have called 'the federal contract'. In searching for the essence of this contract I have explored the history of the federal idea, the ways in which it has been analysed by empirical and theoretical intellectual inquiry, how it must be situated within a broader literature concerning constitutional foundations and the nature of constitutional authority and subjecthood, the specific constitutional purpose of federalism that emerges from these conceptual staging posts, and ultimately the wide variety of institutional forms through which this idea has taken root within constitutional systems that share in common this genus of rule, characterised by a common commitment to the federal idea and its contractual essence.

In Chapter 2 we saw how the voluminous literature on federalism is largely characterised by empirical observation from definitional, institutional, or behavioural perspectives, and that, given the influence of the American prototype upon later constitutional practice, such a methodology has led the search for the federal idea back, not to first principles, but to first practice. I then discussed how, in so far as the federal idea has been the subject of theoretical inquiry, it has often been overlain by moral normativism, another source of distortion that has tended to merge empirical analysis of the federal idea with its promotion as a vehicle for externally derived moral or political values. I argued that these various empirical and theoretical approaches pay insufficient attention to the fact that federalism is at root a constitutional, rather than a political, idea for government; and that its essence can only be uncovered by the specific methodology of constitutional theory—functional normativity. This requires us to identify the common constitutional functionality shared by each federal system that seeks to husband political power to the will of legal authority for a federal purpose; the 'good' in federal government as a genus of constitutionalism is therefore not identifiable from virtues, principles, or tenets derived from political theory but rather from how well or otherwise any particular federal constitution reflects the underpinning purpose of the federal idea.

It is through the prism of constitutional theory that we can therefore explain the federal contract as a constitutional meta-idea, capable of a range of institutional forms, many of which, both in the nineteenth century and in more recent times, have moved away markedly from the US model.

From this methodological starting point I have sought in the rest of the book to uncover systematically the essential foundations of the federal idea as the conceptual bedrock of a discrete form of constitutional praxis, discoverable from a common foundational logic that informs each of its differing institutional manifestations. This task has involved revisiting, from a federal perspective, the theoretical building blocks that characterise our understanding of modern constitutional government—foundations, authority, subjects, purpose, design, and dynamics.

The most fundamental features of modern constitutional theory rest upon the moment of constitutional founding. It is to the original normative act of inception, giving life to the constitution, that the validity of rule must be traced. In addressing the crucial interplay between constituent legitimacy and legal normativity, and how these together give life to the constitutional authority of federal constitutions, it is clear that federal constitutionalism marks a categorical fork in the road within the history of modern constitutionalism. What I have called 'default monist constitutionalism', which rests upon one, purportedly universalisable conception of individualised constituent power, simply will not serve as an account of federal foundations. Federal constitutionalism, as we saw in Chapter 3, is characterised by a fundamentally different concept of original authority: a foundational source of legal validity that derives its legitimacy from its collective territorial constituents, rather than from a conception of a national citizenry, undifferentiated by territorial boundaries. This categorical distinctiveness of the federal idea, emerging *ab initio* within modern constitutionalism, sets federalism on an entirely discrete legal normative path.

The implications of this foundational particularity for constitutional authority were pursued in Chapters 4 and 5; the former exploring how the default account of constitutional sovereignty has been tied intrinsically to both state and nation-building; the latter addressing why constitutional sovereignty within a federal constitution must be understood through the very specific lens of *territorial* constituent authority. Chapter 5 explained that federalism is a specific category of constitutionalism, not of statehood. Although frequently characterised as the latter, this attempt to consign federal polities to theoretical isolation, removing an awkward relative from the comforting familial uniformity of modern constitutional systems, may be theoretically convenient but it is intellectually unconvincing. Federalism, although a highly particular and radically dissonant member of the family, fits squarely within the ménage of modern state constitutionalism. The radical challenge which the federal contract presents to the homogenising assumptions of modern constitutional thinking is to adjust to this fact.

The implications of this challenge became apparent as we turned to constitutional subjecthood in Chapter 6. Federal subjecthood flows from the nature of federal constituent power; the foundational territorial constituents who form the federal constitution are transformed by that act into constitutional territorial subjects, their subjecthood recognised in a number of ways, not least through discrete governments. A federal constitution, like any modern constitution, is normatively transformative, but the fact that the same constituents who found a federal constitution are, in this very moment, constitutionally recognised as legally recreated subjects of the new constitution remains a challenging and potentially destabilising feature of federal constitutionalism. The inter-temporality of a federal constitution's territorial subjects, normatively transformed but not materially supplanted by the constitution, make the ongoing relationship between constituent power and constitutional authority potentially far more real and active than the relationship between individuals—whose founding generation is subject to mortality—and the constitution in a unitary system. The political potential of territorial constituent authority has tended to manifest itself particularly where constituent territories retain a strong sense of societal specificity. We saw this as we traced the unsettled issue of national identity in Canada, culminating as it did in a secessionist crisis in the latter half of the twentieth century and played out dramatically in a seminal reference case before the Supreme Court of Canada. At the same time we saw how territorial subjecthood can diminish in significance, as it has in the United States, calling into question whether, when assessed upon the constituent power–constitutional authority register, the US constitution can still be meaningfully characterised as federal.

At this point in the book, having laid the foundations for what distinguishes federal constitutionalism from monist constitutionalism, I set out in Chapter 7 to articulate the essence of federalism's constitutional purpose. It was argued that federalism is a specific genus of constitutional government for the modern state which, in the act of constitutional union, gives foundational recognition and accommodation to the state's constituent territorial pluralism. The purpose of the federal constitution is both to foster this foundational pluralism and to maintain the constitutional relationship between pluralism and union in the creation and reconciliation of different orders of government. From this purpose a number of principles logically flow. These are not moral principles but rather precepts immanent to the very essence of the federal contract as a discrete order of rule founded upon territorial subjecthood: recognition, autonomous government, associational government, and reciprocity in both vertical and horizontal dimensions. In Chapters 8 and 9 I discussed how each of these principles manifests itself in different ways within any federal constitution. These chapters do not purport to be an exhaustive account of the institutional structure of every federal system but rather they seek to illustrate the degree of variety that attends the manifestation of the federal idea and each of the principles which characterise it. A recurring theme in these chapters is the centralisation of authority within federal systems, whether through a weakening of territorial constituent authority, a constriction of autonomous government through constitutional practice, the overpowering of associational government by the central branch, or the weaponisation of reciprocity in a way that negates territorial individuality and pursues homogeneity in the name of a monistic conception of the demos.[2] This centralising trajectory leaves open to question the very salience of federal constitutionalism in a number of purportedly federal systems today, not only the United States.

Finally, I addressed how federal constitutions change. The significance of the federal contract as a distinctive site of governmental authority is demonstrated by this constitutional feature more than any other. In Chapter 10 we saw the central role played by constituent territories within processes of federal constitutional amendment; how their particular constitutional prerogatives are protected, in some cases beyond the reach of amendment at all; and how the constitution can guarantee a strong role, extending in some cases to a veto, for individual or small numbers of constituent territories in processes of constitutional change. At the same time we also explored the pivotal role of constitutional interpretation and how courts have been significant players on the road to constitutional centralisation, judicial decisions often going against the grain of textual design.

II. The federal contract in the twenty-first century

The divergence between text and interpretation brings to the fore the tension between pluralism and union that lies at the heart of the federal idea. The federal contract is unique because of the centrality of its plural territorial subjects to the authority which their consent to, and participation in, legitimates. But as a form of constitutionalism for the modern state, a federal constitution is also in functional terms designed to foster the integrity of the state within an international legal order of states; a reality of every federal constitution since Philadelphia. This leads to the question of constitutional entrenchment. It is for any constitution in its institutional design to arrive at an appropriate balance between constitutional stability and political flexibility. A federal constitution should entrench the institutional apparatus that is required to give life to its inherent purpose and principles, securing the autonomous government of its constituent territories and guaranteeing their role in meaningful associational government. It should also give life to the two dimensions of reciprocity—vertical and horizontal—requiring the commitment of

[2] This has been a well-recognised trend since at least Kenneth Wheare's analysis in the 1940s. K.C. Wheare, *Federal Government* (Oxford: Oxford University Press, 1946), 4th edn, 1963. For a collection of papers on 'authority migration' in federal systems see E.R. Gerber and K. Kollman, 'Introduction—Authority Migration: Defining an Emerging Research Agenda' (2004) 37 *PS: Political Science and Politics* 397–401, and other papers in that issue of the journal.

each constituent territory to the success of the federal constitution and fostering this by overcoming the deep distortions in relative wealth and power that can unsettle any federal contract. Beyond these principles a federal constitution should remain open to political disagreement and to the resolution of this through political channels. A federal constitution should be wary of crystallising political values as constitutional pre-commitments which, by definition, foreclose the political space within which pluralism can play out. It should afford constituent territories the freedom to develop, foster, and change their own political standards and the policies which emerge from these: this need for political space flows logically from the principles of recognition and autonomy which are accorded foundational constitutional status by the federal contract. Federalism today operates however within a wider environment of muscular constitutionalism which views the constitution as a suitable repository for political values and as a vehicle with which to embed a detailed ideological agenda. This, as I now explore, is one of the most ominous challenges to the federal idea and to the commitment to political pluralism which it bears.

Throughout the book I have sought to take forward—although by no means to complete—the exercise of articulating the federal contract as a discrete form of constitutional ordering. But why, the reader might ask, is this an important task, beyond an exercise in ontology? The answer to that question lies, as it always should for the constitutionalist, in the imperatives of political practice. Today the world is faced with a proliferation of constitutional struggles stemming from the ongoing, and often the intensification of, territorial differences within states. Federalism offers a resource for citizens and political actors struggling with this actuality and it does so because of the constitutional fundamentality that attends a legal-normative federal commitment: a foundational recognition that territory matters and that it does so in ways that do not map perfectly onto the boundaries of existing states. To recognise this is not to make a moral normative claim but merely to observe the nature of contemporary societies, so many of which are plural rather than monist in their demotic composition, and that this inherent territorial pluralism demands a particular form of constitutional ordering if constitutions are to be properly reflective of the peoples they serve.

We see how constitutionalism can respond in nuanced ways to territorial complexity in the history of the Canadian constitution. Canada, in historical perspective, and despite inauspicious beginnings that involved various constitutional experiments in the century leading up to confederation in 1867, constitutes one of the most successful federal systems in the world today. Yet it is also one that, in the past fifty years, has faced severe challenges stemming from the deep territorial diversity upon which it was founded. That it has survived and indeed flourished is highly significant to the very salience of federalism as a constitutional category. Kenneth Wheare observed in the middle of the last century: 'Without federalism Canada could not have come into existence, for the people of Quebec would not otherwise have been prepared to try to be Canadians. Without federalism Canada could not continue to exist, for French-Canadians would not feel that their distinct nationality would be preserved—the basis upon which alone they are prepared to think of themselves as Canadians.'[3] It followed that Canada could not have developed a sense of common national identity were it not for the fact that French-Canadians were reassured that 'Canadian nationality' did not 'exclude or override French-Canadian nationality'.[4] In this we see the complexity of *federal* national identity. Federal nationhood can and indeed must be generated, but it should be a national identity that is open to the possibility of demotic difference: a constitutional form that recognises in its foundational constituent reality how multiple political identities should be allowed to flourish, fostered within the plural territorial and governmental spaces that characterise the federal contract. At root this is more than merely a political commitment; what has sustained the Canadian federal system through troubled times is the constitutional status of this commitment, a status of great legal-normative significance, secured over two centuries by a sense of the fundamentality of the constitution as a binding contract.

The need for both the facilitating and constraining roles of federal constitutionalism is evident today in the number of conflicts that are territorially based. A notable study of global political instability between 1946 and 2019 notes that in 2019 35 countries experienced a civil conflict in their territories. The authors conclude that 'intrastate conflicts have replaced conflict between states'.[5] Despite this evidence of its importance, territory remains under-theorised as a matter of political philosophy in the same way that federalism has remained under-theorised as a matter of constitutional theory.[6] In 1977 Maurice Vile observed that a theory of federalism 'hardly exists today'. Decades of post-war definitionalism had left 'little or no basis upon which to build any sustained theoretical structure'.[7] In the period since then, little has changed. Michael Burgess noted in 2013: 'Since the end of the Cold War we find most of the classic theories of federal state formation and their subsequent maintenance simply redundant.'[8] This is a parlous situation as many political actors in unsettled places turn to federalism to resolve an apparent paradox between the resilient territorial diversity of our time and the

[3] K.C. Wheare, 'Federalism and the Making of Nations', in A.W. Macmahon (ed.), *Federalism: Mature and Emergent* (New York: Columbia University Press, 1955), 28–43, 36.

[4] Wheare, 'Federalism and the Making of Nations', 36.

[5] J. Palik, S.A. Rustad, and F. Methi, 'Conflict Trends: A Global Overview, 1946–2019', Peace Research Institute Oslo Paper, 2020, 35. <https://reliefweb.int/sites/reliefweb.int/files/resources/Palik%2C%20Rustad%2C%20Methi%20-%20Conflict%20Trends%20A%20Global%20Overview%201946-2019%2C%20PRIO%20Paper%202020.pdf>

[6] Discussed in Chapter 2.

[7] M.J.C. Vile, 'Federal Theory and the "New Federalism"', in D. Jaensch (ed.), *The Politics of New Federalism* (Adelaide: Australian Political Studies Association, 1977), 1.

[8] M. Burgess, 'Opening Pandora's Box: Process and Paradox of the Federalism of Political Identity', in A. López-Basaguren and L.E. San Epifanio (eds), *The Ways of Federalism in Western Countries and the Horizons of Territorial Autonomy in Spain* (Berlin: Springer, 2013), vol. 1, 11.

continued existence—and in many cases the consolidation and retrenchment—of strong statehood. Despite the pressing need to understand both the salience of territory and the valence of federalism as a constitutional antidote to territorial conflict '[t]heory has fallen ever further behind as practice has accelerated'.[9]

At the same time as federalism hit the buffers of intellectual endeavour it also found itself undermined by an ideologically driven impetus towards centralisation. This has taken on different manifestations: the revival of the *Staatsvolk* since the turn of the millennium;[10] processes of centralisation within federal constitutional systems; and integrationist approaches to inter-state union, the latter encapsulated in the European Union with its telos of 'ever closer union'.[11] Preston King was aware by the early 1980s that the federal idea is lost when it is seen as a temporary staging post on the road to centralisation. 'The original idea of a federal America or a federal Brazil, or, today, of a federal Europe, was not and is not to divide and disperse, as to centralize and integrate.'[12] The impetus towards supra-state integration extends beyond the EU in ambitions for some notion of global government. The reality of 'globalisation' is however in many ways the unfastening of political and economic power from the democratic guy ropes that constitutionalism has fashioned to control it; fostering economic power, and the exploitation this so often presages, without the constraints of sufficient political accountability.[13] This undermines democratically constituted government, whether federal or unitary, and offers in its place little more than 'fragmented tyranny'.[14]

Federalism is and always has been a constitutional form that challenges the homogenising assumptions of state (and now supra-state) centralisation. Two centuries ago Condorcet wrote dismissively of Montesquieu's defence of the federal idea:

> As truth, reason, justice, the rights of man, the interests of property, of liberty, of security, are in all places the same; we cannot discover why all the provinces of a state, or even all states, should not have the same civil and criminal laws, and the

[9] J.T. Levy, 'Federalism, Liberalism, and the Separation of Loyalties' (2007) 101 *American Political Science Review* 459–477, 459.

[10] B. O'Leary, 'An Iron Law of Nationalism and Federation?: A (Neo-Diceyian) Theory of the Necessity of a Federal Staatsvolk, and of Consociational Rescue' (2003) 7 *Nations and Nationalism* 273–296; M.A. Graber, S. Levinson, and M. Tushnet (eds), *Constitutional Democracy in Crisis?* (Oxford: Oxford University Press, 2018).

[11] P. Mair, *Ruling the Void: The Hollowing of Western Democracy* (London: Verso, 2013).

[12] P. King, *Federalism and Federation* (London: Croom Helm, 1982), 23.

[13] J. Frieden, *Global Capitalism: Its Fall and Rise in the Twentieth Century* (New York: W.W. Norton, 2006).

[14] D. McAdam, S. Tarrow, and C. Tilly, *Dynamics of Contention* (Cambridge: Cambridge University Press, 2001), 266; G. Nootens, 'Autonomy, Boundaries and Trust: Preliminary Remarks', in A.-G. Gagnon and M. Keating (eds), *Political Autonomy and Divided Societies: Imagining Democratic Alternatives in Complex Settings* (Hampshire: Palgrave MacMillan, 2012), 32–48, 45. See also the important new book by E. Christodoulidis, *The Redress of Law: Globalisation, Constitutionalism and Market Capture* (Cambridge: Cambridge University Press, 2021).

same laws relative to commerce. A good law should be good for all men. A true proposition is true everywhere.[15]

It follows that 'there can be nothing normatively interesting to say in favour of a plurality of jurisdictions. A true proposition is, after all, true everywhere.'[16] Modern manifestations of this didactic cosmopolitanism continue to refute the significance of territorial pluralism in the name of purportedly universal values. The projection of moral universalism onto constitutionalism belies however the historical reality of deep and meaningful inter-societal diversity. Therefore, attempts to build federal institutional structures that do not pay sufficient regard to deep multiplicity have largely been unsuccessful in polities where meaningful territorial pluralism is evident. The post-war era saw the collapse of ambitious federal projects that sought to impose constitutional uniformity from Pakistan to Malaysia to the West Indies, while a homogenising constitutional project in the early 1980s, promoted by Prime Minister Pierre Trudeau,[17] nearly brought about the secession of Quebec from Canada. The collapse of the USSR, SFRY, and Czechoslovakia also highlights how decades of *de facto* centralisation based upon the homogenising ambitions of state communism bred only pathological discontent among territorial constituents.

The globalisation of economic power does of course continue apace and commentators try to make sense of how political orders at and below the level of the state can attempt to access the institutions that influence this development, whether through multi-level governance[18] or the rescaling[19] of constitutional authority, adapting to new opportunities beyond the state while seeking greater local control. But it is also the case that the state remains uniquely capable of combining deep pluralism and democratic accountability by fostering a national demos and a responsible government, while also creating meaningful deliberative space for the playing out of societal and governmental difference; offering the nexus between subjecthood (including territorial subjecthood), representation, and accountability that characterises modern constitutional rule.

To appreciate this we must adjust our understanding of the relationship between state and constitution in a democratic age. While the state has often been taken to be the dominant political structure of modernity and the constitution its instrumental bulwark, in fact, when viewed through the relationship between political

[15] M.J.A. Nicolas de Caritat, Marquis de Condorcet, 'Observations on the Twenty-Ninth Book of the Spirit of the Law', appended to D. de Tracy, *A Commentary and Review of Montesquieu's The Spirit of the Laws* Thomas Jefferson (trans.) (New York: Burt Franklin, [1814] 1989)cited by Levy, 'Federalism, Liberalism, and the Separation of Loyalties', 463.

[16] Condorcet, cited by Levy, 464.

[17] S. Tierney, 'Pierre Elliott Trudeau and the Idea of Federalism' (2020) *Supreme Court Law Review* 3–36.

[18] I. Bache and M. Flinders, *Multi-level Governance* (Oxford: Oxford University Press, 2004).

[19] J.-T. Arrighi and D. Stjepanović, *Migrating Borders: Territorial Rescaling and Citizenship Realignment in Europe* (UK: Routledge, 2019).

power and legal authority, the opposite is more true. The state provides a bounded space within which constitutionalism can operate safely and securely as the fundamental validation of legitimate political authority. And in a territorial space that encompasses a number of smaller territorial sites of demotic identity, the state acts as a normatively demarcated playing field, facilitating their interaction through the construction of a complex web of sovereignty and the relationships which sustain it. It is this nexus between constitution and state that allows the federal contract to flourish as a constitutional order of rule. Those who both describe, and indeed prescribe, the withering of the state not only defy political reality, they risk jeopardising meaningful settings for democratic politics. A defence of state-based constitutionalism is not one that reifies the state-nation as a democratic good in itself—I demonstrated the homogenising tendencies of nationalism in Chapter 4[20]—but one that recognises how the state remains the most feasible arena for meaningful democratic constitutionalism, recognised and protected as its autonomy is by international law.[21]

For several decades it has appeared to some that globalisation is a dynamic force that offers new political and democratic opportunities while the state model is sterile, static, and increasingly outmoded. In fact this clichéd assumption is often no more than a fetishisation of the new.[22] States, within which federal systems have taken root and developed over time, can themselves be sites of vigorous political and constitutional innovation and experimentation. It is in fact often at the supra-state level that we see the greatest resistance to change (other than in a centralising and homogenising direction) and the suppression of difference, disagreement, or opposition.[23] Federalism and the diverse and innovative constitutional design which it can offer to each polity remains a vital constitutional toolkit with which to manage subtly the complex identity patterns within many states.[24] Ronald Watts observed in 2008 that 'the federal idea is now more popular internationally than at any time in history',[25] and ascribed this increasing prominence to 'its potential as a

[20] As Lev discusses, '[f]ederalism is inherently *iterable* unlike the public law theory of the state which despite its formality, is tied to its given context.' A. Lev, 'Introduction: Federalism and Public Law Theory', in A. Lev (ed.), *The Federal Idea: Public Law between Governance and Political Life* (Oxford: Hart Publishing, 2019), 1–26, 16.

[21] The sovereignty of the state within international law is of course circumscribed in practice by the political and economic power of non-state forces, but it does provides a vital resource in resisting external domination. G. Simpson, *Great Powers and Outlaw States: Unequal Sovereigns in the International Legal Order* (Cambridge: Cambridge University Press, 2009).

[22] And the not so new, echoing as such an approach does the cosmopolitan dreams of Immanuel Kant: I. Kant, *Perpetual Peace: A Philosophical Essay* [1795] (London: Sonnenschein, 1903).

[23] Mair, *Ruling the Void.*

[24] Research conducted a decade ago suggests an inexorable trend towards the territorialisation of constitutions: An index or regional authority in 42 democracies suggests that 29 countries have regionalized and only two have become more centralized since 1950. L. Hooghe, G. Marks, and A. Schakel, *The Rise of Regional Authority: A Comparative Study of 42 Democracies* (London: Routledge, 2010); and see L. Hooghe et al., *Measuring Regional Authority: A Postfunctionalist Theory of Governance, Volume I*, (Oxford: Oxford University Press, 2016).

[25] R.L. Watts, *Comparing Federal Systems*, 3rd edn (Montreal, QC, Canada: McGill-Queen's University Press, 2008), 7.

way of peacefully reconciling unity and diversity within a single political system'.[26] Among traditional power-houses, the USA and Germany are federal as are three of the four 'BRIC' countries—Brazil, Russian, and India.[27] China is also characterised by deep pluralism, and while it has in recent times attempted to suppress this, it has also in other ways begun to experiment with pluralised governmental arrangements which may evolve in this direction.[28]

It is also clear that the federal idea is highly adaptable. The classical federal systems differ markedly one from another, both in original design and in later development. Among these, the US constitution is categorically different from that of Germany, while many recent innovations within the United Kingdom, Spain, Bosnia and Herzegovina, and Iraq have each taken on very distinctive structures. As Palermo and Kössler put it, 'its evolutions are part of the physiology of federalism'.[29] Erika Arban meanwhile refers to the 'immense and ... unexplored potentialities of federalism';[30] and for Lev, federalism has a 'protean ability ... to invent new political contexts'.[31]

It is in this potential that the real promise of federalism as a constitutional idea lies. If freed from the constraints of institutional uniformity and normative political ideology, it can offer exciting opportunities for constitution-makers in fraught contexts to adapt the federal idea to their circumstances. Federalism does not presuppose a specific institutional structure but it does proffer a particular constitutional disposition, one that views law as a facilitator of, rather than constraint upon, the active engagement of its subjects; an order of rule focused upon empowering rather than inhibiting political deliberation and its outcomes. Federalism can revitalise democracy not only by its sensitivity to territorial difference but by fostering the open political processes necessary for societal pluralism to flourish. To this end it can continue to develop in relation to the complex societies it serves through dynamic and reflexive engagement; a constitutional mentality that accepts and indeed celebrates difference rather than one that seeks to foreclose it in the name of a pre-ordered set of political or moral values.

Given the political potential of federalism as a vehicle for revitalised democratic politics, we return again to the intellectually rich but ultimately distorting influence of the American precedent. In many ways it seems that America never really had faith in federalism. Tocqueville noted during the early years of the Republic

[26] R.L. Watts, 'The Federal Idea and its Contemporary Relevance', in T.L. Courchene et al., *The Federal Idea: Essays in Honour of Ronald L. Watts* (Kingston-Montreal: McGill-Queen's, 2011), 13–27, 14.

[27] Therefore, seven of the eight largest states, in terms of geography, are federal: Canada, the United States, Australia, and Argentina in addition to Russia, India, and Brazil.

[28] K. Tu, 'Towards Constitutional Law of Peoples: China and its Peripheral Societies', PhD thesis, University of Edinburgh, 2011.

[29] F. Palermo and K. Kössler, *Comparative Federalism: Constitutional Arrangements and Case Law* (Oxford: Hart Publishing, 2017), 44.

[30] E. Arban, 'Italian Regionalism and the Federal Challenge', PhD thesis, University of Ottawa, 2014, 8.

[31] Lev, 'Introduction: Federalism and Public Law Theory', 1–26, 16.

that the vernacular commitment of Americans was more to locality than to either states or the Union: 'In America the township was organised before the county, the county before the States, the State before the Union.'[32] It is no surprise therefore that in an era of nation-state-building, the American states came to be supplanted by the centre; subsidiary democracy playing out often more meaningfully at the levels of the city or the county or the district. It also followed that in the elision of the constitution with nationalism, particularly after the Civil War, the US constitution came to embody a model of rigid constitutionalism, possessed not only of a deeply entrenched set of institutional arrangements but also an embedded corpus of political values embodied in the Bill of Rights.[33] Federalism was envisaged by the American founders as a way of constraining rather than pluralising—and thereby valuing—public rule and its potential for popular deliberation. Federalism as an idea therefore came to be co-opted instrumentally as a barrier to public power rather than as a participatory forum for promoting politically engaged territorial pluralism; it is no surprise that the federal idea more generally has largely been lost within processes of constitutionalised state-making in pursuit of similar ideological ends to those promoted by Hamilton and Madison.

Two further aspects of the American model have made its extrapolation to troubled societies unhelpful: the early premise that federalism relies upon demotic uniformity and a concomitant institutional trajectory towards the prioritisation of central over territorial government. Bryce ascribed the success of American federalism to a strong national sentiment.[34] Mill adopted this also as a general principle. For him, a successful federation depends upon homogeneous social preconditions, in particular common sympathies based upon 'race, language, religion' which help foster 'a feeling of identity of political interest.'[35] Dicey is another influential figure in this tradition. Any virtue federalism possessed was to be found in its capacity to foster a strong national state which could only succeed in an environment of societal similitude. Two essential preconditions for a successful federal state flowed from this. First, the existence of 'a body of countries ... so closely connected by locality, by history, by race, or the like, as to be capable of bearing, in the eyes of their inhabitants, an impress of common nationality'; secondly, the existence of 'a very peculiar state of sentiment among the inhabitants of the countries which it is

[32] A. de Tocqueville, *Democracy in America* R.D. Heffner (ed.) (London: The New English Library, 1956), 46.

[33] Over a century ago Dicey observed: 'The United States, is a nation concealed under the form of a federation.' A.V. Dicey, *Introduction to the Study of the Law of the Constitution*, 8th edn (London: Macmillan and Co., 1915), preface.

[34] J. Bryce, *The American Commonwealth, 3 vols* (London: MacMillan and Company, 1888), vol. I, 16–17.

[35] J.S. Mill, 'Considerations on Representative Government', in *Utilitarianism, On Liberty and Considerations on Representative Government* H.B. Acton (ed.) (London: J.M. Dent & Sons, 1972), 367. He continued: 'free institutions are next to impossible in a country made up of different nationalities'.

proposed to unite'.[36] The key goal of federalism was to help manage a large polity through spreading the governmental burden. But in order for these multiple sites of government not to behave centrifugally, the glue of social homogeneity was essential. Federalism, rather than facilitating territorial pluralism, must in fact overcome it to build a coherent policy.[37]

Burgess, a century later, and at a time of strained territorial problems in south eastern Europe and elsewhere, noted that these approaches 'to the modern minds of the new millennium ... have a much more awkward resonance when applied to less socially homogeneous societies'. Astonishingly, but not inaccurately, Burgess also notes that the growth of federal government has 'been the cause of so much discontent in many socially heterogeneous federal societies'.[38] That this is so highlights how processes of centralisation have distorted the federal idea itself, aligning the very concept with an institutional mindset focused upon more 'perfect' union rather than the flourishing of difference; disavowing the premise of federalism as a form of political constitutionalism that should adapt to reflect the demotic composition of the polity it serves. So much did federalism as an idea come to be aligned both with societal homogeneity and institutional centralisation that the Constituent Assembly which drafted the Italian constitution after the Second World War eschewed a federal constitution because it was considered, in light of the American precedent, to be less amenable to local autonomy than a regional arrangement.[39] The centralising impetus of the American model was certainly evident in this period, influencing as it did a form of German federalism that has been almost entirely integrationist in the trajectory of its constitutional practice.

Another trend of recent decades has been external influence, and at times imposition, of constitutional design which echoes processes of post-war constitutional reconstruction in Germany, Austria, Italy, and Japan, and the decolonisation era of the 1950s and 1960s. An example is Bosnia-Herzegovina which has one of

[36] Dicey, *Introduction to the Study of the Law of the Constitution*, 8th edn, 140–141. Schmitt also considered societal homogeneity as essential to the success of a 'bund'. This would help prevent any part asserting sovereignty in relation to others. Discussed by D. Grimm, *Sovereignty: The Origin and Future of a Political and Legal Concept* B. Cooper (trans.) (New York: Columbia University Press, 2015), 67.

[37] Comparatively recent work also, and surprisingly, takes such a view. Watts cites Elazar 1993 as suggesting 'that federations composed of different ethnic groups or nations may be unworkable or run the risk of suffering civil war'. Watts, 'The Federal Idea and its Contemporary Relevance', 26. For a critique of the 'latent ethnocentrism' that remains a feature of mainstream federal thought see W. Kymlicka, 'Is Federalism a Viable Alternative to Secession?', in P.B. Lehning (ed.), *Theories of Secession* (London: Routledge, 2005), 111–150; and also F. Requejo, *Multinational Federalism and Value Pluralism* (Oxford: Routledge, 2004).

[38] Burgess, *Comparative Federalism*, 18.

[39] 'The integrationist pull triggered by this model, entailing for example the principle of supremacy of federal laws upon State laws, could not be embraced by a country which experienced the overarching centralization of the Fascist regime. The regional rather than the federal solution, was considered more suitable to secure the unity of the Republic without compromising the promotion of territorial autonomies and their differentiation.' B. Gustaferro and L. Payero, 'Devolution and Secession in Comparative Perspective: the Case of Italy and Spain', in R. Schütze and S. Tierney (eds), *The United Kingdom and the Federal Idea* (Oxford: Hart Publishing, 2018).

the most complex and innovative federal constitutional arrangements anywhere in the world. The preamble of the constitution asserts that the terms of the constitution have been determined by its three 'constituent peoples'.[40] This remains a fragile system and one that must develop in its own way. However, its credibility has not been enhanced by its origins. As Yee observes, and despite its preamble, the constitutional process emerged from a peace agreement and was largely dominated by international actors.[41]

International influence has bolstered the precedential influence of US federal constitutionalism, in some ways through the elision of the federal idea with its first instantiation, but also in less passive ways with various examples, particularly in Latin America, of federal constitution-building being 'steered' or 'dictated' by the USA.[42] Iraq is another case in point. Its experiment with federal constitutionalism has hitherto been unsuccessful, and one of the reasons is external interference. The drafting of the constitution was shaped by the institutional assumptions of American federalism and by American strategic interests, which at the time included strong support for Kurdish interests,[43] creating a lop-sided and inflexible constitutional system.[44]

The purpose of federal constitutionalism, if it is to live up to the democratic promise which its constituent legitimacy demands, is to reflect the demotic composition of the polity; as the Supreme Court of Canada put it: 'federalism is a political and legal response to underlying social and political realities'.[45] The story of federal systems established from the 1950s and 1960s, and now more recently, is that they risk failure if they are not suited to the vernacular territorial conditions which they serve. Acceptance of internal pluralism was not an easy lesson to learn in an era of homogenising nation-state-building. But it has been a vital one, as James Tully observes:

> There is no irreconcilable conflict between allegiance to the constitution and one's culture or cultures, for the constitution and its public institutions and traditions of interpretation are the protectors, rather than the destroyers, of the cultures and rights of the members . . . The politics of cultural recognition is the response to the

[40] Constitution of Bosnia and Herzegovina 1995, Preamble.

[41] S. Yee, 'The New Constitution of Bosnia and Herzegovina' (1996) 7 *European Journal of International Law* 176–192. See also S. Keil, *Multinational Federalism in Bosnia and Herzegovina* (Farnham and Burlington: Ashgate, 2013).

[42] M. Burgess, *In Search of the Federal Spirit: New Theoretical and Empirical Perspectives in Comparative Federalism* (Oxford: Oxford University Press, 2012), 322.

[43] R. Alkadiri, 'Federalism and Iraq's Constitutional Stalemate', Chatham House Research Paper, 27 November 2020.

[44] Z. Al-Ali, *The Struggle for Iraq's Future: How Corruption, Incompetence and Sectarianism Have Undermined Democracy* (New Haven: Yale University Press, 2014). See also T. Ginsburg, 'Charismatic Fictions and Constitutional Politics', in R. Albert, *Revolutionary Constitutionalism: Law, Legitimacy and Power* (Oxford: Hart Publishing, 2020), 115–131.

[45] *Reference Re Secession of Quebec* [1998] 2 SCR 217, para. 57.

> flouting of this lesson in modern constitutionalism and if the twenty-first century is to be different from the devastating cultural conflicts of the late twentieth century, this lesson will have to be relearned.[46]

Federalism as an idea assumed deep constitutional significance from the eighteenth century onwards as a contract among constituent territorial societies. As such, it is a form of constitutionalism oriented to meet Tully's challenge. However, in practice it has been undercut by a wider approach to constitutionalism that insists upon a universalising mindset and a consequent uniformity of institutional form and behaviour. Federalism remains a vital and adaptable system of democratic constitutional government for our time. But to play this role it must reflect the fundamental idea that gives it this distinct meaning. This is at root a constitutional idea, founded in a dynamic and flexible relationship between authority and democratic legitimacy; an idea of great potential for the societal complexity of today's world. As a consequence it should be freed from the institutional and ideational baggage that has so distorted its essence, and thereupon be reclaimed, revitalised, and put to use as an essential constitutional resource in an age of territorial pluralism.

[46] J. Tully, *Strange Multiplicity: Constitutionalism in an Age of Diversity* (Cambridge: Cambridge University Press, 1995), 198.

Bibliography

Ackerman B., 'The Storrs Lectures: Discovering the Constitution' (1984) 93 *Yale Law Journal* 1013–1072

Ackerman B., *We the People I: Foundations* (Cambridge MA: The Belknap Press of Harvard University Press, 1991)

Ackerman B., *We the People II: Transformations* (Cambridge MA: The Belknap Press of Harvard University Press, 1998)

Ackerman B., 'The New Separation of Powers' (2000) 113 *Harvard Law Review* 633–729

Ackerman B., *Revolutionary Constitutions: Charismatic Leadership and the Rule of Law* (Cambridge MA: Harvard University Press, 2019)

Ackerman B., 'The Race Against Time', in R. Albert (ed.), *Revolutionary Constitutionalism: Law, Legitimacy, Power* (Oxford: Hart, 2020) 377–399

Adam E.C., 'The Constitutional Court of Spain: From System Balancer to Polarizing Centralist', in N. Aroney and J. Kincaid (eds), *Courts in Federal Countries: Federalists or Unitarists?* (Toronto: University of Toronto Press, 2017), 367–403

Adams J., 'A Defence of the Constitutions of Government (1787)', in I. Kramnick and T.J. Lowi (eds), *American Political Thought: A Norton Anthology* (New York: W. W. Norton, 2009), 181–191

Aja E., *Estado autonómico y reforma federal* (Madrid: Alianza, 2014)

Albala A. and J.M. Reniu (eds), *Coalition Politics and Federalism* (Switzerland: Springer, 2018)

Albert R., *Constitutional Amendments: Making, Breaking, and Changing Constitutions* (Oxford: Oxford University Press, 2019)

Aldecoa F. and M. Keating (eds), *Paradiplomacy in Action: The Foreign Relations of Subnational Governments* (London: Frank Cass, 1999)

Alkadiri R., 'Federalism and Iraq's Constitutional Stalemate', Chatham House Research Paper, 27 November 2020

Allen T.R.S., 'The Rule of Law', in D. Dyzenhaus and M. Thorburn (eds), *The Philosophical Foundations of Constitutional Law* (Oxford: Oxford University Press, 2016), 201–220

Allison J.W.F. (ed.), *The Oxford Edition of Dicey* (Oxford: Oxford University Press, 2013), vol. 1

Althusius J., *Politica Methodice Digesta, Atque Exemplis Sacris et Profanis Illustrata*, [1603] F.S. Carney (ed. and trans.) (Indianapolis: Liberty Fund, 1995)

Amar A.R., 'Of Sovereignty and Federalism' (1987) 96 *Yale Law Journal* 1425–1520

Amar A.R., 'Philadelphia Revisited: Amending the Constitution Outside Article V' (1988) 55 *University of Chicago Law Review* 1043–1104

Amar A.R., 'Popular Sovereignty and Constitutional Amendment', in S. Levinson (ed.), *Responding to Imperfection: The Theory and Practice of Constitutional Amendment* (Princeton: Princeton University Press, 1995), 89–115

Amar A.R., *America's Constitution* (New York: Random House, 2006)

Amoretti U.M., 'Introduction: Federalism and Territorial Cleavages', in U.M. Amoretti and N. Bermeo (eds), *Federalism and Territorial Cleavages* (Baltimore: The Johns Hopkins University Press, 2004)

Amoretti U.M. and N. Bormeo (eds), *Federalism and Territorial Cleavages* (Baltimore: Johns Hopkins University Press, 2004)

Anderson B., *Imagined Communities: Reflections on the Origin and Spread of Nationalism* (London and New York: Verso, revised edn, 1991 [1983])

Anderson G., 'The Council of Australian Governments: A New Institution of Governance for Australia's Conditional Federalism' (2008) 31 *University of New South Wales Law Journal* 493–508

Anderson L.M., 'Theorizing Federalism in Iraq' (2007) 17 *Regional and Federal Studies* 159–171

Anderson T., *Creating the Constitution: The Convention of 1787 and the First Congress* (Pennsylvania: Penn. State Press, 1993)

Appleby G. and E.F. Delaney, 'Federalism, Judicial Systems', in A. Harvey (ed.), *Max Planck Encyclopaedia of Comparative Constitutional Law* (Oxford: Oxford University Press, 2017)

Araral E. Jr. et al., *Debate on Federal Philippines: A Citizen's Handbook* (Manila: Ateneo de Manila University Press, 2017)

Arato A., *The Adventures of the Constituent Power: Beyond Revolutions?* (Cambridge: Cambridge University Press, 2017)

Arban E., 'Italian Regionalism and the Federal Challenge', PhD thesis, University of Ottawa, 2014

Arena V., 'Popular Sovereignty in the Late Roman Republic', in R. Bourke and Q. Skinner (eds), *Popular Sovereignty in Historical Perspective* (Cambridge: Cambridge University Press, 2016), 73–95

Arendt H., *On Revolution* (London: Penguin, 2009)

Aroney N., '"A Commonwealth of Commonwealths": Late Nineteenth-Century Conceptions of Federalism and Their Impact on Australian Federation, 1890–1901' (2002) 23 *The Journal of Legal History* 253–290

Aroney N., 'Formation, Representation and Amendment in Federal Constitutions' (2006) 54 *The American Journal of Comparative Law* 277–336

Aroney N., 'Subsidiarity, Federalism and the Best Constitution: Thomas Aquinas on City, Province' (2007) 26 *Law and Philosophy* 161–228

Aroney N., *The Constitution of a Federal Commonwealth: The Making and Meaning of the Australian Constitution* (Cambridge: Cambridge University Press, 2007)

Aroney N., 'Before Federalism? Thomas Aquinas, Jean Quidort and Nicola Casanus', in A. Ward and L. Ward (eds), *The Ashgate Research Companion to Federalism* (Farnham: Ashgate, 2009), 31–48

Aroney N., 'Australia', in L. Moreno and C. Colino (eds), *Diversity and Unity in Federal Countries* (Montreal: McGill-Queen's University Press, 2010), 16–46

Aroney N., 'The Federal Condition: Towards a Normative Theory' (2016) 61 *The American Journal of Jurisprudence* 13–31

Aroney N., 'The High Court of Australia: Textual Unitarism vs Structural Federalism', in N. Aroney and J. Kincaid (eds), *Courts in Federal Countries: Federalists or Unitarists?* (Toronto: University of Toronto Press, 2017), 29–68

Aroney N., 'Constituent Power and the Constituent States: Towards a Theory of the Amendment of Federal Constitutions' (2017) 17 *Jus Politicum: Revue De Droit Politique* 5–31

Aroney N., 'The Federal Condition', in A. Lev (ed.), *The Federal Idea: Public Law between Governance and Political Life* (Oxford: Hart Publishing, 2019), 29–51

Aroney N., 'Christianity, Sovereignty, and Global Law', in R. Domingo and J. Witte, Jr (eds), *Christianity and Global Law* (Abingdon: Routledge, 2020), 267–286

Aroney N. and J. Allan, 'An Uncommon Court: How the High Court of Australia Has Undermined Australian Federalism' (2008) 30 *Sydney Law Review* 245–294

Aroney N. and J. Kincaid, 'Comparative Observations and Conclusions', in N. Aroney and J. Kincaid (eds), *Courts in Federal Countries: Federalists or Unitarists?* (Toronto: University of Toronto Press, 2017), 482–540.

Aroney N. and J. Kincaid (eds), *Courts in Federal Countries: Federalists or Unitarists?* (Toronto: University of Toronto Press, 2017)

Arrighi J.-T. and D. Stjepanović, *Migrating Borders: Territorial Rescaling and Citizenship Realignment in Europe* (UK: Routledge, 2019)

Arrighi J-T. and D. Stjepanović, 'Introduction: The Rescaling of Territory and Citizenship in Europe' (2019) 18 *Ethnopolitics* 219–226

Avbel M. and J. Komárek, *Constitutional Pluralism in the European Union and Beyond* (Oxford: Hart Publishing, 2012)

Bache I., *The Politics of European Union Regional Policy: Multi-level Governance or Flexible Gatekeeping?* (Sheffield: Sheffield University Press, 1998)

Bache I. and M. Flinders, *Multi-level Governance* (Oxford: Oxford University Press, 2004)

Backer L., 'Critical Turnings in Federalism', unpublished paper, ECSA conference, 1999

Backer L., 'The Extra-National State: American Confederation Federalism and the European Union' (2001) 7 *Columbia Journal of European Law* 173–240

Badie B., D. Berg-Schlosser, and L. Morlino (eds), *International Encyclopaedia of Political Science* (Thousand Oaks CA: Sage Publications, 2016), vol. 1

Baker J.W., 'The Covenantal Basis for the Development of Swiss Political Federalism: 1291–1848' (1993) 23 *Publius* 19–41

Bambrick C., '"Neither Precisely National nor Precisely Federal": Governmental and Administrative Authority in Tocqueville's Democracy in America' (2018) 48 *Publius* 586–606

Barber N.W., *The Principles of Constitutionalism* (Oxford: Oxford University Press, 2018)

Barbour C. and G. Pavlich (eds), After *Sovereignty: On the Question of Political Beginnings* (London: Routledge, 2010)

Barry B., *Culture and Equality: An Egalitarian Critique of Multiculturalism* (Cambridge MA: Harvard University Press, 2001)

Beaud O., *Théorie de la Fédération* (Paris: Presses Universitaires de France, 2009)

Beaud O., 'The Founding Constitution Reflections on the Constitution of a Federation and its Peculiarity' (2017) 17 *Jus Politicum; Revue de Droit Politique* 33–63

Beck H. and P. Funk (eds), *Federalism in Greek Antiquity* (Cambridge: Cambridge University Press, 2015)

Bedard E., 'The Centralizing Federalism of Cauchon', in E. Brouillet, A.-G. Gagnon, and G. Laforest (eds), *The Quebec Conference of 1864: Understanding the Emergence of the Canadian Federation* (Kingston/Montreal: McGill-Queen's University Press, 2018), 103–116

Bednar J., *The Robust Federation: Principles of Design* (Cambridge: Cambridge University Press, 2009)

Beeman R., S. Botein, and E.C. Carter II (eds), *Beyond Confederation: Origins of the Constitution and American National Identity* (Chapel Hill: University of North Carolina Press, 1987), 333–348

Beer S., 'The Modernization of American Federalism' (1973) 3 *Publius* 49–95

Beer S., *To Make a Nation: The Rediscovery of American Federalism* (Cambridge MA: Harvard University Press, 1993)

Behnke N. and S. Mueller, 'The Purpose of Intergovernmental Councils: A Framework for Analysis and Comparison' (2017) 27 *Regional & Federal Studies* 507–527

Beland D. and A. Lecours, 'Sub-state Nationalism and the Welfare State: Quebec and Canadian Federalism' (2006) 12 *Nations and Nationalism* 77–96

Bellamy R., *A Republican Europe of States: Cosmopolitan, Intergovernmentalism and Democracy in the EU* (Cambridge: Cambridge University Press, 2019)

Beloff M., 'The "Federal Solution" in the Application to Europe, Asia and Africa' (1953) 1 *Political Studies* 114–131

Benning L., 'James Madison and the Nationalists, 1780–1783' (1983) 40 *The William and Mary Quarterly* 227–255

Bensel R., *Yankee Leviathan: The Origins of Central State Authority in America 1859–1877* (Cambridge: Cambridge University Press, 1990)

Benson G.C.S, *The New Centralization* (New York: Farrar and Rinehart, 1941)

Benson G.C.S. (ed.), *Essays in Federalism* (Claremont: Claremont Men's College, 1961)

Benz A., 'The Federal Constitutional Court of Germany: Guardian of Unitarism and Federalism', in N. Aroney and J. Kincaid (eds), *Courts in Federal Countries: Federalists or Unitarists?* (Toronto: University of Toronto Press, 2017), 193–222

Benz A. and J. Broschek, *Federal Dynamics: Continuity, Change, and the Varieties of Federalism* (Oxford: Oxford University Press, 2013)

Benz A. and F. Knüpling (eds), *Changing Federal Constitutions: Lessons from International Comparison* (Toronto: Barbara Budrich Publishers, 2012)

Bernal A.M., *Beyond Origins: Rethinking Founding in a Time of Constitutional Democracy* (Oxford: Oxford University Press, 2017)

Bhattacharyya H., *Federalism in Asia: India, Pakistan, Malaysia, Nepal and Myanmar*, 2nd edn (London: Routledge, 2021)

Birch A.H., 'Approaches to the Study of Federalism' (1966) 14 *Political Studies* 15–33

Bird R.M., 'The Spending Power in Federal Countries' (2009) SSRN paper, <https://papers.ssrn.com/sol3/papers.cfm?abstract_id=1529322>

Bliss J.M. (ed.), *Canadian History in Documents, 1763–1996* (Toronto: Ryerson Press, 1996)

Bodin J., *The Six Bookes of a Commonweale* [1576] R. Knolles (trans.) 1606, K.D. McRae (ed.) (Cambridge MA: Harvard University Press, 1962)

Bogdanor V., *Devolution in the UK* (Oxford: Oxford University Press, 2001)

López Bofill H., *Law, Violence and Constituent Power. The Law, Politics and History of Constitution Making* (Abingdon: Routledge, 2021)

Bolleyer N., *Intergovernmental Cooperation: Rational Choices in Federal Systems and Beyond* (Oxford: Oxford University Press, 2009)

Bolleyer N. and L. Thorlakson, 'Beyond Decentralization—The Comparative Study of Interdependence in Federal Systems' (2012) 42 *Publius* 566–591

Bowen C.D., *Miracle at Philadelphia: The Story of the Constitutional Convention, May to September 1787* (New York: Little, Brown and Co., 1986)

Braun D., 'Federalism in South Africa—Can it work?' (2009) *Université de Lausanne Travaux de Science Politique/Political Science Working Paper Series*, No. 41

Braun D., 'Multilevel Governance in Germany and Switzerland', in H. Enderlein et al. (eds), *Hand-book on Multi-level Governance* (Cheltenham: Edward Elgar, 2010), 168–183

Breen M.G., 'The Origins of Holding-Together Federalism: Nepal, Myanmar, and Sri Lanka' (2018) 48 *Publius* 26–50

Breen M.G., *The Road to Federalism in Nepal, Myanmar and Sri Lanka: Finding the Middle Ground* (Abingdon: Routledge, 2018)

British North America Act (BNA), 1867, 30–31 Vict., c. 3 (UK)

Broschek J., 'Conceptualizing and Theorizing Constitutional Change in Federal Systems: Insights from Historical Institutionalism' (2011) 21 *Regional and Federal Studies* 539–559

Broschek J., B. Petersohn, and S. Toubeau, 'Territorial Politics and Institutional Change: A Comparative-Historical Analysis' (2018) 48 *Publius* 1–25

Brouillet E., 'The Supreme Court of Canada: The Concept of Cooperative Federalism and its Effect on the Balance of Power', in N. Aroney and J. Kincaid (eds), *Courts in Federal Countries: Federalists or Unitarists?* (Toronto: University of Toronto Press, 2017), 135–164

Brouillet E., A.-G. Gagnon, and G. Laforest, '1864, a Pivotal Year in the Advent of the Canadian Confederation', in E. Brouillet, A.-G. Gagnon, and G. Laforest (eds), *The Quebec Conference of 1864: Understanding the Emergence of the Canadian Federation* (Kingston/Montreal: McGill-Queen's University Press, 2018), 3–25

Brouillet E., A.-G. Gagnon, and G. Laforest (eds), *The Constitutions that Shaped Us: A Historical Anthology of Pre-1867 Canadian Constitutions* (Kingston/Montreal: McGill-Queen's University Press, 2015)

Brouillet E., A.-G. Gagnon, and G. Laforest (eds), *The Quebec Conference of 1864: Understanding the Emergence of the Canadian Federation* (Kingston/Montreal: McGill-Queen's University Press, 2018)

Bryce J., 'Flexible and Rigid Constitutions', in J. Bryce, Studies *in History and Jurisprudence* (Oxford: Oxford University Press, 1901), Part III.

Bryce J., *The American Commonwealth, 2 vols* (London: Macmillan and Co. Ltd, 1888)

Buchanan A., 'Political Legitimacy and Democracy' (2002) 112 *Ethics* 689–719

Buchanan A. and M. Moore (eds), *States, Nations, and Borders. The Ethics of Making Boundaries* (Cambridge: Cambridge University Press, 2003)

Buckner P., 'Canadian Constitution-Making in the British World', in E. Brouillet, A.-G. Gagnon, and G. Laforest (eds), *The Quebec Conference of 1864* (Kingston/Montreal: McGill-Queen's University Press, 2018), 70–101

Bulman-Pozen J. and H.K. Gerken, 'Uncooperative Federalism' (2009) 118 *Yale Law Journal* 1256–1310

Burgess M., 'Federalism and Federation', in M. Burgess and A.-G. Gagnon (eds), *Comparative Federalism and Federation: Competing Traditions and Future Directions* (Hemel Hempstead, UK: Harvester Wheatsheaf, 1993), 3–14

Burgess M., *Comparative Federalism: Theory and Practice* (London: Routledge, 2006)

Burgess M., *In Search of the Federal Spirit: New Theoretical and Empirical Perspectives in Comparative Federalism* (Oxford: Oxford University Press, 2012)

Burgess M., 'Opening Pandora's Box: Process and Paradox of the Federalism of Political Identity', in A. López-Basaguren and L.E. San Epifanio (eds) *The Ways of Federalism in Western Countries and the Horizons of Territorial Autonomy in Spain* (Berlin: Springer, 2013), vol. 1, 11

Burgess M. and A.-G. Gagnon (eds), *Comparative Federalism and Federation: Competing Traditions and Future Directions* (Hemel Hempstead, UK: Harvester Wheatsheaf, 1993)

M. Burgess and A.-G. Gagnon (eds), *Federal Democracies* (London: Routledge, 2010)

Borrows J., *Freedom and Indigenous Constitutionalism* (Toronto: University of Toronto Press, 2016)

Bossacoma Busquets P., *Morality and Legality of Secession: A Theory of National Self-Determination* (London: Palgrave, 2019)

Bossacoma Busquets P., 'Asymmetry as a Device for Equal Recognition and Reasonable Accommodation of Majority and Minority Nations', in P. Popelier and M. Sahadzik (eds), *Constitutional Asymmetry in Multinational Federalism: Managing Multinationalism in Multi-tiered Systems* (London: Palgrave, 2019), 429–460

Bossacoma Busquets P., 'An Egalitarian Defence of Territorial Autonomy' (2021) 62 *Revista catalana de dret public* 90–111

Bussjager P., 'Austria's Cooperative Federalism', in G. Bischof and F. Karlhofer, *Austrian Federalism in Comparative Perspective* (Innsbruck: Innsbruck University Press, 2015), 11–33

Bybee J.S., 'Ulysses at the Mast: Democracy, Federalism, and the Sirens' Song of the Seventeenth Amendment' (1997) 91 *Northwestern University Law Review* 500–572

van Caenegem R.C., *An Historical Introduction to Western Constitutional Law* (Cambridge: Cambridge University Press, 2012)

Caldwell P.C., *Popular Sovereignty and the Crisis of German Constitutional Law: The Theory and Practice of Weimar Constitutionalism* (Durham NC: Duke University Press, 1997)

Canovan M., 'Sleeping Dogs, Prowling Cats and Soaring Doves: Three Paradoxes in the Political Theory of Nationhood' (2001) 49 *Political Studies* 203–215

Canovan M., *The People* (Cambridge: Polity Press, 2005)

Carens J.H., *Culture, Citizenship and Community* (Oxford: Oxford University Press, 2000)

Cartier G.-É., 'Parliamentary Debates on Confederation (7 February, 1865)', W.P.M. Kennedy (ed.), *Documents of the Canadian Constitution, 1759–1915* (Toronto: Oxford University Press, 1918), 559–686

Castells A., 'Catalonia and Spain: Political and Fiscal Conflict' (2014) 40 *Dans Pôle Sud* 59–80 <https://www.cairn.info/revue-pole-sud-2014-1-page-59.htm>

Chagnon R., 'The Fathers of Confederation and the BNA Act: Constitutional Visions and Models', in E. Brouillet, A.-G. Gagnon, and G. Laforest (eds), *The Quebec Conference of 1864: Understanding the Emergence of the Canadian Federation* (Kingston/Montreal: McGill-Queen's University Press, 2018), 29–48

Cheibub J.A. et al., 'Latin American Presidentialism in Comparative and Historical Perspective' (2011) 89 *Texas Law Review* 1707–1731

Chevrier M., 'The Idea of Federalism among the Founding Fathers of the United States and Canada', in A.-G. Gagnon (ed.), *Contemporary Canadian Federalism: Foundations, Traditions, Institutions* (Toronto: University of Toronto Press, 2007), 11–52

Chevrier M., 'The Making of a Dominion: The Completion of a Conquest', in E. Brouillet, A.-G. Gagnon, and G. Laforest (eds), *The Quebec Conference of 1864: Understanding the Emergence of the Canadian Federation* (Kingston/Montreal: McGill-Queen's University Press, 2018), 49–69

Chhibber P. and K. Kollman, *The Formation of National Party Systems: Federalism and Party Competition in Canada, Great Britain, India and the United States* (Princeton and Oxford: Princeton University Press, 2004)

Chignon R., 'The Fathers of Confederation and the BNA Act: Constitutional Visions and Models', in E. Brouillet, A.-G. Gagnon, and G. Laforest (eds), *The Quebec Conference of 1864: Understanding the Emergence of the Canadian Federation* (Kingston/Montreal: McGill-Queen's University Press, 2018), 29–48

Chisholm v. Georgia, 2 U.S. (2 Dall.) 419, 453 (1793)

Choudhry S. (ed.), *Constitutional Design for Divided Societies: Integration or Accommodation* (Oxford: Oxford University Press, 2008)

Choudhry S., 'Migration as a New Metaphor in Comparative Constitutional Law', in S. Choudhry (ed.), *The Migration of Constitutional Ideas* (Cambridge: Cambridge University Press, 2009), 1–36

Choudhry S. and N. Hume, 'Federalism, Devolution and Secession: From Classical to Post-conflict Federalism', in T. Ginsburg and R. Dixon (eds), *Comparative Constitutional Law* (Cheltenham: Edward Elgar, 2011), 356–384

Christodoulidis E., *The Redress of Law: Globalisation, Constitutionalism and Market Capture* (Cambridge: Cambridge University Press, 2021)

Clark C., *Iron Kingdom: The Rise and Downfall of Prussia, 1600–1947* (Cambridge MA: Harvard University Press, 2006)

Cole R.L., J. Kincaid, and A. Rodriguez, 'Public Opinion on Federalism and Federal Political Culture in Canada, Mexico, and the United States' (2004) 34 *Publius* 201–221

Colley L., *Britons: Forging the Nation 1707–1837* (New Haven: Yale University Press, 2005)

Colón Ríos J.I., *Weak Constitutionalism: Democratic Legitimacy and the Question of Constituent Power* (Oxford: Routledge, 2012)

Colón-Ríos J.I., 'Rousseau, Theorist of Constituent Power' (2016) 36 *Oxford Journal of Legal Studies* 885–908

Colon Rios J.I., *Constituent Power and the Law* (Oxford: Oxford University Press, 2020)

Colón-Ríos J.I., 'Arato's Adventures: Between Sovereignty and Constituent Power' (2020) 41 *Revus: Journal for Constitutional Theory and Philosophy of Law* [online], <https://journals.openedition.org/revus/6257>

Corwin E.S., 'The Passing of Dual Federalism' (1950) 36 *Virginia Law Review* 1–24

Courchene T.L. et al., *The Federal Idea: Essays in Honour of Ronald L. Watts* (Kingston-Montreal: McGill-Queen's, 2011)

Craven G., *Secession: The Ultimate States Right* (Melbourne: Melbourne University Press, 1986)

Craven G., 'Would the Abolition of the States be an Alteration of the Constitution under Section 128?' (1989) 18 *Federal Law Review* 85–121

Crenson M. and B. Ginsberg, *Presidential Power: Unchecked and Unbalanced* (New York: Norton, 2007)

Cuesta-López V., 'Intergovernmental Relations in Spain and the United Kingdom: The Institutionalization of Multilateral Cooperation in Asymmetric Polities' (2014) 6 *Perspectives on Federalism* 299–318

Dam I., 'Immigration and Sub-State Nations: Theorizing the Nexus', in K. Detterbeck and E. Hepburn (eds), *Handbook on Territorial Politics* (Cheltenham, Northampton: Edgar Elgar Publishing, 2018), chapter 18

Dardenelli P., 'De/centralization', in J. Kincaid (ed.), *A Research Agenda for Federalism Studies* (Cheltenham: Edward Elgar, 2019), 106–116

Dardanelli P. et al., 'Conceptualizing, Measuring, and Theorizing Dynamic De/Centralization in Federations' (2019) 49 *Publius* 1–29

Davis S.R., 'The "Federal Principle" Reconsidered' (1956) 1 *Australian Journal of Politics and History* 223–244

Davis S.R., *Theory and Reality: Federal Ideas in Australia, England and Europe* (Queensland: University of Queensland Press, 1995)

Dawson R.M., *The Government of Canada* (Toronto: University of Toronto Press, 1949)

Delaney E., 'The Federal Case for Judicial Review', unpublished paper

Detterbeck K., *Multi-Level Party Politics in Western Europe* (Switzerland: Springer, 2012)

Diamond M., 'The Federalist's View of Federalism', in G.C.S. Benson (ed.), *Essays in Federalism* (Claremont: Claremont Men's College, 1961), 21–64

Diamond M., 'What the Framers Meant by Federalism', in R.A. Goldwin (ed.), *A Nation of States: Essays on the American Federal System* (Chicago: Rand McNally, 1964), 24–41

Dicey A.V., *Lectures Introductory to the Study of the Law of the Constitution* (London: Macmillan, 1885); [8th edn (London: Macmillan and Co., 1915)]

Dicey A.V., *The Oxford Edition of Dicey*, J.W.F. Allison (ed.) (Oxford: Oxford University Press, 2013), vol. 1

J.F. Dienstag, 'Between History and Nature: Social Contract Theory in Locke and the Founders' (1996) 58 *Journal of Politics* 985–1009

Dixon R., R. Levy, and M. Tushnet, 'Theories and Practices of Federalism in Deeply Divided Societies' (2019) 46 *Federal Law Review* 481–490

Domingo R. and J. Witte, Jr (eds), *Christianity and Global Law* (Oxford: Oxford University Press, 2020), 267–286

Douglass R., 'Tuck, Rousseau and the Sovereignty of the People' (2016) 42 *History of European Ideas* 1111–1114

Downes P., *Hobbes, Sovereignty, and Early American Literature* (Cambridge: Cambridge University Press, 2015)

Duchacek I.D., *Comparative Federalism: The Territorial Dimension of Politics* (New York: Holt, Rinehart and Winston, 1970)

Duchacek I.D., *Territorial Dimension of Politics: Within, Among, and Across Nations* (Boulder: Westview, 1986)

Dumont H., 'The European Union, a Plurinational Federation in Sensu Cosmopolitico', in A.G. Gagnon and M. Seymour (eds), *Multinational Federalism: Problems and Prospects* (UK: Palgrave MacMillan, 2012), 83–106

Durham Report: 'Lord Durham's Report on the Affairs of British North America' (1839)

Dworkin R., *Justice for Hedgehogs* (Cambridge MA: Harvard University Press, 2013)

Dyzenhaus D., 'Recrafting the Rule of Law', in D. Dyzenhaus (ed.), *Recrafting the Rule of Law: The Limits of Legal Order* (Oxford: Hart Publishing, 1999), 1–14

Dyzenhaus D., *The Constitution of Law: Legality in a Time of Emergency* (Cambridge: Cambridge University Press, 2006)

Dyzenhaus D., 'The Idea of a Constitution: A Plea for Staatsrechtslehre', in D. Dyzenhaus and M. Thorburn (eds), *The Philosophical Foundations of Constitutional Law* (Oxford: Oxford University Press, 2016), 9–32

Dyzenhaus D. and M. Thorburn (eds), *The Philosophical Foundations of Constitutional Law* (Oxford: Oxford University Press, 2016)

Edrisinha R. and A. Welikala (eds), *Essays on Federalism in Sri Lanka* (Colombo: Centre for Policy Alternatives, 2008)

Erk J., *Explaining Federalism: State, Society and Congruence in Austria, Belgium, Canada, Germany and Switzerland* (London: Routledge, 2007)

Elazar D.J., *American Federalism: A View from the States* (New York: Thomas Y. Crowell Company, 1972)

Elazar D.J., *Exploring Federalism* (Tuscaloosa: University of Alabama Press, 1987)

Elazar D.J., 'International and Comparative Federalism' (1993) 26 *PS: Political Science and Politics* 190–95

Elazar D.J., *Federal Systems of the World: A Handbook of Federal, Confederal and Autonomy Arrangements*, 2nd edn (Harlow: Longman, 1994)

Elazar D.J., *Federalism: An Overview* (Pretoria: HSRC Publishers, 1995)

Elazar D.J., 'Covenant and Polity in Biblical Israel', in Daniel J. Elazar (ed.), *The Covenant Tradition in Politics* (New Brunswick: Transaction Publishers, 1995), Volume I

Elazar D.J., 'The United States and Europe: Models for Their Epochs', in K. Nicolaidis and R. Howse (eds), *The Federal Vision: Legitimacy and Levels of Governance in the United States and the European Union* (Oxford: Oxford University Press, 2001), 31–53

R. Epstein and M. Greve (eds), *Federal Preemption: States' Powers, National Interests* (Washington DC: Aei Press, 2007)

Erk J., *Explaining Federalism: State, Society and Congruence in Austria, Belgium, Canada, Germany and Switzerland* (London: Routledge, 2008)

Eulau H., *The Behavioral Persuasion in Politics* (New York: Random House, 1963)

Fafard P., F. Rocher, and C. Cote, 'The Presence (or Lack Thereof) of A Federal Culture in Canada: The Views of Canadians' (2010) 20 *Regional and Federal Studies* 19–43

Falk R., 'Sovereignty', in J. Krieger (ed.), *The Oxford Companion to Politics of the World* (Oxford: Oxford University Press, 1993)

Farrand M., *Records of the Federal Convention of 1787, 4 vols* (New Haven: Yale University Press, 1911–1937)

Feeley M. and E. Rubin, *Federalism: Political Identity and Tragic Compromise* (Ann Arbor: University of Michigan Press, 2008)

Feeley M., 'The Political Theory of Federalism' (2012) 28 *Flinders Journal of History and Politics* 1–15

Feldman N., *The Three Lives of James Madison: Genius, Partisan, President* (New York: Random House, 2017)

Fenna A., 'The Centralization of Australian Federalism 1901–2010: Measurement and Interpretation' (2019) 49 *Publius* 30–56

Ferreres Comella V. and P. Bossacoma Busquets, 'Case Studies in Forms of Self-Determination: A Comparison of the Åland Islands, South Tyrol, the Kurds In Iraq, and Catalonia', Social Science Research Council Working Papers, March 2017 <CPPF_Models of Autonomy_3_Ferreres and Bossacoma.pdf (ssrc.org)>

Filippov M., P.C. Ordeshook, and O. Shvetsova, *Designing Federalism: A Theory of Self-Sustainable Federal Institutions* (Cambridge: Cambridge University Press, 2004)

Fiseha A., 'Constitutional Adjudication through Second Chamber in Ethiopia' (2017) 16 *Ethnopolitics* 295–313

Flinders M., 'Constitutional Anomie' (2010) 44 *Government and Opposition* 383–409

Forsyth M., *Union of States: The Theory and Practice of Confederations* (New York: Leicester University Press, 1981)

Franck T.M. (ed.), *Why Federations Fail: An Inquiry into the Requisites for Successful Federalism* (New York: New York University Press, 1968)

Franks C.E.S, *The Parliament of Canada* (Toronto: University of Toronto Press, 1987)

Freeman E.A., *History of Federal Government V1: From the Foundation of the Achaian League to the Disruption of the United States* (London: MacMillan, 1863)

Freeman E.A., *History of Federal Government in Greece and Italy* J.E. Bury (ed.) (Freeport: Books For Libraries Press, 1972)

Frey R.L. and G. Wettstein, 'Reform of the Swiss Fiscal Equalisation System', CESifo DICE Report 1/2008 <https://citeseerx.ist.psu.edu/viewdoc/download?doi=10.1.1.862.4854&rep=rep1&type=pdf>

Frieden J., *Global Capitalism: Its Fall and Rise in the Twentieth Century* (New York: W.W. Norton, 2006)

Friedman B., *The Will of the People: How Public Opinion Has Influenced the Supreme Court and Shaped the Meaning of the Constitution* (New York: Farrar, Straus & Giroux, 2009)

Friedrich C.J., 'Federal Constitutional Theory and Emergent Proposals', in A.W. Macmahon (ed.), *Federalism: Mature and Emergent* (New York: Russell & Russell, 1962), 510–533

Friedrich C.J., *Trends of Federalism in Theory and Practice* (London: Frederick A. Praeger Publishers, 1968)

Gagnon A.-G. (ed.), *Contemporary Canadian Federalism* (Toronto: University of Toronto Press, 2009)

Gagnon A.-G. and M. Burgess (eds), *Federal Democracies* (London: Taylor and Francis, 2010)

Gagnon A.-G. and M. Seymour (eds), *Multinational Federalism: Problems and Prospects* (UK: Palgrave MacMillan, 2012)

Gagnon A.-G. and J. Tully (eds), *Multinational Democracies* (Cambridge: Cambridge University Press, 2001)

Galligan D.J., 'Constitutional Paradox or the Potential of Constitutional Theory' (2008) 28 *Oxford Journal of Legal Studies* 343–367

Gamper A., 'A "Global Theory of Federalism": The Nature and Challenges of a Federal State' (2005) 6(10) *German Law Journal* 1297–1318

Gamper A., 'Legislative Functions of Second Chambers in Federal Systems' (2018) 10 *Perspectives on Federalism* 117–133

Gardner J.A., 'The Theory and Practice of Contestatory Federalism' (2018) 60 *William and Mary Law Review* 507–588

Gargarella R., 'Constituent Power in a "Community of Equals"' (2020) 41 *Revus: Journal for Constitutional Theory and Philosophy of Law* [online] <http://journals.openedition.org/revus/6436>

Gerber E.R. and K. Kollman, 'Introduction—Authority Migration: Defining an Emerging Research Agenda' (2004) 37 *PS: Political Science and Politics* 397–401

Gerken H., 'Federalism as the New Nationalism: An Overview' (2014) 123 *Yale Law Journal* 1626–2133

Gibson E.L. (ed.), *Federalism and Democracy in Latin America* (Baltimore: John Hopkins University Press, 2004)

Ginsburg T., 'Constitutions as Contract, Constitutions as Charter', in D. Galligan and M. Versteeg (eds), *Social and Political Foundations of Constitutions* (Cambridge: Cambridge University Press, 2013), 182–204

Goldsworthy J., 'Questioning the Migration of Constitutional Ideas: Rights, Constitutionalism and the Limits of Convergence', in S. Choudhry (ed.), *The Migration of Constitutional Ideas* (Cambridge: Cambridge University Press, 2009), 115–141

Golemboski D., 'Federalism and the Catholic Principle of Subsidiarity' (2015) 45 *Publius: The Journal of Federalism* 526–551

Graber M.A., S. Levinson, and M. Tushnet (eds), *Constitutional Democracy in Crisis?* (Oxford: Oxford University Press, 2018)

Gramlich E.M., '"A Fair Go": Fiscal Federalism Arrangements', in R.E. Caves and L.B. Krause (eds), *The Australian Economy: A View from the North* (Sydney: Allen & Unwin, 1984), 231–274

Greaves H.R.G., *Federal Union in Practice* (London: George Allen & Unwin, 1940)

Greenstein F.I. and N. Polsby (eds), *Handbook of Political Science. Volume V: Government Institutions and Process* (Reading MA: Addison-Wesley, 1975)

Grewal B.S., 'Federalism and Fiscal Equalization: Should India Follow the Australian Path?', in I. Copland and J. Rickard (eds), *Federalism: Comparative Perspectives from India and Australia* (New Delhi: Manohar, 1999)

Grewal D.S. and J. Purdy, 'The Original Theory of Constitutionalism' (2018) 127 *Yale Law Journal* 665–705

Grimm D., *Sovereignty: The Origin and Future of a Political and Legal Concept* B. Cooper (trans.) (New York: Columbia University Press, 2015)

Grimm D., *Constitutionalism Past, Present, and Future* (Oxford: Oxford University Press, 2016)

Grodzins M., *The American System* D.J. Elazar (ed.) (Chicago: Rand McNally & Company, 1966)

Gunn J.A.W., *Beyond Liberty and Property* (Montreal and Kingston: McGill-Queen's University Press, 1983)

Gustaferro B. and L. Payero, 'Devolution and Secession in Comparative Perspective: the Case of Italy and Spain', in R. Schütze and S. Tierney (eds), *The United Kingdom and the Federal Idea* (Oxford: Hart Publishing, 2018), 123–150

Habermas J., *Between Facts and Norms: Contributions to a Discourse Theory of Law and Democracy* (Cambridge: Polity Press, 1996)

Habermas J., 'Constitutional Democracy: A Paradoxical Union of Contradictory Principles?' (2001) 29 *Political Theory* 766–781

Habermas J., 'Democracy in Europe: Why the Development of the EU into a Transnational Democracy Is Necessary and How It Is Possible' (2015) 21 *European Law Journal* 546–557

Habermas J., 'Citizen and State Equality in a Supranational Political Community: Degressive Proportionality and the Pouvoir Constituant Mixte' (2017) 55 *Journal of Common Market Studies* 193–202

Hahm C. and S.H. Kim, 'To Make "We the People": Constitutional Founding in Postwar Japan and South Korea' (2010) 8 *International Journal of Constitutional Law* 800–848

Hamilton A., J. Madison, and J. Jay, *The Federalist Papers* C. Rossiter (ed.) (New York: New American Library, 1961)

Hampsher-Monk I., 'Democracy and Federation in the Federalist Papers', in A.-G. Gagnon and M. Burgess (eds), *Federal Democracies* (London: Taylor and Francis, 2010), 29–45

Hanssen K., 'The Constitutionality of Conditional Grant Legislation' (1966) 2 *Manitoba Law Journal* 191–199

Hart H.L.A., *The Concept of Law* (Oxford: Oxford University Press, 1961)

Härtel I., *Handbuch des Föderalismus. Föderalismus als demokratische Rechtsordnung und Rechtskultur in Deutschland, Europa und der Welt* (Berlin: Springer, 2012)

Harvey L.-G., 'Confederation and Corruption: The Republican Critique of the Quebec Resolutions', in E. Brouillet, A.-G. Gagnon, and G. Laforest (eds), *The Quebec Conference of 1864: Understanding the Emergence of the Canadian Federation* (Kingston/Montreal: McGill-Queen's University Press, 2018), 220–232

Heller H., *Sovereignty: A Contribution to the Theory of Public and International Law* D. Dyzenhaus (ed.) (Oxford: Oxford University Press, 2019)

Hendrickson D.C., *Peace Pact: The Lost World of the American Founding* (Lawrence: University of Kansas Press, 2013)

Henry P., 4 June 1788, 'Speech before the Virginia State Ratifying Convention', in H.J. Storing (ed.), *The Anti-Federalist: Writings by the Opponents of the Constitution*, (Chicago: University of Chicago Press, 1985), 296–297

Herzog D., *Sovereignty RIP* (New Haven: Yale University Press, 2020)

Hessebon G.T. and A.K. Idris, 'The Supreme Court of Ethiopia: Federalism's Bystander', in N. Aroney and J. Kincaid (eds), *Courts in Federal Countries: Federalists or Unitarists?* (Toronto: University of Toronto Press, 2017), 165–192

Hicks U.K., *Federalism, Failure and Success: A Comparative Study* (London: Macmillan, 1978)

Hinsley F., *Sovereignty*, 2nd edn (Cambridge: Cambridge University Press, 1986)

Hirschl R., *Towards Juristocracy: The Origins and Consequences of the New Constitutionalism* (Harvard: Harvard University Press, 2007)

Hirschl R., *Comparative Matters: The Renaissance of Comparative Constitutional Law* (Oxford: Oxford University Press, 2014)

Hitch G., 'Scott Morrison says National Cabinet Here to Stay, Will Replace COAG Meetings in Wake of Coronavirus', ABC News, 29 May 2020 <https://www.abc.net.au/news/2020-05-29/coag-scrapped-national-cabinet-here-to-say-coronavirus-update/12300636>

Hobbes T., *Leviathan* [1651] (Cambridge: Cambridge University Press, 1991)

Hodge W.C., 'Patriation of the Canadian Constitution: Comparative Federalism in a New Context' (1985) 60 *Washington Law Review* 585–632

Hogg P.W., *Constitutional Law of Canada* (Toronto: Carswell, 1997)

Hogg P.W. and W. Wright, 'Canadian Federalism, the Privy Council and the Supreme Court: Reflections on the Debate About Canadian Federalism' (2005) 38 *University of British Columbia Law Review* 329–352

Holmes S., 'Precommitment and the Paradox of Democracy', in J. Elster and R. Slagstad (eds), *Constitutionalism and Democracy* (Cambridge: Cambridge University Press, 1988), 195–240

Hont I., 'The Permanent Crisis of a Divided Mankind: "Contemporary Crisis of the Nation State" in Historical Perspective' (1994) 42 *Political Studies* 166–231

Hooghe L. and G. Marks, *Multi-level Governance and European Integration* (London: Rowman and Littlefield, 2001)

Hooghe L., G. Marks, and A. Schakel, *The Rise of Regional Authority: A Comparative Study of 42 Democracies* (London: Routledge, 2010)

Hooghe L. et al., *Measuring Regional Authority: A Postfunctionalist Theory of Governance, Volume I* (Oxford: Oxford University Press, 2016)

Hopkins D.J., *The Increasingly United States: How and Why American Political Behavior Nationalized* (Chicago: University of Chicago Press, 2018)

Horowitz I.L., 'Daniel J. Elazar and the Covenant Tradition in Politics' (2001) 31 *Publius* 1–7

House of Lords Constitution Committee, 'Intergovernmental Relations in the United Kingdom', HL Paper 146, sess. 2014–15, 27 March 2015

House of Lords Constitution Committee, 'The Union and Devolution', HL Paper 149, sess. 2015–16, 25 May 2016

Hueglin T.O., *Early Modern Concepts for a Late Modern World: Althusius on Community and Federalism* (Waterloo: WLU Press, 1999)

Hueglin T.O., 'Federalism: An Alternative Category in Political Thought?', in R. Saxena (ed.), *Varieties of Federal Governance: Major Contemporary Models* (Cambridge: Cambridge University Press, 2012), 3–17

Hueglin T.O., 'Federalism and Democracy: A Critical Reassessment' in G. Skogstad et al. (eds), *The Global Promise of Federalism* (Toronto: University of Toronto Press 2013), 17–42

Hueglin T.O., 'Federalism and Political Theory: A Case of Mutual Neglect?' in J. Kincaid (ed.), *A Research Agenda for Federalism Studies* (Cheltenham: Edward Elgar, 2019), 15–26

Hueglin T.O. and A. Fenna, *Comparative Federalism: A Systematic Enquiry* (Peterborough, Ont.: Broadview Press, 2006) (2nd edn, Toronto: University of Toronto Press, 2015)

Hume D., 'Of the Original Contract', in David Hume, *Essays: Moral, Political, and Literary* (Oxford: Oxford University Press, 1963), Part 2, chapter 12

Hunt G. (ed.), *The Writings of James Madison* (New York: The Knickerbocker Press, 1901)

Hutchinson F., 'Malaysia's Federal System: Overt and Covert Centralisation' (2014) 44 *Journal of Contemporary Asia* 422–442

Inman R.P. and D.L. Rubinfield, 'Economics of Federalism', in F. Parisi (ed.), *The Oxford Handbook of Law and Economics: Volume 3: Public Law and Legal Institutions* (Oxford: Oxford University Press, 2017), Part 1, chapter 5

Inwood G.J., *Understanding Canadian Federalism: An Introduction to Theory and Practice* (Toronto: Pearson, 2013)

Ivison D., 'Pluralism and the Hobbesian Logic of Negative Constitutionalism' (1999) 47 *Political Studies* 83–99

Jackson A., 'The Failure of British and Irish Federalism, circa 1800–1950', in R. Schütze and S. Tierney (eds), *The United Kingdom and the Federal Idea* (Oxford: Hart Publishing, 2018), 29–47

Jacobs N., 'An Experimental Test of How Americans Think about Federalism' (2017) 47 *Publius: The Journal of Federalism* 572–598

Jacobsohn G.J., *Constitutional Identity* (Cambridge MA: Harvard University Press, 2010)

Jacobsohn G.J. and Y. Roznai, *Constitutional Revolution* (New Haven: Yale University Press, 2020)

Jacobsohn G. and M. Schor (eds), *Comparative Constitutional Theory* (Cheltenham: Edward Elgar, 2018), 45–65

Jaensch D. (ed.), *The Politics of New Federalism* (Adelaide: Australian Political Studies Association, 1977)

Jain M.P., 'Nehru and the Indian Federalism' (1977) 19 *Journal of the Indian Law Institute* 392–418

Jennings W.I., *Some Characteristics of the Indian Constitution* (Madras: Oxford University Press, 1953)

Johns C.M., P.L. O'Reilly, and G.J. Inwood, 'Formal and Informal Dimensions of Intergovernmental Administrative Relations in Canada' (2007) 50 *Canadian Public Administration* 21–41

Johnson K.S., *Governing the American State: Congress and the New Federalism, 1877–1929* (Princeton: Princeton University Press, 2007)

Kahn J., *Federalism, Democratization and the Rule of Law in Russia* (Oxford: Oxford University Press, 2002)

Kaiser A. and S. Vogel, 'Dynamic De/Centralization in Germany, 1949–2010' (2019) 49 *Publius* 84–111

Kant I., *Perpetual Peace: A Philosophical Essay* [1795] (London: Sonnenschein, 1903)

Karazivan N., 'Cooperative Federalism v Parliamentary Sovereignty: Revisiting the Roles of the Executive, the Legislative and the Judicial Branches', in A.-G. Gagnon and J. Poirier (eds), *Canadian Federalism and its Future: Actors and Institutions* (Montreal/Kingston: McGill-Queen's University Press, 2019), 291–335

Karmis D., 'Fédéralisme et relations intercommunautaires chez Tocqueville: entre prudence et négation des possibles' (1998) 17 *Politique et Sociétés* 59–91

Karmis D. and W. Norman (eds), *Theories of Federalism: A Reader* (New York: Palgrave-Macmillan Publishing, 2005)

Keating M., *Plurinational Democracy: Stateless Nations in a Post-sovereignty Era* (Oxford: Oxford University Press, 2001)

Keating M., 'Beyond the Nation-State: Territory, Solidarity and Welfare in a Multiscalar Europe' (2021) 9 *Territory, Politics, Governance* 331–345

Keil S., *Multinational Federalism in Bosnia and Herzegovina* (Farnham and Burlington, VT: Ashgate, 2013)

Kellock B.H. and S. LeRoy, 'Questioning the Legality of the Federal "Spending Power"' (2007) 89 *Public Policy Sources* 1–26

Kelly D., 'Carl Schmitt's Political Theory of Representation' (2004) 65 *Journal of the History of Ideas* 113–134

Kelly D., 'Woodrow Wilson and the Challenge of Federalism in World War One', in A. Lev, *The Federal Idea: Public Law Between Governance and Political Life* (Oxford: Hart Publishing, 2017), 167–188

Kelly D., 'Introduction: Carl Schmitt's Critique of Friedrich Meinecke' (2017) 17 *Max Weber Studies* 48–53

Kelsen H., *Allgemeine Staatslehre* (Berlin: Springer, 1925)

Kelsen H., *The General Theory of Law and State* (New York: Russell and Russell, 1945)

Kenyon C., *Men of Little Faith* (Amherst: University of Massachusetts Press, 2003)

Kincaid J., 'From Cooperative to Coercive Federalism' (1990) 508 *The Annals of the American Academy of Political and Social Science* 139–152

Kincaid J., 'Intergovernmental Relations in the United States of America', in J. Poirier and C. Saunders (eds), *Intergovernmental Relations in Federal Systems* (Montreal-Kingston: McGill-Queen's University Press, 2002), 33–44

Kincaid J., 'Introduction', in J. Kincaid (ed.), *A Research Agenda for Federalism Studies* (Cheltenham: Edward Elgar, 2019), 1–14

Kincaid J. (ed.), *A Research Agenda for Federalism Studies* (Cheltenham: Edward Elgar, 2019)

Kincaid J., 'Dynamic De/Centralization in the United States, 1790–2010' (2019) 49 *Publius* 166–193

Kincaid J. and R.L. Cole, 'Public Opinion on Federalism in Canada, Mexico and the USA in 2003' (2004) 34 *Publius* 95–115

Kincaid J. and R.L. Cole, 'Citizen Attitudes Toward Issues of Federalism in Canada, Mexico, and the United States' (2011) 41 *Publius* 53–75

Kincaid J. and G. Alan Tarr (eds), *Constitutional Origins, Structure, and Change in Federal Countries, vol. 1* (Kingston/Montreal: McGill-Queen's University Press, 2005)

King P., *Federalism and Federation* (London: Croom Helm, 1982)

Kirkey C., S. Paquin, and St. Roussel, 'Charting Quebec's Engagement with the International Community' (2016) 46 *American Review of Canadian Studies* 135–148

Kisker G., 'The West German Federal Constitutional Court as Guardian of the Federal System' (1989) 19 *Publius* 35–52

Klarman M.J., *The Framers' Coup: The Making of the United States Constitution* (New York: Oxford University Press), 2016

Knop K., S. Ostry, R. Simeon, and K. Swinton, *Rethinking Federalism: Citizens, Markets and Governments in a Changing World: Citizens, Markets, and Governments in a Changing World* (Vancouver: University of British Columbia Press, 1995)

Koch H.W., *A Constitutional History of Germany in the Nineteenth and Twentieth Centuries* (London: Longman, 1984)

Koggel C., 'The Mediation Committee of the Bundestag and Bundesrat: A Special Institution of German Constitutional Law' (2016) 44 *International Journal of Legal Information* 35–42

Kramnick I. and T.J. Lowi (eds), *American Political Thought: A Norton Anthology* (New York: W. W. Norton, 2009)

Kuznetsov A.S., *Theory and Practice of Paradiplomacy: Subnational Governments in International Affairs* (New York: Routledge, 2014)

Kymlicka W., *Liberalism, Community and Culture* (Oxford: Clarendon Press, 1989)

Kymlicka W., *Multicultural Citizenship: A Liberal Theory of Minority Rights* (Oxford: Oxford University Press, 1996)

Kymlicka W., 'Federalism, Nationalism and Multiculturalism', in D. Karmis and W. Norman (eds), *Theories of Federalism: A Reader* (New York: Palgrave-Macmillan Publishing, 2005), 269–292

Kymlicka W., 'Is Federalism a Viable Alternative to Secession?', in P.B. Lehning (ed.), *Theories of Secession* (London: Routledge, 2005), 111–150

LaCroix A., 'Drawing and Redrawing the Line: The Pre-Revolutionary Origins of Federal Ideas of Sovereignty', University of Chicago Law Occasional Paper, No. 47 (2008)

LaCroix A.L., *The Ideological Origins of American Federalism* (Cambridge MA: Harvard University Press, 2011)

Ladner A., N. Soguel, Y. Emery, S. Weerts, and S. Nahrath (eds), *Swiss Public Administration: Making the State Work Successfully* (Berlin: Springer, 2020)

Landau M., 'Federalism, Redundancy and System Reliability' (1973) 3 *Publius* 173–196

Laforest G., *Trudeau and the End of a Canadian Dream* (Montreal/Buffalo: McGill-Queen's University Press, 1995)

Lane J.E., *Constitutions and Political Theory* (Manchester: Manchester University Press, 1996)

Lang T., 'The Limits of Victorian Federalism: E.A. Freeman's History of Federal Government' (2018) *History Open Access Publications* <https://scholarworks.umass.edu/history_oapubs/3>, 1–18

Larsen S.R., *The Constitutional Theory of the Federation and the European Union* (Oxford: Oxford University Press, 2021)

Lash K.L., 'James Madison's Celebrated Report of 1800: The Transformation of the Tenth Amendment' (2006) 74 *The George Washington Law Review* 165–200

Laski H.J., 'The Pluralistic State' (1919) 28 *Philosophical Review* 562–575

Laski H.J., 'The Obsolescence of Federalism' (1939) 98 *New Republic* 367

Lawson G., *Politica sacra et civilis* C. Condren (ed.) (Cambridge: Cambridge University Press, 2012)

Lawson G. et al., *The Origins of the Necessary and Proper Clause* (Cambridge: Cambridge University Press, 2010)

Leach R.H., *American Federalism* (New York: WW Norton, 1970)

Lecours A., 'Balancing Self-Rule and Shared-Rule: Sources of Tensions and Political Responses in Contemporary Political Systems', in A. López Basaguren and L.E. San Epifanio (eds), *The Ways of Federalism in Western Countries and the Horizons of Territorial Autonomy in Spain, vol. I* (Berlin: Springer, 2013), 103–113

Lecours A., 'Dynamic De/Centralization in Canada, 1867–2010' (2019) 49 *Publius* 57–83

Lecours A., 'Federalism and Nationalism', in J. Kincaid (ed.), *A Research Agenda for Federalism Studies* (Cheltenham: Edward Elgar, 2019), 140–150

Lecours A. and D. Béland, 'Federalism and Fiscal Policy: The Politics of Equalization in Canada' (2010) 40 *Publius* 569–596

Lee D., *Popular Sovereignty in Early Modern Constitutional Thought* (Oxford: Oxford University Press, 2016)

Lev A., 'Sovereignty and Federalism: Inventing and Reinventing Public Law' (2017) 17 *Jus Politicum* 191–208

Lev A. (ed.), *The Federal Idea: Public Law between Governance and Political Life* (Oxford: Hart Publishing, 2019)

Lev A., 'Introduction: Federalism and Public Law Theory', in A. Lev (ed.), *The Federal Idea: Public Law between Governance and Political Life* (Oxford: Hart Publishing, 2019), 1–26

Levinson S. (ed.), *Responding to Imperfection: The Theory and Practice of Constitutional Amendment* (Princeton: Princeton University Press, 1995)

Levinson S., *Our Undemocratic Constitution. Where the Constitution Goes Wrong (And How We the People Can Correct It)* (New York: Oxford University Press, 2005)

Levinson S., 'Reflections on What Constitutes a "Constitution": The Importance of "Constitutions of Settlement" and the Potential Irrelevance of Herculean Lawyering', in D. Dyzenhaus and M. Thorburn (eds), *Philosophical Foundations of Constitutional Law* (Oxford: Oxford University Press, 2016), 75–94

Levy J.T., 'Federalism, Liberalism, and the Separation of Loyalties' (2007) 101 *American Political Science Review* 459–477

Lienhard A., D. Kettiger, J. Bühler, L. Mérillat, and D. Winkler, 'The Federal Supreme Court of Switzerland: Judicial balancing of Federalism without Judicial Review', in N. Aroney and J. Kincaid (eds), *Courts in Federal Countries: Federalists or Unitarists?* (Toronto: University of Toronto Press, 2017), 404–439

Lincoln A., 'Message to Congress in Special Session', in R. Basler (ed.), *The Collected Works of Abraham Lincoln* (New Brunswick, N.J.: Rutgers University Press for the Abraham Lincoln Association, Springfield, Ill., 1953), 421–441

Lindahl H., 'Constituent Power and Reflexive Identity: Towards an Ontology of Collective Selfhood', in M. Loughlin and N. Walker (eds), *The Paradox of Constitutionalism* (Oxford: Oxford University Press, 2008), 9–24

Lindahl H., *Fault Lines of Globalization: Legal Order and the Politics of A-Legality* (Oxford: Oxford University Press, 2013)

Lindahl H., 'Constituent Power and the Constitution', in D. Dyzenhaus and M. Thorburn (eds), *The Philosophical Foundations of Constitutional Law* (Oxford: Oxford University Press, 2016), 141–159

Lively J., *The Works of Joseph de Maistre* (London: Allen & Unwin, 1965)

Livingston W.S., *Federalism and Constitutional Change* (Oxford: Clarendon Press, 1956)

Lloyd H.A., 'Sovereignty: Bodin, Hobbes, Rousseau' (1991) 4 *Revue Internationale de Philosophie* 353–379

Locke J., *The Second Treatise of Civil Government and A Letter Concerning Toleration* (Oxford: Blackwell, 1948)

Loughlin J., J. Kincaid, and W. Swenden, *Routledge Handbook of Regionalism and Federalism* (London: Routledge, 2013)

Loughlin M., *The Idea of Public Law* (Oxford: Oxford University Press, 2003)

Loughlin M., 'Ten Tenets of Sovereignty', in N. Walker (ed.), *Sovereignty in Transition* (Oxford: Hart Publishing, 2003), 55–86

Loughlin M., 'Constitutional Theory: A 25th Anniversary Essay' (2005) 25 *Oxford Journal of Legal Studies* 183

Loughlin M., *Foundations of Public Law* (Oxford: Oxford University Press, 2010)

Loughlin M., 'The Concept of Constituent Power' (2013) 13 *European Journal of Political Theory* 218–237

Loughlin M., 'Why Sovereignty?' in R. Rawlings, P. Leyland, and A. Young (eds), *Sovereignty and Law: Domestic, Regional & Global Perspectives* (Oxford: Oxford University Press, 2013), 34–49

Loughlin M., 'Political Jurisprudence', in M.A. Wilkinson and M.W. Dowdle (eds), *Questioning the Foundations of Public Law* (Oxford: Hart Publishing, 2018), 15–31

Loughlin M. and S. Tierney, 'The Shibboleth of Sovereignty' (2018) 81 *Modern Law Review* 989–1016

Lutz D.S., 'The Articles of Confederation as the Background to the Federal Republic' (1990) 20 *Publius* 55–70

Lutz D.S., 'Toward a Theory of Constitutional Amendment', in S. Levinson (ed.), *Responding to Imperfection: The Theory and Practice of Constitutional Amendment* (Princeton: Princeton University Press, 1995), 237–274

Lutz D.S., 'The Iroquois Confederation Constitution: An Analysis' (1998) 28 *Publius* 99–127

MacCormick N., *Questioning Sovereignty: Law, State, and Nation in the European Commonwealth* (Oxford: Oxford University Press, 2002)

Macedo S., 'Toward A More Democratic Congress? Our Imperfect Democratic Constitution: The Critics Examined' (2009) 89 *Boston University Law Review* 609–628

Madison J., 'Vices of the Political System', in G. Hunt (ed.), *The Writings of James Madison* (New York: The Knickerbocker Press, 1901), 361–369

Mahon P., 'Judicial Federalism and Constitutional Review in the Swiss Judiciary', in A. Ladner et al., *Swiss Public Administration: Making the State Work Successfully* (Lausanne: Palgrave MacMillan, 2018), 137–155

Mair P., *Ruling the Void: The Hollowing of Western Democracy* (London: Verso, 2013)

de Maistre J. (1795) 'Study on Sovereignty', in J. Lively, *The Works of Joseph de Maistre* (London: Allen and Unwin, 1965), 93–129

Majeed A., 'Republic of India', in J. Kincaid and G. Alan Tarr (eds), *Constitutional Origins, Structure, and Change in Federal Countries, vol. 1* (Kingston/Montreal: McGill-Queen's University Press, 2005), 180–207

Malberg R. Carre de, *Contribution à la théorie générale de l'Etat, 2 vols* (Paris: Librairie de la Société du recueil Sirey, 1920)

Marchant S., 'The Historical Traditions of the Australian Senate: the Upper House we had to have', PhD thesis, Australian National University, 2009, 14 <https://openresearch-repository.anu.edu.au/bitstream/1885/49337/2/02whole.pdf>

Marks F.W. III, *Independence on Trial: Foreign Affairs and the Making of the Constitution*, 2nd edn (Baton Rouge: Rowman and Littlefield, 1993)

McAdam D., S. Tarrow, and C. Tilly, *Dynamics of Contention* (Cambridge: Cambridge University Press, 2001)

McGarry J. and B. O'Leary, 'Federations and Managing Nations', in M. Burgess, and J. Pinder (eds), *Multinational Federations* (London: Routledge, 2007), 180–211

McGuire R.A., *To Form a More Perfect Union: A New Economic Interpretation of the United States Constitution* (New York: Oxford University Press, 2003)

McHenry J., 'Papers of Dr. James McHenry on the Federal Convention of 1787' (1906) 11 *The American Historical Review* 595–624

McRoberts K., *Misconceiving Canada: The Struggle for National Unity* (Toronto: Oxford University Press, 1997)

Meierhenrich J. and O. Simons (eds), *The Oxford Handbook of Carl Schmitt* (New York: Oxford University Press, 2016)

Merriman J., *A History of Modern Europe: From the Renaissance to the Present*, 3rd edn (London: Norton, 2010)

Michelmann H. (ed.), *A Global Dialogue on Federalism: Legislative, Executive, and Judicial Governance in Federal Countries* (Kingston/Montreal: McGill-Queen's University Press, 2005)

Michelmann H.J. and P. Soldatos (eds), *Federalism and International Relations: The Role of Subnational Units* (Oxford: Clarendon Press, 1990)

Milkis S.M. and M. Nelson, *The American Presidency: Origins and Development, 1776–2018*, 8th edn (Thousand Oaks: Sage, 2020)

Mill J.S., *Considerations on Representative Government* (London: Parker, Son and Bourn, 1861)

Mill J.S., *Utilitarianism, On Liberty and Considerations on Representative Government* H.B. Acton (ed.) (London: J.M. Dent & Sons, 1972)

Miller D., *On Nationality* (Oxford: Oxford University Press, 1995)

Mitra S.K., 'Language and Federalism: The Multi-ethnic Challenge' (2001) 53 *International Social Science Journal* 51–60

Mogi S., *The Problem of Federalism; A Study in the History of Political Theory* (New York: The Macmillan Company, 1931)

Möllers, C. '"We Are (Afraid of) the People": Constituent Power in German Constitutionalism', in M. Loughlin and N. Walker, *The Paradox of Constitutionalism: Constituent Power and Constitutional Form* (Oxford: Oxford University Press, 2008), 87–106

Montesquieu, C. de Secondat, baron de, 1689–1755, *The Spirit of Laws* (London: Collingwood, 1823)

Moodie G.C., 'The Crown and Parliament' (1956) 10 *Parliamentary Affairs* 256–264

Moore M., *A Political Theory of Territory* (Oxford: Oxford University Press, 2015)

Moreno L., 'Federalization in Multinational Spain' in M. Burgess and J. Pinder (eds), *Multinational Federations* (London: Routledge, 2007), 86–107

Moreno L., *The Federalization of Spain* (London, Portland: Frank Cass, 2001)

Moreno L. and C. Colino (eds), *Diversity and Unity in Federal Countries* (Montreal/Kingston: McGill-Queen's University Press, 2010)

Morgan E., *Inventing the People: The Rise of Popular Sovereignty in England and America* (New York: Norton, 1988)

Morgan I. and P. Davies (eds), *The Federal Nation: Perspectives on American Federalism* (USA: Palgrave MacMillan, 2008)

Mueller S. and S. Keil, 'The Territoriality of Fiscal Solidarity: Comparing Swiss Equalisation with European Union Structural Funding' (2013) 5 *Perspectives on Federalism* 122–148

Murrin J.M., 'A Roof without Walls: The Dilemma of American National Identity', in R. Beeman, S. Botein, and E.C. Carter II (eds), *Beyond Confederation: Origins of the Constitution and American National Identity* (Chapel Hill: University of North Carolina Press, 1987), 333–348

Nagel R.F., *The Implosion of American Federalism* (Oxford: Oxford University Press, 2002)

Natelson R., 'Proposing Constitutional Amendments Through a Convention: Rules Governing the Process' (2011) 78 *Tennessee Law* Review 693–750

National Federation of Independent Business v. Sebelius 567 US 519 (2012)

Neumann F.L., 'Federalism and Freedom: A Critique', in D. Karmis and W. Norman (eds), *Theories of Federalism: A Reader* (Basingstoke: Palgrave Macmillan, 2005)

New South Wales v. Commonwealth 229 CLR 1 (2006)

New State Ice Co. v. Liebmann 285 US 262, 311 (1932)

K. Nicolaidis and R. Howse (eds), *The Federal Vision: Legitimacy and Levels of Governance in the United States and the European Union* (Oxford: Oxford University Press, 2001)

Ninet A.A. and J.A. Gardner, 'Distinctive Identity Claims in Federal Systems: Judicial Policing of Subnational Variance' (2016) 14 *International Journal of Constitutional Law* 378–410

Nicolas de Caritat M.J.A., Condorcet, M. de, 'Observations on the Twenty-Ninth Book of the Spirit of the Law', appended to D. de Tracy, *A Commentary and Review of Montesquieu's The Spirit of the Laws* T. Jefferson (trans.) (New York: Burt Franklin, [1814] 1989)

Niranjan V., 'Legislative Competence: the Union and the States', in S. Choudhry, M. Khosla, and P.B. Mehta (eds), *The Oxford Handbook of the Indian Constitution* (Oxford: Oxford University Press, 2016), Part 5, chapter 26

Nootens G., 'Autonomy, Boundaries and Trust: Preliminary Remarks', in A.-G. Gagnon and M. Keating (eds), *Political Autonomy and Divided Societies: Imagining Democratic Alternatives in Complex Settings* (Hampshire: Palgrave MacMillan, 2012), 32–48

Nootens G., *Popular Sovereignty in the West: Polities, Contention, and Ideas* (London: Routledge, 2013)

Norman W., *Negotiating Nationalism: Nation-Building, Federalism, and Secession in the Multinational State* (Oxford: Oxford University Press, 2006)

Nugent J.D., *Safeguarding Federalism: How States Protect Their Interests in National Policymaking* (Norman: University of Oklahoma Press, 2009)

Okudaira Y., 'Forty Years of the Constitution and its Various Influences: Japanese, American and European' (1990) 53 *Law and Contemporary Problems* 17–49

O'Leary B., 'An Iron Law of Nationalism and Federation? A (NeoDiceyian) Theory of the Necessity of a Federal Staatsvolk and of Consociational Rescue' (2001) 7 *Nations and Nationalism* 273–296

Oliver P., 'Parliamentary Sovereignty, Federalism and the Commonwealth', in R. Schütze and S. Tierney (eds) *The United Kingdom and the Federal Idea* (Oxford: Hart Publishing, 2018), 49–72

Oliver P. and S. Tierney, 'Book Review/Response, Constitutional Referendums: The Theory and Practice of Republican Deliberation', *International Journal of Constitutional Law Blog*, 25 February 2014 <http://www.iconnectblog.com/2014/02/book-reviewresponse-stephen-tierney-and-peter-oliver>

Onuf P. and N. Onuf, *Federal Union, Modern World: The Law of Nations in an Age of Revolutions 1776–1814* (Madison, Wisconsin: Madison House, 1993)

Ostrom V., *The Political Theory of a Compound Republic: Designing the American Experiment*, 2nd edn (Lincoln: University of Nebraska Press, 1987)

Pacific Gas & Electric Co v State Energy Resources Conservation & Development Commission, 461 US 190 (1983)

Palermo F., 'Beyond Second Chambers: Alternative Representation of Territorial Interests and Their Reasons' (2018) 10 *Perspectives on Federalism* 50–68

Palermo F. and K. Kössler, *Comparative Federalism: Constitutional Arrangements and Case Law* (Oxford: Hart Publishing, 2017)

Palik J., Rustad S.A., and Methi F., 'Conflict Trends: A Global Overview, 1946–2019', Peace Research Institute Oslo Paper, 2020, 35. <https://reliefweb.int/sites/reliefweb.int/files/resources/Palik%2C%20Rustad%2C%20Methi%20-%20Conflict%20Trends%20A%20Global%20Overview%201946-2019%2C%20PRIO%20Paper%202020.pdf>

Parisi F. (ed.), *The Oxford Handbook of Law and Economics: Volume 3: Public Law and Legal Institutions* (Oxford: Oxford University Press, 2017)

Partlett W., 'The American Tradition of Constituent Power' (2017) 15 *International Journal of Constitutional Law* 955–987

Patberg M., *Constituent Power in the European Union* (Oxford: Oxford University Press, 2020)

Patterson E., 'The Spending Power after NFIB: New Direction, or Medicaid Exception?' (2015) 68 *Southern Methodist University Law Review* 385–425

Peeters P. and J. Mosselmans, 'The Constitutional Court of Belgium: Safeguard of the Autonomy of the Communities and Regions', in N. Aroney and J. Kincaid (eds), *Courts in Federal Countries: Federalists or Unitarists?* (Toronto: University of Toronto Press, 2017), 69–102

Pelletier B., 'The Future of Quebec within the Canadian Federation', in A.-G. Gagnon (ed.), *Contemporary Canadian Federalism* (Toronto: University of Toronto Press, 2012), 469–482

Philips P.J.J., *The Challenge of Relativism: Its Nature and Limits* (London: Bloomsbury, 2011)

Poirier J., C. Saunders, and J. Kincaid, *Intergovernmental Relations in Federal Systems* (Oxford: Oxford University Press, 2015)

Popelier P., 'Federalism Disputes and the Behavior of Courts: Explaining Variation in Federal Courts' Support for Centralization' (2017) 47 *Publius* 27–48

Popelier P. and K. Lemmens, *The Constitution of Belgium: A Contextual Analysis* (Oxford: Hart Publishing, 2015)

Popelier P. and M. Sahadzic (eds), *Constitutional Asymmetry in Multinational Federalism: Managing Multinationalism in Multi-tiered Systems* (United Kingdom: Palgrave-MacMillan, 2019)

Porter R.B., 'John Stuart Mill and Federalism' (1977) 7 *Publius* 101–124

Preece A.A., 'Financial Powers of Upper Houses' (2002) 4 *University of Notre Dame Australia Law Review* 115–143

'Preserving Independence in the Judicial Appointment System: Report of the Standing Committee on Justice and Human Rights', House of Commons, 39th Parliament, 1st Session, 2007

Rakove J.N., *The Beginnings of National Politics* (New York: Alfred A. Knopf, 1979)

Rakove J.N., *Original Meanings: Politics and Ideas in the Making of the Constitution* (New York: Vintage, 1996)

Rakove J.N., *Revolutionaries: A New History of the Invention of America* (Boston: Houghton Mifflin Harcourt, 2010)

Rakove J.N. and O. Handlin, *James Madison and the Creation of the American Republic* (Glenview: Scott, Foresman/Little, Brown Higher Education, 1990)

Rasch W., 'Carl Schmitt's Defense of Democracy', in J. Meierhenrich and O. Simons (eds), *The Oxford Handbook of Carl Schmitt* (New York: Oxford University Press, 2016), 312–335

Rawls J., *A Theory of Justice* (Oxford: Oxford University Press, 1972)

Rawls J., *The Law of Peoples* (Cambridge MA: Cambridge University Press, 1999)

Requejo F. (ed.), *Democracy and National Pluralism* (London: Routledge, 2001)

Requejo F., 'Is Spain a Federal Country?' 2017 <http://50shadesoffederalism.com/case-studies/spain-federal-country/>

Requejo F., *Multinational Federalism and Value Pluralism* (London: Routledge, 2005)

Riker W.H., *Federalism: Origin, Operation, Significance* (Boston: Little, Brown, 1964)

Riker W., 'Federalism', in F.I. Greenstein, and N. Polsby, (eds), *Handbook of Political Science. Volume V: Government Institutions and Process* (Reading MA: Addison-Wesley, 1975), 93–172

Riker W., *The Development of American Federalism* (USA: Kluwer Academic Publisher, 1987)

Roche J.P., 'The Founding Fathers: A Reform Caucus in Action' (1961) 55 *American Political Science Review* 799–816

Rocher F., 'Opponents of the 1864 Confederation Project: Criticism of the Future Regime', in E. Brouillet, A.-G. Gagnon, and G. Laforest (eds), *The Quebec Conference of 1864: Understanding the Emergence of the Canadian Federation* (Kingston/Montreal: McGill-Queen's University Press, 2018), 179–219

Romney P., *Getting it Wrong: How Canadians Forgot Their Past and Imperilled Confederation* (Toronto: Toronto University Press, 1999)

Romney P., 'Provincial Equality, Special Status and the Compact Theory of Confederation' (1999) 32 *Canadian Journal of Political Science* 21–39

Robertson D.B., *The Original Compromise: What the Framers Were Really Thinking* (New York: Oxford University Press, 2013)

C. Rossiter (ed.), *The Federalist Papers* (New York: New American Library, 1961)

Rosenn K.S., 'Federalism in the Americas in Comparative Perspective' (1994) 26 *The University of Miami Inter-American Law Review* 1–50

Rousseau J.-J., 'The Social Contract', in *The Social Contract and Other Later Political Writings* V. Gourevitch (trans.) (Cambridge: Cambridge University Press, 1997), 39–152

Roznai Y., *Unconstitutional Constitutional Amendments: The Limits of Amendment Powers* (Oxford: Oxford University Press, 2017)

Rubinelli L., *Constituent Power: A History* (Cambridge: Cambridge University Press, 2020)

Rufus Davis S., 'The "Federal Principle" Reconsidered, Part 2' (1956) 1 *Australian Journal of Politics and History* 59–85

Russell P., *Constitutional Odyssey: Can Canadians Become a Sovereign People?*, 2nd edn (Toronto: Toronto University Press, 1993)

Sagar A., 'Constitutional Interpretation in Federations and its Impact on the Federal Balance' (2011) 3 *Perspectives on Federalism* E1–E22

Sahadžić M., *Asymmetry, Multinationalism and Constitutional Law—Managing Legitimacy and Stability in Federalist States* (London: Routledge, 2021)

Sandler R. and D. Schoenbrun, *Government by Decree: What Happens When Courts Run Government* (New Haven: Yale University Press, 2003)

Sarat A. and T.R. Kearns (eds), *Cultural Pluralism, Identity Politics, and the Law* (Ann Arbor: University of Michigan Press, 2014)

Saunders C., 'Commonwealth of Australia', in J. Kincaid and G. Alan Tarr (eds), *Constitutional Origins, Structure, and Change in Federal Countries, vol. 1*, (Kingston/Montreal: McGill-Queen's University Press, 2005), 12–47

Saunders C., 'Constitutional Arrangements of Federal Systems' (1995) 25 *Publius* 61–79

Saunders C., 'The Constitutional Arrangements of Federal Systems: A Sceptical View from the Outside', in J.J. Hesse and V. Wright (eds), *Federalizing Europe? The Costs, Benefits, and Preconditions of Federal Political Systems* (Oxford: Oxford University Press, 1996), 49–69

Saunders C., 'Australia', in K. LeRoy and C. Saunders (eds.), *A Global Dialogue on Federalism, Volume 3: Legislative, Executive, and Judicial Governance in Federal Countries* 128

Saxena R. (ed.), *Varieties of Federal Governance: Major Contemporary Models* (Cambridge: Cambridge University Press, 2012)

Saxena, R., 'The Working of Cooperative and Collaborative Federalism in India: Understanding Intergovernmental Relations', (2021) 67 *Indian Journal of Public Administration* 153–164

Saxena R. and W. Swenden, 'The Indian Supreme Court and Federalism' (2017) 17 *Fédéralisme Régionalisme* 1–12

Scharpf F.W., 'The Joint-Decision Trap. Lessons From German Federalism and European Integration' (1988) 66 *Public Administration* 239–278

Schertzer, R., 'Federal Arbiters as Facilitators: Towards an Integrated Federal and Judicial Theory for Diverse States' (2017) 15 *International Journal of Constitutional Law* 110–136

Schertzer R., *The Judicial Role in a Diverse Federation: Lessons from the Supreme Court of Canada* (Toronto: University of Toronto Press, 2016)

Schiavon J.A., *Comparative Paradiplomacy* (Nueva York: Routledge, 2019)

Schertzer, R., 'Federal Arbiters as Facilitators: Towards an Integrated Federal and Judicial Theory for Diverse States' (2017) 15 *International Journal of Constitutional Law* 110–136Schmitt C., *Constitutional Theory* J. Seitzer (trans. and ed.) (Durham and London: Duke University Press, 2008)

Schmitt N., 'Swiss Confederation', in J. Kincaid and G. Alan Tarr (eds), *Constitutional Origins, Structure, and Change in Federal Countries, vol. 1*, (Kingston/Montreal: McGill-Queen's University Press, 2005), 347–381

Schnabel J., *Managing Interdependencies in Federal Systems: Intergovernmental Councils and the Making of Public Policy* (UK: Palgrave MacMillan, 2020)

Schütze R. and S. Tierney (eds), *The United Kingdom and the Federal Idea* (Oxford: Hart Publishing, 2018)

Scott K., *Federalism: A Normative Theory and its Practical Relevance* (New York: Continuum, 2011)

La Selva S.V., *The Moral Foundations of Canadian Federalism* (London: McGill-Queen's University Press, 1996)

Selway B. and J.M. Williams, 'The High Court and Australian Federalism' (2005) 35 *Publius* 467–488

Sexton J., *A Nation Forged by Crisis: A New American History* (New York: Basic, 2018)

Shaw J., *The People in Question: Citizens and Constitutions in Uncertain Times* (Bristol: Bristol University Press, 2020)

Shaw M., *International Law*, 8th edn (Cambridge: Cambridge University Press, 2017)

Sidgwick H., *The Elements of Politics* (London: Macmillan, 1891)

Sidgwick H., *The Development of European Polity*, 2nd edn (London: Macmillan and Co., Ltd., 1903), 430

Sieyès A.E., 'What Is the Third Estate?' (1789) in O.W. Lembcke and F. Weber (eds), *Emmanuel Joseph Sieyès: The Essential Political Writings* (Leiden: Brill, 2014), 43–117

Sieyes E.J., *What is the Third Estate?* (London: Pall Mall Press, 1963)

Simeon R. and A. Nugent, 'Parliamentary Canada and Intergovernmental Canada: Exploring the Tensions', in H. Bakvis and G. Skogstad (eds), *Canadian Federalism: Performance, Effectiveness and Legitimacy*, 3rd edn (Don Mills: Oxford University Press, 2012), 59–78

Simpson G., *Great Powers and Outlaw States: Unequal Sovereigns in the International Legal Order* (Cambridge: Cambridge University Press, 2009)

Skerry P., 'Many Borders to Cross: Is Immigration the Exclusive Responsibility of Federal Government?' (1995) 25 *Publius* 71–85

Skinner Q., *The Foundations of Modern Political Thought, vol. I: The Renaissance* (Cambridge: Cambridge University Press, 1978)

Skogstad G. et al. (eds), *The Global Promise of Federalism* (Toronto: University of Toronto Press, 2013)

Smiley D.C. and R.L. Watts, *Intrastate Federalism in Canada* (Toronto: University of Toronto Press, 1985)

Smith A.D., *Nationalism and Modernism* (London: Routledge, 1998)

Smith D.E., *The Canadian Senate in Bicameral Perspective* (Toronto: University of Toronto Press, 2003)

Smith H.A., 'The Residue of Power in Canada' (1926) 4 *Canadian Bar Review* 432–439

Smith R., *Civic Ideals: Conflicting Visions of Citizenship in U. S. History* (New Haven: Yale University Press, 1997)

Somek A. and M.A. Wilkinson, 'Unpopular Sovereignty?' (2020) 83 *Modern Law Review* 955–978

Somin I., 'The Supreme Court of the United States: Promoting Centralization More Than State Autonomy', in N. Aroney and J. Kincaid (eds), *Courts in Federal Countries: Federalists or Unitarists?* (Toronto: University of Toronto Press, 2017), 440–481

SoRelle M.E. and A.N. Walker, 'Partisan Preemption: The Strategic use of Federal Preemption Legislation' (2016) 46 *Publius* 486–509

Stein M., 'Federalism', in B. Badie, D. Berg-Schlosser, and L. Morlino (eds), *International Encyclopaedia of Political Science* (New York: Sage Publications, 2016), vol. 1, 897.

Steinberger H., 'Historic Influences of American Constitutionalism upon German Constitutional Development: Federalism and Judicial Review' (1998) 36 *Columbia Journal of Transnational Law* 189–208

Stelzer M., *The Constitution of the Republic of Austria: A Contextual Analysis* (Oxford: Hart Publishing, 2011)

Stepan A., 'Federalism and Democracy: Beyond the U.S. Model' (1999) 10 *Journal of Democracy* 19–33

Stepan A., 'Federalism and Democracy: Beyond the U.S. Model', in D. Karmis and W. Norman (eds), *Theories of Federalism: A Reader* (London: Palgrave Macmillan, 2005), 255–268

Stevenson G., *Building Nations from Diversity: Canadian and American Experience Compared* (Kingston-Montreal: McGill-Queen's University Press, 2014)

Steytler N. (ed.), *Concurrent Powers in Federal Systems: Meaning, Making, and Managing* (Leiden: Brill-Nijhoff, 2017)

Suteu S., *Eternity Clauses in Democratic Constitutionalism* (Oxford: Oxford University Press, 2021)

Swenden W., *Federalism and Second Chambers* (Bern: Peter Lang Publishing, 2004)

Swenden W., *Federalism and Regionalism in Western Europe: A Comparative and Thematic Analysis* (United Kingdom: Palgrave, 2006)

Tamir Y., *Liberal Nationalism* (Princeton: Princeton University Press, 1995)

Tarlton C.D., 'Symmetry and Asymmetry as Elements of Federalism: A Theoretical Speculation' (1965) 27 *The Journal of Politics* 861–874

Taylor A., *American Revolutions: A Continental History, 1750–1804* (New York: W.W. Norton & Co., 2016)

Taylor C., *Sources of the Self: The Making of the Modem Identity* (Cambridge MA: Harvard University Press, 1989)

Taylor C., 'Shared and Divergent Values', in R.L. Watts and D.M. Brown (eds), *Opinions for a New Canada* (Toronto: Toronto University Press, 1991), 53–76

Taylor C., 'The Politics of Recognition', in A. Gutman (ed.), *Multiculturalism: Examining the Politics of Recognition* (Princeton: Princeton University Press, 1994), 25–73

Taylor Q., '"A System Without a Precedent": The Federalism of the Federalist Papers', in A. Ward and L. Ward, *Ashgate Research Companion to Federalism* (Farnham: Ashgate, 2016), 175–192

Tewari M. and R. Saxena, 'The Supreme Court of India: The Rise of Judicial Power and the Protection of Federalism' in N. Aroney and J. Kincaid (eds), *Courts in Federal Countries: Federalists or Unitarists?* (Toronto: University of Toronto Press, 2017), 223–255

Tiebout C.M., 'A Pure Theory of Local Expenditures' (1956) 64 *Journal of Political Economy* 416–424

Tiernan A., 'The Council for the Australian Federation: A New Structure of Australian Federalism' (2008) 67 *Australian Journal of Public Administration* 122–134

Tierney S., *Constitutional Law and National Pluralism* (Oxford: Oxford University Press 2004)

Tierney S., 'Sovereignty and the Idea of Public Law', in E. Christodoulidis and S. Tierney (eds), *Public Law and Politics: Definitions, Debates and Critiques* (Farnham: Ashgate Law Publishers, 2008), 15–26

Tierney S., '"We, the Peoples": Constituent Power and Constitutionalism in Plurinational States', in M. Loughlin and N. Walker, *The Paradox of Constitutionalism* (Oxford: Oxford University Press, 2008), 229–246

Tierney S., 'Federalism in a Unitary State: A Paradox Too Far?' (2009) 19 *Regional and Federal Studies* 237–253

Tierney S., *Constitutional Referendums: The Theory and Practice of Republican Deliberation* (Oxford: Oxford University Press, 2012)

Tierney S., 'Le formalisme constitutionnel strict: la toxine britannique, l'antidote canadien?', in F. Rocher and B. Pelletier (eds), *Le nouvel ordre constitutionnel canadien: du rapatriement de 1982 à nos jours Sous la direction* (Québec: Presses de l'Université du Québec (PUQ), 2013), 291–313

Tierney S., 'Misconceiving Federalism: Canada and the Constitutional Idea', in R. Albert (ed.), *Canada in the World* (Cambridge: Cambridge University Press, 2017), 34–58

Tierney S., 'Brexit and the English Question', in F. Fabbrini (ed.), *The Law & Politics of Brexit* (Oxford: Oxford University Press, 2017), 95–114

Tierney S., 'The Territorial Constitution and the Brexit Process' (2019) 72 *Current Legal Problems* 59–83

Tierney S., 'Pierre Elliott Trudeau and the Federal Idea' (2020) 99 *Supreme Court Law Review* 3–36

Tillin L., *Indian Federalism* (Oxford: Oxford University Press, 2019)

de Tocqueville A., *Democracy in America* (New York: Vintage, 1990 [1835])

Trudeau P.E., 'The Practice and Theory of Federalism, in P.E. Trudeau, *Federalism and the French Canadians* (Toronto: Macmillan of Canada, 1968), 124–150

Truman B., 'Federalism and the Party System', in A.B. Wildavsky (ed.), *American Federalism in Perspective* (Boston: Little, Brown, 1962), 81–109

Tu K., 'Towards constitutional law of peoples: China and its peripheral societies', PhD thesis, University of Edinburgh, 2011

Tuck R., *The Sleeping Sovereign: The Invention of Modern Democracy* (Cambridge: Cambridge University Press, 2016)

Tully J., *Strange Multiplicity: Constitutionalism in an Age of Diversity* (Cambridge: Cambridge University Press, 1995)

Tully J., 'The Imperialism of Modern Constitutional Democracy', in M. Loughlin and N. Walker (eds), *The Paradox of Constitutionalism: Constituent Power and Constitutional Form* (Oxford: Oxford University Press, 2007), 315–338

Tully J., *Public Philosophy in a New Key: Volume I: Democracy and Civic Freedom* (Cambridge: CUP, 2008)

Tully J., 'On Local and Global Citizenship: An Apprenticeship Manual', in J. Tully, *Public Philosophy in a New Key: Volume II, Imperialism and Civic Citizenship* (Cambridge: Cambridge University Press, 2008), 243–310

Tully J., 'Federations, Communities and their Transformations: An Essay in Revision', in A. Lecours and G. Nootens (eds), *Dominant Nationalism, Dominant Ethnicity: Identity, Federalism and Democracy* (Brussels: Peter Lang 2009), 195–212

Tushnet M., 'The Possibilities of Comparative Constitutional Law' (1999) 108 *Yale Law Journal* 1225–1309

Tushnet M., *Weak Courts, Strong Rights* (Princeton: Princeton University Press, 2008)

Umbach M. (ed.), *German Federalism: Past, Present and Future* (London: Palgrave MacMillan, 2002)

Urbinati N., *Representative Democracy: Principles and Genealogy* (Chicago: Chicago University Press, 2006)

Vickers J., 'The Gender-and-Federalism Research Field: Past, Present and Future', in J. Kincaid (ed.), *A Research Agenda for Federalism Studies* (Cheltenham: Edward Elgar, 2019), 117–128

Vile M.J.C., *The Structure of American Federalism* (Oxford: Oxford University Press, 1961)

Vile M.J.C., 'Federal Theory and the "New Federalism"', in D. Jaensch (ed.), *The Politics of New Federalism* (Adelaide: Australian Political Studies Association, 1977), 1–14

Wagner R.E., 'Competitive Federalism in Institutional Perspective', in D.P. Racheter and R.E. Wagner (eds), *Federalist Government in Principle and Practice* (New York: Springer, 2001), 19–37

Walker N., 'Fundamental Law', in *The Laws of Scotland: Stair Memorial Encyclopaedia* (Edinburgh: Butterworths, 2002), 29–82

Walker N., 'Late Sovereignty in the European Union', in N. Walker (ed.), *Sovereignty in Transition* (Oxford: Hart Publishing, 2003), 3–32

Walker N., 'European Constitutionalism in the State Constitutional Tradition' (2006) 59 *Current Legal Problems* 51–89

Walker N., 'Constitutionalism and the Incompleteness of Democracy: An Iterative Relationship' (2010) 39 *Netherlands Journal of Legal Philosophy* 206–233

J.Wallis J. and W.E. Oates, 'The Impact of the New Deal on American Federalism', in M.D. Bordo, C. Goldin, and E.N. White (eds), *The Defining Moment: The Great Depression and the American Economy in the Twentieth Century* (Chicago: University of Chicago Press, 1998), 155–180

Ward A. and L. Ward (eds), *The Ashgate Research Companion to Federalism* (Farnham: Ashgate, 2009)

Watts R.L., *Comparing Federal Systems* (Kingston ON: Institute of Intergovernmental Relations, 1996); (2nd edn, Kingston/Montreal: McGill-Queens University Press, 1999); (3rd edn, Kingston/Montreal: McGill-Queens University Press, 2008)

Watts R.L., 'Federalism, Federal Political Systems, and Federations' (1998) 1 *Annual Review of Political Science* 117–137

Watts R.L., 'Federation as a Method of Ethnic Conflict Resolution', in M. Burgess and J. Pinder (eds), *Multinational Federations* (London: Routledge, 2007), 225–247

Watts R.L., 'The Federal Idea and its Contemporary Relevance', in T.L. Courchene et al., *The Federal Idea: Essays in Honour of Ronald L. Watts* (Kingston-Montreal: McGill-Queen's, 2011), 13–28

Webber C., *Simulating Sovereignty: Intervention, the State, and Symbolic Change* (Cambridge: Cambridge University Press, 1995)

Weber E., *Peasants Into Frenchmen: The Modernization of Rural France, 1870–1914* (Stanford: Stanford University Press, 1976)

Weber M., *Economy and Society* (Berkeley: Berkeley University of California Press, 1978 [1922])

Weinstock D., 'Towards a Normative Theory of Federalism' (2001) 53 *International Social Science Journal* 75–83

Wenman M., *Agonistic Democracy: Constituent Power in the Era of Globalisation* (New York: Cambridge University Press, 2013)

Wheare K.C., *Federal Government* (New York: Oxford University Press, 1946; 4th edn, 1963)

Wheare K.C., 'Federalism and the Making of Nations', in A.W. Macmahon (ed.), *Federalism: Mature and Emergent* (New York: Columbia University Press, 1955), 28–43

Whittington K.E., 'The Political Constitution of Federalism in Antebellum America: The Nullification Debate as an Illustration of Informal Mechanisms of Constitutional Change' (1996) 26 *Publius* 1–24

Whittington K.E., 'Dismantling the Modern State? The Changing Structural Foundations of Federalism' (1998) 25 *Hastings Constitutional Law Quarterly* 483–528

Wiesner C., A. Björk, H.-M. Kivistö, and K. Mäkinen, *Shaping Citizenship: A Political Concept in Theory, Debate and Practice* (UK: Routledge, 2019)

Wildavsky A., B. Swedlow, D. Schleicher, and D. Elazar (eds), *Federalism and Political Culture* (New Jersey: Transaction Books, 1997)

Wilson W., *The State* (Boston: DC Heath & Co., 1918)

Wood G., *The Creation of the American Republic, 1776–1787* (Chapel Hill: University of North Carolina Press, 1969)

Yarbrough J., 'Rethinking "The Federalist's View of Federalism"' (1985) 45 *Publius* 31–53

Yee S., 'The New Constitution of Bosnia and Herzegovina' (1996) 7 *European Journal of International Law* 176–192

Zackin E., 'What's Happened to American Federalism?' (2011) 43 *Polity* 388–403

Zaid A.A., *The Struggle for Iraq's Future: How Corruption, Incompetence and Sectarianism Have Undermined Democracy* (New Haven: Yale University Press, 2014)

Zimmerman J.F., *Federal Preemption: The Silent Revolution* (Ames: Iowa State Univ. Press, 1991)

Index

For the benefit of digital users, indexed terms that span two pages (e.g., 52–53) may, on occasion, appear on only one of those pages.